STUDIES IN THE EARLY HISTORY OF BRITAIN

General Editor: Nicholas Brooks

Social Identity in Early Medieval Britain

Social Identity in Early Medieval Britain

Edited by William O. Frazer and Andrew Tyrrell

Leicester University Press

London and New York

Leicester University Press
A Continuum imprint
Wellington House, 125 Strand, London WC2R 0BB
370 Lexington Avenue, New York, NY 10017-6503

First Published 2000

British Library Cataloguing-in-Publication Data

A catalogue record for this book is available from the British Library.

ISBN 0 7185 0084 9 (hardback)

Library of Congress Cataloging-in-Publication Data

Social identity in early Medieval Britain/edited by William O. Frazer and
Andrew Tyrrell.
     p. cm. – (Studies in the early history of Britain)
    Includes bibliographical references and index.
    ISBN 0-7185-0084-9 (HB)
     1. Group identity–Great Britain–History. 2. Community life–Great
Britain–History. 3. Ethnicity–Great Britain–History. 4. Social classes–
Great Britain–History. 5. Great Britain–History–Medieval period,
1066–1485. 6. Civilization, Medieval. I. Frazer, William O. II. Tyrrell,
Andrew, 1970- III. Series.

HN385.5 .S577 2000
305.5'0941–dc21
                                       99-086100

Typeset by BookEns Ltd, Royston, Herts
Printed and bound In Great Britain

Contents

Foreword

The aim of the *Studies in the Early History of Britain* series is to promote works of the highest scholarship which open up new fields of study or which bridge the barriers of traditional academic disciplines. As scholarship becomes ever more specialized, interdisciplinary studies are needed not only by students and general readers but also by professional scholars. This series therefore includes research monographs, works of synthesis and collaborative studies of important themes by several scholars from different fields. Our knowledge of the early Middle Ages will always be limited and fragmentary, but progress can be made if the work of the historian has secure foundations in philology, archaeology, geography, literature, numismatics, art history and liturgy – to name only the most obvious fields. The need to cross and to remove academic frontiers also explains the extension of the geographical range of this series to include the whole island of Britain, where its predecessor had been limited to 'Early English History'. The change would have been welcomed by the previous editor, the late Professor H.P.R. Finberg, whose pioneering work helped to inspire, and to provoke, the interest of a new generation of early medievalists in the relations of Britons and Saxons. The approach of this series is therefore deliberately wide-ranging – early medieval Britain can only be understood in the context of contemporary developments in Ireland and on the continent.

Few issues seized scholarly interest in the late 1990s so comprehensively as 'social identity'. The way in which groups, communities and individuals come to define themselves in relation to others lies at the root of all political and social organization. Our television screens and our newspapers make clear to us every day how deeply rooted are some identities and how transitory others under the pressure of events. This long-standing concern of sociologists and social anthropologists has become a dominant issue in archaeological theory, while historians (particularly early medievalists) have begun to find in these ideas new approaches to the thought-world of their sources. When two young research students from the Department of Archaeology and Prehistory of the University of Sheffield approached Leicester University Press with a well-conceived proposal for an interdisciplinary volume on this theme, we were therefore delighted to encourage them. William O. Frazer and Andrew Tyrrell are to be congratulated on their visionary skill in assembling a powerful team of contributors and their persistence in bringing the volume to fruition. They were determined to produce a book that would stand rigorous scrutiny from social scientists, archaeologists and historians but would also be accessible to non-specialists, both students and general readers. No single theory of how national, ethnic, class, family, monastic, corporeal and gender identities were constructed in the early Middle Ages is set out here, but these studies are brimming with new interpretations and insights. They provide a rich introduction to the social history (in its widest sense) of early medieval Britain. It is a privilege to welcome to the series a volume which pulls together in a most exciting fashion key problems in interpreting the material culture and conceptual world of that period. I am proud to introduce to the series a volume which integrates some of the approaches of social science, of archaeological science and of history into a stimulating volume full of important reassessments.

Nicholas Brooks
University of Birmingham
September 1999

Acknowledgements

This book was produced while we the editors were immersed in our doctoral research. Such difficult logistic circumstances created many unforeseen obstacles (and some which we could not have envisaged even were we not relatively new scholars). In the end the success of the volume has been due not only to our own tenacity but also to all those others who have helped and persevered along the way. The end result would have been considerably poorer without the collaboration of many of our friends and colleagues, and the editors would like to offer their thanks and appreciation to all those concerned in the conception and production of this volume. However, some deserve special thanks. First, and most importantly, to all those who contributed to the volume. As editors, we have both been extremely grateful for your erudition and patience and hope that the volume fulfils all of your expectations. We would also like to extend our warmest thanks to the series editor Professor Brooks who has always been amiable and supportive. Janet Joyce at Leicester University Press has also provided much assistance in the facilitation of the book's production for which we are also indebted.

Andrew Tyrrell: I would particularly like to thank the Natural Environment Research Council (NERC) for funding the research which ultimately led to my chapter, and which also enabled me to spend time editing this volume. Furthermore I would like to thank my supervisor Dr Andrew Chamberlain for being congenial enough to accept that sometimes my other work was not always going to be as prompt as he might have liked. I would also like to thank Jenny Moore for initially helping us into the world of publishing and all those others at the University of Sheffield, Department of Archaeology and Prehistory c. 1994 who provided much of the impetus for a publication and gave up their time to allow us to discuss various ideas. Particularly valued for their contributions at that time are Kathryn Denning, Kurtis Lesick and Alex Woolf. A huge thank you to Bill for all his tireless, and often thankless, work on the volume and for having the courage to go ahead with it in the first place. Lastly the greatest thanks go to my fabulous wife Alison. Without her constant support and love this volume would not have been completed. At least, not with my involvement.

x *Acknowledgements*

William O. Frazer: I would like to thank the University of Sheffield and the UK Committee of Vice Chancellors and Principals for funding my research during the editing of this volume, with the Wightman Scholarship and an Overseas Research Studentship. Like my co-editor, I would like to thank Jenny Moore for her publishing advice and Alex Woolf for his many useful suggestions during early brainstorming sessions. John Moreland was an excellent sounding board for much of the theory that underpins this book. The spirit of interdisciplinary scholarship which I learned from Clark Maines, who first interested me in archaeology, is at the centre of this book, and I would particularly like to thank him for his friendship and tutelage. Without the intelligence and hard work of Andy Tyrrell, this volume would not have come to fruition; my greatest thanks to him also for his genuine commitment to intellectual cooperation, something increasingly rare in academia today. Finally a heartfelt thanks to Clodagh Tait for her insight and support during the final stages of production.

Contributors

Julia Crick is Lecturer in the Department of History, School of Historical, Political and Sociological Studies, University of Exeter.

Catherine Cubitt is Lecturer in Early Medieval History, Centre for Medieval Studies, University of York.

Stephen Driscoll is Senior Lecturer in Archaeology, School of History and Archaeology, University of Glasgow.

William O. Frazer is Landscape Archaeologist for Eachtra Archaeological Projects in Ireland and a PhD student at the University of Sheffield.

Dawn Hadley is Lecturer in Historical Archaeology, Department of Archaeology and Prehistory, University of Sheffield.

Christopher Knüsel is Lecturer in Biological Anthropology, Department of Archaeological Sciences, University of Bradford.

John Moreland is Senior Lecturer, Department of Archaeology and Prehistory, University of Sheffield.

Nerys Thomas Patterson is currently an independent scholar; she has held lectureships at a number of institutions, most notably Harvard where she carried out most of the research for her chapter.

Kathryn Ripley holds a BSc in archaeology from the Department of Archaeological Sciences, University of Bradford.

Tom Saunders is currently an independent researcher.

Andrew Tyrrell has recently completed his PhD at the University of Sheffield.

Alex Woolf is Lecturer in Celtic and Early Scottish History, University of Edinburgh.

Barbara Yorke is Reader in Medieval History and Archaeology, recently King Alfred's College, Winchester.

Figures

Abbreviations

ASE	*Anglo-Saxon England*
Bon. Ep.	*S. Bonifatii et Lulli Epistolae*, ed. M. Tangl, *MGH, Epistolae selectae*, I (Berlin, 1916)
Bede, *HA*	Bede, *Historia abbatum*, in *Venerabilis Baedae, Opera Historica*, ed. C. Plummer (1896)
Bede, *HE*	*Bede's Ecclesiastical History of the English People*, ed. and trans. R. Mynors and B. Colgrave (rev. edn, 1991)
CCSL	*Corpus Christianorum Series Latina* (Turnholt, in progress)
ECMS	*Early Christian Monuments of Scotland*
EHD I	*English Historical Documents, I, c. 500–1042*, ed. D. Whitelock (2nd edn, 1979)
EHR	*English Historical Review*
Harmer, *SEHD*	*Select English Historical Documents of the 9th and 10th Centuries*, ed. F.E. Harmer (1914)
HF	*Historia Francorum*
JEH	*Journal of Ecclesiastical History*
MGH	*Monumenta Germaniae Historica*
Robertson, *Charters*	A.J. Robertson, *Anglo-Saxon Charters* (1939)
TRHS	*Transactions of the Royal Historical Society*
Whitelock, *Wills*	D. Whitelock, *Anglo-Saxon Wills* (1930)

1 Introduction: Identities in Early Medieval Britain[1]

William O. Frazer

The genesis of this book was in 1994, when several younger scholars at the University of Sheffield became interested in the concept of social identity. From intense dialogue in cramped offices (when perhaps we ought to have been working) to animated discussions in neighbouring pubs (when perhaps we ought to have been relaxing), the idea for a more careful investigation of historical ideas about 'identity' grew from a series of linked concerns in our respective research interests to plans for a conference on the topic and eventually to musings about the value of an edited volume such as this. At the centre of these concerns was the very open and friendly atmosphere that permeated much of Sheffield's Department of Archaeology and Prehistory at that time, the interesting ideas that different backgrounds fed into the discussions, and the strong interdisciplinary background of both editors. The latter, we realized, was something that many colleagues appeared to regard with alarm and something that, as junior scholars, we felt concerned to justify. More important than this, however, was our desire to reconcile apparently disparate ideas in adjacent fields of study that seemed to us to be of value beyond narrow disciplinary confines. We also wished to broaden the project beyond those fields already familiar to us and to include others that we recognized harboured fertile ideas for a better understanding of how people thought of themselves and each other in early medieval Britain.

Only relatively recently have historians and archaeologists studying Britain begun to approach the study of medieval society using the

1. I would like to thank Andrew Tyrrell for his coediting of this book, his general cooperation in the project since we first conceived it in 1994, and for his comments on and criticisms of this chapter. I would also like to thank the series editor Nicholas Brooks for his patience, assistance, comments and criticisms, and the contributors to the volume for their participation in the project. I was partly maintained during the research for this book by a Wightman Scholarship from the University of Sheffield, and by an Overseas Research Studentship. In the notes that follow, I have tried to provide key references that I find particularly useful for interdisciplinary understanding.

methodology and terminology of the social sciences. Two themes
permeate the book: first the integration of sophisticated theories into
the often atheoretical realm of early medieval studies; secondly
relating these different understandings of our past to the broader
realm of contemporary culture where regionalism and national identity
(and their 'origins') have become increasingly topical and heated. Over
the past decade or so, both medievalists and the media have
increasingly employed terms such as identity and ethnicity without
always being clear about the meaning of these terms.

The contributors to this book have drawn particularly upon
sociocultural anthropology, social theory and sociology to address
more particular issues and debates within history, archaeology and
physical anthropology. Although we were never able to host a
conference on the topic, we have edited the chapters as part of a
single holistic project – there are many complementary ideas which
shade into one another in different chapters, in spite of the fact that
authors sometimes disagree on specific issues. Each author was asked
by the editors to focus upon a particular topic (what we call some of the
'structuring principles' of early medieval identity) – ethnicity, national
identity, social location, subjectivity/personhood, political organization, kinship, the body, gender, age groups, proximity/regionality,
memory and ideological systems. All the contributors are innovative
and critical in their approach and all have attempted to make their
work accessible to people outside their specialization. Several
summarize complicated ideas in a discipline or sub-field speciality so
that non-specialists can understand and follow the logic of the
argument. In some cases, this attempt at communication across
disciplinary boundaries is the first such example of which I am aware.

Thinking about identity

A variety of abstract theoretical ideas about identity have influenced
the contributors. It is difficult to address all these ideas in a manner
that is still accessible to the wide range of disciplines from which they
are drawn, but, nevertheless, a number of similar understandings of
identity underpin all the chapters in this volume. At the most basic
level, all the chapters recognize that the term identity has been under-
theorized in historical studies. Even in many anthropological and
sociological texts concerned with history, while there have been
diverse ideas about the formation of 'collective' or 'group' identity and
the nature of collective action, there remains a tendency to see groups
as a coming together of pre-formed 'selves'.[2] The relationships which

---

2. S. Mennell, 'The function of we-images: a process theory', in *Social Theory and
    the Politics of Identity*, ed. C. Calhoun (1994), 175–97, at 175. Roger Rouse has
    noted the manner in which we unthinkingly tend to universally assign modern

exist between self and group identities have been neglected. It is possible, however, both to acknowledge the dynamics between individual and group identities, and to investigate the nature of those dynamics in specific situations, by employing the more general term 'social identity' to encompass both the individual and the group.

Furthermore, it is fruitful to recognize explicitly the broad concept 'social identity' as multi-layered and to understand that identities derive from the circumstances of social interaction. This re-emphasizes the vital, active role which the formation of social groups has on the formation of individual identities ('subjectivities'). It begins to reconnect the two. We might begin to think about social identity as akin to the phrase 'second nature' – made up of acquired tendencies that have become largely instinctive. This taken-for-granted under-standing is useful in comprehending the formation of groups. Aspects of one's own group identity, for example, seem to be inherent, innate, 'natural', while their absence or difference seems correspondingly unnatural. Nevertheless, 'social identity' also implies a more conscious awareness by members of a group than that allowed by second nature. In other words, certain second nature aspects of social identity are brought to the fore in certain social interactions, emphasized and manipulated by individuals in ways that are much more conscious and deliberate.[3] We are forced to engage with these two aspects of social identity to avoid the tensions that arise from an 'either-or' theorization of the concept: *either* as always 'given', 'taken-for-granted', *or* as absolutely changeable and subject to no factors apart from each individual's will ('voluntarism').

The advantage of considering both group and individual identities in such a way – as created through social action and contingent upon social relations – is that it confronts notions both of identity as naturally given and as produced exclusively by the unfettered exercise of individual will. It also acknowledges the connection between group and individual identity, and begins to theorize how that connection works. Such considerations, called 'social constructionism', also 'challenge "essentialist" notions that individual persons can have singular, integral, altogether harmonious and unproblematic identi-ties'.[4] These approaches can call into question understandings of group identities as based upon some common 'essence'.[5] This latter issue is of particular significance when considering material culture,

---

contd.
    characteristics of bourgeois liberal democracy to contemporary group identities, in 'Questions of identity: personhood and collectivity in transnational migration to the United States', *Critique of Anthropology* 15(4) (1995), 351–80. This is also a problem with many studies of past group dynamics.
3. Mennell, 'We-Images', 177.
4. C. Calhoun, 'Social theory and the politics of identity', in *Social Theory and the Politics of Identity*, ed. C. Calhoun (1994), 9–36, at 13.
5. *Ibid.*, 13.

since there is still an inclination among archaeologists to view artefact 'kits' as signifiers of straightforward, unchanging group identities, rather than as the expressions of identities in particular social interactions, in which the acts of expressing are also the acts of identity formation.[6]

It might clarify these abstractions about social identity and about its place within social life, if we think of the latter as 'storied'.[7] Several implications follow from such a model. First, that such stories of social life, to some extent, steer action. People form multiple, changing, biographical identities by placing themselves or being placed within a series of emplotted stories. Second, the model implies that experience itself is created through these stories. That is, that people make sense of what has happened and what is happening to them by trying to gather or integrate these happenings within one or more stories. And finally, that people are guided to act in particular ways on the basis of the projections, expectations and memories derived from a number of different but ultimately limited series of available stories. Identities are important influences on human activity. Examining them in a theoretically sophisticated way, one could argue, holds the potential to help us understand both the people and the events of the past in new and useful ways. The idea of social life as a bundle of interconnected

---

6.   Dell Upton has recently warned against the 'kit' understanding of material culture in relation to ethnicity; D. Upton, 'Ethnicity, authenticity and invented traditions', *Historical Archaeology* 30(2) (1996), 1–7. See also: R.H. McGuire, 'The study of ethnicity in historical archaeology', *Journal of Anthropological Archaeology* 1 (1982), 159–78; B.R. Penner, 'Old World traditions, New World landscapes: ethnicity and archaeology of Swiss-Appenzellers in the colonial South Carolina backcountry', *International Journal of Historical Archaeology* 1(4) (1997), 257–321; and S. Jones, *The Archaeology of Ethnicity: Constructing Identities in the Past and Present* (1997). For other perspectives on archaeology and social identity, see: S. Shennan (ed.), *Archaeological Approaches to Cultural Identity* (1989); P.L. Kohl and C. Fawcett (eds), *Nationalism, Politics and the Practice of Archaeology* (1995); and J.A. Atkinson, I. Banks and J. O'Sullivan (eds), *Nationalism and Archaeology* (1996). Accounts of the dangers of mapping ethnicity or race directly onto archaeology can be found in: B. Arnold, 'The past as propaganda: totalitarian archaeology in Nazi Germany', *Antiquity* 64 (1990), 464–78; and B. Trigger, *A History of Archaeological Thought* (1989).

7.   Much of this paragraph paraphrases and simplifies arguments in M.R. Somers and G.D. Gibson, 'Reclaiming the epistemological "Other": narrative and the social construction of identity', in *Social Theory and the Politics of Identity*, ed. C. Calhoun (1994), 37–99, at 38–9. Hayden White has previously argued that narrative modes of representing knowledge (telling historical stories) were representational *forms* imposed by historians on the 'chaos' of lived experience; see *ibid.*, 38; and H. White, 'The question of narrative in contemporary historical theory', *History and Theory* 23, 1–33. For additional perspectives on the narrative (storied) nature of social life, see: P. Ricoeur, 'Narrative time', in *On Narrative*, ed. W.J.T. Mitchell (Chicago, 1981), 165–86; *idem, Time and Narrative*, trans. K. McLaughlin and D. Pellauer (2 vols, 1984, 1986); V.W. Turner and E.M. Bruner (eds), *The Anthropology of Experience* (Urbana, 1986); J. Bruner, 'Life as narrative', *Social Research* 54(1), 11–32; T.R. Sarbin (ed.), *Narrative Psychology: The Storied Nature of Human Conduct* (New York, 1986).

stories allows us, on the one hand, to acknowledge the influence of our social surroundings on our identities, but, on the other, to explain great differences in identities between people who are ostensibly from similar cultural and social situations, from similar historical contexts. Within this model, we might observe that identities are formed through reflexive processes, which means that people's perception of how others see them plays a paramount part in how they think of themselves.[8]

Analyses which allow people in certain early periods of history this reflexive savvy, this ability to participate in social life as active, thinking people, are not common.[9] This is especially true for the first millennium AD, a period of European history in which contact between different groups was becoming more frequent, and a period that is portrayed in most European national historiographies as the font of today's national identities. With the exception of several widely cited texts analysing nationalisms as sociocultural phenomena,[10] important theoretical texts examining identity have tended to neglect the historical specifics of medieval Europe in favour of in-depth analyses of more recent and contemporary social and cultural circumstances. In particular, viewing 'pre-modern State' social identities only as opposites against which we then contrast modern identities and nationalisms is problematic. In popular culture, these 'pre-modern State' identities are often romanticized as being radically different, 'kin-based', universal and unchanging until some poorly understood but crucial historical break such as 'the Enlightenment', 'modernity' and 'industrial capitalism'.[11] Defining portions of the past, without close historical scrutiny, as opposites to the present does little to help us genuinely understand that past. It has led to a situation in which critical analyses of the construction of social identity that are both historical and focused upon an era pre-dating the formation of modern

---

8. Mennell, 'We-Images', 179.
9. For an exception, see S. Greenblatt, *Renaissance Self-Fashioning* (1980). On the wider relevance of Greenblatt's historically-specific idea of 'self-fashioning' identities, also see J. Clifford, 'On ethnographic self-fashioning: Conrad and Malinowski', in *The Predicament of Culture: Twentieth-Century Ethnography, Literature and Art* (1988), 92–113.
10. For example: B. Anderson, *Imagined Communities: Reflections on the Origin and Spread of Nationalism* (1983); L. Colley, *Britons: Forging the Nation 1707–1837* (1996); L. Greenfield, *Nationalism: Five Roads to Modernity* (1992); E. Hobsbawm, *Nations and Nationalism since 1780: Programme, Myth, Reality* (1990); R. Samuel (ed.), *Patriotism: The Making and Unmaking of British National Identity* (3 vols, 1989). Three notable anthropological takes on nationalism and ethnicity are: F. Barth, *Ethnic Groups and Boundaries: The Social Organization of Culture Differences* (Boston, 1969); T.H. Eriksen, *Ethnicity and Nationalism: Anthropological Perspectives* (1993); and R. Jenkins, *Social Identity* (1996).
11. See Mennell, 'We-Images', 179–80 for a discussion of the 'prevalence of egocentric models of the "individual" and "society" [in which] "society" beyond the face-to-face group or community has remained undifferentiated'.

State apparatuses, that explore the manner in which social identity is constituted, are very much needed.

Based upon ethnographic, sociological and historical research, several 'structuring principles' within which societies organize their social identities suggest themselves. These structuring principles relate to the understanding of social identity and social life outlined above – that the formulation of social identity, as an action undertaken by knowing, active people, is enabled and constrained by such principles. Although by no means comprehensive, or perhaps even applicable in every social circumstance, these structuring principles serve as useful abstractions upon which we can begin to build our historical interpretations. Such generalities are of little applicability without a more thorough grounding in historical detail: the ways in which these principles actually structure identity and the significance these identities have with regard to power and access to knowledge, are most usefully considered through a focus on the particular.

Structuring principles such as ethnicity, nationalism, social location,[12] subjectivity/personhood, political organization (e.g. legal definitions), kinship, the human body, gender, age groups, proximity/regionality, memory and ideological systems (e.g. spirituality and religious belief) all help to constitute both the way modern scholars think about early medieval Britain, and how they construct early medieval people's perceptions of themselves and others. Ethnicity, because of its importance in national historiographies and in contemporary scholarly debate, figures prominently in several of the chapters.

The structure of this book mirrors the structuring principles of early medieval identity. The principles interpenetrate, as will become clear from the contributions to this book; the usefulness of considering them discretely aids scholarly understanding but we should be careful not to separate them into distinct, bounded categories.

Chapters 2 to 6 comprise studies of how we have come to understand social identity in early medieval Britain – the theories underpinning our scholarship. Several authors consider how these differ from earlier understandings of social identity by reconstructing early medieval perspectives on 'the self' and 'the other'. Chapters 7 to 12 undertake more specific empirical studies which address the dynamics of one or more structuring principles of early medieval

---

12. I use the phrase 'social location' as a shorthand to encompass terms from different disciplines that overlap but are not exactly the same – social 'role' (analogous to 'enactment') and social 'status' (analogous to 'subject-position') – while simultaneously avoiding some of the pitfalls of sociology's role theory (such as the tendency to see an individual as separate from, and pre-existing, her/his 'roles' rather than as constructed through them; or the manner in which role theory obscures the fact that individuals have multiple identities). For a fuller discussion, see Calhoun, 'Social theory', especially 12–14.

identity, and the manner in which those articulated with other aspects of social life. These later chapters, especially, provide detailed microanalyses which challenge some of the received general wisdoms about social identity. Moreover, in combination with earlier chapters, they mark out a route between historical specifics and theory, suggesting guidelines and possibilities for future scholarship in other eras.

Past and present views on early medieval people

John Moreland, in Chapter 2, points out the problems which have developed in medieval studies often because of the lack of theorization of ethnicity and material culture, and of the relationships between the two. Like other aspects of social identity, ethnic groupings of past societies have become fundamental to the constitution of modern identities, and national identities in particular. Moreland develops a familiar critique of the 'culture history' approach, which is still widespread in medieval archaeology and in the interdisciplinary literature which draws upon it, observing that archaeological 'cultures' do not equal so-called ethnic cultures. There is a broader problem here which Moreland touches upon tangentially – a misunderstood conception of culture in which societies are conceived as 'small, self-contained, and culturally homogeneous'.[13] In much medieval archaeology, variation in the patterning of material culture is still liable to be explained in terms of 'ethnicities' or 'group identities', in which these categories are thought of as discrete, miniature cultures, rather than as a complex web of inter-woven, heterogeneous, fluid social relationships. One of the problems such a conception of group identity engenders is a profound difficulty in addressing the actions of interest groups *within* that larger collectivity.[14] When culture and group identity are considered to be conscriptive and monolithic, variety of belief and

---

13. J.H. Steward, 'Introduction', in *The People of Puerto Rico: A Study in Social Anthropology*, eds J.H. Steward, R.A. Manners, E.R. Wolf, E. Padilla Seda, S.W. Mintz and R.L. Scheele (1956), 1-27, at 5; and W. Roseberry, 'The cultural history of peasantries', in *Articulating Hidden Histories: Exploring the Influence of Eric R. Wolf*, eds J. Schneider and R. Rapp (1995), 51-66, at 52-4.
14. This problem is explored in more depth in B. Frazer, 'Reconceptualizing resistance in the historical archaeology of the British Isles', *International Journal of Historical Archaeology: Archaeologies of Resistance in Britain and Ireland, Part I* 3(1), ed. B. Frazer (1999), 1-10, where I draw upon the critique of cultural 'authenticity' outlined in Clifford, *The Predicament of Culture*, 222 and *passim*. For comment on the attacks upon anthropological 'relativism' – that discipline's tendency to focus on the 'exotic' and to stress cultural difference – see C. Geertz, 'Anti-Anti-Relativism', *American Anthropologist* 86(2) (1984), 63-78. I do not believe, however, that the concept of 'culture' itself is always suspect, always fetishizing the 'other', always assessing difference hierarchically (*contra* L. Abu-Lughod, 'Writing against culture', in *Recapturing Anthropology: Working in the Present*, ed. R.G. Fox (1991), 137-62). A strong case for a

practice within a group is considered unimportant and aberrant.[15] This raises problems because it presumes a top-down social model for the group in which most members behave like sheep. In addition to being politically abhorrent, the model is extremely difficult to sustain on evidence from either history or sociocultural anthropology.

With his notion of 'restricted ethnicity' (present, he argues, by the end of the seventh century) Moreland begins to get at the specifics of this denial of agency and power to marginalized people ('subalterns') in early medieval Britain. He also develops a potent critique of modern ideas about the homogeneity and German-ness of 'the English'. Moreland notes that ethnic adjectives, notably those used in association with the term *gens*, were rarely used for individuals. Typically, they apply to 'a dominant and restricted social elite, a minority'. For those lower on the social scale, he suggests that social location as well as geographical location would perhaps have been more important than any putative 'ethnic' identity. 'Given the lack of archaeological evidence for a massive rupture in the countryside of late Roman Britain,' Moreland argues, 'we must assume that the vast majority of the population were not of Germanic origin/descent'. Further, 'a more continuous process of assimilation into the decentralized and personalized power structures of sub-Roman Britain means that we cannot even assume that the elites were primarily Germanic'. Although Moreland does not situate such notions within broader post-colonial discourse, the trope of an uninhabited landscape waiting to be 'taken' by European colonists is a recurrent theme in colonial descriptions from the early modern period right up until the present day.[16] In a similar manner, Moreland introduces many of the issues which are developed further in later chapters.

The early medieval person's individual notion of self is the subject of Nerys Patterson's critical historical sociology in Chapter 3.

---

contd.

'borderland' understanding of culture 'without otherness', in which differences come from different histories as much as different cultures, and in which anthropological associations of culture with authenticity and bounded distinction are reconsidered, is made in S.B. Ortner, *Making Gender: The Politics and Erotics of Culture* (Boston, 1996). These issues are also touched on succinctly, from a sociological perspective, in Calhoun, 'Social theory', especially 14.

15. B. Barnes, *The Elements of Social Theory* (1995), 10–36 summarizes the strongest criticisms, and delivers his own damning critique of the excesses of individualism. For the historical situatedness of contemporary Western ideas about 'the individual', see M. Mauss, 'Une catégorie de l'esprit humain: la notion de la personne, celle de "moi"', in *Sociologie et Anthropologie* (Paris, 1950), 333–61. An overemphasis in history on dominant power is famously critiqued in M. Foucault, *Discipline and Punish* (New York, 1977) and *idem*, *Power/Knowledge: Selected Interviews and Other Writings*, ed. C. Gordon (1980).

16. For elaboration upon this and other lexical and tropic inventions characteristic of a European colonial gaze, see: P. Hulme, 'Polytropic man: tropes of sexuality and mobility in early colonial discourse', and J. Rabasa, 'Allegories of the atlas', both in F. Barker *et al.* (eds), *Europe and Its Others* vol. 2, 1–16 and 17–32,

Patterson argues that modern cultures tend to explore the events of the body, and the mind's emotions about those events, exclusively 'evading and obfuscating the question of what is happening to the broader field of social relationships'. This is problematic when considering early medieval subjectivities, especially through a 'phenomenological' focus on the day-to-day lived experiences of 'self' which concern Patterson. Modern understandings of self, she argues, are 'in contrast to early medieval cultures – which deal with marriage and death as packages of related changes'. Anxiety about such transformative junctures in human life cycles was expressed in early medieval societies as 'loss'. This loss, in turn, was solved or soothed by 'filling the void with monetary or material compensations'. This is an avenue yet to be explored by archaeologists of the early medieval period, yet what Patterson argues from traditional historical sources could have dramatic repercussions for our understanding of material culture, particularly in the context of funerary ritual. 'Medieval people,' she asserts, 'approached not only the changes accompanying marriage and death but the entire relationship of the self and others, in all its complexity, as transactions where loss of one kind (personal, physical and emotional) was compensated by gain of another kind (in personal, material and instrumental).' She tells us that 'this way of handling subjective experience and its representation as a "self" is closely tied to aspects of early European social structure, particularly the mode of agrarian production'. Patterson uses Ireland (and *Crith Gablach*) as a model for England, transcending the influence of national historiography in the process of her analysis, and presenting a

contd.

respectively; L. Montrose, 'The work of gender in the discourse of discovery', *Representations* 33, 1–41; and E. Shohat, 'Imaging terra incognita: the disciplinary gaze of empire', *Public Culture* 3: 41–70 (1993). E. Said's *Orientalism* (1978) and *Culture and Imperialism* (1993) are important watersheds in the development of critical analyses of colonial discourse, following on from A. Césaire, *Discourse on Colonialism*, trans. J. Pinkham (New York, 1972); F. Fanon, *The Wretched of the Earth*, trans. C. Farrington (1965); *idem, A Dying Colonialism*, trans. H. Chevalier (New York, 1967). Also significant in the corpus of postcolonial discourse are other articles in F. Barker *et al.*, *Europe and Its Other* (2 vols, 1984) and P. Chatterjee, *Nationalist Thought and the Colonial World: A Derivative Discourse* (1986). It would be interesting to further explore the link between nineteenth-century notions of empire and the discourse of early Anglo-Saxon studies, as, for example, has been done for antiquarian ideas in Britain concerning prehistory and the Romans – see S. Smiles, *The Image of Antiquity: Ancient Britain and the Romantic Imagination* (1994), especially 113–28; and A.B. Ferguson, *Utter Antiquity: Perceptions of Prehistory in the Renaissance* (1993). See also, for the issue of Anglo-Saxon scholarship and notions of 'race': H.A. MacDougall, *Racial Myth in English History: Trojans, Teutons and Anglo-Saxons* (1982); R. Horseman, 'Origins of racial Anglo-Saxonism in Great Britain before 1850', *Journal of the History of Ideas* 37(3) (1976), 387–410; and J.W. Burrow, *A Liberal Descent: Victorian Historians and the English Past* (1981).

comparison which will, no doubt, elicit criticism from some scholars. Yet the comparison is valid, not least for its fundamentally significant generalizations on understandings of the self across early medieval Europe: 'the self was viewed as socially embryonic – needing to be equipped with many attributes and possessions in order to have much worth'. Her argument that individualistic accumulation was a fundamental aspect of the highly individualized mode of production in early northern Europe avoids the classic anachronistic projections of contemporary individualism onto the past. It does so by connecting the existence of certain notions of self directly to the experience of agricultural production and rural quotidian life at the time. This issue begs for further explorations in other specific contexts, employing both historical and archaeological material. Patterson begins to situate, historically and culturally, the individualistic materialism which has come to represent contemporary Western society more broadly. Historically, the impulse cannot simply be explained as a product of capitalism, modernity, the Enlightenment, the Industrial Revolution or of commodity culture[17] (although clearly, contemporary individualism relates to all of these) – it has earlier antecedents.

In Chapter 4, Barbara Yorke touches upon many of the issues raised in Moreland's chapter, but from a perspective which focuses on the nature of early medieval political organization. She takes the work of

---

17.   Equally problematic are claims that 'individualism' and other 'English' or 'Anglo-Saxon' characteristics are not subject to the vicissitudes of time or space (and therefore extend from at least the early medieval period forwards) and are the cause of capitalism, modernity, etc.: e.g. see A. MacFarlane, *The Origins of English Individualism: The Family, Property and Social Transition* (1978); *idem*, *The Culture of Capitalism* (1987); and R. Hodges, 'Anglo-Saxon England and the origins of the modern world system', in *Anglo-Saxon Settlements*, ed. Della Hooke (1988), 211–304. Both Alan MacFarlane and Richard Hodges confuse eurocentrism and English ethnocentrism with analyses of specific circumstances in western Europe which led to particular historical events. The argument, implied or explicit, for structural cohesiveness over a millennium or longer, across the whole of medieval Europe, is one which I find untenable – P. Zumthor, *Speaking of the Middle Ages* (1986, Lincoln), and J. Le Goff, 'For an extended middle ages', in *The Medieval Imagination* (1988), 18–23 argue for such a situation; R. Balzaretti, 'The creation of Europe', *History Workshop Journal* 33 (1992), 181–96, and J. Moreland, 'Through the looking glass of possibilities: understanding the middle ages', in *Die Vielfalk der Dinge: Neue Wege zur Analyse mittelalterlicher Sachkultur (Internationaler Kongress Krems an der Donau 4. bis 7. Oktober 1994)* (Forshungen des Instituts für Realienkunde des Mittelalters und der frühen Neuzeit: Diskussionen und Materialien Nr 3, Vienna, 1998), 85–116, at 103–9 critique such a notion. Jack Goody makes a strong general case against the 'uniqueness of the West', in terms of teleological tendencies towards capitalism, addressing the work of Karl Marx, Max Weber, and numerous sociologists and historians of Europe: J. Goody, *The East in the West* (1996). Goody, who could be accused of downplaying cultural specificity too much, is at least right to point out the problematic 'orientalism' of both Marx and Weber; see also Said, *Orientalism* and articles in C.A. Breckenridge and P. van der Veer (eds), *Orientalism and the Post-Colonial Predicament: Perspectives of South Asia* (Philadelphia, 1993).

Bede, and argues that we must understand the context in which classical terms were being used for political figures and organizations, and how their meanings changed through time. What terms should historians today employ in their discussions of the early medieval past? Yorke expands on some of the difficulties with the anthropological term 'chiefdom', namely its disjuncture with the terminology of the time. The term risks glossing over contextual nuances necessary for a detailed study and it also risks drawing too crude a contrast between early 'chiefdom' Anglo-Saxon England and later Anglo-Saxon 'state' society.[18] Similarly, the general term 'polity' is not very descriptive. If we are to consider the nature of political identity during the first millennium in Britain, it is perhaps best approached through a detailed analysis of the meanings that the terms then in use held. For example, what did the early medieval term 'peoples' mean and what was its relation to political structures? Towards this end, Yorke delivers a fine-grained analysis of Bede's terminology, situating a textual reading within an historical anthropological mileu and moving on to consider charter evidence, the Tribal Hidage and religious hagiographies.

Alex Woolf (Chapter 5) questions the autonomy of *regiones* in early England as independent, embryonic kingdoms, building a critique of evolutionary archaeological models ('an obsession with small beginnings') which parallels that of Yorke in Chapter 4. Nevertheless, Woolf approaches his material from a 'structural functionalist' perspective, explaining both the use of contemporary early medieval terms and the value of modern terms such as 'social network' according to the purpose(s) they might serve in a 'social system'. Social network, for example, Woolf uses along the lines of a more enlightened anthropological definition of 'kin': 'to designate the unit of kin and friends who actually aid a litigant in bringing a dispute to resolution. ... The social network ... is ... fluid in its constituency ... its extent being modified by pragmatic affiliations and absences, and a more situational identification of interest.'

Again, like Yorke, Woolf is critical of understandings of the Tribal Hidage which overemphasize the significance, in terms of structural power and control over land, of smaller *regiones* and -*saete* groupings, suggesting that our contemporary concerns with cultural and political 'disunity' (as Woolf terms it) may have more to do with our own cultural and political mileu than with evidence we have from the past.

---

18. The source for this problematic evolutionary schema ('band', 'tribe', 'chiefdom', 'state'), albeit an indirect one for many medievalists, is E. Service, *Primitive Social Organization: An Evolutionary Perspective* (New York, 1962), which draws upon the economics of Karl Polanyi. Service recanted and altered his schema, something almost universally ignored by archaeologists; *idem*, 'Our contemporary ancestors: extant stages and extinct ages', in *Cultural Evolution* (New York, 1971), 151–7; for this observation in another context, see A.B. Kehoe, *The Land of Prehistory: A Critical History of American Archaeology* (1997), 166–7.

In this respect, Woolf's chapter might be taken as a prompt for a more critical scrutiny of the theories of knowledge ('epistemological' bases) upon which so many of our arguments about early medieval Britain rest.

Woolf employs a Norwegian comparison to argue that the 'hundred', 'plebs' or 'vicaria' were probably all based upon face-to-face contact (although he is quick to note the important distinctions from a kin group, whose boundaries would have been far more fluid). He hypothesizes that the *regiones*-based *gens* was likely based upon assemblies mustered at regular intervals. If this was indeed the case, Woolf argues, then wealthier inhabitants of a given area would have been able to attend more often and to acquire the social contacts, political voice and power which came with such attendance. While this line of thinking is clearly reductive, Woolf plays it up to stress a significant point: 'At root, the *gens* itself, long recognized to have little basis in shared descent, is, indeed, nothing less than a giant social network of this sort!' It is only when a group reaches a level of social organization at which face-to-face familiarity can no longer be maintained – because of population, geographical distance, etc. – that 'ethnic' identifiers, Woolf argues, begin to appear (e.g. the larger *regiones* and more populous *gens*).

In Chapter 6, Dawn Hadley sets out to examine the belief that Scandinavian settlers in England were ethnically and culturally distinct through a consideration of apparently incompatible historical, material culture and place-name evidence, including a review of the scholarly literature which relates to these topics. Although the documentary evidence for viking[19] settlement is slight, much scholarly literature has assumed that such settlement had a significant impact. Regions of Scandinavian settlement in the ninth and tenth centuries were characterized at a later date and to different degrees by Scandinavian place-names; Scandinavian legal and administrative offices and institutions names; distinctive legal and administrative organization; large numbers of free peasants (sokemen); a prevalence of large, multi-vill estates (sokes); and artefact evidence with Scandinavian iconographic influences. Such evidence was used, by Frank Stenton and Henry Loyn amongst others,[20] to argue for quite separate identities for Danish and English people residing in northern and eastern England. In contrast, scholars such as Peter Sawyer have downplayed any significant impact which Scandinavian settlers may have had, arguing that the numbers of viking settlers were minute.[21] Linguists especially have maintained that regardless of the size of the viking armies, it is unlikely that they could have been responsible for the great

---

19. With a small 'v', Hadley insists.
20. F.M. Stenton, *Anglo-Saxon England* (3rd edn, 1971); H. Loyn, *The Vikings in Britain* (1977).
21. P.H. Sawyer, *The Age of the Vikings* (2nd edn, 1971).

Scandinavian influence on the place-names, personal names and speech of Anglo-Saxon England.[22] Instead, such linguistic influence has come to be regarded as the consequence of a second, unrecorded wave of peasant Scandinavian immigrants.

Hadley argues that much of this literature, particularly that which downplays the Scandinavian influence and emphasizes a swift assimilation into existing society, to some extent begs the question of 'what was the nature of the society of the Danelaw'. 'People do not integrate and adopt the social structures and belief systems of others by a process of unconscious osmosis,' she says. Rather, 'real and relevant decisions must be made, survival strategies adopted, and resistance encountered. A consideration of this has been lacking from recent work on the Danelaw.'

Hadley observes that there are but 150 or so loan words from Scandinavian languages in Old English, most of which relate to legal and administrative spheres. In contrast, Middle English has many thousands of Scandinavian loans, of a sort which can only realistically be accounted for by the existence of a mixed-speech community across a broad spectrum of social locations. In comparable ethnographic and historical contexts such linguistic influence requires: mutual intelligibility, bilingualism and a period of co-existence of two languages. What the linguistic evidence reveals is not the scale of the Scandinavian settlement but rather the degree of contact between Scandinavian and English speakers.

How do these observations relate to place-names, in terms of place-name elements which are Scandinavian in origin, and in terms of pronunciation changes? For the former, when we consider legal and administrative Scandinavian loan words, we must question why major settlements and administrative centres tend to have conspicuously Old English names. Moreover, the bulk of Scandinavian place-names are in sparsely-settled regions and on the periphery of estates. As Hadley argues, a division of the countryside into areas of English and areas of Scandinavian settlements on the basis of place-name evidence is problematic, depending as it does upon 'assumptions about "ethnic" separation and continuity that are difficult to sustain'. In a similar manner, 'Scandinavian' sculpture does not mark out Scandinavian inhabitation on a simple one-to-one basis. Concerning the religious conversion of the Scandinavians, we may posit a similar explanation relating to power, if we make an anthropology-based distinction between private conversion and public Christianization ritual. (Scholars of comparative religion have termed this distinction 'orthopraxy' and 'orthodoxy', respectively.[23]) For Hadley, the survival

---

22. See Hadley's relevant chapter, note 9.
23. For a discussion of 'orthopraxy' and 'orthodoxy' in medieval Europe, see: J. Nelson, 'Society, theodicy and the origins of heresy: towards a reassessment of the medieval evidence', in *Schism, Heresy and Religious Protest*, ed. D.J. Baker (Studies in Church History, vol. 9, 1972), 65–77 and J.C. Russell, *The*

of Old English estate names was part of a strategy which also included the issuing of coinage, the forging of relations with native lords and ecclesiastics, the adoption of Christianity and the patronage of monumental stone sculpture. It was a way to control and legitimate rule by reference to existing systems of power and social organization.

Structuring social identities

In Chapter 7, Andrew Tyrrell, co-editor of this book, initiates the case-study-oriented section with a discussion of the body and ethnic identity in early medieval Britain. Understanding the body as a window on society, Tyrrell stresses 'corporeality' (our sense of bodily experience) as a structuring principle for both individual and group identity. He notes the marginalization, in some humanities and social sciences, of biological studies in interrogating ethnicity, and develops his own specific critique of 'genes equals people' arguments in early medieval archaeology.

This marginalization of biology has resulted partly from the elision of ethnicity and race and the mistaken assumption that both are biological givens. Modern scholarship has consequently failed to treat the subject of human variation critically or thoroughly, leaving it more open to bogus manipulation.[24] By deconstructing previous texts and incorporating both Erving Goffman's concept of 'body idiom' and Pierre Bourdieu's understanding of 'doxa', Tyrrell seeks to clarify misunderstandings about the relationship between biological descent, material culture and ethnicity.[25] This is particularly important for the early medieval period because of the significance which misunderstandings of that period have had as bases for nationalist discourses. Too frequently, in interpretations of early medieval Europe and Britain, 'origins' have become confused with 'ethnicity'.

Tyrrell begins with a critique of the frequent assumptions about the label 'Anglo-Saxon' – what was it in the past and what meanings does the use of the term convey today? His own understanding of ethnic

---

contd.

Germanization of Early Medieval Christianity: A Sociohistorical Approach to Religious Transformation (1994). A number of scholars have discussed the desire to acquire more 'foreign' knowledge among indigenous people in contexts where such education may be seen as valuable to facilitate increased, status-generating contact with foreign powers; e.g., G. Lienhardt, 'The Dinka and Catholicism', in *Religious Organization and Religious Experience*, ed. J. Davis (1982), 81–95; B. Frazer, *Tintagel, Justinian and the Material Culture of Missions*, unpublished MA thesis, University of Sheffield (1994), especially 36–42; R.C. Trexler, 'From the mouths of babes: Christianization by children in 16th century New Spain', in *Religious Organization and Religious Experience*, ed. J. Davis (1982), 115–36.

24.   Calhoun, 'Social theory', 17; see also D. Haraway, *Simians, Cyborgs and Women* (1991).

25.   E. Goffman, *The Presentation of Self in Everyday Life* (1969); P. Bourdieu, *The Logic of Practice* (1990).

groups as socially constructed, self-reflexive and changing serves as a basis for his chapter, drawing upon Patrick Geary and Goffman's 'body idiom'.[26] Any genuine correspondence between physicality and genetic relatedness, Tyrrell notes, is irrelevant to those who perceive an imagined community based upon a common origin, law or language. What is more significant for us in understanding the past is how, why and when material culture (including aspects of body idiom) was used to symbolize identity in early medieval Britain. This question does not entail the equation of biology or material culture directly with ethnic identity, nor the practice of mapping ethnicity onto geographical variation in archaeological data and dubbing it 'ethnic symbolism'. Our patterns and links are as much artefacts of the ways we study material as they are observations of the material we are studying.

What it does entail is a deconstruction of existing texts and a critical reappraisal of some of the specific issues upon which early medievalists have foundered. Tyrrell undertakes such a re-evaluation of the manner in which early medieval bodies articulated with ethnicity by a critique of several ground-breaking articles by Heinrich Härke.[27]

Christopher Knüsel and Kathryn Ripley, in Chapter 8, address aspects of the relationships between gender identity and the body in early medieval Britain through a reconsideration of select archaeological funerary remains. By mapping 'discrepancies' between biological sex from skeletal analysis and grave goods associations in early medieval adult cemetery populations from Buckland, Dover, Kent; Sewerby, East Yorkshire; Norton, Cleveland; and Portway, Andover, Hampshire, the two authors begin to query the normative assumptions made by many scholars about the existence and extent of a female/male gender polarity in early medieval society, and about gender divisions in social roles and activities at the time. They elaborate upon the existence of supposedly 'male' skeletons (delivering a succinct analysis of the methodology of osteological sexing in the process) with purportedly 'female' grave goods, systematically running through the possible explanations for such 'incongruities'. Typically, these skeletally 'male' people have been explained away as 'female' individuals, supposedly in accordance with their grave goods, a conclusion that says more about the rigidity of today's contemporary normative understandings of masculinity than it necessarily does about Anglo-Saxon identity.[28] The difficulty lies, they conclude, with a

---

26. P.J. Geary, 'Ethnic identity as a situational construct in the early middle ages', *Mitteilungen der Anthropologischen Gesellschaft in Wien* 113 (1983), 15–26.
27. H. Härke, ' "Warrior graves?" The background of the Anglo-Saxon weapon burial rite', *Past and Present* 126 (1990), 22–43; *idem*, 'Finding Britons in Anglo-Saxon graves', *British Archaeology* 10 (1995), 7; *idem*, 'Weapon burials and knives' in *Berinsfield and Didcot*, eds A. Boyle, A. Dodd, D. Miles and A. Mudd, Thames Valley Landscapes Monograph No. 8 (1995), 67–74.
28. On this rigidity of Western definitions of masculinity over the last several centuries (and its comparison to changing normative conceptions of femininity), see *Radical History Review* 71 (1998), especially L. Gordon and A. Hunter, 'Not

problematic conception of gender which does not allow for the likelihood of more than two genders in early medieval Britain and views male and female as immutable, bounded categories, unaffected and separate from other aspects of identity such as social location and age. Conceptualizing gender as 'an element of human social relations based on culturally perceived and culturally uninscribed differences and similarities between and among males and females', and drawing comparisons from a wide variety of temporal and geographical scenarios, Knüsel and Ripley posit an explanation for at least some of the 'ambiguous' individuals that sees them as *sacerdos* – shamanistic religious figures central to pagan Anglo-Saxon society.

Briefly exploring the possibilities of the usefulness of the concept of social identity in early medieval studies, Julia Crick (Chapter 9) is critical of the manner in which identity has frequently been understood in historical studies – as sentiment, or (dominant) consciousness or solidarity. Apart from glossing over intra-group difference in problematic ways, Crick argues that such understandings tend to treat identity and kinship systems in 'pre-industrial' contexts as little more than foils for modern definitions of social identity.

Crick then specifically considers the relationship between family and social identity among some elites in pre-Conquest England through a consideration of *post obit* arrangements, as revealed in wills, charters and dispute settlements from circa 800 to 1066. She argues that evidence from Anglo-Saxon wills suggests a significantly different understanding of death than that typical in late-industrial, western (secular) culture today, in which it was comprehended as a liminal age category characterized by an extreme state of (dis)embodiment.[29]

Such *post obit* arrangements provide us with some detailed insight into intra-group power relations within families, and, in particular, to the tensions between 'the rights of the individual' and 'the rights of the family'. Crick argues that while individuals behaved as members of kin groups – which she conceptualizes along the lines of Weberian status groups in terms of behaviour towards non-kin – 'the interests of groups are upheld by the actions of individuals'. In others words, it is through social interaction that those group interests manifest themselves. 'Families constantly fragment into multiple groups', often along obvious tension lines (e.g. a woman's natal kin and her husband's family), demonstrating intra-group power dynamics within the family

---

contd.

all male dominance is patriarchal', 71–83. See also J. Tosh, 'What should historians do with masculinity? Reflections on nineteenth-century Britain', *History Workshop Journal* 38 (1994).

29.   The notion of such 'liminal' interstices of society, developed by Victor Turner, is associated with 'anti-structure' outside or in between the Durkheimian structures of group social life; see V.W. Turner, *The Ritual Process: Structure and Anti-Structure* (Hawthorne, 1969).

collectivity. Frequently, it appears that natal groups, conjugal units and affinal relatives are sub-units in term of power relations. Rifts along generational lines, in particular, are typically more complex in the manner in which they articulate with power, since, as we have observed, 'kinship' pious obligations extend in some cases beyond the confines of the kin group or family to include the future owner of an estate. This is particularly significant – interlocking, as it does, with the observations of Patterson (Chapter 3) – in signalling the importance of property: 'The system of pious obligation turned not on blood but on land, not on belonging but on ownership.' It shows the plasticity and situatedness of kinship relations, often presented by historians (and especially archaeologists) as strictly bounded in pre-industrial societies. Crick argues that the familiar analytical categories of 'individual' and 'family' or 'kin' have fallen short in explanations regarding the constitution of society, demonstrating the value of a fluid concept of social identity which is contingent upon social interaction.

In Chapter 10, Tom Saunders employs a Marxist understanding of 'class' to consider some ways in which social location was central to early medieval identities. Outlining his Marxist definition of 'feudalism', Saunders examines the formation of feudal identities in early medieval England in order to shed light upon both the link between land and power and the social use of space. Conceptualizing class as a 'structural relationship', notably after the work of G. E. M. de Ste Croix,[30] but also as 'historical process', Saunders maintains that this is in contrast to a Weberian understanding of 'status' as static and ascribed. Moving on to define 'feudalism' alongside recent work reconsidering the term,[31] he argues both that the bounding and regulation of space 'lies at the heart of an archaeology of feudalism' and that it 'was one of the key structuring principles behind the construction of class identities'. Under feudalism, 'the class relationships between lords and peasants were "anchored to specific territories and specific spaces"'. In particular, Saunders is concerned to scrutinize transformations from dispersed rural settlements to nucleated villages and shifts from ports-of-trade to regional urban centres.

In the first of these two concerns, Saunders observes the increasing prominence which bounded space began to play in the spatial organization of rural sites. From the late ninth century and through the tenth, dispersed and 'fluctuating' farmstead patterns in the East Midlands were replaced by a 'network of fewer large-scale and more permanent settlements'. In spite of some arguments to the contrary,[32] Saunders maintains that the earliest planned villages and hamlets tended to appear on royal estates or those of powerful bodies such as the Church, and that we may take this as an indication of primarily top-down organization. Saunders sees a breaking down of kinship ties

---

30. G.E.M. de Ste Croix, *The Class Struggle and the Ancient Greek World* (1983).
31. E.g., S. Reynolds, *Fiefs and Vassals: The Medieval Evidence Reinterpreted* (1994).

within the peasantry during this period, and believes this to be fundamental to changing relationships between farmers and land. However, such arrangements, through proximate relations and collective farming, also engendered local village communities which 'cast limits on the powers of lordship'. There were constraints to feudal strategies of power – many tenements at both Raunds and West Cotton in Northhamptonshire were not initially occupied and, as well, peasants had some control over their own plots and holdings. Saunders views lordly patronage in the construction of churches, particularly during the consolidation of the parish system in the tenth and eleventh centuries, as not only symbolic of inequalities in wealth and competition between members of the aristocracy, but also as ideological legitimation for what was in actuality a highly fragmented ruling class. He is, however, quick to point out that differences between villages were indicative of the individualization of class power in varying local circumstances.

In the second of his concerns, Saunders views the so-called 'birth of the medieval town' from the seventh through the eleventh centuries through a similar lens – as intricately 'intertwined with the articulation of new class relations and the construction of feudal identities'. In the seventh and eighth centuries, *wics*, royal foundations which served as emporia, were located along the coasts and major waterways of England. The shift to a growing network of more insular, regional centres, boroughs (*burhs*), has been argued to be one result of a transformation from a gift-exchange economy to a more market-orientated economy.[33] Building upon challenges to this normative historical interpretation developed by Rodney Hilton and Guy Bois,[34] Saunders maintains that such medieval urbanization was 'thoroughly feudal' and intimately linked to aristocratic, Church and state interests. Emblematic of new landed social relations, *burhs* served as nodal points in a fragmented feudal structure and played a formative role in the institution and projection of state power. Their built environments were permeated by the enforcement and display of class relations. Towns, Saunders argues, were 'not competitive commercial enterprises'; trade was based upon monopoly and exclusion. They were 'important meeting places for a fragmented feudal aristocracy', 'specialized centres' for the collection of agricultural surpluses, and 'administrative markets for the production and exchange of prestigious items', and these objectives were effected through the design of their urban environments. Early medieval towns 'were a product of

---

32. E.g., C.C. Dyer, 'Power and conflict in the medieval English village', in *Medieval Villages: A Review of Current Work*, ed. Della Hooke (1985), 27–32.
33. R. Hodges, *Dark Age Economics* (1982); *idem, The Anglo-Saxon Achievement* (1989).
34. R. Hilton, *English and French Towns in Feudal Society: A Comparative Study* (1992); G. Bois, *The Transformation of the Year One Thousand: The Village of Lournand from Antiquity to Feudalism* (1992).

feudalism', asserts Saunders, 'but also a *producer* of new social relations and conditions'. Their very diversity relates not only to the complexity of the social construction of urban entities, but also 'allude[s] to the active and transformative nature of the urbanizing process'. As with nucleated villages, however, the feudal interests of an aristocratic class that were effected through the built environment of towns were fraught with tensions: 'as towns expanded, less organized and regulated space grew up in the back streets and behind fronts of tenements'. Not simply physical manifestations of a dominant feudal ideology, the irregular suburbs that grew outside the walls of early medieval towns, as well as the unseen spaces behind tenement frontages, provided locales where structural power could be 'resisted and defied'. More precisely, the transformative role that the construction of both rural and urban space played in the formation and continuing renegotiation of feudal class identities – what I have more broadly called social location – was not simply dictated by the principal agents of early medieval structural power, lords, monarchs and ecclesiastical elites. Rather, ever-changing urban and rural landscapes served as normative frameworks within which both elites and, albeit with greater difficulty, peasants worked and reworked their understandings of groups and individuals.

In Chapter 11, Stephen Driscoll considers how 'ethnic' differences were expressed from the sixth to the twelfth centuries in Scotland by critically scrutinizing a non-military arena of political discourse, sculptured stone monuments. Taking ethnicity to be a socio-cultural construct, and explaining his understanding of the term (he is critical about whether our contemporary notions of ethnicity were relevant in the past), Driscoll moves on to consider sculptured stone monuments as markers of regional variation. Arguing that ethnicity in early medieval Scotland is fundamentally bound up with political capital and structural power, he considers that the process of producing and maintaining regional identity is also the process by which it is transformed.

Following Robert Bartlett, Driscoll understands ethnicity in and around the tenth century to relate to language, law and custom.[35] Within Bartlett's custom category, Driscoll focuses on three social institutions in which custom resides: housing, attire and religious practice. For the latter, he argues that the propagation of different saints' cults in different areas is linked to local concerns both political and ethnic (in Bartlett's medieval understanding of the term), as well as conflict between competing powers within the Church. The large number of Christian monuments erected between the seventh and the tenth centuries AD suggest, through regional differences and links to high-status metalworking, that schools of sculpture were linked to secular patronage (and, ultimately, to royal houses). Moreover, in

---

35. R. Bartlett, *The Making of Europe: Conquest, Colonization and Cultural Change, 950–1350* (1993).

Pictland, representations of the elite as warriors and hunters upon stone media are common, providing support for arguments claiming aristocratic patronage for stone sculpture. The regional differences in sculptural form and composition are corroborated by historical and place-name studies (for which the author provides examples), but Driscoll suggests that these interpretations are problematic because they are not fine-grained enough. In the early Christian monuments of Scotland, the stones were used to define the political landscape, in part through the symbolic content of the sculpture. Using several examples of saints' dedications, Driscoll demonstrates a correspondence between religious dedications and regional schools of stone sculpture. While his suggestion that concentrations of such dedications might therefore be 'eroded footprints of ancient polities' remains to be demonstrated (and similar ideas popular among archaeologists and historians of England are critiqued by both Crick and Woolf), Driscoll's assertion that 'the monumental stone sculpture of early Scotland shares many qualities of early texts such as charters, sagas and saints' lives' is more resilient: '[they] not only recorded events or beliefs, but were actively used to mediate social relations'. More precisely, Driscoll asserts that they contributed to the development of estates and a concomitant shift in structural power from military conquest to, more clearly, the control of agricultural production.

The appearance and decline of early Christian monument stones initially indicate, Driscoll argues, the legitimation of an emerging (locally-based) aristocracy, a process which peaked in the ninth century. The result of this, maintains the author, was a 'nation' of small regional polities accentuating natural topographic differences. Although replaced by the aristocratic sponsorship and construction of stone churches by AD 1000, monumental sculptured stones fundamentally marked 'a social distinction within groups' who identified as local communities, regional political units or Bartlett's early medieval 'ethnicities' far more significantly than they ever marked distinctions between modern conceptions of 'the Picts and the Scots'.

Catherine Cubitt, in the final chapter, is concerned to examine the role of memory in the formation of identity, specifically religious identity in early medieval monasteries in England. She takes, as her starting point, Janet Coleman's arguments about medieval monastic memory: that a collective monastic memory robustly structured by time regulation was substituted for lay memories based upon personal experience.[36] Cubitt is critical of such a simplified dualism. Conflicts in early medieval monasteries, particularly between abbot and brethren, illustrate that monks were, in fact, concerned to some degree with comfort in daily life. Further, the intra-group differences in how members conceptualized their individual identities in relation

---

36. J. Coleman, *Ancient and Medieval Memories: Studies in the Reconstruction of the Past* (1992), 129–36.

to the monastic community do not fit Coleman's generalizations. *Pueri* and those entering monasteries as child oblates clearly have a different identity than those coming to monasteries late in life, and this relates fundamentally to intragroup power relations. Bede, among other writers, gives some indication of the scorn with which less academic later entrants were sometimes considered by better readers. Throughout a monk's life cycle, time was not only structured by the liturgical calendar, but also by both age categories and associated social locations within the community, and special roles and responsibilities. All of these were inherently hierarchical, mirroring, for the most part, rigid ascribed hierarchies in the secular world at the time. Moreover, historical writing also emphasizes the continuing contact between monasteries and the surrounding area, in contrast to Coleman's distinct division. The experiential aspect of monastic life is also evident from memories recounted in historical material, with regard to music, rituals and all-important teacher–student social relations. In accounts of the latter, some sense of both affection and power conflicts is evident, with the clear message that senior members were meant to serve as models of monastic life for younger brethren. Cubitt argues that idealized memories in many of these accounts fit into narrative archetypes (the 'topos of the deathbed scene', for example) when former (famous) members of a monastic community were concerned, but that such memories were also personalized in situations where the deceased had been known directly. Death, in particular, appears to have served as a 'central mnemonic moment in monastic life', and one frequently associated with specific material culture: relics and reliquaries; land donations; and church furnishings such as altar vessels, crosses, pictures and books. As a rite of passage to the liminal age category of 'deceased' (drawing upon Crick's analysis in Chapter 10), the importance of deathbed accounts about senior members of monasteries may provide a hint as to the significance of other formal rites of passage, and a hint of the strict hierarchical boundedness of age categories and other structuring principles of individual identity on membership status within the group. In a setting of comparative disciplinary strictness, in terms of the liturgical structuring of all aspects of everyday life, it is perhaps unsurprising that punctuated moments within the routine of monastic existence appear to have taken on such gravity with respect to intra-group identity and power differences.

From the documentary data, Cubitt extracts several general observations about the structures important in the creation and renegotiation of both collective and individual monastic memories. First, the nature of the foundation – royal or noble – appears to have been significant with respect to traditions of venerable fathers and founding figures. Second, the built environment of the monastic enclosure, including its portable material culture, as well as the surrounding landscape, were vital structuring factors in the nature of monastic memory and identity. The specifics of liturgical practice also clearly played a prominent role in influencing the day-to-day experiences of monks. Finally, the influence of abbots also played a powerful role – through the oral transmission of rule interpretation, as an exemplary model, and through the exercising of dominant power. In short, Cubitt argues for a dramatic interplay between the oral, physical and written aspects of monastic existence. While Coleman is right to emphasize the profound effect that texts had upon monastic memory, such texts could be experienced in a variety of starkly different ways – as part of the liturgy, as public reading in the refectory, and so forth. The written was inseparable from physical discipline, complementary to experiential memory, rather than substitutive.

Conclusion

In summary, the chapters cover a number of aspects of social identity which were significant to inhabitants of early medieval Britain and have remained important to more recent perspectives of Britain in the first millennium AD. By exploring understandings of many of the structuring principles of early medieval identity – ethnicity, national identity, social location, subjectivity/personhood, political organization, kinship, the body, gender, age groups, proximity/regionality, memory and ideological systems – the aim is not merely to broaden our comprehension of a particular period of history, although that is certainly part of our project. It is also to contribute to wider ongoing discussions about the nature of social identity: critiquing and revising often problematic depictions of 'pre-industrial' social life which have formed an historical Other against which contemporary Western social identities have tended to contrast themselves.

2 Ethnicity, Power and the English[1]

John Moreland

'The eternal stream of blood binds us across the ages'[2]

In his *Travels in Hyperreality*, Umberto Eco suggested that all our contemporary 'hot' problems have their source in the Middle Ages, and argued that 'we go back to ... [*the Middle Ages*] every time we ask ourselves about our origin'; that 'people started dreaming of the Middle Ages from the very beginning of the modern era'.[3] In one such dream, the blood of the *gentes* (peoples) of the early Middle Ages still flows in the veins of their modern kin. The issue of origins is 'hot' because there are still people who believe that there *is* an eternal stream of blood linking them to their 'ethnic' ancestors and the 'homeland'. For many that 'blood' flows from the early Middle Ages. They further believe that archaeological and historical evidence can be used to demonstrate this, and can confirm them in their ancestral homelands or show them where those homelands are. In this chapter I

1. I dedicate this article to my uncle Sean Ritchie who died while it was being written. While he might not have favoured the focus on the English, I hope he would have approved of the sentiments which underpin this work. The editors of this book displayed a Job-like patience waiting for this contribution and their comments on early drafts contributed greatly to whatever merits this final version may have. I very much appreciate their efforts and support. I must also thank the series editor, Professor Nicholas Brooks, for his firm editorial hand and valued comments. Richard Jenkins, Alex Woolf, Heinrich Härke, Vanessa Toulmin, Richard Hodges and Mark Pluciennik enhanced my perspectives on ethnicity and the English. Participation in the European Science Foundation's *Transformation of the Roman World* project enabled me to meet and discuss some of the issues with scholars from across Europe. In the light of the problems addressed in this article it seems more than appropriate to thank all those involved in this trans-national venture. My deepest thanks, however, go to Prue for helping me through a very difficult time.
2. H. Reinerth, *Das Federseemoor als Siedlungsland des Vorzeitmenschen* (Leipzig, 1936), 5; cited in B. Arnold, 'The past as propaganda: totalitarian archaeology in Nazi Germany', *Antiquity* 64 (1990), 468.
3. U. Eco, 'Dreaming of the Middle Ages', in *Travels in Hyperreality* (1987), 65.

want to begin a study of the way in which these 'dreams' of the Middle Ages have contributed to the construction of the English.[4]

As archaeologists and historians we have to investigate these issues because we can *show* that in the Middle Ages – that place to which people so often return in their dream-world – ethnicity was not based on 'blood'.[5] The 'eternal stream of blood' binds neither the English nor any other modern people across the ages to their ethnic forebears.[6] We can *demonstrate* this. It is true that 'medieval peoples ... seem frequently to have *believed* that they belonged to nations (*nationes*) and peoples (*gentes*)', and that 'since a people was formed by descent, blood was the vehicle for its consolidation and expansion from one generation to the next'.[7] However, it is also true that these 'peoples' were 'imagined communities'[8] bound together by *belief* in common descent and *actual* common interests.[9] The *gentes* of the early Middle Ages came to *believe* that they constituted 'blood-communities' as a *result* of social and political solidarity.[10] As Richard Jenkins argues, people come to believe that they share a common ancestry as a *consequence* of acting together.[11]

This does not mean that ethnicity did not exist in the early Middle Ages; it did. But it was bound up with other forms of identity, and particularly with relationships of *power* and domination. The imposition of *our* concept of a discrete and objective ethnicity on the early Middle Ages may provide the *medieval* concept of ethnicity with a power in the structuring of society and the life of the individual which it never had at the time. The consequence of our imposition is that we ignore or devalue factors which were then of greater importance in the construction of society and the self. An awareness of this provides us with a very different image of the Middle Ages and a very different understanding of the 'dreams' we can responsibly draw from it.

It is easy to appreciate the role of ethnicity in the wars that have ripped through the Balkans; many people can, perhaps, come to see the Northern Ireland 'Troubles' as an ethnic as opposed to (or as well

---

4. That study will appear in more complete form in my forthcoming book, *Myths of the English*.
5. This is despite the implications of much of the recent work on genetics and archaeology. See P. Sims-Williams, 'Genetics, linguistics, and prehistory: thinking big and thinking straight', *Antiquity* 72 (1998), 505–27.
6. W. Pohl, 'The Barbarian successor states', in *The Transformation of the Roman World AD 400–900*, ed. L. Webster and M. Brown (1997), 47.
7. R.R. Davies, 'The peoples of Britain and Ireland 1100–1400, 1. Identities', *Transactions of the Royal Historical Society* 6th ser. 4 (1994), 4, 6, emphasis added.
8. *Ibid.*, 4.
9. P. Amory, 'Names, ethnic identity, and community in fifth- and sixth-century Burgundy', *Viator* 25 (1994), 4.
10. S. Reynolds, 'What do we mean by "Anglo-Saxon" and "Anglo-Saxons"?', *Journal of British Studies*, 24 (1985), 405.
11. R. Jenkins, *Rethinking Ethnicity. Arguments and Explorations* (1997), 10.

as?) a religious conflict. However, we have a tendency to see ethnicity not as part of *our* make-up, but as something particular to the 'Others'.[12] With characteristic forthrightness, Michael Ignatieff states that at the end of his 'Journeys into the New Nationalism' he had to confront

> the central conceit which cosmopolitans everywhere, and the British in particular, have about the tide of ethnic nationalism destroying the fixed landmarks of the Cold War world: everyone else is a fanatic, everyone but us is a nationalist.[13]

With these insights in mind, I want to begin digging into the myths of the English. I want to question commonly held ideas about their origins and to counter the implicitly held notion that the emergence of England and Englishness was part of some *inevitable* process.[14] In particular I will question the constitution of the 'peoples' – the Angles, Saxons and Jutes – who, largely on the basis of one short paragraph in Bede's *Ecclesiastical History of the English People*,[15] are deemed the ancestors of the English, and assess what kind of identities we can read from their material culture.

One of the strongest and most persistent 'myths of the English' is that they are descended from these three Germanic peoples. In the late nineteenth century Francis Gummere argued that 'Germanic invaders' provided the foundation of English national life;[16] in the late twentieth century Professor Sir Geoffrey Elton asserted that 'the mixed collection of Germanic raiders ... [became] ... subsumed under the name of the English'.[17] However, one of the conclusions of this chapter is that the 'English' are not biologically descended from the Germanic stock of Bede's account. The belief that they are is a myth that draws heavily on 'dreams' of the Middle Ages. It is a myth that is perpetuated through a misreading of historical and archaeological evidence, and through the imposition of modern concepts of identity onto the Migration Period past. It is a myth that has penetrated to the core of many peoples' beliefs about their 'origins', and it is the source of many of the characteristics that they feel to be peculiarly 'English'.

---

12. *Ibid.*, 14.
13. M. Ignatieff, *Blood and Belonging: Journeys into the New Nationalism* (1994), 11.
14. J.G.A. Pocock, 'British history: a plea for a new subject', *Journal of Modern History* 47 (1975), 609. See also P. Wormald, 'Bede, the *bretwaldas* and the origins of the *gens Anglorum*', in *Ideal and Reality in Frankish and Anglo-Saxon Society*, ed. P. Wormald (1983), 104.
15. *Bede's Ecclesiastical History of the English People*, eds B. Colgrave and R.A.B. Mynors (1969), I.15 (Hereafter Bede, *HE*). See also M. Hunter, 'Germanic and Roman antiquity and the sense of the past in Anglo-Saxon England', *Anglo-Saxon England* 3 (1974), 31.
16. F. Gummere, *Germanic Origins: A Study in Primitive Culture* (1892), 1–2.
17. G. Elton, *The English* (1992), 1. The 'conquest myth' is examined by H. Härke, 'Material culture as myth: weapons in Anglo-Saxon graves', in *Burial and Society: The Chronological and Social Analysis of Archaeological Burial Data* (1997), 120–4.

Of course, historians have questioned the myth, in whole or in part.[18] However, such criticisms have proved unattractive to English historians, since they attack the 'English national story'.[19] Today, while historians and archaeologists have expressed the belief that they have a sophisticated understanding of the Migration Period, when it comes to the sources for the 'English national story' many scholars 'still seem far too willing to suspend their disbelief'.[20]

In other parts of the world we can see that 'ethnic dreams' of the Middle Ages are of more than academic concern. At a time when the former governing party has been reduced to a purely English heartland; when the people of Scotland and Wales have voted for devolution; when the Labour government is not dependent on Unionist votes in Westminster and the future of Northern Ireland within the Union is again being considered; and when Norman Tebbit has argued that the failure of 'minority' cultures to integrate into British/English culture would result in disintegration and the 'Balkanization' of Britain,[21] an appreciation of the *constructed* nature of English identity may be timely.

Like many others, Lord Tebbit believes that there is a *single* English culture into which the Others must integrate. However, it is clear that what cultures, languages, and histories there are within England are the product of the history of the *many* peoples who have lived (and fought) there. They are not the product of some mythical, coherent, homogeneous, ancient people called the *English*.

Standing outside the myth of Englishness, I will assess the evidence from England. Throughout this chapter, however, I will also draw upon the archaeological and historical evidence from across Migration Period Europe. That is the world from which the supposed ancestors of the English emerged. Further, this information can serve to put the laconic 'English' sources into context,[22] and can assist in overcoming that insularity of outlook which has dominated early Anglo-Saxon studies, and contributed to assumptions about the 'inevitability' of England and the 'uniqueness' of the English.

---

18. P. Sims-Williams, 'The settlement of England in Bede and the *Chronicle*', *Anglo-Saxon England* 12 (1983), 1.
19. *Ibid.*, 1.
20. *Ibid.*, 39.
21. M. White, 'Hague fury at Tory "dinosaurs" ', *The Guardian* (8 October 1997), 1; interview with Lord Tebbit, *Today* programme, BBC Radio 4, 8 October 1997. See also D. Lowenthal, 'British national identity and the English landscape', *Rural History* 2 (1991), 205–30.
22. For an assessment of these sources, see David Dumville, 'Essex, middle Anglia, and the expansion of Mercia in the south-east Midlands', in *The Origins of Anglo-Saxon Kingdoms*, ed. S. Bassett (1989), 123, 126. Also, C. Scull, 'Archaeology, early Anglo-Saxon society and the origins of Anglo-Saxon kingdoms', *Anglo-Saxon Studies in Archaeology and History* 6 (1993), 65–6; R. Hodges, *The Anglo-Saxon Achievement* (1989), 22–3.

In addition, I will argue that much misunderstanding of Migration Period England is a consequence of the absence of theorization of some of the key concepts we use – in particular of ethnicity, material culture, and the relationship between them. I will therefore attempt to provide such a 'theorization', drawing upon recent archaeological, anthropological and sociological theory and on fresh readings of some of the documentary and archaeological evidence.

The aim here is not to destroy the feelings of belonging (and security?) which this story bestows but to show that the English, just like the Others, are constructed through myth; and that the myth of the English, like other national myths, owes more to culture and history than to blood and manifest destiny. In addition, if we deconstruct this story we can produce a history of the English which is more in tune with their heterogeneous past and their multicultural present.

Archaeological cultures and 'peoples'

Susan Reynolds has suggested that the 'most difficult problems of all in what we think of as Anglo-Saxon history come right at its very beginning, with what is traditionally called the Anglo-Saxon settlement'.[23] In one of the most powerful 'dreams' of the English, this is where they were born.

The problems of studying this period are indeed difficult and are made more so by the inadequate theorization of concepts. The archaeological evidence is comparatively sparse and difficult to interpret. The same can be said of the documentary sources. However, this difficulty in interpretation has not always been recognized and past scholarship is littered with uncritical readings of the historical sources and attempts to situate the archaeological evidence within them.[24] To initiate this discussion, however, we have to go back to Reynolds' 'very beginning'.

---

23. Reynolds, 'What do we mean', 400.
24. References and discussion are provided in D. Austin, 'The "proper study" of medieval archaeology', in *From the Baltic to the Black Sea*, eds D. Austin and L. Alcock (1990), 9–42. Many people have now reassessed the historical evidence and we can read it in a more 'realistic' fashion. See, among others, B. Yorke, 'Fact or fiction? The written evidence for the fifth and sixth centuries AD', *Anglo-Saxon Studies in Archaeology and History* 6 (1993), 45–50; D. Dumville, 'Kingship, genealogies and regnal lists', in *Early Medieval Kingship*, eds P. Sawyer and I. Wood (1977), 72–104; Sims-Williams, 'Settlement of England'. The archaeological evidence is considered by (again, among many others) S. Esmonde Cleary, *The Ending of Roman Britain* (1989), 130–87; C.J. Arnold, *The Archaeology of the Early Anglo-Saxon Kingdoms* (second edition 1997); N.J. Higham, *Rome, Britain and the Anglo-Saxons* (1992); C. Hills, 'The archaeology of Anglo-Saxon England in the pagan period: a review', *Anglo-Saxon England* 8 (1979), 297–329; C. Scull, 'Early Anglo-Saxon society', 65–82; J. Hines, 'The Scandinavian character of Anglian England: an update', in *The Age of Sutton Hoo:*

In the early eighth century, Bede, in his *Historia Ecclesiastica Gentis Anglorum*, provided us with an account of the settlement of England by the Angles, Saxons and Jutes:

> the race of the Angles or Saxons, invited by Vortigern, came to Britain in three warships ... They came from three very powerful Germanic tribes, the Saxons, Angles and Jutes. The people of Kent and the inhabitants of the Isle of Wight are of Jutish origin and also those opposite the Isle of Wight, that part of the kingdom of Wessex which is still today called the nation of the Jutes. From the Saxon country, that is, the district now known as Old Saxony, came the East Saxons, the South Saxons, and the West Saxons. Besides this, from the country of the Angles, that is, the land between the kingdoms of the Jutes and the Saxons, which is called *Angulus*, came the East Angles, the Middle Angles, the Mercians, and all the Northumbrian race (that is those people who dwell north of the river Humber) as well as the other Anglian tribes. *Angulus* is said to have remained deserted from that day to this. Their first leaders are said to have been two brothers, Hengist and Horsa.[25]

This is the account of the Anglo-Saxon settlement which has so beguiled generations of archaeologists, historians, politicians and Churchmen. It provides the historical context within which many archaeologists have sought to situate their evidence. Thus J.N.L. Myres, one of the greatest Anglo-Saxon archaeologists of the twentieth century, began his investigation of the continental background of the 'English settlements' with Bede's statement, and argued that it was possible to accommodate this with the archaeology, especially with the cremation pottery to whose study he devoted his life.[26] For Myres, commencing his studies in the 1920s, it appeared natural to use the cremation urns as ethnic signifiers. Much the same approach of matching the pottery and jewellery from English cemeteries with that from northern Germany and southern Scandinavia, and then applying 'ethnic names' drawn from the historical sources, has been followed more recently by Martin Welch and (to some extent) John Hines.[27]

---

contd.

    The Seventh Century in North-Western Europe, ed. M. Carver (1992), 315–29; J.N.L. Myres, *The English Settlements* (1986). Language is considered by J. Hines, 'Philology, archaeology and the *adventus Saxonum vel Anglorum*', in *Britain 400–600: Language and History*, eds A. Bammesberger and A. Wollmann (1990), 17–36; and *idem*, 'The becoming of the English: identity, material culture and language in early Anglo-Saxon England', *Anglo-Saxon Studies in Archaeology and History* 7 (1994), 49–59.

25. Bede, *HE* I.15.
26. Myres, *English Settlements*, 46, 63.
27. M. Welch, *Anglo-Saxon England* (1992), 11. See also Hines, 'The Scandinavian character' and J. Blair, *Anglo-Saxon Oxfordshire* (1994), 7–8; B. Yorke, *Wessex in the Early Middle Ages* (1995), 44. For Hines, see nn.24 and 79.

These archaeologists write within what is known as the culture–history approach. This kind of archaeology/history is based on the premise that we can link the distribution of clusters of archaeological artefacts with the 'peoples' referred to in the historical sources.[28] In culture–history, Archaeology's subservience to History is reproduced, and archaeologists continue to labour under the 'tyranny of the historical record'.[29] David Austin suggests that 'the archaeologist feels bound ... by the rules of historical practice laid down by documentary historians'.[30] Historians set the agenda for the study of the period and when archaeologists have contributed they have tended to 'accept unchallenged the "truth" of [the] documentary information and its interpretations as the unquestioned framework of the discussion'.[31] One of the results, says Austin, is that 'archaeology has followed for most of this century an ethnocentric, and racial, view of early medieval Britain as the political and cultural product of conquest and colony'.[32] I hope that in the course of this chapter it will become clear that many historians and archaeologists have indeed constructed a racial and ethnocentric view of early English history. Most, however, are unaware that they have done so.

It is necessary to draw out the implications of the kind of history which culture–history produces:

1. There is a direct relationship between ethnicity and material culture, despite the protestations of archaeologists for at least the last decade.
2. The Angles, Saxons and Jutes existed as discrete groupings in their Continental homelands and remained so in the early period of their settlement in England.
3. Somehow these discrete groupings gradually coalesced or were absorbed to form the nation we know as England and the people we know as the English.

As archaeologists we really should know by now that there is no immediate and direct relationship between ethnicity and material

---

28. Some of the problems with the culture–history approach are discussed below, and in Austin, 'Proper study'; S. Jones, *The Archaeology of Ethnicity: Constructing Identities in Past and Present* (1997), 15–26, 135–44; S. Shennan, 'Introduction: archaeological approaches to cultural identity', in *Archaeological Approaches to Cultural Identity*, ed. S. Shennan (1988), 1–32; B. Trigger, *A History of Archaeological Thought* (1989), 148–206.
29. T. Champion, 'Medieval archaeology and the tyranny of the historical record', in Austin and Alcock, *Baltic to the Black Sea*, 91.
30. Austin, 'Proper study', 12. See also J. Richards, 'Style and symbol: explaining variability in Anglo-Saxon cremation burials', in *Power and Politics in Early Medieval Britain and Ireland*, eds S. Driscoll and M. Nieke (1988), 145; Hills, 'Archaeology in the pagan period', 325, 328.
31. Austin, 'Proper study', 25. Lotte Hedeager, *Iron Age Societies: From Tribe to State in Northern Europe 500 BC to AD 700* (1992), 181, has identified the same problem in Danish archaeology.
32. Austin, 'Proper study', 15.

culture. Stephen Shennan tackles this problem head on. He points out that archaeologists have identified what are called 'archaeological cultures' – a range of artefacts associated in time and space – and have linked these to the names of peoples given in the written sources. The archaeological cultures are thus regarded as material manifestations of discrete and autonomous ethnic groups, of peoples.[33] The implication is that 'peoples' in the past signalled their affinity (and primarily their ethnic affinity) *directly* in the material objects they used, and that we can trace the pattern of movement of these 'peoples' through the changing distribution of distinctive artefacts.[34] This is a seriously flawed argument but is one which contributes to the 'stream of blood' theories to which I referred earlier. It has to be challenged.

Shennan shows that to link archaeological cultures with historically-recorded (so-called) ethnic groups is mistaken since 'we cannot assume that the "peoples" described in the sources correspond to the *self-conscious identity groups* which are essential to the definition of ethnicity'.[35] In addition, if we are fixated with the idea that late antique and Migration Period material culture should be seen only as ethnic group signifiers, we miss other, perhaps more important, meanings which can be read from this material, and ignore the *active* role of material culture postulated by so many post-processual archaeologists. We should also be aware of the parallel arguments concerning the ways in which archaeologists construct 'cultures', and especially the fact that 'in many instances such entities are purely constructs devised by archaeologists'.[36] As Siân Jones further points out, we have to be aware of the 'unfortunate implication ... that archaeologists, and other social scientists, may have developed paradigms to explain that which they have themselves created'.[37]

Dominic Janes has examined the relationship between brooch form and imperial status in late antiquity.[38] He argues that, because of the power of the State – what he calls its 'golden clasp' – the aristocracy of the late Empire wore golden cross-bow brooches. These brooches were worn as emblems of allegiance, *regardless* of ethnic affiliation.[39] They relate to the power structures of the late Roman empire rather than to the ethnic identity of their wearers. They bespeak identity, but not ethnic identity. We miss such important insights into the relationship between material culture and *other* forms of collective identity when we assume a direct and inflexible link between it and

---

33. Shennan, 'Introduction', 6.
34. For an extreme example, see V. Bierbrauer, H. Büsing, and A. Büsing-Kolbe, 'Die Dame von Ficarolo', *Archaeologia Medievale* 20 (1993), 686.
35. Shennan, 'Introduction', 15, emphasis added.
36. Jones, *Archaeology of Ethnicity*, 108–9, 131.
37. *Ibid.*, 139.
38. D. Janes, 'The golden clasp of the late Roman state', *Early Medieval Europe* 5 (1996), 127–53.
39. *Ibid.*, 146–8.

ethnicity. We might examine the 'chip-carved' belt fittings from late Roman Britain in the same light.

The documentary sources tell us that Germanic mercenaries were employed in the defence of late- and sub-Roman Britain, and attempts have been made to link these belt-fittings directly with these early 'Germanic' settlers.[40] Such objects are found throughout the empire, especially along the Rhine-Danube frontier,[41] and it has been argued that the similarity between those from the latter area and those in England was archaeological evidence for early Germanic occupation.[42] Further it was suggested that this 'Germanic' settlement might in fact be 'Anglo-Saxon' since 'it is ... assumed that the most likely source for the Germanic *foederati* was the Anglo-Saxon homelands'.[43] The 'chip-carved' belt fittings thus became early Anglo-Saxon ethnic identifiers.

However, much doubt has now been cast on this interpretation. It has been pointed out that these artefacts are probably from 'official issue' belts, which may have been worn by the 'officials of the administrative and financial bureaucracies charged with the smooth running of the diocese'.[44] Catherine Hills accepts that some types of buckles *may* have been associated with the military, but notes that this is 'not the same as accepting that they were worn *only* by Germanic soldiers'.[45] Kevin Leahy makes the point that 'there has been a tendency to overemphasize their Germanic nature', and argues that 'the dolphins that decorate them are more closely related to late Roman, rather than Germanic tastes'.[46]

Frequently, these objects are found in the excavation of burials, and Simon Esmonde Cleary points out that a new burial rite appeared around the middle of the fourth century. Male graves contained belt fittings at the waist, a cross-bow brooch at the shoulder and an 'offering' by the right foot.[47] In his study of the same phenomenon in northern Gaul, Guy Halsall has pointed out that the burial rite, similar to the one we have been describing – 'the standard Roman form of burial but with the addition of more numerous grave-goods, including weaponry and belt-sets for the men and jewellery for the women' – is

---

40. A principal source for this discussion is still Hills, 'Archaeology in the pagan period'.
41. *Ibid.*, 298.
42. S. Hawkes and G. Dunning, 'Soldiers and settlers in Britain, fourth to fifth century', *Medieval Archaeology* 5 (1961), 1–70; Hills, 'Archaeology in the pagan period', 299.
43. Esmonde Cleary, *Ending of Roman Britain*, 56.
44. *Ibid.*, 55. G. Halsall, 'The origins of the *Reihengräberzivilisation*: forty years on', in *Fifth Century Gaul: A Crisis of Identity?* eds J. Drinkwater and H. Elton (1992), 200.
45. Hills, 'Archaeology in the pagan period', 305, emphasis added. Also Halsall, '*Reihengräberzivilisation*', 200–1.
46. K. Leahy, 'The Anglo-Saxon settlement of Lindsey', in *Pre-Viking Lindsey*, ed. A. Vince (1993), 30.
47. Esmonde Cleary, *Ending of Roman Britain*, 55.

significantly different from those of Free Germany.[48] Halsall has extracted similar belt fittings from a 'Germanic' context and sees them instead as 'symbols of authority'.[49] He argues that the burials in which they occur took place in the context of challenges to Roman authority at times when that authority was weakened. Importantly, it is argued that while such opposition might come from 'Roman' or 'German' sources, the people who mounted the challenges were doing so largely within 'the accepted imperial idioms of authority'.[50] In this context it should come as no surprise that they, and their contemporaries in Britain, also used material symbols of that authority.

There may have been 'Germanic' mercenaries in Britain in the fourth century. This would not be unexpected and it need not have taken an 'invitation' from Vortigern to bring them. There had been 'Germanic' soldiers in Britain in the period of Roman occupation and it is possible that many stayed at the end of empire. It is generally assumed that the Roman army was withdrawn in the early fifth century,[51] but 'the only firm evidence we have for troop withdrawals comes in 401/2 ... [when] Stilicho removed a British legion ... to help in the defence of Italy against Alaric's invasion'.[52] Procopius tells us that after the suppression of the revolt of the 'emperor' Constantine in 409, the Romans could no longer maintain their hold on Britain and it was then ruled by 'tyrants'. However, as Averil Cameron points out, it is unlikely that Roman rule ended so abruptly.[53]

We might instead imagine a situation in Britain in the late fourth century much like that argued for Italy in the seventh century by Tom Brown. Here the structures of the State remained in place for much longer, but as cash payments to the army became a problem in the late sixth and early seventh centuries, soldiers began to acquire land and live off its produce, a process which 'gave troops a major incentive towards the vigorous defence of their own properties and communities'.[54]

In Britain, coins (especially silver and gold) are extremely rare from 378.[55] In this context we might see Roman soldiers (Germans and others) immersing themselves in the local power structures of late imperial Britain. Increasingly these were power structures which bore an antagonistic but dependent relationship to the authority of Rome. The onerous late Imperial demands for taxation, among others factors, had eroded the effectiveness of *Romanitas* as a binding mechanism, and the elite increasingly opted out of the State, preferring to develop

---

48. Halsall, *'Reihengräberzivilisation'*, 202.
49. *Ibid.*, 205.
50. *Ibid.*, 204.
51. Higham, *Rome*, 215.
52. M. Millett, *The Romanization of Britain* (1990), 215.
53. A. Cameron, *Procopius and the Sixth Century* (1985), 213–14.
54. T. Brown, *Gentlemen and Officers: Imperial Administration and Aristocratic Power in Byzantine Italy AD 554–800* (1984), 88.
55. Millett, *Romanization*, 219.

their 'private' powers as landowners and landlords.[56] It is in this context
– fragmentation of state authority and consolidation of private power –
that the 'chip-carved' belt fittings belong. At this stage the 'ethnic'
identity of the wielders of this localized power mattered little; nor was
it to matter for some time. What did matter was the construction of
power in and against a relationship with the authority of Rome.

We are therefore now in a position to see these belt sets, and the
burials in which they are incorporated, in a late Roman and not
specifically 'Germanic' context. Like the cross-bow brooches studied
by Janes, they have connections with the late Roman state. Like the
crossbow brooches, the belts were symbols of collective identity, but
not ethnic identity. The belt fittings and cross-bow brooches belong in
a world of transition where identities and loyalties were complex and,
at times, contradictory. To see them only as symbols of Germanic
ethnicity is not only to ignore the evidence while labouring under the
'tyranny of the historical record',[57] it is also to misunderstand the
complex web of identities that existed at the time.

Tackling this issue from another direction, we might accept *for the
moment* that the material record of the Migration Period in England is
indeed a reflection of past ethnicity. If we assume that the Angles,
Saxons, and Jutes were bounded, discrete, homogeneous cultural
groups who reflected their identity through material culture, we might
expect clear distinctions in the archaeology of their respective
'settlement areas'. While it is the case that there are parts of England
where so-called Anglian or Saxon material culture dominates, this is
not always true. Hines has noted that in the period up to *c.* 475 early
'Saxon' material is found 'across the whole of the area from north of
the Humber to Sussex, with the exception of Kent east of the Medway,
where Jutish material ... is predominant'.[58] Barbara Yorke suggests
that 'archaeological evidence suggests that the material culture of the
Hampshire Jutes was not strikingly different from that of their Saxon
neighbours'.[59] On the same theme, Hills points out that in the pagan
Anglo-Saxon cemeteries of East Anglia, although there are objects
which resemble those from the 'continental Anglian areas ... There
are also applied brooches of Saxon types and bone combs paralleled
both in the Elbe-Weser region and further west'. She concludes that
attempts to locate discrete Anglian, Saxon and Jutish groups in
England is fruitless since on the Continent these groups were really
'loose confederations drawn from a variety of people'.[60]

---

56. C. Wickham, 'The Other Transition: from the ancient world to feudalism', *Past
and Present* 103 (1984), 3–36; Higham, *Rome*, 213–14; Scull, 'Early Anglo-Saxon
society', 70.
57. Champion, 'Tyranny of the historical record', 91.
58. Hines, 'Philology', 27.
59. B. Yorke, 'The Jutes of Hampshire and Wight and the origins of Wessex', in
Bassett, *Anglo-Saxon Kingdoms*, 92.
60. Hills, 'Archaeology in the pagan period', 317. See also Scull, 'Early Anglo-Saxon
society', 71.

Usually such 'anomalies' to the expected 'Bedan' pattern are simply noted and ignored; where explanation is attempted, this is couched in culture-historical terms with all the implications to which I have already referred. For example, Leahy argues that 'the people who settled Lindsey during the 5th century were predominantly Angles but with the addition of some Saxons and other elements'.[61] From time to time the recognition of such anomalies within the culture-historical framework results in further 'anomalies' and necessitates somewhat tortuous explanations. Thus, we are told that the earliest evidence for the presence of 'Saxons' in Wessex is at Hod Hill, where they had 'arrived by the mid-fifth century'. However, it appears that the 'Saxon' finds emerge from a 'British' context and the strict association assumed between material culture and ethnic group necessitates the conclusion that 'the fifth century objects from Hod Hill may have belonged to the families of Saxon warriors in British employ'![62] Bruce Eagles also argues that a particular type of 'hand-made organic-, often grass- or chaff-tempered pottery' provides 'one of the few pointers to the British population'. In essence, it becomes an ethnic identifier for an undifferentiated 'British' people. However, we are also told that it was found on 'Anglo-Saxon' sites such as Portchester; was associated with 'a possible Anglo-Saxon sunken-featured building' at Hucklesbrook, and was 'recovered from Anglo-Saxon burials at Ford, Petersfinger and Winterbourne Gunner'.[63]

Here we should also note the evidence for more localized 'material cultures' within the so-called Anglian and Saxon settlement areas. Yorke points out that in the sixth century in Wessex, 'no two cemeteries are identical and ... each community had patterns of burial ritual or dress peculiar to itself'.[64] Several scholars have pointed to the existence of differentiation within individual cemeteries.[65] Ellen Pader well illustrates the scale and 'proximity' of difference –

> the populations buried at Westgarth Gardens and Holywell Row did not choose to differentiate between children and adults in the

61. Leahy, 'Lindsey', 37.
62. B. Eagles, 'The archaeological evidence for settlement in the fifth to seventh centuries AD', in *The Medieval Landscape of Wessex*, eds M. Aston and C. Lewis (1994), 27.
63. *Ibid.*, 18.
64. Yorke, *Wessex*, 44–45. Also, Richards, 'Style and symbol'.
65. See H. Härke, 'The shield in the burial rite', in *Early Anglo-Saxon Shields*, eds T. Dickinson and H. Härke (1992), 65; E. Pader, 'Material symbolism and social relations in mortuary studies', in *Anglo-Saxon Cemeteries 1979*, eds P. Rahtz, T. Dickinson and L. Watts (1980), 147–9, 157; C. Arnold, 'The Anglo-Saxon cemeteries of the Isle of Wight: an appraisal of nineteenth-century excavation data', in *Anglo-Saxon Cemeteries: A Reappraisal*, ed. E. Southworth (1990), 168; J. Huggett, 'Social analysis of early Anglo-Saxon inhumation burials: archaeological methodologies', *Journal of European Archaeology* 4 (1996), 348–58, 362; C. Scull, 'Before Sutton Hoo: structures of power and society in early East Anglia', in Carver, *Age of Sutton Hoo*, 15.

same manner or to the same degree. Nor did they always use the same objects (e.g. knives for females). Yet both are on tributaries of the River Lark, are only some 19km apart, and overlap temporally.[66]

However, these are only anomalies if we persist in believing in bounded and homogeneous 'ethnic' groups in the past, and if we continue to interpret the archaeological record through the methodologies of culture-history. A fresh look at the evidence, combined with a reconsideration of the nature of ethnicity in the early Middle Ages, suggests that processes other than (as well as?) those of ethnic 'signalling' were at work in the fifth- and sixth-century regions of England.

Ethnicity and heterogeneity

Contrary to common understanding, it would be a gross error to assume that the Angles, Saxons and Jutes possessed discrete identities in their so-called tribal homelands and maintained them in the early part of their settlement in England. However, in his recent volume on *The English*, Sir Geoffrey Elton tells us that 'the Anglo-Saxons did not intermarry with the indigenous population ... [and] did not mix significantly with the Celts (Britons)'.[67] In a similar vein, Welch has 'real problems' accepting the idea that the *adventus Saxonum* was in fact made up of

> a small number of well-armed warrior bands ... [who] married native British women and that they and their *mixed-blood* "Anglo-Saxon" progeny are the occupants of the many so-called Anglo-Saxon burial grounds studied by archaeologists

and argues instead that the invaders brought their wives with them.[68] The same view is implicit in the writings of those who argue for the 'separateness' and 'distinctiveness' of Anglian and Saxon groups up to the sixth century.[69]

However, some archaeologists and historians now question the assumed racial purity, and integrity of Migration Period groups.[70] Thus, Herwig Wolfram reminds us of the vast array of 'peoples' in the fourth

---

66. Pader, 'Material symbolism', 158. See also Hodges, *Anglo-Saxon Achievement*, 37-8.
67. Elton, *The English*, 3.
68. Welch, *Anglo-Saxon England*, 11 (emphasis added). Also N. Higham, *The English Conquest: Gildas and Britain in the Fifth Century* (1994), 168. For a useful corrective, see Arnold, *Anglo-Saxon Kingdoms*, 24.
69. See below , notes 89 and 90.
70. Austin, 'Proper study', 16, referring to W. Goffart, *Barbarians and Romans AD 418-584: The Techniques of Accommodation* (1980). Also E. James, 'Burial and status in the early medieval West', *Transactions of the Royal Historical Society* 5th ser., 39 (1989), 25.

century Ostrogothic 'kingdom' of Ermanaric. More generally, he argues that 'the sources attest the basically polyethnic character of the *gentes*. Archaic peoples are mixed ... Their formation ... is not a matter of common descent but one of political decision'.[71] The presence of 'Romans', or former 'Romans', in these 'barbarian' groups should be emphasized.[72] The situation detected by Patrick Amory where small cultivators who joined the army of Theodoric the Great would have *become known as* Goths by 493, was surely more widespread than the areas of Pannonia, Moesia, and northern Italy.[73] In this context we might remember that Orosius, 'writing of the irruption of Germans into Gaul and Spain early in the fifth century, could say that some Romans preferred to live among the "barbarians", poor in liberty, rather than endure the anxiety of paying taxes in the Roman empire'.[74] In the changing world of late antiquity people were making *active* choices, and those choices were no longer (if they ever had been) between Roman and barbarian. With the transformation of Empire, and of the institutional structures which formed it, 'people were forced to choose loyalties from among the new smaller communities within which they found themselves'.[75] In addition, it is not at all clear that *ethnic* identity formed the basis of these new communities. In the Burgundian kingdom many members of the Roman elite prospered under the new regime. After the fall of the Burgundian kingdom in 534 some remained prominent under the Franks. Significantly,

> none of them has left any record of feeling different or special due to their *Roman* descent. Their prominence and self-conscious pride were due to their *senatorial* descent, a more specialized category than an ethnic group.[76]

The fact that they remained in position throughout the changes in 'ethnic' control in the region suggests that social and economic *power* rather than ethnic identification or exclusion was an essential element in the construction of their identity – as a people apart. Significantly, it appears that Burgundian or Germanic 'ethnicity' was not the most important factor for those members of the elite with Germanic names. They too lived in and through the structures formed from the political demise of the Roman empire.[77]

---

71. H. Wolfram, *History of the Goths* (1988*)*, 7–8; *idem*, 'Origo et religio. Ethnic traditions and literature in early medieval texts', *Early Medieval Europe* 3 (1994), 21. See also T. Anderson, Jr, 'Roman military colonies in Gaul, Salian ethnogenesis and the forgotten meaning of the *Pactus Legis Salicae*', *Early Medieval Europe* 9 (1995), 136; and E. James, 'The origins of barbarian kingdoms: the continental evidence', in Bassett, *Anglo-Saxon Kingdoms*, 48.
72. Wolfram, *History of the Goths*, 8.
73. Amory, 'Names, ethnic identity', 5, emphasis added.
74. G.E.M. de Ste Croix, *The Class Struggle in the Ancient Greek World* (1981), 481.
75. Amory, 'Names, ethnic identity', 5.
76. *Ibid.*, 22.
77. *Ibid.*, 19.

Where then do the Angles, Saxons, and Jutes as coherent peoples fit into this picture of 'bewildering heterogeneity' and overlapping identities? Although the prominence given to Bede's statement about the Angles, Saxons and Jutes has foreclosed much discussion of alternatives, the very fact that all Migration Period groups were characterized by fluidity and heterogeneity makes it extremely unlikely that the 'ancestors of the English' were any different. Some of the late Antique sources speak of 'peoples' other than the Angles, Saxons and Jutes taking part in the 'settlement' of England.[78] Hines has suggested that there is archaeological evidence for an undocumented movement of people from 'southern and western Norway about the beginning of the last quarter of the fifth century',[79] although we must be mindful here of slipping into culture-historical arguments. We might also cite the reference that in 527,

> pagans came out of Germany, and occupied East Anglia ... from where some of them invaded Mercia and waged many wars against the Britons: but because their leaders were many, they have no name.[80]

This is interesting not because it records 'another' migration but because of the implications it has for the structure of the 'warbands'. 'Their leaders were many' might suggest a heterogeneous group made up of individuals attached to their own 'warleader'. We might envisage a similar structure in the groups which *ultimately* became known as the Angles, Saxons and Jutes. The fact that the latter 'had a name' (and that those recorded in 527 did not) may have more to do with the late seventh- and early eighth-century political circumstances in which Bede was writing than with the actual homogeneity of the original group.[81]

In England in the fifth century, we do have evidence for the migration of people from north-western Europe. It would be perverse to deny this. But it cannot be emphasized strongly enough that these population movements were part of the European pattern of *Völkerwanderungen*, and given the evidence cited for the heterogeneous

---

78. Procopius (*History of the Wars*, 8.20, translated by H.B. Dewing, 1928) records the Frisians as one of the peoples of Britain. For discussion, see E.A. Thompson, 'Procopius on Brittia and Britannia', *Classical Quarterly* 30 (1980), 498–507; Cameron, *Procopius*. See also Hines, 'Becoming of the English', 50 for the problems with using another comment by Bede (*HE* V.9) as a list of the Migration Period settlers of England.
79. Hines, 'Philology', 29. See also his *The Scandinavian Character of Anglian England in the Pre-Viking Period* (1984) and 'Scandinavian character: an update'.
80. Cited in T. Williamson, *The Origins of Norfolk* (1993), 63; Nicholas Brooks (pers. comm.) reminds me of the rather dubious authority of the original source. For discussion, see W. Davies, 'Annals and the origin of Mercia', in *Mercian Studies*, ed. A. Dornier (1977), 17–29; Scull, 'Before Sutton Hoo', 5; P. Stafford, *The East Midlands in the Early Middle Ages* (1985), 81.
81. See Yorke, and Woolf, this volume.

constitution of the Continental *gentes*, we cannot expect the 'people' who *became known as* the Angles, Saxons and Jutes to have been any different. Additionally we have to understand that the 'Bedan' account of the 'migration' is likely to represent a condensation in time of a long-term process.[82] The fire and sword scenario painted by many for the *adventus Saxonum* is unlikely to have occurred; there was no confrontation between coherent, homogenous Anglo-Saxons and an equally coherent and homogenous British 'people' in a few cataclysmic years.

It is equally important to remember the context into which these 'migrants' inserted themselves. This was one of decentralized power held by members of the 'Roman' elite, and probably the army, some of whom may have been of 'Germanic' extraction. But as already argued, the 'ethnicity' of the powerful was not important; power was. And here we must understand the nature of the societies from which the migrants came. These were not the egalitarian, free, Germanic communities of Tacitus' construction. Archaeological evidence from Denmark and northern Germany clearly shows that the communities from which the 'Angles', 'Saxons' and 'Jutes' emerged were hierarchically structured,[83] and there is no reason to believe that they lost this structure in the journey across the North Sea. These were not the free, German, yeoman stock of English mythology.

Nicholas Higham has argued that the archaeological evidence from parts of southern England shows clear links with southern Denmark and north-west Germany, areas which he considers as 'not already much affected by cultural contacts with Rome', and 'reached Britain unaffected by Romanizing influences'.[84] It would appear that such comments are the product of an overly insular perspective. It is well recognized by Danish and other Continental scholars that although Denmark lay well beyond the *limes*, and beyond the 'buffer-zone' of 'Romanized tribes', its people were profoundly affected by trade and exchange networks and other forms of interaction with 'Rome'. Some of them had served in the Roman army. These connections resulted in the flow of Roman objects into Denmark. The flow was controlled by Danish elites and the objects, and the control over their distribution, were used in strategies which reproduced and transformed social relations within Danish society.[85] These people were not Romanized,

---

82. Scull, 'Before Sutton Hoo', 8. For a parallel situation in early historic Scotland, see Margaret Nieke and Holly Duncan, 'Dalriada: the establishment and maintenance of an early historic kingdom in northern Britain', in Driscoll and Nieke, *Power and Politics*, 6–21.

83. See below, notes 85 and 86.

84. Higham, *Rome*, 173; also 226.

85. These ideas are discussed in detail by Lotte Hedeager, 'Empire, frontier and barbarian hinterland: Rome and northern Europe AD 1–400', in *Centre and Periphery in the Ancient World*, eds M. Rowlands, M. Larsen, and K. Kristiansen (1987), 125–40; 'Kingdoms, ethnicity and material culture: Denmark in a European perspective', in Carver, *Age of Sutton Hoo*, 281–2; *idem, Iron-Age*

but they used Roman material culture and experience of Rome in the construction of self and society.

It is also apparent from the archaeology that relationships with the Roman Empire were not the only factors in the construction and reproduction of the power of the elites in Denmark. The material culture from Funen, for example, illustrates the especially strong contacts with the peoples of south-eastern Europe.[86] The point is that the societies from which the 'Germanic' settlers of England emerged were complex and stratified. These were not the 'hill-billies' or 'backwoodsmen' of the Germanic migrations.[87] The basis of elite power appears to have lain in their control over the acquisition and distribution of objects and knowledge from Other peoples, across a wide geographical area. The recognition of the importance and wide-ranging nature of such relationships should further undermine notions of the existence of discrete and bounded 'ethnic' units in the fourth to sixth centuries, and of the archetypal yeoman farmer of English mythology.

What is clear is that we can no longer see the 'peoples' of the Migration Period as discrete, homogeneous, autonomous groups. It is fairly depressing to note that this much is recognized, and then ignored, by scholars.[88] Thus John Blair can assert that 'it would be anachronistic to envisage separate races with separate cultures ... or to imagine them colonizing England in large, politically coherent groups which kept their identity in isolation from others',[89] and can then concur with Tania Dickinson's statement that 'the Thames was a major line of communication for the Upper Thames region with *other Saxon* communities'[90] – implying separate communities of Saxons, using Saxon material culture, communicating with each other.[91] As

contd.

    Societies. See also the papers in *The Archaeology of Gudme and Lundeborg*, eds P. Nielsen, K. Randsborg and H. Thrane (Copenhagen, 1994); and K. Randsborg, 'Beyond the Roman Empire: Archaeological discoveries in Gudme on Funen, Denmark', *Oxford Journal of Archaeology* 9 (1990). M. Todd, *The Early Germans* (1992), 88–103 gives some idea of the range of Roman objects which passed into 'Free Germany' and beyond.

86. See B. Storgaard, 'The Årslev grave and connections between Funen and the Continent at the end of the later Roman Iron Age', in *Archaeology of Gudme and Lundeborg*, 160–8; C. Fabech, 'Reading society from cultural landscape: South Scandinavia between sacral and political power', in *Archaeology of Gudme and Lundeborg*, 178.

87. *Contra* Higham, *Rome*, 226.

88. Sims-Williams, 'Settlement of England', 39.

89. Blair, *Anglo-Saxon Oxfordshire*, 7; see also note 90.

90. T. Dickinson, *The Anglo-Saxon Burial Sites of the Upper Thames Region, and Their Bearing on the History of Wessex, c. AD 400–700* (Unpublished Oxford DPhil thesis, 1976), 415–17 emphasis added, cited in Blair, *Anglo-Saxon Oxfordshire*, 8. For the same phenomenon see also Arnold, *Anglo-Saxon Kingdoms*, 23–30.

91. See also Blair, *Anglo-Saxon Oxfordshire*, 14–16.

Reynolds observes, many scholars seem able to accept the hetero-geneous nature of these groups but still hold to the idea that 'each tribe or people that had (or has) a separate name formed some kind of cultural entity'.[92]

Constructing ethnicity

It is clear that there are serious problems in using the culture-history approach as the basis for interpretation, and major deficiencies in our understanding of the nature and composition of 'Germanic' groups (both on the Continent and in England). However, it is also apparent from recent work in archaeology, anthropology and sociology that it would be a debilitating step to move from the rejection of a direct and inflexible link between ethnic identity and material culture to argue that there is *no* relationship.[93] As I have already suggested, many of the problems in this area lie in an inadequate theorization (and therefore understanding) of ethnicity and material culture.

If we abandon (as we must) the notion of ethnic groups as unchanging, bounded entities, a minimal definition of ethnicity might be 'a collective identification that is *socially constructed* with reference to *putative cultural similarity and difference*'.[94] This 'putative cultural similarity and difference' is used in a series of social strategies to classify people as belonging (or not), and to define membership (or otherwise) of a collectivity. As a result 'identity is a matter of the *outs* as well as the *ins*'; it is a matter of 'social closure'.[95] It is one of the strengths of Richard Jenkins' work that he emphasizes the creation of 'outsiders' through ethnic closure. However, he does more than this since he argues that *power* is inherent in this relationship,[96] and that the process of closure, of categorization as 'outsider', can be used by 'outsiders' in the process of constructing their own identity.[97]

Ethnic identity, therefore, is *constructed* through the process of interaction between people. Cultural traits are implicated and manipulated in this process.[98] Archaeologists understand that material culture was actively drawn upon in the very *creation* and reproduction of relations of power, identity, and gender.[99] It also provided a 'basis

---

92. Reynolds, 'What do we mean', 400.
93. See Jenkins, *Rethinking Ethnicity;* Jones, *Archaeology of Ethnicity.*
94. Jenkins, *Rethinking Ethnicity*, 75, emphasis added.
95. *Ibid.*, 10, 11. Emphasis in the original.
96. *Ibid.*, 52–63, 71–2.
97. *Ibid.*, 70.
98. *Ibid.*, 10. See also Amory, 'Names', 4–5; Jones, *Archaeology of Ethnicity*, 128.
99. See my 'Method and theory in medieval archaeology in the 1990s', *Archaeologia Medievale* 18 (1991), 7–42; and 'Through the looking glass of possibilities: understanding the Middle Ages', in *Die Vielfalt der Dinge. Neue Wege zur Analyse mittelalterlicher Sachkultur*, eds H. Hundsbichler, G. Jaritz, and T. Kühtreiber (1998), 85–116.

and resources for ethnic closure';[100] it was the 'objectification of cultural difference'.[101]

The recognition that ethnic identity is frequently constructed in a process of categorization which excludes the 'Others', and that material culture can be implicated in this process, might allow us to predict the situations in which material symbols of similarity and difference would be brought to the fore (although it should be clear that material culture is not activated as part of the process of ethnic identity construction only in such 'contact' situations. The process is continuous and changing[102]). With the *adventus Saxonum* we might expect both the 'invaders/settlers' and the 'natives' to do just this, since in the still dominant interpretation of the *adventus* we have the remnants of Romano-British society being challenged by migrating 'peoples' ('Angles', 'Saxons' and 'Jutes') from continental Europe. The migrants were supposedly confronted by the 'British' who were ultimately defeated and either killed or driven into the fastness of Wales and the West.[103] Conflict and war with the 'barbarian' Other might be expected to enhance significantly the ethnic identity, and the feeling of 'Us-ness', among the first generations of 'Angles', 'Saxons' and 'Jutes'.

This, however, does not appear to have been the case. The detail of the fifth century archaeological material from the so-called settlement areas of the Angles, Saxons and Jutes does not suggest that 'material symbols of similarity and difference' were being emphasized by 'peoples' at this early date. I have already referred to the fact that in the period up to c. 475 'Saxon' material is found across most of England 'from north of the Humber to Sussex', with 'datable Anglian material ... [being] largely confined to cruciform brooches'.[104] Speaking of the 'Jutes' of Kent and the Isle of Wight, Hills points out that although this area had a distinctive material culture, this was not in the period of the Migrations as we would expect if 'Jutish ethnicity' was being signalled in this period of 'contact'; rather it was in the sixth century.[105] Even the architecture of the early 'Anglo-Saxon' house is no longer seen as distinctively Germanic.[106]

---

100. Jenkins, *Rethinking Ethnicity*, 10.
101. Jones, *Archaeology of Ethnicity*, 120.
102. *Ibid.*, 122.
103. See Higham, *Rome*, 2–15; Sims-Williams, 'Settlement of England', 2. Also E. John, *Reassessing Anglo-Saxon England* (1996), 7–8.
104. Hines, 'Philology', 27–8.
105. Hills, 'Archaeology in the pagan period', 313; See also, H. Geake, 'Burial practice in seventh- and eighth-century England', in Carver, *Age of Sutton Hoo*, 92; Sims-Williams, 'Settlement of England', 25. For a European perspective, see I. Wood, 'The European Science Foundation's programme on the transformation of the Roman World and the emergence of early medieval Europe', *Early Medieval Europe* 6 (1997), 224.
106. See among several others, P. Dixon, 'How Saxon is a Saxon house?', in *Structural Reconstruction*, ed. P. Drury (1982), 275–87; and S. James, A. Marshall, and M. Millett, 'An early medieval building tradition', *Archaeological Journal* 141 (1984), 182–215.

Given our expectation that in the fifth century, in the context of 'contact' with the British Other, if at any time, specific Anglian, Saxon and Jutish identities should be signalled, our failure to find such evidence forces us to reconsider the traditional picture of the *adventus Saxonum*, and the images of conflict, battle and devastation which have played such an important part in explanations for the emergence of the English from Germanic stock.

Arguments for ethnic conflict between homogeneous and coherent 'peoples' – Angles, Saxons, Jutes and Britons – leading to ethnic cleansing and decimation are not supported by the archaeological, environmental, or historical evidence. Equally we cannot accept the more 'moderate' view which does away with the 'fire and sword' imagery but still postulates coherent and discrete 'peoples' – Angles, Saxons and Jutes – maintaining their separate and distinctive identities through time to become the English.

We must accept that people constructed their identities through a dialectic between past experience and current social, economic and (in particular) power relationships. We must understand that material culture was actively drawn upon in the construction and reproduction of those relationships. The people who lived in England in the fifth and sixth centuries acted and created within the emerging structures of society. If we examine the sixth-century evidence more closely we may be able to see how material culture was actively used in the construction of identity at that time. It is surely not coincidental that it is also in the sixth century that we get archaeological and documentary evidence for the emergence of overarching systems of power and authority.

On page 63 of his *Anglo-Saxon England*, Welch provides us with an image of 'three women dressed in regional fashions of the sixth century'. Ignoring the fact that the women are presented as very much alive, while the reconstructions are based on cemetery evidence, we should pay particular attention to the dress of the 'Anglian' woman –

> The well-dressed woman in the Anglian regions ... would be similarly dressed [to the Saxon woman], except that the range of brooches was somewhat different and the undergarment had long tailored sleeves fastened by cuff-link-like fittings called wrist clasps. These small hook-and-eye metal fittings were sown on either side of a split sleeve and are extremely rare in England outside this region. Keys and mock keys called girdle hangers also play a prominent role in Anglian dress.[107]

The image presented is a static one in which material culture (in life as in death) *reflected* Anglian ethnic identity. In fact, the archaeological evidence shows that such a picture is profoundly misleading. What appears in the sixth century as 'Anglian' dress is very much a

---

107. Welch, *Anglo-Saxon England*, 62–4.

construction, a *creation* of that time. It does not stem from the migration *into* England of the Angles in the middle of the fifth century, but from the construction of a sense of identity in the particular social and political circumstances of the sixth century *in* England.

Hines shows how, within a few generations of the *adventus*, a 'new, consistent and distinctive Anglian English culture was ... put together out of a remarkably diverse range of sources'.[108] He argues that this material culture assemblage should not be seen simply as an indicator of the extent of Anglian occupation, but rather as 'a means by which people could both claim their membership of the new group and promulgate the conditions by which membership was established'.[109] Scull has pointed out that not only were many of the known cemeteries established two to three generations after the *adventus*, but also that much of the material culture had by then taken on a 'distinctively *insular* character'.[110] In other words by the time we get the emergence of these distinctively regional sets of material culture, some of the objects are the product of a mixture of 'traditions'. They have been called 'Germanic offshoots out of the late-Roman craft tradition'.[111]

In the sixth century material culture was being activated in the construction and signalling of 'cultural similarity and difference', not by simply drawing upon a set of fixed ethnic signifiers stemming from a supposed Continental inheritance, but through a mixture of adoption, selection, creativity and continuity.

In a recent reassessment of the cemetery evidence from the Isle of Wight, Chris Arnold has examined the evidence for a supposed 'Jutish' settlement of that island from Kent. He points out that when we look at the total assemblages from the graves, few of them have distinctively 'Kentish' objects, such as brooches. In those that do, these Kentish objects are rarely associated with other 'Kentish' artefacts. In addition many of the objects in the graves are of types which are generic to most of southern England. Arnold concludes that the material evidence may represent 'nothing more than the movement of people or objects between families maintaining a traditional link between Kent and the island'.[112]

I would go further, and suggest that if this 'traditional' link existed, it was incorporated as one element in a series of 'traditions', 'memories', or 'aspirations' which were used in the construction of regional identities in the sixth century. The 'memory' or myth of

---

108. J. Hines, 'Cultural change and social organisation in early Anglo-Saxon England', in *After Empire: Towards an Ethnology of Europe's Barbarians*, ed. G. Ausenda (1995), 81.
109. *Ibid.*, 81.
110. Scull, 'Early Anglo-Saxon society', 71, emphasis added; Hills, 'Archaeology in the pagan period', 316.
111. Hines, 'Philology', 23. See also, Arnold, *Anglo-Saxon Kingdoms*, 192; Arnold, *Roman Britain to Saxon England* (1984), 103.
112. Arnold, 'Anglo-Saxon cemeteries of the Isle of Wight', 170.

'Jutishness' may have been one aspect of that construction. Detailed analysis, at the regional level, elsewhere in England might show the active construction of similar 'material cultures'. The possibility of recognizing these, and then interpreting them, is severely hampered by the traditional practice of focusing on the highly diagnostic artefacts ('Anglian', 'Saxon' or 'Jutish') within individual grave assemblages.[113] A spurious uniformity is thereby imposed on a potentially more heterogeneous and 'constructed' assemblage, resulting in an equally spurious reading of the past.

If these regional patterns really are markers of group identity (and I think that they are), then we have to remember that 'identity is a matter of the *outs* as well the *ins*'; it is a matter of 'social closure'.[114] Who then were the 'outs'; against whom was the 'closure' designed to operate? A conventional response would be the Britons. But then we would have to ask why it took several generations (of conflict?) to produce these strategies and symbols of exclusion. In fact it might be argued that, in the context of the sixth-century Anglo-Saxon world, the Others meant *each other*. Given what I have already said about problems with historical sources such as the early sections of the *Anglo-Saxon Chronicle*,[115] I hardly dare mention that the first strife recorded between the 'English' is in the sixth century, 568 – 'In this year Ceawlin and Cutha fought against Ethelbert, and drove him in flight into Kent'.[116]

It can also be argued that the strategies of inclusion and exclusion, in which the material culture we have been considering played a part, were the product of the emergence of regional structures of *power*. I shall return to this later. For the moment I want to emphasize once again that the symbols of group identity in sixth-century England were a product of processes current *in* sixth-century England. It was in this context that new identities, ethnicities if you like, were *constructed*.

Ethnicity and power

If we can agree that it is anachronistic to envisage separate races as the basis for a sense of ethnic identity in the early Middle Ages, we have to ask what formed the basis for such identity? Patrick Geary argues that in the early Middle Ages

> one concludes that ethnicity did not exist as an objective category but rather as a subjective and malleable category by which

113. *Ibid.*, 167.
114. Jenkins, *Rethinking Ethnicity*, 11. Emphasis in the original.
115. See note 24.
116. *The Anglo-Saxon Chronicle*, trans. and ed. D. Whitelock (1961), 13. Also, Arnold, 'Wealth and social structure: a matter of life and death', in Rahtz, Dickinson and Watts, *Anglo-Saxon Cemeteries*, 84. Reynolds, 'What do we mean', 402.

various preexisting likenesses could be manipulated symbolically to mold an identity and a community.[117]

We have a tendency to see ethnicity as discrete and *objective* and as a major force in the construction of individuals and peoples in the past.[118] By contrast, as Jenkins does for the present, so Geary argues that in early medieval Europe ethnicity itself was *constructed*, 'molded' in the context of the operation of *power* relationships.[119] Examining the historical sources for the contexts in which an 'ethnicity' is appended to named individuals, Geary discovered that very few people are ever so identified.[120] Further, it became clear that 'the terms *Franci, Alamanni, Burgundiones, Gothi* and the like appeared in connection with kings and with war'.[121] Geary concludes that

> the peoples of the migration period acquired their identity through their adherence to particular royal or ducal families alongside whom they fought and whose traditions they adopted.
> The actual circumstances in which ethnic designations seem to have been felt most acutely were largely *political*.[122]

This discussion takes us back to the heart of the question of concepts of ethnicity in the early Middle Ages. We have a tendency to assume that *all* members of a particular social grouping constituted the *ethnos*. In fact it seems likely that such a sense of belonging was more socially circumscribed. Wolfram tells us that '[a]rchaic peoples are mixed; they never comprise all potential members of a *gens*';[123] 'the *gens* is the people in arms';[124] 'a *gens* is a large group as much as a clan, a fraction of a tribe as much as a confederation of several ethnic units'.[125] In the Burgundian law codes the terms 'Roman' and 'Burgundian' always refer to the upper ranks of society – 'the *nobiles* and *mediocres*. The *coloni* and slaves, whatever their familial origins, do not get ethnic adjectives'.[126] More generally, where we can extract 'identities' from the Burgundian sources, these are usually constructed on the basis of politics and power, not 'blood'.[127]

Peter Heather argues that Gothic identity (or 'Gothicness') was focused on a caste of 'freemen' – 'a dominant and restricted social

---

117. P. Geary, 'Ethnic identity as a situational construct in the early middle ages', *Mitteilungen der Anthropologischen Gesellschaft in Wien*, 113 (1983), 16. See also Amory, 'Names', 29.
118. See Arnold, *Anglo-Saxon Kingdoms*, 21.
119. Geary, 'Ethnic identity', 24–5; Jenkins, *Rethinking Ethnicity*.
120. Geary, 'Ethnic identity', 21, notes 26–8. Also Amory, 'Names', 3.
121. Geary, 'Ethnic identity', 22.
122. *Ibid.*, 22–4, emphasis added.
123. Wolfram, '*Origo*', 21.
124. Wolfram, *History of the Goths*, 7.
125. *Ibid.*, 11.
126. Amory, 'Names', 4, 8.
127. *Ibid.*, 3.

elite: a minority ... within the total adult male population of groups calling themselves Gothic'.[128] He goes on to point out that this obviously left the majority of the population as an 'underclass'. Their commitment to 'Gothicness' cannot really be measured from the historical or archaeological sources, but it is surely noteworthy that when the nobles were killed in battle the rest of the Gothic population simply surrendered.[129] We cannot know the 'ethnic allegiance' (if it existed) of the vast majority of the Gothic (or Burgundian) population, but with Amory we can suggest that 'for the lowest classes, social role and geographic location were more important defining traits than ethnic identity'.[130]

This all suggests that when the historical sources speak of a *gens* – a people like the *gens Anglorum* – they are not referring to *all* the inhabitants of England, or even of any of the 'settlement areas'. They are referring to an *elite* within that larger entity. We might call this 'restricted ethnicity' but ultimately, they are talking about *power*.

This concept of 'restricted ethnicity' has important implications for our understanding of the operation of early 'English' society. The problem we have in discussing 'restricted ethnicity' in the case of Anglo-Saxon England derives, once again, from the nature of the sources. As I have already noted, contemporary English documentary sources for the fifth and sixth centuries do not exist and later sources must be read with a deep awareness of their context.[131] As Reynolds succinctly puts it,

> we do not know how consistently the Germanic-speaking invaders of Britain behaved like a group or felt themselves to be a group during the fifth and sixth centuries. We do not know what they called themselves, if indeed they had any collective name.[132]

However, Higham argues that there is evidence in Bede for an *exclusive* understanding of what/who constituted the *gens Anglorum* in the seventh century. Higham shows that there are remarkably few references to the lower orders in Bede's text and argues that they were beneath Bede's attention.[133] He would not have had them in mind when he spoke of the *gens Anglorum*.

Bede tells us that in 679 a battle was fought, 'near the river Trent', between the Northumbrian king Ecgfrith and the Mercian king

---

128. P. Heather, *The Goths* (1996), 301.
129. *Ibid.*, 301.
130. Amory, 'Names', 4.
131. Dumville, 'Essex', 123. See also Sims-Williams, 'Settlement of England', 1–41; Scull, 'Early Anglo-Saxon society', 65–6; Hodges, *Anglo-Saxon Achievement*, 22–3; B. Yorke, *Kings and Kingdoms of Early Anglo-Saxon England* (1997, reprint of 1990 original), 1–4; *idem*, 'Jutes of Hampshire and Wight', 84–8.
132. Reynolds, 'What do we mean', 401.
133. N. Higham, *An English Empire: Bede and the Early Anglo-Saxon Kings* (1995), 218–19.

Æthelred during which the former's brother Ælfwine was killed.[134] In the course of the battle Imma, a *miles* of Ælfwine, was wounded, and after lying for some time among the dead on the battlefield

> he was found and captured by men of the enemy army, and taken to their lord, who was a *gesith* of king Æthelred. On being asked who he was, he was afraid to admit that he was a thegn; but he answered instead that he was a poor peasant and married; and he declared that he had come to the army in company with other peasants to bring food to the soldiers. The *gesith* took him and had his wounds attended to ... When he had been a prisoner with the *gesith* for some time, those who watched him closely realized by his appearance, his bearing, and his speech that he was not of common stock as he had said, but of noble family.[135]

Higham argues that the deception perpetrated by Imma was designed to prevent his being killed by the Mercians in revenge for the losses they had incurred. More significantly for our purposes, the fact that

> the *miles* was considered by both parties to be an appropriate object of such revenge, but the *rusticus* not, implies that the former, but not the latter, was considered to be a full member of the appropriate *gens* (people) – so vulnerable to a blood feud which that *gens* had incurred *en masse*.[136]

It is also significant that the Mercians eventually recognized Imma to be of noble birth from 'his appearance, clothing and speech'. We might conclude that such signs distinguished him from the lower orders who supported him in battle, if only by way of bringing provisions to the army.

Such perceptions of the significance of the lower orders were not restricted to Bede. In a letter to Æthelheard, Archbishop of Canterbury, written after the Viking destruction of the monastery at Lindisfarne in 793, Alcuin urges the English to reform themselves so that the same might not happen again. The clergy are reminded of their spiritual duties; those best able to do battle (we might call them the *bellatores*) are to protect the clergy (*oratores*). However, Alcuin 'does not name those who labor; they have no role during a time of crisis'.[137] These may only be the perceptions of the clergy, but they are reinforced by the evidence of the seventh- and eighth-century law-codes of kings Æthelberht of Kent and Ine of Wessex,[138] and in any case they are the only literary perceptions we have. What they suggest is that in the seventh century the *gens Anglorum* comprised a

---

134. Bede, *HE* IV.21.
135. Bede, *HE* IV.22.
136. Higham, *English Empire*, 225–6.
137. Howe, *Migration*, 24.
138. Higham, *English Empire*, 235–40.

restricted secular and ecclesiastical elite who exercised extensive power over the vast majority of the population.[139]

In this summary Higham returns us to the link between the 'peoples' named in the historical sources and relationships of power and domination – Imma claimed he was a *peasant* bringing provisions to the Northumbrian *militia*. However, he does so by imposing a crude 'ethnic' (in its biological sense) hierarchy on to what is clearly a social/cultural one. Thus he argues that the '*gens Anglorum* was a political, military and cultural elite, atop a community which remained otherwise quite British even up until the early eighth century'.[140] I would suggest that the social and political hierarchy was not so clearly constructed on biological grounds.

Higham's argument for a socially restricted sense of *gens Anglorum* is echoed by others.[141] At a different level, Hines, discussing the meaning of named late sixth- and earlier seventh-century political units for their inhabitants, suggests that

> we have little reason to suppose that they expressed in any consensual way the group-identity of most of these inhabitants, and that consequently a group name like the Hæstingas is not to be conceived of as representing some comfortably clannish system in which all the people of Hæst were one as if part of some extended family and thus united by their ethnic identity at least: it could rather be an administrative, *possessive, imposed* description – the people who belong to N.[142]

In the past it was thought that these *-ingas* names were evidence for the earliest settlement of England by Germanic families, with the family head providing the prefix (*Hæstingas* = the kin of Hæsta). It is now recognized that they belong to a rather later phase of early English history, one associated with 'consolidation and demarcation'.[143] Hines' observation removes the assumption of 'familiarity' and consensus which has frequently been associated with these names, and places them in the context of developing power relations, which also involved 'consolidation and demarcation'. The suggestion that it could have been an imposed term also removes the necessity to assume 'blood' links between (for example) the members of the *Hæstingas*.

There are, therefore, indications that in the seventh century and later, the term *gens* referred to elite identity. The Continental evidence suggests that it would not be surprising if the concept of restricted ethnicity (in which the membership of a *gens* was socially circumscribed) *did* apply in England in the fifth and sixth centuries. Despite

---

139. *Ibid.*, 255.
140. *Ibid.*, 254, emphasis added.
141. See, for example, Sims-Williams, 'Settlement of England', 24.
142. Hines, 'Cultural change', 82, emphasis added.
143. Blair, *Anglo-Saxon Oxfordshire*, 35. Also Yorke, *Wessex*, 40–3.

the often cited differences in the economic and political situation in fifth-century Britain and Gaul (for example),[144] and in the 'non-Romanized' nature of the 'invaders' of England, 'it seems implausible that the customs of ... [the Germanic-speaking settlers of England] differed so much from those of other Germanic-speaking barbarians of north-western Europe'[145] as to render inappropriate the application of insights drawn from the Continent.

Conclusion: Germanic kin?

The material cultures which culture-historians link with the peoples named in Bede's one paragraph on the Germanic ancestors of the English were the product of actions taken in England in the sixth and seventh centuries. They were the product of interactions between emerging regional networks of power, both 'Anglo-Saxon' and 'British'. Their style was determined by late Roman forms associated with the authority of Rome and by memories and myths of a 'Germanic' homeland. But the main point is that they were *constructed* in the context of sixth- and seventh-century regional *power* structures. The emergence of such structures is manifest in the archaeology of cemetery and settlement. In the cemeteries there is increasing evidence for stratification and hierarchy in the second half of the sixth century,[146] while in the seventh century this is more clearly marked, especially in the individual barrow burials.[147] The settlements of the fifth and early sixth century are marked by a profound lack of differentiation, both internally and across regions. Richard Hodges points to the contrast between the fortified hill-top centres of western Britain where the scale of refurbishment, the presence of 'high status' imports from the Mediterranean, and the nature of some of the structures and argues for their occupation by an elite, and the 'egalitarian quality of ... [the] modest farmsteads' of contemporary early Anglo-Saxon England.[148] Just such an apparently egalitarian picture emerges from the excavations of the mid-fifth-century phases of the settlement at Mucking in Essex. Here the 'absence of large, "high

---

144. Many of these differences are summarized in H.R. Loyn, *The Making of the English Nation: From the Anglo-Saxons to Edward I* (1991), 10–17; also Welch, *Anglo-Saxon England*, 104.
145. S. Reynolds, *Fiefs and Vassals: The Medieval Evidence Reinterpreted* (1994), 325.
146. Hodges, *Anglo-Saxon Achievement*, 38.
147. J. Shephard, 'The social identity of the individual in isolated barrows and barrow cemeteries in Anglo-Saxon England', in *Space, Hierarchy and Society*, eds B. Burnham and J. Kingsbury (1979), 47–79; M. Carver, *Sutton Hoo: Burial Ground of Kings?* (1998).
148. Hodges, *Anglo-Saxon Achievement*, 34; also Scull, 'Early Anglo-Saxon society', 72; D. Hinton, *Archaeology, Economy and Society: England from the Fifth to the Fifteenth Centuries* (1990), 2; Yorke, *Wessex*, 22; L. Alcock, *Cadbury Castle, Somerset: The Early Medieval Settlement* (1995), 150.

status", or obviously central buildings' and the 'lack of any obvious structure or planning within the settlement' were used to argue for 'the absence of an overall, regulating authority'.[149] There *is* evidence for differentiation within Anglo-Saxon period settlements, and for the kind of structure and planning so evidently absent at West Stow and the early phases at Mucking, but this appears in the late sixth and seventh centuries;[150] at the same time as we get the construction of distinctive regional material cultures. I would argue that there is an intimate connection between these two phenomena, and that the forms of identity we find expressed in the regional material cultures are those of affiliation and allegiance to regional 'aristocratic' elites.

Five generations after the supposed *adventus Saxonum* the 'blood ethnicity' of these elites would have been hard to determine, even if it mattered.[151] Given the lack of evidence for a massive rupture in the countryside of late Roman Britain, however, we must assume that the vast majority of the population was *not* of Germanic origin/descent. Abandoning the notions of homogeneous groups of Anglo-Saxons 'invading' and destroying a coherent entity, in favour of a more continuous process of assimilation into the decentralized and personalized power structures of sub-Roman Britain, means that we cannot even assume that the elites were primarily Germanic.[152] What matters is that the heterogeneous peoples of the regions of England came to *see themselves* as having a common identity. They did so as a consequence of collective action and interaction with other British and Anglo-Saxon entities. It *may* be at this time (in the late sixth and seventh centuries) that this identity came to be seen as Anglian, Saxon, etc. but we still have to recognize that we have no idea what the peoples of fifth- and sixth-century England called themselves 'if indeed they had any collective name'.[153] It *may* be that this sense of identity – of 'Anglian-ness', 'Saxon-ness' etc. – was restricted to a social elite, and it seems that this concept of 'restricted ethnicity' existed by the end of the seventh century.[154] It is probably of some importance that, in the eighth century, succession to the throne was linked to descent from a sixth-century 'ancestor'.[155] But as we have already noted, a concomitant of ethnicity is *power* and this must be especially true of 'restricted ethnicity'. The elites of the kingdoms of 'Anglo-Saxon' England may have emphasized their Anglo-Saxon origins from the

---

149. H. Hamerow, 'Settlement mobility and the middle-Saxon shift: rural settlements and settlement patterns in Anglo-Saxon England', *Anglo-Saxon England* 20 (1991), 8–9; and her *Excavations at Mucking, Volume 2: The Anglo-Saxon Settlement* (1993), 89.
150. Hodges, *Anglo-Saxon Achievement*, 58–65. Scull, 'Before Sutton Hoo', 21; Hinton, *Archaeology, Economy and Society*, 27.
151. Reynolds, 'What do we mean', 402–3.
152. *Contra* Higham *English Empire*, 254.
153. Reynolds, 'What do we mean', 401.
154. See Higham, *English Empire*, 225–6.
155. Dumville, 'Kingship', 73.

seventh century onwards, drawing upon a common mythical past to promote a common sense of belonging and so create what Shennan has called 'the self-conscious identity groups which are essential to the definition of ethnicity'[156]; but, as with Heather's Goths, the ethnic identity of the mass of the population is unclear and likely to have been at least ambivalent. The reality for them, as it was for Imma, was economic, social and political subordination.

---

156. Shennan, 'Introduction', 15.

3 Self-worth and Property: Equipage and Early Medieval Personhood[1]

Nerys Thomas Patterson

Understanding the way in which people in other cultures experience their personhood is the quintessential anthropological project. Its success has always depended on the total alienation of the field worker through perceptual saturation in the exotic and the reintegration of the anthropologist's own self-in-society after returning to his or her point of departure for the study. Earlier historical phases of Western societies in some ways resemble 'exotic' contemporary societies, with even their most lumpishly obvious remains – houses, streets and fields – challenging our assumptions about their function and meaning. But the lived experiences of individuals in the past are less accessible than those of the peoples visited by anthropologists. There is no total context in which the historian can lose his or her former sense of self and start to live as a member of another society. Historical reconstruction is inevitably contaminated by projections of the present onto the past.

In this regard the anthropological approach may be of practical help, for the anthropologist's problem of ethnocentricity is of a similar nature to anachronistic misunderstanding. Anthropologists are drawn to what is hard to fathom in the host society, frequently seeking out what they perceive to be the most bizarre and repulsive aspects of foreign cultures and societies. By establishing the intelligibility in their context of such practices as cannibalism, exhumation of the dead, and genital mutilation, anthropologists have attempted to illuminate the entire composition of the society and culture they seek to understand. It is precisely the outrageous that often serves as a central thread in the seeming design of the social fabric: pull it and the relationships emerge. Similarly, the mundane relics of the past, once seen in conjunction with something that shocks, may take on quite new aspects.

1. I gratefully acknowledge the financial aid for this research received from the H. B. Earhart Research Fellowship 1992–93 and the Harvard University Fellowship in Law and Liberal Arts 1992–93.

In this chapter I have taken just such a route into the intricacies of early medieval Western subjectivity, seeking to show the meaning of what appears to be coarse materialism in the accepted behaviour of normal men and women of this period. I have chosen for discussion two examples of early medieval attitudes towards the economic aspects of close personal relationships. These concern social transactions occasioned by sexual relations and by death. From a modern perspective the nuptial and mortuary practices described below seem rudely instrumental and materialistic, but their analysis offers an avenue into the quite exotic landscape of feelings, beliefs and symbols that made up the early medieval person's individual experience of self.

Medieval coarseness is not a new subject, of course, but one that has been much discussed, most notably perhaps by Norbert Elias.[2] But the crudeness of medieval (early and later) cultures and societies seems to be better recognized than understood. Elias himself does not go beyond showing that 'they' were less artificial and were closer to nature in their presentation-of-self than are 'we'. But it is possible that far from being merely primitive harbingers of our own modern selves, early medieval individuals experienced their subjectivity in ways quite different from our own. It is the aim of this chapter to set forth an outline of the elusive interior world of the early medieval self – a *weltanschauung* obscured by the assumption that rough manners indicate an absence of other types of complexity in the encoding of experience.[3]

The sources of my examples of 'crude materialism' are medieval Celtic language texts, primarily legal tracts. These depict regional varieties of European social institutions, differing in some ways, but in general substantially conforming to, the main lines of Western cultures and societies. They constitute the richest vernacular sources of information on early medieval European social structures. The manuscripts themselves, however, are no earlier in date than the twelfth century. Where contents are assigned to the early middle ages, this is usually on grounds of linguistic archaism. On the whole, therefore, it is dangerous to base arguments about chronologies of social change on these sources and safer to emphasize that the texts reflect a form of society whose distinctive features (notably the blood-feud and honour-price) had faded away in England between the late Anglo-Saxon and early Norman period. On these grounds one may say that the practices described below reflect an early medieval *mentalité*, but with some additions of later elements.[4]

---

2. N. Elias, *The Civilizing Process* (New York, 1978) and *The History of Manners* (New York, 1982).
3. I employ *weltanshauung* in the general sense of a 'cultural world view' and that view's reflexive relationship with the actions undertaken by early medieval individuals.
4. A full discussion of the Irish texts appears in F. Kelly, *A Guide to Early Irish Law* (1988). For the Welsh law texts see H. Pryce, *Native Law and the Church in Medieval Wales* (1993); T.M. Charles-Edwards, *The Welsh Laws* (1989);

Nuptial and mortuary practices in early medieval Wales and Ireland

Nuptial and mortuary practices express the social interpretation of changes to individuals' bodies, and also the changes in social relationships consequent on individual transitions. First intercourse at marriage and the passage of heirship during the dying process are crucial points in the lives of social groups, for this is when new bonds are forged and old ones severed, altering the future membership of the group. Modern societies and cultures, however, acknowledge only the events of the body at these times and the mind's emotions about those events, evading and obfuscating the question of what is happening to the broader field of social relationships, especially as these are affected by changes in the distribution of property as a marriage begins or a life ends. In contrast, early medieval cultures and societies dealt with marriage and death as packages of related changes, each aspect valid and worthy of recognition, the economic no less than the personal. This recognition was expressed in ways that would be deeply offensive to modern sensibilities.

Marriage: the worth of sexuality and the pricing of sex

The modern view, enshrined in both the religious and the legal codification of marriage, is that the marital relationship is first and foremost an emotional contract in which the mutual exchange of comfort and support are paramount: marriage is all about *love. Comfort* obviously includes sex and support implies the provision of *worldly goods*, but since divorce was for centuries prohibited by the Church and almost unobtainable at law, the marriage contract makes no mention of *how many* worldly goods, let alone *how much* sex, each partner has the right to expect of the other. 'For richer, for poorer' has long been the basic religious-legal rule on this matter, so that the question of the economic basis of the marriage was left, among the rich, to private legal contract, while the poor looked to community norms. Likewise, the nature of the sexual relationship was unspecified – for example, English common law did not until recently recognize rape in marriage.

The substance of the economic and sexual transactions that were the subject of the marriage contract were thus neglected by the main regulative mechanisms of the state – the Church and the law – yet it was these agencies that gave voice to ideas of morality and propriety.[5]

---

contd.
> D. Jenkins, *The Law of Hywel Dda* (1990). I discuss the difficulties of assigning historical provenance to the social institutions represented in the Irish law tracts in *Cattle-lords and Clansmen: The Social Structure of Early Ireland* (Notre Dame, 1994), as does R.C. Stacey, *The Road to Judgment: From Custom to Court in Medieval Ireland and Wales* (Philadelphia, 1994).

If they were silent on the question of the economic obligations of spouses in marriage what were people supposed to think? One clear implication was that self-respecting people were not supposed to marry to satisfy their financial and sexual needs, much less exchange financial favours for sexual ones. They were to marry for sentimental reasons and the relationship was to be a sentimental one. Actual behaviour has always departed from this ideal, but nevertheless this *was* the ideal: good people only marry 'for love', and only have sex in a loving marriage. To show interest in the material basis of sexual relations was either reviled as prostitution or scorned as gold-digging (when it was a woman with such interests), or culturally denied where the spouses and the marriage were conventional and the husband monopolized economic interests in the marriage.

This ideal still informs current debates in Britain on 'family values', condemning most people to guilt about their actual experiences of need and want in relationships. Paradoxically, the modern ideology that emotions should be the basis of relationships is associated with the suffocation of actual emotions in order to preserve the institutional framework of relationships which ought (one day) to bring happiness to married couples and their offspring.

The medieval self was not so troubled. Nothing could contrast more starkly to modern coyness about the material worth of marriage partners to each other than the explicitness of the provisions for a married woman's economic establishment found in the texts of the medieval Welsh law books.[6] These provisions were several: a dowry from her family of origin; property accumulated mutually during the marriage and divisible upon divorce according to a pre-nuptial agreement based on a customary formula; property accruing to the wife due to marital offences by the husband (infidelity and violence) and inalienable from her; and property assigned only to a virgin bride on account of her virginity on the occasion of the wedding. The latter payment, *cowyll*, is the subject of the present analysis.

Welsh *cowyll* was similar to Germanic and Anglo-Saxon 'morning gift': it was supplied by the husband and in medieval Wales it formed the most substantial element in that part of a married woman's

---

5. L. Stone, *Uncertain Unions and Broken Lives: Marriage and Divorce in England. 1660–1857* (1995). In *The Road to Divorce: England 1530–1987* (1990) Stone shows how the confusion in law and Church doctrine stimulated the growth of divorce in early modern Europe. This picture needs to be viewed against evidence that divorce and valid remarriage was a feature of early medieval society, well documented as a legal institution in Welsh and Irish law; see Patterson, *Cattle-lords*, 310 ff. Absence of documentation from other parts of early Europe reflects ecclesiastical control of writing, which leaves open the question of the cultural acceptability of *de facto* divorce in these areas.
6. Text editions, translations and analytical essays on marriage in medieval Wales are found in D. Jenkins and M. Owen (eds), *The Welsh Law of Women* (1980).

property which was inalienably hers.[7] It was important to women and to their families, for otherwise a woman who was divorced on account of her own faults might otherwise have been rendered destitute by the husband's retention of her share of the assets of the marital household. It is in the way that *cowyll* was handled that we see dramatically revealed the cultural gulf between modern bashfulness at the material interests of people in their close personal relationships and medieval explicitness. In the first place, the condition of female virginity had a clear-cut *minimum price* which the man who ended it was obliged to pay, whether he did this in the context of a marriage, a liaison, or rape. The price was stipulated in the law-books according to the rank of the bride's father. So, for example, the *cowyll* of a king's daughter was £8, that of a landowner's daughter £1, and that of a serf's daughter 80d.[8]

But a woman could demand more than the minimum payment due to her rank. Bargaining could have occurred as part of the general negotiations that would have preceded a marriage agreement, but the texts also clearly envisage further bargaining going on in seclusion between the bride and groom before intercourse.[9] A startling picture presents itself: the groom rising from the marriage bed to declare to the wedding guests what amount he had agreed to pay to his future wife for her permission to let him deflower her, and that he had got what he had paid for. So entrenched was this custom that a woman who contracted her own semi-formal marriage by eloping with a man was legally expected/advised to demand 'what will you give me?' before having first intercourse.[10] A sworn statement by the woman at a later date, in the event of desertion by the man, was enough to secure her this sum, regardless of the absence of witnesses.

Unless the bride was in her early teens she was viewed as sexually mature and unlikely to be a virgin. (Adulthood was regarded as starting for women with menstruation, which was expected at twelve.)[11] For this reason there was deep suspicion about women's claims of virginity and demands for *cowyll*. The family of a nubile bride was required to provide an oath as to her virginity before the would-be husband agreed to pay *cowyll* at all. If, after all this, the bride proved sexually experienced, the husband had the right to repudiate her at once: according to one text he was entitled to jump out of bed, light candles, call the wedding guests and denounce the bride. Then he (or someone) should cut off her clothing to waist-level and drive her out into the night.[12] On the other hand (since men were envisaged as being as

---

7. *Ibid.*, 76ff.
8. *Ibid.*, 76.
9. *Ibid.*, 77.
10. *Ibid.*, 153, no. 23.
11. *Ibid.*, 77.
12. *Ibid.*, 153.

deceptive as women), if he slept the entire night with his non-virgin bride he forfeited his rights to denounce her next morning and was required to pay her *cowyll* no matter what her state of pre-marital sexual experience.

The contrast between these customs and present-day views on sexual self-worth could hardly be greater: only prostitutes nowadays bargain for the amount of money it will cost a man to have sexual intercourse, and only pimps – not wedding guests – express interest in the agreed amount. Yet in Welsh medieval culture a mercenary transaction accompanied what was the most important event in the making of kinship, namely marital intercourse and the ensuing formation of a new nuclear family. What does this difference mean as to the worth of an individual's sexuality in early medieval societies?

On the face of it, the practices surrounding *cowyll* would suggest a brash shamelessness about sex – intercourse and virginity seem to have been openly commodified. The texts might signify, then, nothing more than an extreme case of medieval coarseness, and the whole function of *cowyll* may have been nothing more than to make it too costly for young men to have pre-marital intercourse with virgins, leaving them pregnant and hard to marry off. Yet the texts also refer to a young girl's 'shame' at being told by her father that he had 'given her to a man'. Indeed another element in the women's property complex is explained in the texts as due to a bride on three occasions: first, as recompense for the shame described above; second on the actual loss of her virginity; and third when she faced the wedding guests on the morning after the wedding night.[13] Sex was understood to be capable of shaming a woman in another way also, that is, if it became known that her husband had sexual intercourse with another woman. For this she could demand a fine from him (*gowyn*) on up to three occasions, keep the proceeds, and on the third occasion divorce him while retaining all her other property rights intact.[14]

Far from being 'shameless' about sex, then, medieval Welsh women were meant to feel shame under some circumstances and to receive payments (in livestock) to 'make up' for the shame. But it would be a mistake to transpose modern prurience to the medieval consciousness and construe these two examples of expected sexually-caused shame as shame *about* sex. Had there been such a notion one would have found

---

13. *Ibid.*, 159, no. 65. The 'women's property complex' refers to the variety of pre-mortem transmissions of property to women on the occasion of marriage (usually first marriage). Principal elements are dowry stemming from the bride's own family, trousseau accumulated by the bride through her own labour and voluntary gifts from friends and relatives, and dower – a settlement on the bride by her husband in anticipation of his prior decease. Female inheritance on the death of kin in the family of origin is not excluded from this count, but was ancillary to the main forms of provision. See J. Goody and S. J. Tambiah, *Bridewealth and Dowry* (1973), and J. Goody, *The Development of the Family and Marriage in Europe* (1983).
14. Jenkins and Owen, *Welsh Law*, 171, no. 51.4.

it cropping up in all aspects of a woman's life. But, on the contrary, mature women were regarded as sexual by nature and not in need of reparation if seduced by a man. Indeed the notion of seduction is not present in the laws, only rape or other forced sexual attention.

The 'shame' attributed to women in the instances mentioned above must thus have been experienced on account of other aspects of the cultural construction of the meaning of sex. Most likely, the married woman was viewed as shamed by her husband's adultery because of the public exposure of the sexual insufficiency of the marriage, while the virgin was shamed by the exposure of her inexperience. In both cases it was the opening to public gaze of private, usually concealed, feelings of sexual inadequacy that required compensation. These provisions imply that the normal adult woman's self-esteem included inner assurance and public acceptance of her sexual competence – not just fertility, but (as Irish law put it) ability to perform 'the woman deed'. Less surprisingly (to us), the adult male could also claim compensation for loss of self-esteem if his wife 'cast aspersions on his beard', i.e. told others he was not virile enough. Both men and women were expected to be sexually whole, i.e. competent rather than 'pure', and if they were depicted otherwise the 'hole' in their self-esteem required filling up with compensating payments of livestock, goods or coins.[15]

Death: family love and family property[16]

Modern embarrassment about the financial basis of marriage is matched or even exceeded by contemporary coyness about the role of property in the bond of inter-dependence between parents and children. In the absence of a will, heritable property in the UK is transmitted to the surviving spouse, who precludes children's claims, while inheriting children preclude siblings of the deceased. As there are no provisions that enjoin sharing between members of different heirship categories, it is possible that in the absence of a will a second spouse may entirely shut out the claims of the children of the deceased's first marriage. Similarly, a surviving member of a childless intestate couple may involuntarily transmit on his or her death the other spouse's estate to his or her own siblings or parents, excluding the other spouse's siblings – even when the couple had obtained property through inheritance from the other spouse's parents. In view

---

15. So omni-present was the notion that damage was a loss that could be restored through 'filling up' whatever had been breached that in early Ireland even pollution of arable land by a dog's droppings was remedied in this way: the owner was to remove the faeces and dig a hole where they had been, then fill the hole with emollients – butter and new milk; see Patterson, *Cattle-lords*, 73.

16. References in the following section are to citations from primary sources and discussion in Patterson, *Cattle-lords*.

of such possibilities it is striking that the vast majority of people in contemporary Britain (about 80 per cent) do not make a will.[17] Consciously or not, kin seem to want to avoid thinking about the relationship between property and family feelings.

The awkwardness of those faced with the question of making a will is matched by the embarrassment of those anticipating inheritance. A common source of problems for modern heirs is the disparity between the amount of 'caring' undertaken by the different children of a parent who has become dependent. Since 'love' in the family is supposed to be unconcerned with reciprocity, the child's service is not supposed to entitle her (sometimes him) to more of a share of inheritance than other children.[18] Parents, similarly, are not supposed to have favourites, even when one child is making far more of an effort than others. Failure to adjust inheritance to filial efforts often leads to family tensions.[19]

Modern inheritance, then, is a one-sided affair: the norm is that the dying leave their assets to successors, willy-nilly and unconditionally. The dying parent is a total giver, and the child as heir is a total receiver of material goods. Even in the realm of affection – the giving and receiving of love – where reciprocity would seem a reasonable expectation, *exchange* of affection is not the model. The emotional ideal is, instead, a coincidence of similar but unilateral feelings. For example, modern parents (are supposed to) love their children even when, as is not uncommon, the child expresses dislike of the parents, rejects the parents's values, or seeks therapy. But while it is culturally acceptable for a child to reject parents on the grounds that they did not love him or her enough, the reverse is culturally inadmissible. Given this massive imbalance between parental giving and filial taking it is not surprising that guilt clings to the modern heir, and vengeance may be subtly exacted by the old through manipulation of unexpressed hopes of inheritance.[20]

As with sex, so with death: early medieval people were less at odds with themselves. Medieval people were explicit about the economic consequences of death, treating the inevitable fact of future parental ageing and death as the foundation stone of the relationship *in life* between parents and children. Their attitudes were informed by clear-cut expectations as to the parent's duty to convey inheritance and the child's reciprocal duty to provide care for the parent during sickness and frailty. The Irish law texts stipulated that those who failed in this duty towards parents lost their legal status in society, while those who

---

17. J. Finch, *Family Obligations and Social Change* (1989), 18.
18. *Ibid.*, 13–56.
19. D. Merrill, 'Conflict and cooperation among adult siblings during the transition to the role of filial caregiver', *Journal of Social and Personal Relationships* 13(3) (1996), 399–413.
20. H.B. Gibson, *The Emotional and Sexual Lives of Older People* (1992), 113ff.

abandoned even distant relatives suffering from mental illness stood to lose the right to inherit their land.[21]

The equation of the right to inherit with the duty to care is also attested in thirteenth-century English manorial records which describe contracts between older people and younger ones, usually close kin, in which food and care are promised in return for inheritance of the house.[22] This custom persisted until the present century in many rural regions of Ireland. Here the inheriting son was obliged to delay marriage until the age of his father's retirement from farm management, after which the parents resided in the west room and the new wife saw to their personal needs.[23] As in manorial England, parents often made contracts with their children as to their economic entitlements following the transmission of property to the heir.[24] These rights were formalized and written down by a local scholar, cultural descendant of the pre-conquest native lawyer. In addition to written rights, parents had customary expectations for provision by the heir that were strong enough to elicit protests at their non-fulfilment to the Poor Inquiry in the 1830s.[25]

One contrast between early medieval and later norms of inheritance, then, was that the former was a two-way street between the social relationships of the past (the generation of the dead and dying) and those of the present and future,[26] while the latter is one-sided and a potential source of feelings of guilt and inadequacy. Another contrast resides in the fact that earlier heirs had on-going services to provide to the deceased: death did not end the exchanges between them. The main duty of the heir was the obligation to fund the religious memorialization of the dead out of the heritage. This could take the simple form of paying for candles and prayers, or more expensively, paying for masses or even endowing a church with land or chattels. The on-going nature of these donations was linked to the on-going struggle of the deceased to make his or her way through limbo and purgatory and on to heaven. The dead were imagined as struggling to achieve promotion in much the same way as the early medieval farmer struggled, as he matured, to acquire more and more property and status (see below, p. 63). In Ireland, much of what he acquired came from collateral inheritance, so it is hardly surprising that the other life and this one were seen as highly continuous. Through prayers and other offerings, the living were to assist the dead in their battle to improve their social standing; the dead in turn helped the living with

21. F. Kelly, *A Guide to Early Irish Law* (Dublin, 1988) and Patterson, *Cattle-lords*.
22. G. Homans, *English Villagers of the Thirteenth Century* (New York, 1941).
23. C. M. Arensburg, *The Irish Countryman* (Gloucester, Massachussetts, 1959).
24. D. Fitzpatrick, 'The modernisation of the Irish female', in *Rural Ireland: Modernisation and Change 1600-1900*, eds P. O'Flanagan, P. Ferguson, and K. Whelan (1987), 171-2.
25. Fitzpatrick, 'Modernisation', 172.
26. See J. Crick in this volume, for more on death as an age category.

their struggle for status and security by bequeathing heritage and a good family name to them.

In the various streams of Celtic law the Irish texts give the fullest evidence on the relationship between social structure on earth and imagined social structure after death. The dying were allowed to bequeath a proportion of their estate away from the heirs of their body to the church.[27] The church, which would have been a local monastic church, usually related by kinship to local landowning families, was not entitled to alienate this land, but neither could the heirs of the deceased reclaim it (in theory). As local churches accumulated such property, their estates not only supported the souls of deceased secular kin but also provided a livelihood for their living descendants. As the early medieval Irish clergy were non-celibate (a holy man was 'a bishop of one wife'), the monasteries became, with some exceptions, the hereditary estates of clerical families.[28] The funding of the ancestors' well-being after death and the funding of social relations here on earth were thus intermingled. Moreover, the social unity effected by the transmission of heritage existed in the ultimate time-frame: the Irish believed that the dead would arise on the day of atonement wherever they had been buried – surrounded, then, by kith and kin on the family lands. Over much of Europe, this ancient imagined socio-economic exchange between the dead and the living persisted until the Reformation.

The 'stuffed self': an overview of early medieval selfhood

The early nuptial and mortuary customs described above show that the emotions caused by powerful experiences of sexuality and mortality had quite different possibilities of expression in medieval and modern Western cultures. Medieval people expressed their anxiety at change as 'loss', and soothed this anxiety by 'filling the void' with monetary or material 'compensations' which represented the worth of different aspects of their own and others' selves. Thus, when a girl 'lost' her virginity she gained her *cowyll*; when a man 'lost' his father he gained his inheritance. Both the bride and the heir could be openly proud of their material gains.

Modern men and women have a different structure of sentiments for these same experiences – a structure of heightened sentimentality and diminished practicality in which economic interests are diametrically opposed to all that is good in marital and parent–child relationships. It is impossible for anyone nowadays to show open satisfaction in the expensiveness of an engagement ring, for example, or the amount of a legacy: these are unmentionable things. Moderns are left experiencing

---

27. Kelly, *Irish Law*, 122–3.
28. K. Nicholls, *Gaelic and Gaelicized Ireland* (Dublin, 1972), 91 ff.

a normative dichotomy between love and money, and between emotional and instrumental connection – even though, in actual social life, no such dichotomy is ever experienced as authentically present, only as required. More precisely, we should say that modern loss is inconsolable – there is no culturally prescribed way to fill the void created by whatever is experienced as causing loss, only personal, idiosyncratic ways. Medieval people, in contrast, approached not only the changes accompanying marriage and death but the entire relationship of the self and others, in all its complexity, as transactions where loss of one kind (personal, physical and emotional) was compensated by gain of another kind (impersonal, material and instrumental). As we shall now see, this way of handling subjective experience and its representation as a 'self' is closely tied to aspects of early European social structure, particularly the mode of agrarian production.

The fullest early medieval picture of a relationship between agricultural organization, ownership of property, and the worth of individuals is found in an Old Irish law tract called *Crith Gablach* (*CG*), which was written in the midlands or north of the island in the eighth or ninth century.[29] Although Ireland was wetter and more pastoral in its agriculture than many other parts of western Europe, *CG* was written in one of its more fertile arable areas and describes a model of farming that presumes the use of a four-ox plough. On the whole, it is reasonable to assume that some aspects of its basic outline of farming society would apply to many parts of early medieval northern Europe, particularly Britain. There is, for example, a striking similarity between *CG* and the eleventh-century Anglo-Saxon tract, *Rectitudines Singularum Personarum*.[30]

CG describes the ranks of male society from the bottom up, beginning with immature boys, and climbing through the ranks of holders of small plots of land who shared a plough with their kith and kin, through the ranks that were self-sufficient, and on to those who were able to extend credit to others. Leaving the 'plebeians' it continued to climb upward, listing the ranks of those who performed judicial and military services for the social group (the *tuath*, or petty clan-kingdom). Among farmers, each rank-level was associated with ever-increasing amounts of land, livestock, and gear. At each rise in the

---

29. D. A. Binchy (ed.), *Crith Gablach* (1941); E. MacNeill (trans.), 'Ancient Irish law: the law of status or franchise', *Proceedings of the Royal Irish Academy* 36C (1923), 265–315. *Crith Gablach* is obscurely translated as 'the branched purchase', with 'branches' referring to the lineages of a clan or petty kingdom, *tuath*, and 'purchase' somehow alluding to possessions. Binchy's authoritative edition of the text does not include a translation into English. MacNeill's edition does offer a translation but is not entirely reliable. The translation offered in 'Ancient Irish Law' is almost unintelligible. This important text requires reassessment as a historical document.
30. H.R. Loyn, *Anglo-Saxon England and the Norman Conquest* (1962), 189 ff.

level of ownership, the tract indicates that a person's social worth also increased. That is, with regard to the entire range of recognized social transactions and of possible offences, the amount due to a man (and to a woman, at half a male peer's rate) was linked to the amount that he held as an owner of a part of the group's total material assets. Likewise, the importance of the issues to which a man could give testimony in a legal dispute (as eye-witness or oath-giver) was linked to his status as farmer. Indeed, rank affected every aspect of who he or she was and what he or she could do.

In addition to the *CG* treatment of the relationship between possessions and legal privileges, other Old Irish tracts exist that make connections between status and type of marriage, military capacity, clerical grade, and degree of expertise in a craft. In this society, then, individuals could not think of themselves and of other's selves as whole beings with a fixed essence (such as an astrological fate, a totem, or an ancestrally-given identity). The early medieval Irish individual was rather a bundle of personal attributes, comprising his or her age, gender, rank by birth, rank by occupation, and rank by level of wealth. Even in death (due to homicide), the worth of a whole person had several different expressions, since payments of compensation for the dead body were made to relatives according to the closeness of the genealogical relationship.

Such rank-related atonement payments (often known by the Germanic term 'wergeld') were common all over early Europe.[31] There can be little doubt that they reflected social distinctions similar to those applied in the Old Irish law tracts, though we have no means of knowing how fluid and finely graded these classifications were in other regions. They indicate that in early medieval Europe the self was viewed as socially embryonic – needing to be equipped with many attributes and possessions in order for it to have much worth. The mature individual, properly equipped, was him- or herself valued as an assemblage of many useful parts, and was in turn one component of the corporate body in which his or her rank had its basis. In such a universe, where material worth bound everything and everyone together in a charted web of relative worth and costs, social transactions surrounding sex and death would *inevitably* have been marked by the making of payments, as described earlier in this chapter.

The links between individual social worth and agricultural capacity point to an origin for the early medieval concept of the individual self in the social organization of farm production. As Max Weber and Karl Wittfogel both argued, the material springboard of cultural development in Western Europe was never a zone of intensive mono-crop production by gang labour (no rice paddies or maize terraces), as it was in the other epicentres of civilizational growth. Uniquely, Western

---

31. B. Phillpotts, *Kindred and Clan in the Middle Ages and After: A Study of the Sociology of the Teutonic Races* (1913).

development occurred in a temperate, naturally well-watered zone of mixed farming in which the unit of food production was ideally a diversified, self-sufficient farm, run by one male head with his family and other dependent labour.[32]

How this ideal, so clearly cherished in *CG*, actually sat on the ground in a real landscape is best envisaged for the early Middle Ages in northern Europe in the model of the multiple estate.[33] Multiple estates consisted of a core of rich arable, surrounded by zones of varying agricultural potential. Individual farmers held fields and strips in all the different types of lands owned by the group as a whole. Sometimes the ownership was physically demarcated, but sometimes it was abstract and notional. Sometimes the estate might be managed by a clan head, but multiple estates might also be held (as they were in medieval Wales) as the farms of kings and princes, worked by bondsmen. The essence of this pattern of land use was not status-relations but work organization: each person engaged in production should apply him- or herself (and his or her equipment and dependent personnel) to every element in the unit's total collection of agrarian resources. This pattern of labour deployment and use of land probably dates back to episodes in the pre-Roman development of farming in Europe when cultivation of heavy soils required the social strategies of production associated with multiple estates – joint ploughing, common arable and 'stinted' pasture.[34]

Traces of the multiple estate have been found in several areas of early medieval north-western Europe.[35] Nevertheless it is difficult to say how common or typical was this pattern of agrarian organization before the spread of slave-run Roman estates into late Iron Age northern Europe. Rather than argue that multiple estates were statistically dominant, the presence of this type of regime in the historical record is best treated as one known example of how early farming produced the kind of *mentalité* discussed in this chapter – an experience of the self as an individual made known and recognizable to others as a bundle of attributes, *comparable to the bundle of resources*

---

32. K. Wittfogel, *Oriental Despotism* (New Haven, 1957); M. Weber, *The Agrarian Sociology of Ancient Civilizations*, trans. by R.I. Frank (1976). Intensive Greek arboriculture and Roman *latifundia* seem to have developed only after the emergence of large-scale slavery. See M. Finley, *Slavery in Classical Antiquity* (1960).
33. G.R.J. Jones, 'Nuclear settlement and its tenurial relationships: some morphological implications', in *Villages, Fields and Frontiers: Studies in European Rural Settlement in the Medieval and Early Modern Periods*, eds B.K. Roberts and R.E. Glasscock (1983), British Archaeological Reports, International Series 185, 153–67.
34. *Stinting* meant that the farmer could put no more head of stock on the common pasture than his measure of arable permitted. It was a way of ensuring that for each plough beast required by the farmer's arable land there were set numbers of beasts in his herd.
35. Jones, 'Nuclear settlement'.

farmed by the individual. The existential project of this individual was to acquire as much as possible of these attributes in order to do better (economically and politically) and be better (socially and morally) than others. *CG* shows a farming system in which a farmer could never have too much of anything, and a society, therefore, in which sacrifice, gift-exchange, and potlatch were of quite limited social importance. The real game of the farmer, indeed of everyone in early Western economies was accumulation beyond the level of subsistence consumption in order to invest in social relationships with dependents. The farmer strove first to marry and reproduce a small labour force; then to become self-sufficient; and then, once independent, he or she sought to accumulate a surplus of chattels (livestock, gear, or land) and to attract borrowers. These would become all-purpose clients. Individualistic accumulation was thus an integral aspect of a highly individualized mode of food production in early northern Europe.

One of the main symbolic high points of early farming systems was the primitive Western feast, provided by underlings to their lord, in which honour accrued *to the receiver* of the food, not to the providers.[36] It is true that the lord shared the feast with his entourage and guests – after all, he alone could not consume the mountains of food brought by clients – but the point is that in these social systems, high-status people did not distribute food downwards or laterally through exchange mechanisms, but drew resources inwards and consumed or retained them within an inner circle of supporters. The 'spirit of the gift' is not really present in early Europe: the social obsession was with permanent relationships of domination, not temporary superior prestige in reciprocal exchange. Feasts demonstrated the ability to dominate, for they were the deployment in display of a surplus that remained after maximum use had been made of resources in investment in clientship contracts.

My view is that the materialism of the cultures of early medieval Europe utterly and thoroughly permeated every facet of social and personal experience. Long before capitalism the early medieval farmer had the *mentalité* of the counting-house. How long ago? Weber suggested that different types of subjectivities emerged in the Old World as distinctive forms of social organization of production came into being. He located the roots of Chinese bureaucracy and Indian caste, and their associated ways of cultivating the individual self, in the first millennium BC. Perhaps, then, during the same period, Western European socio-economic development also resulted in a crystallization of social values into a systematized cultural code having expression (as in China and India) both in law and in religion.

Evidence on this question is hard to come by, for the development of society and culture in 'Iron Age' Europe was totally transformed by

---

36. Patterson, *Cattle-lords*, 127 ff.

the rise of the Roman Empire, by the failure of that Empire to stabilize its cultural forms, and by its transformation into an apostolic religious organization (Christianity). The notorious social fluidity of the West (its 'freedom'), and the sharp contrast this presents to the highly durable social and cultural systems found in China and India, arose from these processes of predatory imperial expansion – processes which mask, rather than reveal, whatever was the bedrock of social experience in non-imperial and uncolonized 'Iron Age' communities in Western Europe.

But there is one thing we can say with certainty about social life before the impact of the Roman phenomenon: it was not innocent of money. Abundant and widely distributed coin hoards have been found that date to the late Iron Age in northern Europe. Of these Daphne Nash writes: 'It is a common misconception to identify ancient coins too closely with trade. In antiquity significant trade was conducted by barter ... The likelihood is that coinage was first required for such purposes as tribute, taxation, fines, dowries, and offerings, rather than transactions in the market place.'[37] Money existed before the supra-local market, serving as the currency for adjustment of social worth as well as for mundane local sales and purchases. It is not unlikely that the kind of self experienced by early medieval women who demanded payment for sex, and by adult children who expected legacies in return for piety to parents, was much older in cultural history than the early Middle Ages. The shattering of this system of self-management at the end of the Middle Ages left in its wake a deep confusion as to the way in which individuals should properly value each other. It has also left us with only a dull appreciation of those early cultures and societies so commonly trivialized as 'barbarian', and people whose lives are dismissed as not only short, but nasty and brutish.

---

37. D. Allen, *The Coins of the Ancient Celts* (1980), 2.

4 Political and Ethnic Identity: A Case Study of Anglo-Saxon Practice

Barbara Yorke

The problem of how to conceptualize and describe early medieval political organization is nothing new. Here is Gregory of Tours writing in his *History of the Franks* at the end of the sixth century, despairing at making sense of his source, Sulpicius Alexander:

> When he says *regales* or 'royal leaders', it is not clear if they were kings or if they merely exercised a kingly function ... a few pages on, having given up talk of *duces* and *regales* he states clearly that the Franks had a *rex*, but he forgets to tell us what his name was.[1]

More recent commentators have, of course, often faced the same problems when endeavouring to interpret medieval writers such as Gregory himself or Bede. Do these writers use terminology consistently, and can we understand the distinctions they appear to draw? Gregory and Bede, of course, inherited their vocabulary from the classical world and concern has been expressed that classical terms may have been shoehorned to fit an early medieval political structure which they could not adequately delineate.[2] This has in turn led to debate about what vocabulary modern historians should use when writing about the early Middle Ages. 'Kingdom' may seem a safe enough term for provinces which are known to have been controlled by 'kings', but may prejudge the issue for those units which possessed *subreguli* or *principes* who, like Gregory's *regales*, might be suspected of possessing only some of the attributes of the *rex*; hence recourse to the conveniently non-judgemental 'polity' when wanting to generalize

---

1. L. Thorpe (trans.), *Gregory of Tours: History of the Franks* (1974), II, 9 (adapted).
2. On the problems of borrowing terminology from the Roman world, see E. James, 'The origins of barbarian kingdoms: the continental evidence', in *The Origins of Anglo-Saxon: Kingdoms*, ed. S. Bassett (1979), 40–52; T. Champion, 'Power, politics and status', in *The Celtic World*, ed. M.J. Green (1995), 85–94.

about such units.[3] Some recent writers, though, would prefer use of
the term 'chiefdom', as defined in certain anthropological studies to
describe a political organization anterior to that of the centralized
state.[4] Although valuable insights have been gained from viewing early
Anglo-Saxon society alongside other cultures at comparable stages of
development,[5] many of these models are potentially too rigid in their
unilinear determinism. The term 'chiefdom' also has the disadvantage
of not resembling terminology used by the Anglo-Saxons themselves
nor allowing for the fine-tuning which is necessary in any discussion of
the early Anglo-Saxon political framework.[6]

As is well known, the Anglo-Saxons not only portrayed themselves
as living in units such as kingdoms, but also described themselves as
'peoples' – another example of modern terminology which is not
without its problems, but one which is surely preferable to a loaded
term such as 'tribe'. Investigation of Anglo-Saxon political structures
therefore needs to explore the relationship between 'peoples' and the
units into which they were organized. Selection of terminology is
particularly difficult here for, as will become apparent, 'people' units
could exist at a number of different organizational levels in Anglo-
Saxon England, not all of which necessarily had a 'political' dimension.
The Anglo-Saxons were not unusual in having such group terminolo-
gies. They were a mode of classification that was in use throughout
Europe and had been since the earliest written records we possess.[7]

It is with the terminology for 'peoples' who seem to have been
envisaged as definitely having a political identity in early Anglo-Saxon
England that this chapter will begin. As with so many aspects of
seventh- and early eighth-century history, Bede must be our primary
guide, though his usages can be paralleled by that of other early Anglo-
Saxon writers of Latin. We shall begin with Bede's application of the

3. For example, C. Arnold, 'Territories and leadership: frameworks for the study of
    emergent polities in early Anglo-Saxon southern England', in *Power and Politics
    in Early Medieval Britain and Ireland*, eds S.T. Driscoll and M.R. Nieke (1988),
    111–27.
4. For a convenient summary of basic concepts see T. Earle, 'Chiefdoms in
    archaeological and ethnohistorical perspective', *Annual Review of Anthropology*
    16 (1987), 279–308. For application of the chiefdom model to Anglo-Saxon
    England, see C. Renfrew, 'Post collapse resurgence: culture process in the Dark
    Ages', in *Ranking, Resource and Exchange: Aspects of the Archaeology of Early
    European Society*, eds C. Renfrew and S. Shennan (1982), 113–15; D. Pelteret,
    Slavery in Early Medieval England (1993), 24–37.
5. For example, R. Hodges, *Dark Age Economics: The Origins of Towns and Trade
    AD 600–1000* (1982).
6. To describe early Anglo-Saxon England as a chiefdom society and that of later
    Anglo-Saxon England as a state society is to risk drawing too crude a contrast
    between them, especially as the West Saxon kings based their control of
    England by expanding structures (e.g. the shire system) which they had
    developed successfully in Wessex during the eighth and ninth centuries.
7. H.D. Rankin, *Celts and the Classical World* (1987).

Latin term *gens*,[8] which for Bede, following classical usage, had a variety of connotations.[9] The terms *natio* or *populus* were alternatives to *gens* which Bede – like Isidore of Seville – used interchangeably.[10]

The gens Anglorum

In the first chapter of his *Historia Ecclesiastica*, Bede describes how the languages of five different *gentes* were spoken in the Britain of his day, namely those of the English, the British, the Irish, the Picts and the Latins.[11] He draws a parallel with the five books of the Pentateuch, and it is presumably no coincidence that his own History was divided into five books. Indeed, one of his motives in writing was to show how the *gens Anglorum* were the true heirs of the *gens Latinorum* – that is, the Church of Rome – and were able to play an instrumental role in returning the other *gentes* of Britain to the true customs of the universal church.[12] In this aspect of his work, Bede draws upon one of the distinguishing facets of a *gens* in classical and medieval thought, namely that they might share a common language.[13] This consciousness of a link between language and national identity may be found in Old English itself where *þeod* means 'the people', but *geþeode* designates both language and people.[14] Bede also appears to indicate that English identity was in part formed by a consciousness of difference from other peoples in Britain, a consciousness in which language must have played a part, especially because of the contrast between the Anglo-Saxons' own Germanic dialects and the language of their Celtic neighbours.[15] The British must have contributed to defining the 'otherness' of the incomers. Bede reveals that the Anglo-Saxons

8. G. Loud, 'The *Gens Normannorum*: myth or reality?', *Proceedings of the Battle Conference of Anglo-Norman Studies* 4 (1981), 104–16.
9. In addition to the usages discussed below, *gens* might also be used in the early Middle Ages to designate a kin-group or family. When Abbess Eangyth of Kent wrote to Boniface, concerning a kinsman, that *rex noster eius gentem multum exosam habet*, 'our king has a great hatred of his line', she was presumably using *gentem* with that sense – M. Tangl (ed.), *S. Bonifatii et Lulli Epistolae*, MGH *Epistolae Selectae* I (Berlin, 1916), 23 [henceforth, *Bon. Ep.*].
10. P.F. Jones, *A Concordance to the Historia Ecclesiastica of Bede* (Cambridge, 1929); S. Reynolds, *Kingdoms and Communities in Western Europe, 900–1300* (1984), 250–5.
11. B. Colgrave and R.A.B. Mynors (eds), *Bede's Ecclesiastical History of the English Peoples* (1969) [henceforth Bede, *HE*], I.1.
12. H.E.J. Cowdrey, 'Bede and the "English People"', *Journal of Religious History* 11 (1981), 501–27.
13. S. Reynolds, 'Medieval *origines gentium* and the community of the realm', *History* 68 (1983), 375–90, especially 383.
14. T. Charles-Edwards, 'Language and society among the insular Celts, AD 400–1000', in *The Celtic World*, ed. M.J. Green (1995), 703–36, especially 733, n. 161.
15. Charles-Edwards, 'Language and society', 730–3; R.R. Davies, 'Names, boundaries and regnal solidarities', *Transactions of the Royal Historical Society* (hereafter *TRHS*), sixth series, 5 (1995), 1–20.

were collectively referred to by the British as *Garmani*.[16] Gildas also treats the Germanic settlers as one *gens* and, again following a classical convention, assigns them various national characteristics which, in their case, are of a ferocious and bestial nature.[17] Bede further underlines the distinctiveness of his five *gentes* by providing a mythic account for each of them of their migration to Britain.[18]

Much interest has been focused on why Bede preferred to use the term *Angli* when, as he himself acknowledged, the incomers came *de tribus Germaniae populis*, namely the Saxons, Angles and Jutes.[19] He also knew from Egbert, a Northumbrian living in Ireland who had close links with early Anglo-Saxon missionaries in Germany, that the *Angli vel Saxones* of Britain in fact derived from many different *nationes* of *Germania*.[20] In this passage Bede seems to show awareness that the identity of Angles and Saxons (and presumably the Jutes), although partly the result of heavy migration from certain areas in the Germanic homelands, was also the product of a certain rationalization and regrouping of identity which occurred within Britain itself, something with which current archaeological analysis would be broadly in agreement.[21] As in that extract, Bede sometimes refers to the Angles or Saxons as if these could be used as interchangeable terms, but if he only uses one name his preference is clearly for *Angli*.[22] British, Irish and Frankish writers, on the other hand, preferred *Saxones* as the collective term for the Germanic incomers of Britain.[23] As Patrick Wormald has so persuasively shown, Bede's usage (and that of the Church in Canterbury) is likely to have been influenced by that of Rome and particularly by that of Pope Gregory the Great, who in his letters concerning the Augustine mission always refers to the Germans of Britain as *Angli*.[24] One advantage of *Angli* over *Saxones* was that it clearly distinguished the Anglo-Saxons of Britain from the 'Old Saxons' of Saxony who remained obstinately pagan in spite of the ministrations

---

16. Bede, *HE* V.9; see K. Jackson, *Language and History in Britain* (1953), 281.
17. M. Winterbottom (ed.), *Gildas: The Ruin of Britain and Other Documents* (1978); N.J. Higham, *The English Conquest: Gildas and Britain in the Fifth Century* (1994), 35–66.
18. N. Howe, *Migration and Mythmaking in Anglo-Saxon England* (New Haven, 1989), 49–71.
19. Bede, *HE* I.15; J.N.L. Myres, 'The Angles, the Saxons and the Jutes', *Proceedings of the British Academy* 56 (1970), 145–74.
20. Bede, *HE* V.9.
21. J. Hines, 'The becoming of the English: identity, material culture and language in early Anglo-Saxon England', *Anglo-Saxon Studies in Archaeology and History* 7 (1994), 49–59.
22. Jones, *Concordance*, 29–31, 481–2.
23. E. James, *The Franks* (1988), 101–3; D.P. Kirby, *The Earliest English Kings* (1991), 12–14; D. O'Murchadha, 'Nationality names in the Irish annals', *Nomina* 16 (1992–93), 49–70.
24. P. Wormald, 'Bede, the *Bretwaldas* and the origins of the *Gens Anglorum*', in *Ideal and Reality in Frankish and Anglo-Saxon Society*, ed. P. Wormald, with D. Bullough and R. Collins (1983), 99–129.

of Anglo-Saxon missionaries and became increasingly demonized in Frankish sources.[25] Boniface, in particular, in his correspondence seems to be aware of the desirability of distancing the Christian *Angli* from the pagan *Saxones*,[26] and the importance of his example should not be underestimated. A united English Church under the Archbishop of Canterbury therefore added to the sense of an English identity which Anglo-Saxons had already begun to form as a result of their consciousness of an 'otherness' which distinguished them from the Celtic-speaking inhabitants of Britain. But arguably this sense of Englishness did not receive a political dimension until King Alfred saw the advantages of stressing the unity of the *Angelcynn* over which he and his successors intended to exercise control.[27]

The English *gentes*

Although Bede was keen to stress the unity of the English Church under one archbishop,[28] and recognized common cultural character-istics which marked out the *gens Anglorum* from their Celtic neighbours, he did not believe that there was a common English political identity. He certainly did not seek to promote the wide-ranging overlordship achieved by some of the more powerful Anglo-Saxon rulers in such a way.[29] He makes clear that although these kings ruled over a number of different *gentes*, their control was personal and temporary and did not eclipse the separate political identities of the individual kingdoms.[30] When he wrote of the political structure of the

25. See for instance Einhard, *Vita Caroli*, trans. L. Thorpe (1969), ch. 7, 61–3; Eigil, *Life of Sturm*, ch. 22 (*Charlemagne: Translated Sources*, ed. P. King (1987), 332–3); *History of the Franks, sub annis* 795 and 798 (*op. cit.*, 9 and 91). In contrast, Isidore described the chief characteristic of the Saxons as their agility – *Isidori Hispalensis Episcopi, Etumologiarum sive originum librum XX*, ed. W.M. Lindsay, 12 vols (1911), IX, ii, 100. Another advantage of *Angli* over *Saxones* was that there was no group remaining in Europe who identified themselves as *Angli*. Bede in *HE* I.15 believed that the former province of *Angulus* had become deserted because all the *Angli* (he seems to imply) had crossed to Britain.
26. See, for instance, Tangl, *Bon. Ep.* no. 73, 146–54, where the lax moral behaviour of Æthelbald of the Christian *Angli* is made all the more shocking because it would not be tolerated by the pagan *Saxones*. For the influence of Pope Gregory I and Bede on Boniface, see Howe, *Migration and Mythmaking*, 125–42.
27. P. Wormald, '*Engla Lond*: the making of an allegiance', *Journal of Historical Sociology* 7 (1994), 1–24; S. Foot, 'The making of *Angelcynn*: English identity before the Norman Conquest', *TRHS*, 6th series, 6 (1996), 25–50.
28. For instance, Bede *HE* IV.2 where Theodore is described as the first archbishop whom *omnis Anglorum ecclesia* agreed to obey.
29. Bede, *HE* II.5; Wormald, 'Bede and the *Gens Anglorum*', S. Keynes, 'Rædwald the bretwalda', in *Voyage to the Other World: The Legacy of Sutton Hoo*, eds C.B. Kendall and P.S. Wells (Minneapolis, 1992), 103–23.
30. S. Fanning, 'Bede, *imperium* and the bretwaldas', *Speculum* 66 (1991), 1–26, argues that Bede would have used *imperium* in *HE* II.5 specifically to indicate a ruler who claimed authority over other *regna* and *gentes*.

Anglo-Saxons, the primary unit for Bede was the individual kingdom, for which his normal term was *provincia*, whose inhabitants could also be designated as a *gens*.[31] In Bede's account the kingdoms were also significant units of religious administration and the equation of *gens*, *provincia* and bishopric was so central to Bede's conception of the natural order of things that he felt obliged to comment if the conventions were not followed. Thus he evidently believed that the Jutes of Wight, who inhabited a distinct *provincia* with their own kings, should have had their own bishopric in spite of their conquest and incorporation into the kingdom of Wessex. He notes the failure to set up the appropriate bishopric when Cædwalla conquered the island in 686, and in 731 recorded that the *episcopatus Uectae* had been assigned to the bishopric of Winchester, even though no separate *episcopatus* had ever been created for the island.[32] The Middle Angles seem to have been another *gens*. Bede believed they should have their own bishopric even though they were not always politically or episcopally independent.[33] A people, to Bede's mind, would not flourish as Christians unless they were controlled by their own king and bishop. He does not blame the Mercians for rebelling against the direct rule of the Northumbrians, for 'being free and having their own king, they rejoiced to serve their true king, Christ', and were appropriately helped to do so by the establishment of their own bishopric.[34]

Therefore to Bede's mind there existed in the Anglo-Saxon territories of the seventh and eighth centuries both the wider concept of the *gens Anglorum* and the political reality of the several *gentes* who inhabited *provinciae* and were ruled by kings. Bede seems to have had a clear distinction in mind between the *provinciae* ruled by kings and the lesser units into which kingdoms were divided and which were managed by individuals subject to kings, some, but not necessarily all, of whom may also have been members of royal houses. It is true that Bede does on occasion apply *provincia*, his preferred term for a kingdom, to a subdivision of a kingdom which he would normally designate as a *regio*.[35] That was, of course, quite in keeping with the meaning of *provincia* in classical Latin. But what Bede does not do is

---

31. J. Campbell, *Bede's Reges and Principes* (Jarrow lecture, 1979), 3–4; reprinted in *Essays in Anglo-Saxon History* (1986), 85–98. There are a few instances where *natio* and *populus* were used by Bede to indicate the inhabitants of a kingdom; Jones, *Concordance*, 311–12, 403–4.
32. Bede, *HE* IV.16 and V.23.
33. Bede, *HE* III.21. For the debate over whether the Middle Angles were a relatively recent creation of Penda of Mercia for his son Peada or an older established province, see: W. Davies, 'Middle Anglia and the Middle Angles', *Midland History* 2 (1973–4), 18–20; Campbell, *Reges and Principes*, 4–5, 14; D.N. Dumville, 'Essex, Middle Anglia and the expansion of Mercia', in *The Origins of Anglo-Saxon Kingdoms*, ed. S. Bassett (1989), 123–40. The implication of Bede's terminology in III.21 and I.15 is that he considered the Middle Angles were a *gens* in the way that the Mercians or the Northumbrians were.
34. Bede, *HE* III.24.
35. Campbell, *Reges and Principes*, 3–4.

ever describe a 'people', whether *gens, natio* or *populus*, as living in a *regio*.[36] The distinction is clearly brought out in a passage where the *provincia Meanuarorum* is identified as being *in gente Occidentalium Saxonum*.[37] Bede is similarly careful with his use of *rex*, which was a term reserved for those who ruled a *gens*. Collectively kings could be described as *principes*, perhaps particularly when in the company of individuals who might not fully qualify for the term *rex*,[38] but a *princeps* was normally someone who was answerable to a *rex*. There are instances where a complex political situation has to be carefully decoded, but Bede emerges as consistent in his usage. Peada, ruler of the Middle Angles, was a particularly difficult case for Bede because he ruled a people whom Bede considered a distinct *gens* who should have been controlled by a *rex*,[39] but he was evidently subject to his father, Penda of Mercia, who had placed him in control of the province (*praelatus est a patre regno gentis illius*).[40] The relative positions of Penda and Peada seem to have been decisive for Bede in deciding how he would designate Peada for he is never directly referred to as *rex*, only as *princeps*.[41] Bede was careful to distinguish such cases of subordination, even when they involved members of the royal house, from genuine power-sharing where two or more individuals might rule jointly as occurred on a number of occasions among the East Saxons. Thus Sæberht of the East Saxons is said to have left his three sons as joint heirs so they are jointly described as *reges*,[42] and Sigehere, *rex*, ruled with another *rex*, Sebbi, *socius eius et coheres regni* – 'his colleague and joint inheritor of the kingship'.[43] The complexities of the Anglo-Saxon political system and the lack of a sufficient variety of Latin terms to reflect the situation adequately, may cause problems in interpretation for modern commentators, but Bede seems to have been clear in his own mind about the difference between a *gens* ruled by a *rex*, what we would designate as a kingdom, and the lesser

36. *Ibid.* gives a reference to *regionem Geuissorum* in Bede, *HE* IV.16 as a possible exception, but here Bede is referring to Gewissan territory as a subdivision of what by his day had become the kingdom of the West Saxons, and is comparing it with lands of the Jutish province which had also been absorbed to form Wessex; see B.A.E. Yorke, 'The Jutes of Hampshire and Wight and the origins of Wessex', in *The Origins of Anglo-Saxon Kingdoms*, ed. S. Bassett (1989), 84–96.
37. Bede, *HE* IV.13; however, Bede does not always specifically identify such *regiones/provinciae* as subdivisions of kingdoms.
38. Jones, *Concordance*, 421. The only individuals given the designation of *princeps* are Peada of the Middle Angles and Tondbert of the Gyrwe, for whom see further below. For subsequent use of *princeps* for royal officials, see A.T. Thacker, 'Some terms for noblemen in Anglo-Saxon England', *Anglo-Saxon Studies in Archaeology and History* 2 (1981), 201–36.
39. See note 33 above.
40. Bede, *HE* III.21. See also Campbell, *Reges and Principes*, 3.
41. Bede says Peada was worthy of the name and office of king, but in III.21 and the *recapitulatio* in V.24 refers to him only as *princeps*.
42. Bede, *HE* II.5.
43. Bede, *HE* III.30.

provinciae or *regiones* into which a kingdom might be divided and which might be controlled by *principes* and *subreguli*.[44] If we take provinces which Bede either designates as being the territory of *gentes*, or which appear to fit what seems to have been Bede's definition of a *gens* as having its own royal house and a bishopric (or the potential to become a bishopric), we can identify thirteen such units in the pages of the *Historia Ecclesiastica* – Kent, East Saxons, East Angles, West Saxons, Mercia, Hwicce, South Saxons, Deira, Bernicia, Isle of Wight, Lindsey,[45] Middle Angles,[46] and '[populi] qui ultra amnem Sabrinam ad occidentem habitant'.[47] Of these, only the first seven plus Northumbria (formed from the amalgamation of Bernicia and Deira) can be definitely stated to have still had royal houses in 731 when Bede made his final survey of the state of the country.[48]

The view from the kingdoms

The central role which Bede identifies for kings in defining their *gentes* is also stressed in two surviving genres, the genealogy and origin myth, which presumably originated at the royal courts themselves. The earliest surviving form of a genealogy is that for the kings of Kent provided by Bede in the *Historia Ecclesiastica* which traces their descent from Woden 'from whose stock the royal families of many kingdoms claimed their descent'.[49] Bede's statement is supported by the Anglian collection of genealogies, which was probably assembled in the later eighth century and traces the descent of the royal houses of Bernicia, Deira, Mercia, Lindsey, Kent, the East Angles and the West Saxons.[50] All claimed descent from Woden, but most of the genealogies also exhibit considerable elaboration beyond Woden with inclusion of

---

44. The term *subregulus* was only applied by Bede to rulers in Wessex; Jones, *Concordance*, 514. For the problems of interpreting these references, see D.P. Kirby, *The Earliest English Kings* (1991), 49–53; B.A.E. Yorke, *Kings and Kingdoms of Early Anglo-Saxon England* (1990), 185–6; idem, *Wessex in the Early Middle Ages* (1995), 79–84.
45. S. Foot, 'The kingdom of Lindsey', in *Pre-Viking Lindsey*, ed. A. Vince (1993), 128–40.
46. See note 33 above.
47. Bede does not give any information on a royal house for this province, but see K. Pretty, 'Defining the Magonsæte', in *The Origins of Anglo-Saxon Kingdoms*, ed. S. Bassett (1989), 171–83.
48. Bede, *HE* V.23.
49. Bede, *HE* I.15; for commentary see N. Brooks, 'The creation and structure of the kingdom of Kent', in *The Origins of Anglo-Saxon Kingdoms*, ed. S. Bassett (1989), 55–74; E. John, 'The point of Woden', in *Anglo-Saxon Studies in Archaeology and History* 5 (1992), 127–34.
50. D.N. Dumville, 'The Anglian collection of royal genealogies and regnal lists', *Anglo-Saxon England* 5 (1976), 23–50.

additional gods, and mythical and classical heroes.[51] The same tendency is seen in the collection of East Saxon genealogies, which must also have been compiled in the latter part of the eighth century, though they stressed descent from the Saxon god Seaxneat rather than Woden.[52] The culmination of genealogical elaboration was, of course, achieved by the West Saxons in the ninth century when the Germanic and classical progenitors were joined by a biblical contingent to create the genealogy of Æthelwulf in the *Anglo-Saxon Chronicle* for 855, of which several other versions are known.[53]

Several versions of a Kentish origin myth seem to have existed by the ninth century, suggesting that as an embryonic saga it enjoyed considerable popularity.[54] For other kingdoms we have much briefer accounts incorporated into the *Anglo-Saxon Chronicle*, presumably by its ninth-century compilers.[55] The West Saxon account naturally receives most attention, but origin myths for Kent, the South Saxons, the Jutes of Wight and Hampshire – all of which had been incorporated into Wessex by the ninth century – are also included. No doubt similar accounts once existed for the other kingdoms; there are scattered remembrances of a Bernician one and hints of others.[56] In essence the myths depict the arrival within Britain of a pair of related warrior leaders, often with comparable, alliterating names, who, with a small number of ships, defeat British rulers and establish themselves as kings and the founders of royal dynasties. Although this is not always explicitly stated, these accounts were probably meant to embody the foundation of the whole *gens*. This seems to be clearly signalled in the *Anglo-Saxon Chronicle* annal for 514, a duplication of the entry for the arrival of Cerdic and Cynric in 495, which reads 'in this year the West Saxons came to Britain with three ships'.[57] It is also implied by Wihtgar, one of the founders of the royal house of Wight, bearing a name which clearly derives from the Latin name of the island and is in a form which was used to designate its inhabitants, namely the 'Wihtgara'.[58] Therefore these sources help us to understand further

51. K. Sisam, 'Anglo-Saxon royal genealogies', *Proceedings of the British Academy* 39 (1953), 287–348.
52. B.A.E. Yorke, 'The kingdom of the East Saxons', *Anglo-Saxon England* 14 (1985), 1–36, at 3–4, 13–16.
53. Sisam, 'Anglo-Saxon royal genealogies', 299–322; D.N. Dumville, 'The West Saxon Genealogical Regnal List: manuscripts and texts', *Anglia* 104 (1986), 1–32.
54. Brooks, 'Kingdom of Kent', 58–64.
55. J. Bately, 'The compilation of the Anglo-Saxon Chronicle, 60 BC to AD 890: vocabulary as evidence', *Proceedings of the British Academy* 64 (1978), 93–129.
56. P. Hunter Blair, 'The origins of Northumbria', *Archaeologia Aeliana*, 4th series, 25 (1947), 1–51; W. Davies, 'Annals and the origins of Mercia', in *Mercian Studies*, ed. A. Dornier (1977), 17–29; Kirby, *Earliest English Kings*, 14–16.
57. *The Anglo-Saxon Chronicle*, eds and trans. D. Whitelock *et al.* (1961). For duplications of annal entries see K. Harrison, 'Early Wessex annals in the Anglo-Saxon Chronicle', *English Historical Review* 86 (1971), 527–33.
58. For the significance of Wihtgara and its relationship with Wihtwara, see H. Kökeritz, *The Place-Names of the Isle of Wight* (Uppsala, 1940), xlvii–lvi.

Bede's linking of identity as a *gens* with possession of a royal house, for in this version of a kingdom's history it was the royal founders who had led the people to a new land and instigated the creation of a new *gens*. It is also likely that the inhabitants of Anglo-Saxon kingdoms, like many other early medieval peoples, believed that they had a common descent, as, in the words of Isidore of Seville, 'a *gens* is a multitude sprung from one principle ... a *gens* is named from *generatio*'.[59]

The origin myths in the eighth- and ninth-century contexts in which they have been preserved can be seen as fulfilling one of the classic functions of myth, namely 'to mediatize contradiction'.[60] For instance, by placing the arrival of Cerdic and Cynric, the supposed founders of the West Saxon dynasty, in the Solent, the West Saxons were laying prior claim to an area that they only in fact acquired by defeating the Jutish dynasties in the course of the seventh century.[61] All the indications are that the West Saxon dynasty in fact originated in the upper Thames region. Their 'claims' to the kingdom of Wight are further supported by the statement that Stuf and Wihtgar were kinsmen of Cerdic and Cynric who installed them as rulers of Wight.[62] Genealogies and origin myths were undoubtedly being developed in England in the course of the eighth and ninth centuries to bolster the self-images of the surviving royal dynasties. The clerical role in the elaboration of genealogies is particularly apparent, and may be suspected in the development of origin myths as well. The earliest account of an Anglo-Saxon foundation legend is after all that given by Gildas, and only a few additions were needed to customize it for the Kentish royal house in the *Historia Ecclesiastica*.[63] There is an increasing belief that the genealogies and origin myths preserved for Germanic dynasties of other parts of Europe were developed in an educated milieu rather than being simply the result of recording oral traditions.[64] Jordanes carried out this role for the Goths,[65] Fredegund and others for the Franks,[66] and Dudo for the Normans.[67]

---

59. Isidore, *Etymologia*, IX, ii, 1; Loud, 'The *Gens Normannorum* myth', 109.
60. G.F. Kirk, *Myth: Its Meaning and Function in Ancient and Other Cultures* (1970), 254–6. On political uses see also D.N. Dumville, 'Kingship, genealogies and regnal lists', in *Early Medieval Kingship*, eds. P. Sawyer and I.N. Wood (1977), 72–104.
61. Yorke, 'The Jutes of Hampshire and Wight'.
62. *Anglo-Saxon Chronicle*, *sub anno* 534.
63. P. Sims-Williams, 'Gildas and the Anglo-Saxons', *Cambridge Medieval Celtic Studies* 6 (1983), 1–30; Howe, *Migration and Mythmaking*, 33–71.
64. Reynolds, 'Medieval *origines gentium*'; W. Goffart, *The Narrators of Barbarian History, AD 550–800* (Princeton, 1988).
65. P. Heather, *Goths and Romans 332–489* (1991).
66. J.M. Wallace-Hadrill, *The Long-Haired Kings* (1962), 71–94; I.N. Wood, *The Merovingian Kingdoms 450–751* (1994), 33–5; J. Barlow, 'Gregory of Tours and the myth of the Trojan origins of the Franks', *Frühmittelalterliche Studien* 29 (1995), 86–95.
67. Loud, 'The *Gens Normannorum* myth'.

Does this mean that we should see Anglo-Saxon attempts to boost the kings as embodiments of their *gentes* as something that was created in the post-conversion phase, perhaps to support the idea of identification of one people under king and bishop which seems to have been a key part of Bede's political thinking? Anglo-Saxon churchmen may have played important roles in the development of origin myths and genealogies, but there is evidence to suggest that they were merely taking forward something which already existed and had had an important function in the creation of Anglo-Saxon political identities during the sixth century, if not even earlier. Although Gildas provided the archetypal written version of the Anglo-Saxon foundation legend, there remains the question of how he acquired his material. There are other signs, such as his use of the Germanic *cyulis* for their ships and a reference to a Germanic prophecy that they would remain 300 years in the island, that Gildas had information that ultimately came directly from the Anglo-Saxon settlements.[68] Whatever the ultimate origins of the Anglo-Saxon foundation myth, it is likely to have been transmitted for Gildas to use via a Germanic oral source. One could also argue that the foundation myths of the Jutish peoples of the Solent must have originated in a pre-Christian context, for these peoples seem to have lost their political independence to the West Saxons *before* their conversion to Christianity.[69]

The claim that Woden was the progenitor of the royal houses must also have been made in the pre-Christian period, notwithstanding how his presence may have been rationalized by ecclesiastics.[70] Bede's concern to play down the attractions of pre-Christian cults does not disguise the fact that there was a close association between them and the royal houses,[71] nor that, in order to gain acceptance, the Christian God had to be presented as an effective god of battles, which one presumes had previously been one of Woden's specialities.[72] Further demonstration of the importance of the link with Woden seems to come from the small, naked figures with belts, spears and bird-headed

---

68. Sims-Williams, 'Gildas and the Anglo-Saxons', 1–30; Higham, *The English Conquest*, 35–66.
69. Yorke, 'The Jutes of Wight and Hampshire'. For a broader argument for genuine origin myths lying behind literary embellishments, see H. Wolfram, '*Origo et religio*: ethnic traditions and literature in early medieval texts', *Early Medieval Europe* 3 (1994), 19–38.
70. See note 49.
71. See for instance Bede, *HE* II.13 (Edwin); II.15 (Rædwald); and R. North, *Heathen Gods in Old English Literature* (1997).
72. W.A. Chaney, *The Cult of Kingship in Anglo-Saxon England: The Transition from Paganism to Christianity* (1970); E. Hoffmann, *Die heiligen Königen bei den Angelsachsen und den skandinavischen Völkern* (Neumünster, 1975); L.E. von Padberg, 'Odin oder Christus?', *Archiv für Kulturgeschichte* 77 (1995), 249–78; A.T. Thacker, 'Oswald, "most holy and victorious king of the Northumbrians"', in *Oswald: Northumbrian King to European Saint*, eds C. Stancliffe and E. Cambridge (1995), 97–127.

helmets displayed on the Sutton Hoo helmet and the Finglesham buckle whose iconography can be closely paralleled in Scandinavia and seems to have been associated with the cult of Woden.[73]

The grave-good deposit from Sutton Hoo mound 1 is eclectic. It is not simply that it includes objects that have been imported from different parts of Europe, but rather that ways of symbolizing royal power from a variety of milieux have been integrated to make what could be interpreted as a claim that the Sutton Hoo ruler was the heir of Germanic, Celtic and Roman predecessors.[74] The impressive ensemble of helmet, belt-fittings and surcoat with its unique shoulder-clasps derives its form from Roman military dress, but utilizes Germanic iconography.[75] The gold-and-garnet jewellery and the great gold buckle inlaid with niello are masterpieces of the Germanic craftsman's art and use techniques to be found at the most prestigious Germanic courts in Europe.[76] Two objects which are generally interpreted as signifiers of royal power, the standard and the whetstone, have established pedigrees in the late Roman and contemporary Byzantine world,[77] but the whetstone and the stag which probably surmounted it, in particular, also have their closest parallels with similar items from insular Celtic provinces.[78]

Much attention has been focused on the links which exist between the Sutton Hoo mound 1 grave-goods, comparable material from Sweden and passages in the Old English poem *Beowulf* whose action likely takes place in Southern Scandinavia and includes the deposition of the dead in ships furnished with grave-goods.[79] The shared elements have been sufficient to suggest that the East Anglian royal house could have been of Geatish/Swedish origin.[80] What we may instead be seeing

---

73. R.L.S. Bruce-Mitford, *The Sutton Hoo Ship-Burial Volume II, Arms, Armour and Regalia* (1978), 186–220.
74. R. Farrell and C. Neuman de Veguar (eds), *Sutton Hoo: Fifty Years After*, American Early Medieval Studies 2 (Oxford, 1992); W. Filmer-Sankey, 'The "Roman" emperor in the Sutton Hoo ship-burial', *Journal of the British Archaeological Association* 149 (1996), 1–9; M. Archibald, M. Brown and L. Webster, 'Heirs of Rome: the shaping of Britain AD 400–900', in *The Transformation of the Roman World AD 400–900*, eds L. Webster and M. Brown (1997), 208–48.
75. Bruce-Mitford, *Sutton Hoo Ship-Burial*, II, 220–4, 532–5, 564–81.
76. B. Arrhenius, *Merovingian Garnet Jewellery: Emergence and Social Implications* (Stockholm, 1985); I.N. Wood, 'The Franks and Sutton Hoo', in *People and Places in Northern Europe 500–1600*, eds I.N. Wood and N. Lund (1991), 1–14.
77. Bruce-Mitford, *Sutton Hoo Ship-Burial*, II, 311–431.
78. C. Hicks, 'A note on the provenance of the Sutton Hoo stag', in Bruce-Mitford, *Sutton Hoo Ship-Burial*, II, 378–82; M.J. Enright, 'The Sutton Hoo whetstone sceptre: a study in iconography and cultural milieu', *Anglo-Saxon England* 11 (1983), 119–34.
79. R. Bruce-Mitford, 'Sutton Hoo and the background of Beowulf', in *Aspects of Anglo-Saxon Archaeology: Sutton Hoo and Other Discoveries* (1974), 253–61; S. Newton, *The Origins of Beowulf and the Pre-Viking Kingdom of East Anglia* (1993).
80. J.L.N. O'Loughlin, 'Sutton Hoo: the evidence of the documents', *Medieval Archaeology* 8 (1964), 1–19; Newton, *Origins of Beowulf*.

here is not true migration, but allusion to one of the most prominent Germanic origin myths of the early Middle Ages which may derive ultimately from classical ethnographers – what one might term the 'out of Scandinavia myth'.[81] Already by the end of the sixth century Jordanes had improved upon Gothic oral traditions to present them as a politically and culturally united people who had migrated from Scandinavian homelands, when it would appear that the Goths came originally from the other side of the Baltic.[82] The same classical influences, or perhaps the prestige of the Goths, was sufficient for other Germanic peoples of Europe, such as the Burgundians, to want to claim Scandinavian origins too.[83] It is perhaps in this context we should view the aspects of Scandinavian dress and decoration that were adopted in Anglian provinces and Jutish Kent.[84] The Kentish royal house may have gone further to claim direct links with the Goths.[85] Oisc, reputedly the *cognomen* of Oeric son of Hengest, has a name cognate with that of the Ostrogothic demigods, the Ansis, referred to by Jordanes, while Irminric/Eormenric, the father of Æthelbert I, bears the name of one of the most renowned of the early Gothic heroes. Asser was aware that the Jutes claimed a Gothic identity when he described Alfred's maternal grandfather Oslac as 'a Goth by race (*natione*), for he was descended from the Goths and the Jutes', for Oslac claimed Stuf and Wihtgar, the supposedly Jutish founders of the kingdom of Wight, as his ancestors.[86]

This brief survey suggests that the genealogies and origin myths which were recorded in the eighth and ninth centuries were not a new way of looking at the past introduced by churchmen for their own political or antiquarian reasons. Rather, well before their conversion and direct exposure to literary culture, royal houses seem to have been developing ways of linking themselves, and the *gentes* they ruled, with

---

81. Reynolds, 'Medieval *origines gentium*', 375–80. The possible relevance of these myths to interpreting archaeological evidence from Anglo-Saxon England was brought to my attention through a lecture given by Leslie Webster in conjunction with the British Museum's exhibition 'The Heirs of Rome' (1997).
82. Heather, *Goths and Romans*; P. Heather, *The Goths* (1996), 9–50.
83. I.N. Wood, 'Ethnicity and the ethnogenesis of the Burgundians', in *Typen der Ethnogenese unter besonderer Berücksichtigung der Bayern* 1, eds H. Wolfram and W. Pohl (Vienna, 1990), 53–69.
84. S. Chadwick Hawkes, 'Anglo-Saxon Kent *c.* 425–725', in *Archaeology in Kent to AD 1500*, ed. P.E. Leach (1982), 64–78; J. Hines, *The Scandinavian Character of Anglian England in the Pre-Viking Period* (1984); J. Hines, *Clasps: Hektespenner, Agraffen* (Stockholm, 1993); C. Behr, 'Material and textual evidence for an early Anglo-Saxon kingdom in Kent' (*Early Medieval Europe*, forthcoming).
85. H. Kleinschmidt, 'Bede and the Jutes: a critique of historiography', *North-Western European Language Education* 24 (1994), 21–46, at 26–8.
86. *Asser's Life of King Alfred*, ed. W.H. Stevenson (1904, repr. 1959), ch. 2; S. Keynes and M. Lapidge, *Alfred the Great* (1983), 68. For the context of Alfred's interest in his possible Scandinavian ancestry, see A.C. Murray, 'Beowulf, the Danish invasions and royal genealogy', in *The Dating of Beowulf*, ed. C. Chase (Toronto, 1981), 101–12.

the most powerful peoples of Europe, both past and present. Surviving iconography suggests that their strategies may not be represented fully by the extant written Anglo-Saxon origin myths.[87] The Christian Church was able to add a further dimension of Biblical ancestors and to flesh out allusions to the Roman world from their book-learning, but it would appear the ecclesiastical writers were working within established genres, not creating entirely new ones.

Kingdoms and *regiones*

Charters support Bede's picture of *regiones* as subdivisions of kingdoms and of a clear distinction in status between kings and their *subreguli* and *principes*,[88] though it must also be stressed that the number of surviving charters from the period covered by the *Historia Ecclesiastica* is small and the majority of them only survive in later copies which may not always reproduce their exact original form.[89] Charters enable us to extend the list of *regiones* and *subreguli* that can be compiled from the *Historia Ecclesiastica*, but do not provide grounds for adding to Bede's list of kingdoms. Nevertheless there has been much speculation over whether *regiones* had once been independent *gentes* in their own right which had been subsumed by more successful dynasties before they could make an impression upon written records. A model for the development of kingdoms, that has found favour in archaeological circles in particular, sees 'tribal' units (*regiones*) evolving from the settlement areas of extended families, and kings emerging from competition between the leaders of such groups.[90] That enigmatic document the 'Tribal Hidage' has been cited in support of such theories. The 'Tribal Hidage' survives in three different recensions preserved in manuscripts of the eleventh century or later.[91] It provides a list of names with an assessment in hides for each. The larger groupings are attested kingdoms such as the East Angles and the East Saxons; among the middling and smaller groupings are

---

87. H. Moisl, 'Anglo-Saxon royal genealogies and Germanic oral tradition', *Journal of Medieval History* 7 (1981), 215–48.
88. Campbell, *Reges and Principes*.
89. P. Wormald, *Bede and the Conversion of England: The Charter Evidence* (Jarrow lecture, 1984).
90. Bassett, 'In search of the origins', 17–24; C. Scull, 'Archaeology, early Anglo-Saxon society and the origins of Anglo-Saxon kingdoms', *Anglo-Saxon Studies in Archaeology and History* 6 (1993), 65–82.
91. W. Davies and H. Vierck, 'The contexts of Tribal Hidage: social aggregates and settlement pattterns', *Frühmittelalterliche Studien* 8 (1974), 223–98; D.N. Dumville, 'The Tribal Hidage: an introduction to its texts and their history', in *The Origins of Anglo-Saxon Kingdoms*, ed. S. Bassett (1989), 225–30; A. Rumble, 'An edition and translation of the Burghal Hidage, together with Recension C of the Tribal Hidage', in *The Defence of Wessex: The Burghal Hidage and Anglo-Saxon Fortifications*, eds D. Hill and A. Rumble (1996), 14–35.

identifiable *regiones*, many of which lie on the eastern and southern borders of Mercia, but there are also a number of names which are unintelligible or otherwise only attested in place-name evidence. There is no indication of the purpose of the document. The most favoured recent explanations would see it as a tribute list for a seventh-century overlord from either Northumbria or Mercia, but over the years a wide range of dates and interpretations have been placed upon it.[92] Simon Keynes has recently urged caution in making such assumptions and points out that, in the form in which we have it, it is as likely to have been compiled out of scholarly interest as in response to an administrative fiat.[93]

It is, therefore, only one interpretation out of a number of possibilities which argues for the 'Tribal Hidage' showing a number of 'peoples' who were treated as the same type of unit when being assessed for tribute by a powerful early Anglo-Saxon overlord. Are we justified in saying that because some of the 'peoples' of the 'Tribal Hidage' were ruled by kings that all must have been, or at least possessed some other means of defining themselves as distinct *gentes*? It is true that one of the smallest units of all, that of the *Wihtgara* assessed at 600 hides, is usually interpreted as designating the inhabitants of the Isle of Wight which did possess a royal dynasty with its own origin myth.[94] But that may be the exception which proves the rule, for Wight was an island, and therefore of circumscribed size, and had an unusual strategic importance because it controlled one of the shortest crossing-points to Francia. Probably for this reason its dynasty was closely connected with that of Kent, perhaps in a mutually beneficial alliance with Francia.[95] Unusual circumstances may therefore have allowed the emergence of a kingdom in such a small territory. The only other smaller 'Tribal Hidage' unit which has some supporting evidence for once having been a kingdom is that of the South Gyrwe whose *princeps* Tondbert married the East Anglian princess Æthelthryth.[96] Their fenland position gave the Gyrwe

---

92. For a summary of views to date, see A. Rumble, 'The Tribal Hidage: an annotated bibliography', in *Defence of Wessex*, 182–8.
93. S. Keynes, 'England, 700–900', in *The New Cambridge Medieval History II, c. 700–c. 900*, ed. R. McKitterick (1995), 18–42, at 21–5.
94. Kökeritz, *Place-Names of the Isle of Wight*, xlvii–lvi; Davies and Vierck, 'Contexts of Tribal Hidage', 232.
95. K. Ulmschneider, 'Archaeology, history and the Isle of Wight in the middle Saxon period', *Medieval Archaeology* 43 (1999), 19–44.
96. Bede, *HE* IV.19. Princesses tended to marry other royalty at this time, but while this might suggest Tondbert was of royal birth, it need not mean that he was from a Gyrwean royal house. Like Bede's only other *princeps*, Peada of Mercia, he could have been a member of a foreign royal house appointed to rule newly conquered territory. Additional, but still equivocal, support for a former kingdom of the Gyrwe comes from *HE* III.20 where Bishop Thomas of the East Angles is described as coming from *provincia Gyruiorum* – Bede normally cites a kingdom when giving an individual's regional origin, but possibly Thomas's East Anglian origins may have seemed too obvious to state as he had become bishop

something approximating to an island location, but final proof of kingly status is lacking.

What is more striking is the lack of confirmation for the majority of the lesser units of the 'Tribal Hidage' having ever had the status of independent polities. The names of a number of the peoples have the suffix -*sætan/-sæte*, usually combined with a topographical feature, and so indicating the 'dwellers' of a certain district. Other, non-'Tribal Hidage',-*sæte* units appear to postdate the formation of kingdoms and to have been created for purposes of administration and taxation. For instance, the people living in the West Saxon shires of Dorset, Somerset and Wiltshire were designated as -*sæte* 'dwellers' with a suffix derived from the name of the towns from which they were administered. These shires were essentially units of adminstration created in the early eighth century from a reorganization of territories which had come under West Saxon control.[97] Other -*sæte* names belonging to groups occupying territory along the border between Mercia and Welsh principalities and in the vicinity of Offa's dyke may be the result of administrative arrangements made by Mercian kings, perhaps in the eighth century.[98]

Other Anglian units, listed in the 'Tribal Hidage' and elsewhere, have names, often simple nouns, which relate them to rivers or other topographical features (e.g. Gifle, Gyrwe), as do the names in -*ware* found in the Jutish districts (e.g. Meonware, Merscware), and many of those in -*ge* (e.g. Lyminge).[99] Some of the names in -*ingas* also have a topographical suffix, though in a number of cases the first element seems best explained as a personal name.[100] These latter names have attracted much attention in the past and were once seen as primary settlement groups, preserving the name of their pioneer leader.[101] That interpretation was exploded by John Dodgson,[102] but a satisfactory explanation for the use of a personal name plus the -*ingas* suffix for these early district names has yet to be made. They appear to be the name-formation favoured in Saxon areas (though also appearing in some Anglian districts) for units which elsewhere are monothemes or have suffixes indicating the inhabitants of a particular area, though they can be applied to smaller units within *regiones* as well as to

contd.
    of the province. For location of the Gyrwe, see P. Courtney, 'The early Saxon fenland: a reconsideration', *Anglo-Saxon Studies in Archaeology and History* 2 (1981), 91-9.

97.   Yorke, *Wessex in the Early Middle Ages,* 84-90.

98.   M. Gelling, *The West Midlands in the Early Middle Ages* (1992), 118-19.

99.   B. Cox, 'Place-names of the earliest English records', *English Place-Name Society Journal* 8 (1975/6), 12-66.

100.   E. Ekwall, *English Place-Names in -ing* (Lund, 1923); M. Gelling, *Signposts to the Past* (1978), 106-29.

101.   J.M. Kemble, *The Saxons in England* (2 vols, 1849), I, 35-71; J.R. Green, *A History of the English People* (4 vols, 1877-80), I, 8-27.

102.   J.M. Dodgson, 'The significance of the distribution of English place-names in -*ingas*, -*inga*- in southern England', *Medieval Archaeology* 10 (1966), 1-29.

regiones themselves.[103] That 'people' names of these types were identified with specific geographic territories is supported by the way in which Bede and other writers refer to locations within them. His references to events occurring *In Berecingum*, *In Getlingum* and *In Gyruum*, etc. suggest units that are distinct areas and, as with the shires, it would seem likely that the locations to which the district names became attached (i.e. Barking, Gilling and Jarrow) were the places from which they were administered.[104]

Many of the attested kingdoms of the seventh and eighth centuries also used the names of 'peoples' with a locational element, but there are reasons for thinking that names of the East, West and South Saxon type are not primary kingdom names, and only came gradually into use, probably under the influence of the Church wanting to define clear territorial boundaries for its bishoprics.[105] A secondary substitution is attested in the cases of Northumbria, whose name was adopted probably only after the amalgamation of Bernicia and Deira,[106] and of Wessex, whose dominant Saxon element were originally known as the Gewisse before their conquest of the Jutish provinces of the Solent area.[107] In both cases the geographical qualifier does not seem to have become current immediately; the Northumbrians may initially have used the form 'Humbrenses' while the West Saxons seem to have begun by calling themselves 'the Saxons'. The name Gewisse is of particular interest. It may mean something like the 'sure' or 'reliable' ones,[108] and it may be a name appropriate for a group whose strength was in its warriors, comparable to the names of other Germanic groups such as the Franks.[109] The Hwicce may also have a name of this type, but the etymology is uncertain.[110]

The other form of kingdom name which is presumed to be early is that derived from a Roman or British name. Kent is the only kingdom to continue the name of a Roman *civitas*,[111] but the name of Lindsey is presumed to derive from that of its *civitas* capital.[112] Wight is a

---

103. See maps in *Origins of Anglo-Saxon Kingdoms*, ed. Bassett, especially at 70, 99 and 116.
104. J. Campbell, 'Bede's words for places', in *Names, Words, and Graves: Early Medieval Settlement*, ed. P.H. Sawyer (1978), 34–54, at 48.
105. Kirby, *Earliest English Kings*, 20–3.
106. P. Hunter Blair, 'The origins of Northumbria', *Archaeologia Aeliana*, 4th series 25 (1947), 1–51.
107. H.E. Walker, 'Bede and the Gewissae: the political evolution of the Heptarch and its nomenclature', *Cambridge Historical Journal* 12 (1956), 174–86.
108. R. Coates, 'On some controversy surrounding *Gewissae/Gewissei*, Cerdic and Ceawlin', *Nomina* 13 (1989/90), 1–11.
109. James, *The Franks*, 2–10, 35.
110. A.H. Smith, 'The Hwicce', in *Medieval and Linguistic Studies in Honour of Francis Peabody Magoun, Junior*, eds J.B. Bessinger and R.P. Creed (1965), 56–65; Sims-Williams, *Religion and Literature*, 29–30.
111. Brooks, 'Kingdom of Kent', 57–8.
112. S. Bassett, 'Lincoln and the Anglo-Saxon see of Lindsey', *Anglo-Saxon England* 18 (1989), 1–31, with appendix on the name of Lindsey by M. Gelling, 31–2.

Germanization of the Latin name of the island,[113] and Bernicia and Deira are thought to be originally British district names.[114] This is but part of the evidence which could suggest that it is unnecessary to envisage the Roman provinces of eastern Britain dissipating to such an extent that it was necessary to begin the process of state-formation all over again beginning with extended family networks. Rather, as is being increasingly accepted for western Britain, kingdoms may have emerged in the east of Britain based on the Roman infrastructure of *civitas* capitals and other significant subunits of the Roman provinces.[115]

Some administrative subdistricts within these new kingdoms may also have had Roman antecedents,[116] but the degree of survival at this level was probably variable and *regiones* are likely to have been of different dates, sizes and origins. Like all such Germanic units they bore the name of 'peoples', but that did not make them *gentes* in the sense in which this term was used in England in the early Middle Ages, and names of this type are not necessarily early. It is certainly possible that some of these units may have been territories of some significance in the fifth and sixth centuries, but it should not be assumed automatically that they represent some sort of early tribal or settlement district. Neither the form of their names nor the way they are described in seventh- and eighth-century documents mean that they *have* to be interpreted in such a way, and at least some *regiones* may have been created for administrative purposes after the stabilization of kingdoms.

Expressing personal identities

Unfortunately we lack the type of written sources which enable us to see how individuals defined their own political or regional identities. The *discipulus Umbrensium* who edited 'The Penitential of Theodore' is unusual in identifying himself in this way.[117] The writers of letters in the seventh and eighth centuries rarely give a direct indication of their home province, and as a result there has been considerable debate

---

113. See note 58 above.
114. Jackson, *Language and History*, 701–5.
115. S. Bassett, 'Church and diocese in the West Midlands: the transition from British to Anglo-Saxon control', in *Pastoral Care Before the Parish*, eds J. Blair and R. Sharpe (1992), 13–40; K.R. Dark, *Civitas to Kingdom: British Political Continuity 300–800* (1994).
116. M. Gelling, 'English place-names from the compound *wicham*', *Medieval Archaeology* 12 (1967), 87–104; G. Foard, 'The administrative organization of Northamptonshire in the Saxon period', *Anglo-Saxon Studies in Archaeology and History* 4 (1985), 185–222; C.J. Balkwill, 'Old English *wic* and the origins of the hundred', *Landscape History* 15 (1993), 5–11.
117. *Councils and Ecclesiastical Documents Relating to Great Britain and Ireland*, eds A.W. Haddan and W. Stubbs (3 vols, 1869–71), III, 173.

about where to locate the correspondents of Boniface and Lull whose letter-collections provide the bulk of letters written by Anglo-Saxons in this period.[118] Authors of hagiographical works were not as interested as Bede in tracing the regional origins of individuals. Neither Stephanus nor Felix refers to his own regional identity when introducing himself in the prologue of, respectively, *The Life of Wilfrid* and *The Life of Guthlac*.[119] The authors of *Lives* of Anglo-Saxons sainted on the Continent go no further than identifying their subjects as 'Saxon' or 'Anglian' in origin.[120] The only individuals who are regularly given a regional identification in prose works, other than those written by Bede, are the kings – which rather supports the conclusions already offered that the identification of *gentes* was intimately linked with that of their royal houses. The link emerges particularly clearly in Felix's *Vita Guthlaci* where Penwalh, the father of Guthlac and of royal descent, is described as being *de egregia stirpe Merciorum* – 'of the distinguished stock of the Mercians' – which seems to imply an identification of the royal house of Mercia with the Mercian people as a whole.[121] Similarly he introduces King Æthelbald as being *de inclita Merciorum prole*.[122] On the other hand, Hwætred, who was not of royal birth, is described as being 'noble' and 'East Anglian', but he is not said to be 'of the noble stock of the East Anglians',[123] which was presumably, to judge from Felix's other usages, a form of description only applicable to members of royal houses.

When individuals in the Boniface-Lull correspondence wished to identify themselves and establish common bonds, they made use of personal links. So when Leoba sent a letter to Boniface introducing herself, she reminded him of their kinship and his friendship with her father.[124] Ecgburh referred to Boniface's affection for her dead brother, and she also had a call upon him because she was formerly his pupil.[125] Lull wrote in terms of the greatest respect to his former abbess Cyneburh, whom he still regarded as his 'lord', and whose help he expected to enlist.[126] Such personal ties of kinship, association and lordship are undoubtedly what really mattered to the Middle Saxon aristocracy and dictated the pattern of their lives. For the aristocracy the personal would also have been political, since links with kings, or

---

118. Tangl, *Bon. Ep. passim*. For discussion of the provenance of correspondents, see B.A.E. Yorke, 'The Bonifacian mission and female religious in Wessex', *Early Medieval Europe* 7 (1998), 145–72.
119. *The Life of Bishop Wilfrid by Eddius Stephanus*, ed. B. Colgrave (1927), 2–3; *Felix's Life of Saint Guthlac*, ed. B. Colgrave (1956), 60–5.
120. G. Wieland, 'England in the German legends of Anglo-Saxon saints', in *Words, Texts and Manuscripts*, ed. M. Korhammer (1992), 193–212.
121. *Life of Guthlac*, ch. 1, 72–3.
122. *Ibid*. ch. 40, 124–5.
123. *Ibid*. ch. 41, 126–7.
124. Tangl, *Bon. Ep.* no. 29.
125. *Ibid*. no. 13.
126. *Ibid*. no. 49.

other members of the royal house, would have been a key element of their existence. The importance of royal relationships is brought out in Bede's account of the thegn Imma which is so informative about many facets of Middle Saxon life.[127] Imma was a thegn of Queen Æthelthryth of Northumbria and had fought on the Northumbrian side at the battle of the River Trent in 679. His Mercian captor sold him to a Frisian merchant who took him to London, where Imma was eventually given parole in order to raise a ransom. This he was able to obtain from King Hlothere of Kent, on the grounds that he was a thegn of Hlothere's aunt (herself a member of the East Anglian royal house by birth). Imma's story gives a good indication of the importance of royal links for the aristocracy, through which they would have a primary identification with a particular kingdom. It also reminds us that as the royal houses intermarried in the seventh and eighth centuries, their own kin and personal links which extended by association to their followers cut across kingdom boundaries. This must have contributed to the idea of a common Anglo-Saxon identity which has already been discussed.

Conclusion

The Anglo-Saxon evidence seems to fit with Benedict Anderson's classic definition of a nation as 'an imagined community'.[128] Ethnic identity in the sense of membership of a *gens* could be defined in more than one way in early Anglo-Saxon England and could indicate membership of a kingdom, of a broader regional grouping such as the Angles, Saxons or Jutes, or an 'English' identity. Such identities were underpinned by origin legends, but not necessarily by actual biological descent.[129] They were constructed identities which through being adopted by various lineages and their followers as actualities became 'real' identities. The apparently 'Germanic' *gentes* must have included a significant proportion of those descended from the indigenous inhabitants of Roman Britain, and even those who migrated from Germanic homelands would not necessarily have brought with them a specifically Anglian, Saxon or Jutish identity. But identity was not just a state of mind; it was above all, in early Anglo-Saxon England, a question of allegiance. By recognizing the authority of a particular king one became a member of his *gens* and so by definition eligible for inclusion in the broader groupings of *gentes* as well. Of course, this identity may have been of more significance to some sectors of society

---

127. Bede, *HE* IV.22.
128. B. Anderson, *Imagined Communities: Reflections on the Origins and Spread of Nationalism* (1983).
129. F. Barth, *Ethnic Groups and Boundaries: The Social Organisation of Cultural Difference* (Oslo, 1969); A.D. Smith, *The Ethnic Origin of Nations* (1986).

than to others, and references to 'British' peasants living in Anglo-Saxon kingdoms in accounts of the seventh century confirm that, as is so often the case in medieval sources, the 'people' were those with some influence, an elite group of nobility and freemen.[130] One suspects that Anglo-Saxon England could be an example of warfare – in this case membership of a warband or king's army – having a key role in providing new ethnic identities.[131] Even among the upper classes political identity was but one of a series of significant identities, and for the lower orders district, lordship and family must have been even more important units of self-identity. Those living in the more localized districts, which may very well have been significant units governing many aspects of their lives, might be identified as 'peoples', but were not described by Bede and other Anglo-Saxon writers of Latin as *gentes* – that is, political units such as kingdoms. The *gentes* predominate in the written sources, and within them concepts of political and ethnic identity were intimately linked with and promoted by the royal courts. Alfred and his successors may have been the first to claim the title *rex Anglorum*, but in yoking together political and ethnic identities they were following a path already laid out by their Middle Saxon predecessors.

---

130. N.J. Higham, *An English Empire: Bede and the Early Anglo-Saxon Kings* (1995), 218–60.
131. A.D. Smith, 'War and ethnicity: the role of warfare in the formation, self-images and cohesion of ethnic communities', *Ethnic and Racial Studies* 4 (1981), 375–95.

5 Community, Identity and Kingship in Early England[1]

Alex Woolf

The history of Western Europe in the second half of the first millennium of the Christian Era is frequently characterized as a period in which the nation states, with which we are so familiar today, emerged from the fragmented anarchy of the fallen Roman Empire and its barbarous neighbours. Such a view presents the more barbaric regions, such as Britain, Ireland, Scandinavia, 'Free' Germany and the Slavonic world, as gradually being united into medieval kingdoms through a long history of competitive warfare, with the winners taking all. Indeed, a recent collaborative volume on Anglo-Saxon England opened with an extended analogy, by the editor, based on the model of a football league.[2] This approach to the emergence of medieval kingdoms tends to divert attention from the fact that long before executive structures emerged, with the tightening control of the reins of power by kings, many of the 'nations' of Europe were clearly visible to their contemporaries. Concentrating on Anglo-Saxon England, but drawing analogies and comparisons with other European regions, I wish to investigate what exactly it was that allowed early medieval people to recognize the unity of groups like *Gens Anglorum* before any of the structures of statehood had clearly emerged. How did people know that they themselves, or others, were English?

While the existence of small *regiones* within the larger provincial kingdoms is beyond dispute, and is attested by both Bede and early charter sources, it is open to question whether the assertion that 'the *regio* of the Stoppingas [an area of some 50 square kilometres in north Worcestershire] and all other such settlement areas should be recognised as distinct polities – indeed, embryonic kingdoms'.[3] The

1. I would like to thank the following for comment, discussion and encouragement: Nicholas Brooks, Chris Cumberpatch, Simon Keynes, John Moreland, Mike Parker Pearson, Ron Ross, Jane Stevenson, Ross Samson, Kath Thompson and Chris Wickham, and Patrick Wormald. Eccentricities and errors remain my own.
2. S. Bassett (ed.), *The Origins of Anglo-Saxon Kingdoms* (1989), 3–28.
3. Bassett, 'In search of the origins of Anglo-Saxon kingdoms', in *ibid.* 19 [*et passim*].

first part of this statement, with minor reservations, is perfectly acceptable and while a social interpretation of the *regio* over the proprietorial interpretations of either Glanville Jones's multiple estate or T.H. Aston's manor is to be applauded, we must consider whether the recognition of a community's status as a socio-political entity necessarily demands that we should see it as an embryonic kingdom glorying in its independence and isolation.[4] The disturbing supposition is that all words referring to socio-political entities are synonymous with 'kingdom', or at least that we have no alternative to the view that dynastic hegemonies emerged as the result of militaristic expansion out of tiny locales, and that if we can identify the birth place of a dynastic progenitor we can identify the core of a kingdom. While it is clear that every royal ancestor must have been born within a local *regio*, this does not necessarily demand that that *regio* is in any sense a core territory, for a myriad of different kinds of community existed in the medieval period.[5] Not all of these communities can be categorized as kingdoms.

Kingship is an office, and while the obligations and privileges that go with kingship may vary from case to case, it is by its very nature distinct from any position within a dynastic structure. The idea of fixed kin groups as static units passing through time – and thus dominating local politics – is untenable, as every birth, marriage and death changes the equilibrium, and many individuals would have had responsibilities within a number of social networks.[6] The descent group, or lineage, is clearly distinct from any practical socio-political structure. Were early medieval kingdoms based upon tightly defined kin groups, any set of laws which invoked the kindred (as all the barbarian codes do) would be a nonsense since everyone under the jurisdiction of the code would share the same kindred. Even in the archaic Irish *rúath*, whose members were almost certainly quite

---

4. For a summary of Glanville Jones's views on multiple estates see his 'Multiple estates and early settlement' in *Medieval Settlement: Continuity and Change* (1976), ed. P. Sawyer. For T.H. Aston on pre-Viking Age manors see 'The origins of the manor in England', *Transactions of the Royal Historical Society*, 5th series, vol. 8 (1958), 59–83.
5. For a full discussion on the subject see Susan Reynolds', *Kingdoms and Communities in Western Europe, 900-1300* (1990), esp. 1–36.
6. I use the term 'social network' to designate the unit of kin and friends who actually aid a litigant in bringing a dispute to resolution. Such networks and the variety of functions they performed are described by J.L. Byock in his *Feud in the Icelandic Saga* (Berkeley, 1982). The social network, as I intend it, is far more fluid in its constituency than any empirically defined kin group, its extent being modified by pragmatic affiliations and absences, and a more situational identification of interest. The Icelandic material has been examined in a more explicitly social historical context by W.I. Miller under the heading 'Practical Kinship,' in his *Bloodtaking and Peacemaking: Feud, Law and Society in Saga Iceland* (Chicago, 1990), esp. 155–78. Obviously lineages and stories, true or mythical, of shared descent can have a role in political legitimation but they are rarely structures that can be utilized in daily interaction.

closely related, a clear distinction was drawn between the *ágae fine* or *cenn fine*, the head of kin, and the *rúaithe*, the elected leader of the polity.[7] Indeed, I would go so far as to suggest that the primary, though not sole, function of a polity and its magistrates, of whom the king is the principal, in the kinds of societies that interest us here, is to mediate *between* kin groups. Kingship, legitimized through ritual linkage with the supernatural, may indeed have originated as a face-saving device developed by the *optimates* of the polity to allow them to turn away with honour from otherwise destructive direct conflict.[8] Any study of the origins of Anglo-Saxon kingdoms must therefore start by identifying the parameters of kingship and also clarify the distinction between the roles of the king as the magistrate of the republic and of the king as tyrant: kings and kingdoms are not like chickens and eggs, the king always comes first.

The Old English word for king, *cyning*, is of unknown provenance and etymology. Herwig Wolfram claims that it derives from a Germanic *kuningaz* and described the same phenomenon as the Gothic *reiks*, the magistrate of a small region, similar to the Irish *rí*, but there is little substantial evidence for this.[9] In England the word does not appear in any useful context until well into the eighth century when social structures had undergone considerable change; and so, rather than waste time in speculation, it is probably best to ignore *cyning* and to concentrate, in the first instance, upon the Latin word *rex*.

Whatever its precise semantic import in the prehistoric Italian context to which it owes its origin, the word *rex* had by the sixth and seventh centuries obtained a meaning that is immediately accessible to us. In the Latin translations of the Bible it was the word used to describe the leading men in Israel and Judah between Saul and the Babylonian captivity. In the contemporary world it was used to describe the rulers of the Visigoths and the Franks, and some of the leaders of the Langobards; it was also occasionally used of the Augustus at Constantinople. It described a monarch, a sole leader, who held office indefinitely (abdication and deposition were possible but there was no question of an agreed fixed term). The *rex* held office within a defined constituency usually identified as a *gens* or people, such as the Goths, the Langobards, etc. The Franks are often said to have practised partible kingship whereby more than one son could

---

7. See F. Kelly, *A Guide to Early Irish Law* (Dublin, 1988), esp. 1–14, and T.M. Charles-Edwards, *Early Irish and Welsh Kinship* (1993). For the archaic *naithe* see my unpublished MPhil thesis *The Transition from Late Prehistoric to Early Historic Social and Political Structures amongst the Irish* (University of Sheffield, 1991), 24 ff.
8. The last decades of the Icelandic *Frístat*, the notorious 'Sturlung Age', were riven by bloody conflict precisely because there was no device by which the pre-eminent citizen of the commonwealth could legitimize his superiority.
9. H. Wolfram, 'The Shaping of the Early Medieval kingdom', *Viator* 1 (1970), 1–20, esp. at 6.

split the kingship of their father between them, but this interpretation is open to question.[10] It is possible that the large amounts of imperial *fisc* extant in Gaul at the time of Clovis led to this development; the *fisc* land may have been inherited partibly as private property and yet recognition that the holder of *fisc* was the monarch was maintained. This then is the context of the usage of the term *rex* in the period under discussion.

Those of us who spend much of our time pondering the pages of early British and Irish history have become used to thinking about the leaders of the seventh-century Anglo-Saxons in the terms Bede uses to describe them, *reges* or, by convention, kings, but perhaps we should pause and consider how they earned this status (in linguistic if not in social terms). Edward James, picking up on Bassett's football analogy, suggests that to continental teams the Anglo-Saxons must have appeared to be 'knocking a ball around in some corner',[11] and indeed he has a valid point. If the model *reges* were the Visigoths, Franks and Langobards how on earth did the leader of the South Saxons or the Cantware qualify? While in the football model these latter polities are second-division 'big' kingdoms, neither one of them is any larger than the average continental *civitas*, dozens of which might comprise a kingdom. Of course we can look back in history to Tacitus or other ancient authors and find the term *rex* used for the leaders of very small units, but is that a historically justifiable methodology? The writers of the earlier Middle Ages arranged their classifications according to their own experience, not with reference to a broad range of comparative ethnography.

The word *rex* is first used with reference to an Englishman in a letter addressed to Æthelbert *Rex Anglorum*.[12] We are used to thinking of this man as a king of Kent, but our source for this assumption is Bede, writing one hundred years or more after the man's death. Gregory always refers to Æthelbert as *Rex Anglorum*, 'king of the Angles', and the law code ascribed to him in *Textus Roffensis*, unlike those ascribed to Hlothere and Wihtred, makes no mention of Kent in its preamble.[13] Certainly from a continental perspective it would seem far more reasonable to refer to Æthelbert as *rex* with reference to an office held in relation to the Angles as a whole rather than to the province of the Cantware alone, and this seems to be the contemporary usage. I would contend then that the contemporary evidence of the early seventh century suggests that the term *rex*, as introduced to the

---

10. For a recent discussion see Ian Wood, *The Merovingian Kingdoms, 450–751* (1994).

11. E. James, 'The origins of barbarian kingdoms', in Bassett, *Origins of AS Kingdoms*, 40.

12. 'Gregorii I Papae Registrum Epistolarum XI', in *MGH Epist.* 2 vols. Berlin, 1891 and 1899, ed. P. Ewald and L.M. Hartmann (henceforth G.E.).

13. F. L. Attenborough, *The Laws of the Earliest English Kings* (1922). Æthelbert's is at 4–17, Hlothere's at 18–23 and Wihtred's at 24–31.

English, referred initially only to the leader who held *imperium* over the various provinces.[14] Pope Gregory seems always to have envisaged the conversion of the Angles as a nation, and not province by province, which might suggest that the contemporary view, at least from Italy, was of a more unified community than recent scholarship would allow.

Peter Hunter-Blair, in discussing the course of Augustine's journey to Britain, suggested that in not consecrating the missionary in Rome himself Gregory recognized the possibility that the mission would not cross the channel if conditions were not right.[15] Augustine then used Gregory's *licentia* to get the Austrasian bishops to consecrate him when he realized that he did indeed have a chance of success. Hunter-Blair suggests that the information Augustine received was that Bertha and her episcopal chaplain Liudhard were at Canterbury, yet it surely seems unlikely that news of the whereabouts of a Merovingian princess and a bishop could have escaped Augustine when he first entered Gaul, especially since the marriage of Æthelbert and Bertha must have been nearly a decade old at least. A more likely sequence of events is that it was the presence of lady and bishop, and perhaps even letters from the latter (Gregory had heard that the English wished to be Christians[16]), that prompted the mission, possibly following the demise of Ceawlin, and that what Augustine discovered in 596 was that Æthelbert was apparently secure in the office that Frankish latinists termed *Rex Anglorum*, and that Liudhard could now get him access to the whole nation and not just to an already semi-Frankish toehold in the extreme south-east.

Before moving on to discuss what the term *Rex Anglorum* denoted in the early seventh century, we should consider how it came to be that by the time Bede wrote his works, and indeed somewhat earlier, the term *rex* had come to be applied, ordinarily, to the leaders of provinces rather than of the *gens* as a whole. (Although Bede is not fully consistent in his terminology he generally uses *provincia* to mean those larger units which tended to form the basis of dioceses and which most scholars would accept had the right to be called kingdoms at one time or another; for these polities I shall follow that usage.) The history of the word *rex* in England is intimately tied up with the history of the Latin language, and that of course is bound to England's ecclesiastical history. To continental churchmen the term *rex* signified scale as much as anything, as James shows in his discussion of Gregory of Tours' inability to come to terms with the concept of non-national kings among fourth-century Germans,[17] and so they applied it to the most highly placed leader in the *Gens Anglorum* regardless of how insubstantial the structure supporting his office might be. After the

---

14. Bede's *australibus provinciis* of *HE* II.5.
15. *The World of Bede* (1970), 49–58.
16. G.E. VI.
17. James, *op. cit.* 41–3.

death of Edwin, however, in 632, the influence of continental churchmen outside of the south-east, which in any case had been pretty superficial, disappeared for a generation. Christian missionary work continued of course, and spread throughout the country, from Malmesbury and Bradwell to Lindisfarne (or rather *vice versa*); the difference was that these missionaries were Irish, or Irish-trained (which came to the same thing with regard to their approach to Latin).

Because Ireland had never been fully integrated into the Roman Empire, and because the conversion of the Irish to Christianity was not undertaken by a well-organized mission with interactive support from a major ecclesiastical centre on the Continent, the Latin used by its saints and scholars developed a different set of usages from those current in the sub-Roman west.[18] In Hiberno-Latin the term *rex* was used to gloss the native word *rí* (just possibly still Primitive Irish *rōx* at the time of transmission), the title of the leading magistrate of the *tœath*,[19] a small polity of two or three thousand souls which was known in Hiberno-Latin as a *plebs*. The important question is, with a greater awareness of the outside world and, more importantly, without the homophonic relationship between *ríx* and *rex*, (often pronounced 'rix' in Late Latin),[20] would the Irish have ended up using the term *rex* for the headman of a simple *tœath*?[21] Patrick Wormald has argued that, once one gets beneath the superficial differences in the source material, Celtic and Anglo-Saxon kingship were not so different as traditional historiography would have us believe, a view which I would wholeheartedly endorse.[22] Further, if one were to rewrite Irish history reserving the term *rex* for *ruiri* and using some term such as *satrap* or *maior* for the simple *rí*, the Irish might look a lot more like Germanic barbarians. That the inventors of Hiberno-Latin saw things in this way is perhaps confirmed by use of the term *plebs*, rather than *regnum* or *provincia*, for the *túath*.[23] We must pause to ask ourselves whether explicit or implicit assumptions of objective categorization have affected our interpretation of the sources.

If this is the case, is it any surprise that in the Latin propagated in the ecclesiastical establishments which sprang up among the English during the *imperia* of Oswald and Oswiu, the word *rex* was used for a less exalted position than that recognized by the Italians at Canter-

---

18. See J.B. Stevenson, 'The beginnings of literacy in Ireland', *Proceedings of the Royal Irish Academy* (1989C), 6–165, esp. at 152 ff. and the citations therein.
19. Kelly, *A Guide*, at 3–6 and 17–26. In oblique cases the Latin stem is *reg-* while the Irish is *ríg-*.
20. Wolfram, 'The Shaping', at 8.
21. Cf. Welsh *breyr*, glossed as *nobilis*, from *brogo-rix* (*brogo-* referring to territory).
22. C.P. Wormald, 'Celtic and Anglo-Saxon Kingship' in *Sources of Anglo-Saxon Culture*, ed. by P.E. Szarnach with V.D. Oggins, *Studies in Medieval Culture 20* (1986).
23. Professor Ó Corráin has touched on these matters in his paper 'Nationality and Kingship in pre-Norman Ireland' in *Nationality and the Pursuit of National Independence*, ed. T.W. Moody (Historical Studies 11, Belfast, 1978), 1–35.

bury? It is, perhaps, more surprising that it was used for so few people. Nevertheless, by the time the Continental Church seized the initiative once more – in the time of Archbishop Theodore (668–90) – the English, for linguistic rather than constitutional reasons, had become a people of many kingdoms rather than one. (The term heptarchy was never appropriate and I fear dodecarchy, though more accurate, will never catch on.) If this sounds outlandish, I suggest that one should pause to contextualize Augustine, Mellitus, Lawrence and Paulinus along with their fellow missionaries and their chief at home. These people were Italians.

In 568 Italy was invaded by the Langobards, led by a *rex*, Alboin. As the country fell to them, provinces were taken over by *duces*. In 572 Alboin was murdered by an internal faction. A new *rex*, Cleph – as far as we know, not a relative of Alboin – was elected. He too was killed in faction fighting (574) and for ten years each of the *duces* ruled his own province with no need of a *rex*. Then, in the face of a Frankish invasion, they elected a new *rex*, Authari (584–90). He happened to be Cleph's son, but when he died his successor Agilulf (590–616), was no relation, although he did marry Authari's widow.[24] The *Gens Langobardorum*, with which Gregory and his missionaries were probably far more familiar than they might have wished to be, was thus superficially very similar in its structure to the *Gens Anglorum* they set out to convert. *Reges* were elected for their leadership qualities from any one of a number of families (dynastic kingship would not be established until the second half of the seventh century), while the most durable organizational structures were at a provincial level under the leadership of *duces*, who seem to have been drawn from established local dynasties. Not all the *duces* participated in all the collective activities of the *gens*, and some almost never did. Fighting between *duces* was almost constant and only those whose provinces were immediately adjacent to the power base of a *rex* could really be said to be his subjects rather than his colleagues.

If we accept that this was the understanding of a barbarian *gens* that the Augustinian missionaries carried north with them in 596, then the historiography of early English kingship becomes clearer. The Italian regime at Canterbury ended with the death of Archbishop Honorius in 653, coinciding neatly not only with Bede's horizon of reliable witnesses – a man born *circa* 635 might be an adult participant in events of the 650s and still only in his sixties when Bede set out on his academic career – but also with the mid-point in the reign of Oswiu, the last of Bede's seven kings of *Gentis Anglorum* who 'ruled over the southern provinces'.[25] Bede tells us in the Preface of his *Ecclesiastical*

---

24. This information comes from Paul the Deacon's *Historia Langobardorum*, but is usefully summarized and discussed in C. Wickham's *Early Medieval Italy: Control, Power and Local Society* (1981), 28–47.
25. Bede, *HE* II.5.

History that the 'principal authority and helper in this modest work has been the revered Abbot Albinus'[26] of St Peter and St Paul (St Augustine's) at Canterbury who obtained from 'written records', as well as oral tradition, 'all that the disciples of Gregory had done in the province of Cantwara as well as in the neighbouring *regiones*'.[27] These were brought to Jarrow by Nothelm, both in writing and orally, and later Nothelm went to Rome and collected letters from the papal archive. The result of this was that the major part of the documentary sources that Bede possessed for English history before 650 were written in a Latin informed by the Italian *mentalite* outlined above. Bede, however, had no choice but to impart to the vocabulary from which his sources were constructed the meanings derived from his experiences of the semantic tradition current in the *scriptoria* of Angelcyn in his day, and for most of the previous three-quarters of a century. Bede's early eighth-century expectations of government were based upon his experience of provincial leadership and, increasingly, rule in the period between about 660 and 725. Seeing the same vocabulary used to describe national leaders in the late sixth and earlier seventh centuries he naturally assumed that they had attained a level of organizational control at a national level unparalleled in his own day. As Simon Keynes has pointed out, Bede seems less happy with Oswiu's status than with that of the six previous *imperium* holders.[28] This is exactly what we might expect, since for Oswiu he would have had alternative 'Italian' and 'Irish' sources, and the lack of correspondence would have been apparent. This might go some way towards explaining the absence of modern 'Bretwaldas' from Bede's world. Bede's much vaunted anti-Mercian stance, often used to explain the absence of Icling monarchs from the list of *imperium* holders, is a modern myth – he disapproved of Penda, but that was because Penda was a pagan. Peada, Wulfhere and Æthelred are all treated generously and fairly; indeed, as Wormald points out, the remarkable thing about the English in this period was the persistence of their sense of national fellowship despite provincial partisanry.[29] It may well be, as Wormald suggests, that it is in part the long shadow of the Canterbury tradition (though his interpretation of what that entails differs somewhat from mine), but if that is so the task remains to identify the light source from which that shadow was cast. Just what was the *Gens Anglorum* that the Canterbury scribes identified and who were its *reges*?

The major point on which I differ from models that present medieval kingdoms growing out of competition between *plebes* and *regiones* is

---

26. *Ibid.*
27. *Ibid.*
28. S. Keynes, 'Rædwald the Bretwalda' in *Voyage to the Otherworld: The Legacy of Sutton Hoo*, ed. C.B. Kendall and P.S. Wells (Minneapolis, 1992), 103–24.
29. C.P. Wormald, 'Bede, the Bretwaldas and the origins of *Gens Anglorum*' in *Ideal and Reality in Frankish and Anglo-Saxon Society: Studies Presented to J.M. Wallace-Hadrill*, ed. Wormald, Bullough and Collins (1983), esp. at 122–3.

their apparent obsession with small beginnings. This is not merely a problem with Bassett's model; he is working within a strong tradition and one particularly popular among archaeologists. Rejection of the obviously legendary accounts of the fifth-century invasions dates back to Kemble,[30] but more recently it seems as if some scholars believe that proving that the invasions did not happen *as they were described* in later sources is the same thing as proving that they did not happen at all. Hodges, for example, conjures up an image of a North Sea cultural sphere of increasing travel and communications, but no migrations, in which 'given the political complexity [i.e. fragmentation] of the old province, and bearing in mind its material poverty, it is not difficult to envisage the tensions such contacts might have created and, in some cases, the avid adoption of alien ideas and goods'.[31]

Of course I have no desire to resurrect the image of millions of Britons suffering genocide at the hands of slavering hordes of innumerable Germans (though late twentieth-century events in the Balkans might suggest that such genocide would not have been implausible), and in any case it is not my intention to discuss fifth-century events here, but it is curious how political and cultural disunity has become so attractive to modern scholars. In the same chapter of his *Anglo-Saxon Achievement* from which the last quotation was drawn, Hodges implies that the *Tribal Hidage* represents a patchwork of some thirty small tribal units.[32] This is a gross misrepresentation. While it is true that there are thirty-four named territories in the document, 88.89 per cent of the hidage is attributed to a mere ten of them (even if we remove the absurdly high reckoning for Wessex the remaining nine big provinces still account for 81.19 per cent). It is clear, indeed, that it is the fragmentation of the east midlands that requires special explanation since it contrasts so clearly with the general rule of provincial-level organization. Contrary to Hodges' assertion, the *Tribal Hidage* shows us a country already divided into large, multi-regional provinces, some of which were surrounded by small, contested territories.

Our earliest contemporary reference to a group we can identify as *Gens Anglorum* is in the writings of the Greek historian Procopius in his *Gothic War*: 'Three very populous nations inhabit the island of Brittia, and *one king* is set over each of them. And the names of these nations are Angles, Frisians and Britons who have the same name as the island'.[33] Bede, in turn, tells us that 'from the country of the Angles came the East Angles, the Middle Angles and the Mercians and all the Northumbrian race (*progenies*) as well as the other Anglian *populi*'.[34]

---

30. J.M. Kemble, *The Saxons in England* (1849).
31. R. Hodges, *The Anglo-Saxon Achievement* (1989), 10–42.
32. *Ibid.*, 25.
33. Bede, *HE* VIII.20, 6.
34. Bede, *HE* I.15.

By other Anglian *populi* Bede probably means the dominant groups in those provinces which were colonized by the Mercians, such as the Hwicce and the Magonsæte. The question is, what constituted being an Angle? I am not interested here in origins, nor even invasions, but in a historical present. What difference did being, or not being, an Angle make to someone who was, or was not, one?

Cemetery archaeology of the fifth century seems to show a bias towards cremation over inhumation in the areas identified by Bede, excluding Bernicia (in which Angle identity may have been a relatively late import), following a rite, and accompanied by jewellery characteristic of south Jutland and north Germany, the putative homeland of the Angles.[35] On the other hand, in the Thames basin and on the Channel coasts, inhumation is more common, as are signs of contact with Roman and Frankish fashions.[36] This would seem to suggest that some sort of community did exist in the Anglian part of Britain which wished to signal commonality, and also to display signs that could be associated with the part of the continent traditionally associated with the Angles. It does not prove immigration or descent but it may prove ethnicity; the people who burned and urned these bodies probably thought of themselves as Angles. We can thus say, with some safety, that in the period prior to the Augustinian mission the Angles inhabited the territory of four early Anglo-Saxon provinces: Deira, Lindesfarona, Mierce, East Anglia and also of the region known as Middle Anglia (the region of maximum fragmentation in the *Tribal Hidage*). South of here there may have been a British polity in the Chiltern region[37] and beyond that the various provinces ascribed to Frisians by Procopius and to Saxons and Jutes by Bede. This confused situation in the south-east is no doubt reflected by the failure of clearly dominant mortuary ritual to emerge, and its history may be marginally closer to the model suggested by Hodges. The term Saxon which had come into use for the Thames Valley Germans may reflect the late creation of an ethnic group in opposition to indigenous Britons for whom the term Saxon indicated any German in Britain. That they were late starters in attaining any kind of group identity may go some way towards explaining why *Gens Anglorum* was eventually to attain dominance as an expression of national identity.

What was the nature of Angle unity? Well, of course it was nothing like Visigothic unity in Spain or like Frankish unity after Clovis. In Spain and Gaul German *Heerkönige* had taken over up-and-running provincial and Imperial structures and used them to enhance their own

---

35. For a fuller and far more sophisticated discussion of the Anglian diagnostics of pre-Viking Age England see J. Hines, *The Scandinavian Character of Anglian England in the Pre-Viking Period*, British Archaeological Reports, British Series 124 (1984).

36. N. Higham, *Rome, Britain and the Anglo-Saxons* (1992), 172–4.

37. K. Rutherford Davis, *Britons and Saxons: The Chiltern Region 400–700* (1982), and now K.R. Dark, *Civitas to Kingdom* (1994).

positions within the *gentes*. In Britain the Imperial government had been ejected a generation or two before the *gens* became established so this was not possible. But how might the situation on the island have compared with that of the Franks before the mid-fifth century, or the Alamanni in the time of Ammianus, or the Old Saxons in the time of Bede? Edward James has discussed such phenomena.[38] The vocabulary varies in time and place, but essentially each nation is divided into a number of units (those of the Terving Goths were called *phylai* by the Greeks, a word indicating common descent), each with a permanent 'chief magistrate', usually of a particular lineage. In times of crisis a leader was elected from among them. This is of course what we saw among the Langobards in the time of Gregory, where the provincial magistrates are *duces* and the elected leader a *rex*. Among the Tervingi the provincial magistrates were *reguli* and the elected leader a *judex*; among the Old Saxons Bede calls the provincial magistrates *satrapes* and carefully avoids using a noun to describe the allotted leader. James concludes his discussion of these kinds of structure by returning to Gregory of Tours's account of how, after he had secured control of Gaul, Clovis used his armed might, based on his position within Gallo-Roman – if not Imperial – society, to eliminate all the 'provincial' Frankish magistrates (called *reges* in this case) and make himself *Rex Francorum*. He goes on to suggest that this is what might have happened in sixth-century England.[39] Once again, however, one must stress the problem of scale. When Gregory talks about the Frankish *reges* of the time before the death of Clovis[40] he locates them, if at all, with reference to Gallo-Roman *civitates* – Childeric with Tournai, Ragnachar with Cambrai, Sigibert with Köln and so forth. Similarly the subdivisions of the continental Saxons were peoples like the Westfali, Ostfali and Angrarii.[41] Consider also the scale of the Langobardic *ducati*. If we are to find an equivalent to these divisions in sixth-century Angelcyn, then they are not the *regiones* but the *provinciae* – Deira, Lindesfarona, Mierce and East Anglia.

Before moving on to look at *Gens Anglorum* in more detail let us consider a little further the nature of the *gens* as a phenomenon. Was there anything more to it than elected military leadership? How was the extent of the franchise decided? Most of the work that has been published and discussed dealing with this subject in recent times has concentrated upon the experiences of the barbarian *gentes* within the old Imperial frontiers.[42] In these more complex situations contact and

38. E. James, 'The origins of barbarian kingdoms' in Bassett, *Origins of AS Kingdoms*, 40–52.
39. *Ibid.*, 45–6.
40. *HF* II, *passim*.
41. F. Seebohm, *Tribal Custom in Anglo-Saxon Law* (1911), at 213.
42. E.g. R. Wenskus, *Stammesbildung und Verfassung* (1981), Cologne; H. Wolfram, 'Gothic History and Historical Ethnography' in *Journal of Medieval History* 7 (1981); and P.J. Geary, 'Ethnic identity as a situational construct in the Early

collaboration with alternative power structures was already undermining traditional forms of political activity. To take one example, in the face of a Frankish invasion of Italy the Langobard *duces*, or some of them, gave half of their *substantiae* to Authari to create a *fisc*, something that had obviously not been thought necessary before and which was probably a direct emulation of imperial practice.[43] As an alternative I should like to turn to less romanized parts of Europe – to Scandinavia and Ireland – to see if a more rounded picture can be discerned.

Norwegian historiography has long been aware of a phenomenon known in the modern literature as the *lovsamfund*, literally the 'law union'. Medieval Norway was divided into a number of distinct cultural regions each of which operated under its own laws right up until the sixteenth century. At least three of these *lovsamfund* had their origins in the Viking Age or earlier. These three had their assemblies at Eid, in Oppland, at Gula, in the Vestland, and at Frosta, in Trøndelag. It is on Frosta and Trøndelag, the best known of the regions, that I wish to concentrate here. In 1967, Jørn Sandnes published a survey of what he called Trøndelag's oldest political history and that will serve as the basis of my account.[44]

The Trønder were a *gens* of great antiquity who may be mentioned in *Widsith*,[45] usually reckoned to be one of the earliest of Old English poems. In the early historic period the *gens* of the Trønder was divided into eight *fylker*, or provinces, all of which shared some access to Trondheimsfjord. Until the tenth century, each *fylke* seems to have had its own king (*rex* or *konungr* in Latin and Icelandic respectively), and its own assembly place where all free farmers (*bonder*) met to settle disputes and decide upon communal action. Norway being a country possessing what one might term enhanced topography, the boundaries of the Trønder *fylker* were in general clearly circumscribed and probably changed little over time. Five of the *fylker* – Orkdal, Gauldal, Støjrdal, Verdal and Sparbyggja – were centred along river valleys, each being between fifty and a hundred kilometres in length, while the remaining three – Strinda, Skeyna and Eyna – were more closely associated with the fjord itself (each being divided internally by open water). The distance between the southern point of Orkdal and the northern extremity of Sparbyggjafylke (that is to say the breadth of Trøndelag) is about two hundred and sixty kilometres (the distance between Oxford and York).[46] In terms of communications (that is to say

contd.
    Middle Ages', in *Mitteilungen der Anthropologischen Gesellschaft in Wien*, 113 (1983), 15–26.
43. Wickham, *Early Medieval Italy*, at 32.
44. J. Sandnes, 'Trøndelags eldste politiske historie' in *Historisk Tidskrift*, 46 (1967), Oslo.
45. l.64; *ond mid Throwendum*.
46. For maps showing the internal divisions of Trøndelag see K. Sognnes, *Sentrumsdannelser i Trøndelag: En kvantativ analyse av gravmaterialet fra yngre jernalder* (Trondheim, 1988).

travelling time) if not in demography and productivity, these Trønder *fylker* are comparable in extent to Anglo-Saxon provinces such as those of the Hwicce or the East Saxons. Ease of communication is most likely to have been the determining factor in communities that were governed by collective decision-making. Public assemblies would have had to have been held in generally accessible locations.

Within each *fylke* there were also much smaller units, each known as a *herað*.[47] These districts often form the basis for modern parish organization but are generally made up of dispersed farms. It is these units that equate most nearly with the Stoppingas type of *regio* or *plebs*. Each year, at the beginning of August, after the harvest was gathered in, an assembly for the whole *samfund* of Trondheim ('Home of the Trønder' – only later was the name applied to the city of Nidaros) was held at Frosta, a site on a peninsula in the middle of the fjord. In theory any Trønde *bonde* could take part in the proceedings at which, as well as litigation, 'friendships and political alliances were initiated, continued or broken; information was passed on; promises were given; stories told; and business was transacted'.[48] It was association through the medium of the Frostating and it was the links that were established there which identified one as a Trond.

Functionally, the *samfund* and its constituent tiers of social organization must have been intended, primarily, to mediate and ameliorate tension. Each *herað* must have possessed shared hunting, grazing and other 'forest' rights,[49] and the problems of straying cattle or irresponsible action by community members could be dealt with at a local level. This is the type of structure familiar throughout western Europe under a variety of names such as hundred, *plebs* or *vicaria*.[50] The community was one of extreme familiarity and day-to-day contact, but it should be noted that its members would not necessarily have made up a discrete kin or descent group. The *herað*, or *plebs*, was located through spatial proximity and its boundaries may have been relatively static through long periods of time, whereas social networks, the horizontally structured units which articulate a 'kin-based' society will be in constant flux (as, of course, will 'estates' in societies which

---

47. See Sawyer and Sawyer, *Medieval Scandinavia: From Conversion to Reformation circa 800-1500* (1993).
48. This is from Jesse Byock's *Medieval Iceland* (1988) at 61, discussing the analogous Icelandic Althing.
49. For these see C.J. Wickham, 'European forests in the Early Middle Ages', *Settimane di Studio*, 37 (Spoleto, 1990), 479-548.
50. The workings of the *plebs* are discussed in graphic detail by Wendy Davies in her *Small Worlds* (1988), and by Susan Reynolds in chapter 5 of her *Kingdoms and Communities*, pages 101-54. For archaeological discussion of such units in barbarian Europe see H. Steuer, 'Archaeology and history: proposals on the social structure of the Merovingian Kingdom' in *The Birth of Europe*, ed. K. Randsborg (Rome, 1989), esp. at 117 ff. Also see H.T. Waterbolk, 'Mobilität von Dorf, Ackerflur und Gräberfeld in Drenthe seit der Latènezeit', *Offa*, 39 (1982), 97-137.

practise partible inheritance). Certainly the socio-political preoccupations of the leading characters within a *herað* may often have been to assert their own dominance, as individuals, in the community through the manipulation of kin relations, but even where total domination of the land by one group is achieved, segmentation will inevitably follow. Quarrels, after all, are between individuals; kinship merely forms a convenient starting point for mustering auxiliaries.[51]

The *fylke* fills the same niche within the social ecosystem[52] as the Langobard *ducatus*, the Old Saxon satrapy or the Anglo-Saxon provincial kingdom. In spatial terms it represents, broadly, the area from which an assembly or social centre can be reached by a day's travel by horse or boat (rather than the 'hour's walk' radius of the *herað*). The communities within each *fylke* will have shared some common resources such as highways, rivers and perhaps heathland. In terms of personal familiarity the *fylke* itself probably represents a community whose membership know of, if not actually know, everybody and can locate them on the social map. While the *fylke* obviously functions to stabilize social relations between the *plebes*, it also serves to enhance emerging social distinctions. Time is, of itself, a commodity (labour), and attending a *fylke* assembly is obviously more labour-intensive for most people than participating in the local *herað* meeting. The poorer farmer, whose own personal labour is indispensable to the day-to-day running of his farm and who must return home each evening to milk the cow, chop the firewood or whatever, will not be able to attend functions organized at the *fylke* level as regularly as his better-off neighbours. Consequently he will not have the opportunity of establishing himself within the same kind of network of kin ties and friendships that will allow them to mesh into a social network capable of operating potently at the *fylke* level. When issues that are very important to him as an individual are in the air he

---

51. Thomas Charles-Edwards discusses the relationship between a ruling kindred, who may give their name to their *plebs*, and other groups in his *Early Irish and Welsh Kinship* (1993), esp. with reference to the Corcu Duibne of West Kerry. Like the Stoppingas they gave their name to their *plebs*, but the preponderance of Ogham inscriptions in the district commemorating individuals of other descent groups shows that they were not the sole proprietors nor even the sole family of substance in the district, esp. at 157 ff.

52. For those who are worried that I am generating generally applicable rules of social structure and claiming too direct an equivalence for Norse, Saxon, Celtic and Roman structures, the metaphor of the niche within an ecosystem is probably the most useful heuristic device. Although remaining quite distinct animals the kangaroo and the gazelle fulfil similar roles within similar environments. In terms of size, habitat, reproductive capacity, diet, protein conversion capability, mobility they are extremely similar; evolutionary particularism has made them superficially extremely different. This is the kind of relationship I visualize existing between, for example, the *byggd* and the *plebs*. Any taxonomic precision, even within one society, is of course purely academic; people in pre-literate or semi-literate societies do not classify the structures of everyday life so neatly.

may make a special effort to attend, and his membership of the *fylke* will not be denied, but he will find himself at an operational disadvantage. The permanent magistrate emerges at this level precisely because the community has expanded and the immediate familiarity of all its members with one another cannot be maintained. By travelling around the *fylke* and enjoying the '*feorm* of one night' the magistrate was able to enter into relationships of honour and hospitality with the whole community and to become, ideally, a link in every social network. He was thus bound to support each member of the community and to labour for reconciliation and the common wealth. Similarly, each individual was bound to support him in his disputes. Through the magistrate everybody becomes the friend of a friend.

At the level of the *samfund* the participatory restrictions of labour requirements are further intensified, and a smaller group would have regularly attended the annual general assembly which, with travelling time included, may have taken up several weeks. Among the Trønder the Frostating was held at the beginning of August and lasted a week. Although in Iceland the Althing was held in June, this was probably due to the extreme environmental conditions, and August seems to have been a more usual time for holding assemblies. Certainly in Ireland where the *samfund* concept also seems to have been in operation (the term *côiced* was used[53]) the great assemblies of Óenach Tailten, Óenach n-Emne and Óenach Colmáin (respectively those of the Uí Néill, the Ulaid and the Laigin) were also held then, commencing on the feast of Lugnasad.[54] The increased size of the community represented at the *samfund* level, together with the decrease in the proportion of the population who could have become regular participants at the assembly, would have meant that personal familiarity with or cognizance of one's fellows would have decreased extraordinarily and this may explain why it is at this level that ethnic signifiers of the sort identified by archaeologists and ethnologists appear.[55]

Although in Trøndelag and the other Norwegian *lovsamfund* – as among the Old Saxons – there does not seem to have been a permanent magistrate at this level, this is not necessarily a general

---

53. For a discussion of the systems at work in Ireland see my MPhil thesis *The Transition from Late Prehistoric to Early Historic Social and Political Structures amongst the Irish* (University of Sheffield, 1991).
54. D.A. Binchy, 'The Fair of Tailtiu and the Feast of Tara', *Friu*, 18 (1958), 113–38.
55. I am thinking here of conscious signifiers, styles of dress, haircut, weapon type, etc., rather than of the unconscious signs of homogeneity which develop through the medium of the constant exchange with, and influence of, friends and neighbours.
56. The *Lade Jarl*, the leading man in tenth- and eleventh-century Trøndelag, was a product of the state formation process and does not seem to have been an officer of the republic.

rule.[56] Most surprising of all, even in Iceland, where the constitution seems to have been deliberately arranged to avoid the gravitation of power towards kingship by ensuring that three chieftains jointly held office at the level which equates with the *fylke*, a permanent hereditary 'head of state', the *Allsherjargoði*, existed.[57] As his title implies, this officer, who was also the farmer at Reykjavik (and the heir of the alleged first settler), was envisaged as the leader of the national host, but as Iceland never went to war, he never rose to prominence (although in the pagan period he was responsible for hallowing the site of the Althing before each year's assembly). Among the Uí Néill the office of *Rí Temra* seems to have been envisaged as permanent, but its permanence may have been linked with the tradition of the *boruma*, the ritualized war waged regularly (if not annually) against the Laigin. (In fact this was a glorified cattle raid, but all the Uí Néill were supposed to take part as a sign that they endorsed the choice of *Rí Temra*.[58]) However, our understanding of 'over-kingship' among the more traditional *coíceda* of Ireland, the Laigin and the Ulaid, might benefit from considering the possibility that, up until at least *c.* 800, a system more like that in vogue among the continental Saxons prevailed.[59]

Essentially, the key to the *gens* must have been the assembly, or some analogous shared experience such as the Frankish *Marchfeld*, an annual mustering of the *gentile* host. How else could anything approaching group identity have been maintained? The important dynamics would revolve around the establishment of, and competition between, social networks operating at this assembly level. While competition for greater control of resources and people would be played out at more local levels, be it *plebs* or province, the advantage would go to those who could mobilize external, higher-level support. From the earliest historical period, we are aware of provincial elites contracting marriages across the breadth of Angelcyn and even beyond. The function of such alliances was doubtless to secure entry into a social network which would intimidate one's competitors at one's own level of primary activity; thus Sledd, the East Saxon dynast, married Ricula of Kent[60] not to forge an alliance between the Cantwara and the East Saxons but to gain prestige among the East Saxon *optimates*, just as Æthelbert himself obtained a Merovingian wife to enhance his status at home. The social network is formed through community of interest; the kin have a stake in the protagonist's patrimony while the friends may have more short-term pragmatic reasons to care. The value of individuals to any social network,

57. Byock, *Medieval Iceland*, 60.
58. F.J. Byrne, *Irish Kings and High Kings* (1973), 144–6.
59. For a recent discussion of early Irish social organization see T.M. Charles-Edwards, *Early Irish and Welsh Kinship* (1993).
60. B. Yorke, *Kings and Kingdoms of Early Anglo-Saxon England* (1990), 28.

however, depends upon their being recognized as members of the wider community. The social network is not designed primarily to promote conflict but to avert it,[61] and this is best done if its members are tied into as wide a variety of relationships within the community as possible. A disputant is far more likely to come to terms if he knows that his opponent's social network includes his next-door neighbour or his wife's brother than if it contained the same number of able-bodied men with whom he himself has no ties. The social network, ideally, encourages good citizenship and relies upon as broad a base of common familiarity as possible.[62] This level of common acquaintance and interest is served by recourse to general assemblies and other shared 'rituals'; the rituals, doubtless, becoming more theatrical as personal familiarity between the participants declines. At root the *gens* itself, long recognized to have little real basis in shared descent,[63] is, indeed, nothing less than a giant social network of this sort!

The question for us as Anglo-Saxonists is: did *Gens Anglorum* maintain its identity, at least in part, through the mechanism of a summer assembly or regular hosting? That this was the case would seem to be implied by the existence of Bede's seven *imperium* holders for at least as long as the *gens* continued to function as such. The astute reader will have noticed that while my discussion has centred upon a *Gens Anglorum* comprising the 'truly' Anglian provinces of Britain, Bede's list of *imperium*-holders includes non-Anglian southerners. A simple explanation might be that at about the time of the Augustinian mission the *gens* was expanding from the sixth-century identity so clearly evident in the funerary archaeology[64] to include all the Germans in Britain. Bede may have known of Anglian '*reges*' before the latter part of the sixth century, but they did not hold *imperium* over all the 'southern provinces'. Quite possibly it is only from the time of Ceawlin, with the disappearance of British polities from the South-East, that the 'Saxons' and 'Jutes' became incorporated into *Gens Anglorum*.

The relationship between the recent recruits to Angelcyn, Bede's Saxons and Jutes, and the original *Angli*, cannot have been without its problems. The seventh-century phenomenon of the Gewisse and Bede's assertion that the Cantwara did not accept Edwin's leadership are hints of this, but by and large, for all their differences, the Angles and the southerners probably had far more in common with one another than either had with the Britons or the Franks. No doubt genealogical relationships had to be established to prove a long lost

---

61. P.J. Wormald, 'Bloodfeud, Kindred and Government in Early Modern Scotland', in *Past and Present* 87 (1981), 54–97; and of course Gluckman, 'Peace in the feud'.
62. Cf. the Cleisthenic reform of the Athenian constitution which bound all citizens into 'electoral colleges' which cut across residential zones.
63. H. Wolfram, *A History of the Goths* (1987).
64. See Hines, *Scandinavian Character*, *passim*.

cousinhood, and it may be no coincidence that while the Cerdicingas and Æscingas could claim to be Woden-born along with the other Angle stems, the Seaxnetingas, who never provided an *imperium*-holder, could not.[65]

Having considered the beginning of Bede's list of seven kings, let us now consider the end. Earlier, it was suggested that Latin semantics played a part in the disappearance of the *Rex Anglorum*, but perhaps this was not the only factor. The *gens* leader, whether a Terving *judex* or a Langobard *rex*, was in some sense an elected magistrate, a *primus inter pares*. His main function was to mediate with external powers, whether supernatural, in the field of ritual, or mortal, on the field of battle, on behalf of the *gens*. Was the Iclingian *imperium* different? Aside from his pagan aspect, one striking feature of Penda's career marks him out from the magnificent seven. He fought alongside non-Angles (indeed non-Germans) and, as far as we know, exclusively against members of the Germanic-speaking community in Britain. Before Æthelbald (716–757) there is no evidence of Penda or any of his successors on the Mercian throne fighting against the Britons. Might we not consider the possibility that the Iclingas were tyrants rather than archons, that their power was based on explicit threat and domination and not on the idealized image of a *primus inter pares* leading the *gens* against common foes?[66]   This is the difference between Edwin and Penda – the Iclingian *imperium* was not of the same character as that held by Ælle, Ceawlin and Æthelbert. Why and how Penda came to take these steps is beyond the scope of the present chapter, but a more detailed examination of how his career differed from that of Bede's *imperium*-holders would certainly be profitable.

This has been a wide-ranging essay, but I hope that I have been able to raise some questions about the way in which our sources and our perceptions of the English Nation vary across the time-span of Bede's narrative. I also hope to have gone some way towards redressing the trend to seek small beginnings for all the early Anglo-Saxon institutions and towards identifying the need to recognize that medieval people were capable of retaining, contemporaneously, a whole series of separate identities on a variety of scales, each valid within its own context. A lot more work needs to be done to approach an understanding of the origins of Anglo-Saxon kingdoms, but I would like to suggest that we should not be enslaved by a nationalist agenda which merely charts territorial expansion but should concentrate on the evolution of executive power and ask ourselves why particular levels of identity seem to attract this evolution in different societies. If

---

65. For the redrawing of genealogies in this way see, most recently, Charles-Edwards, *Early Irish*, 111–34.
66. This is the distinction that Aristotle draws between a tyrant and a king, that while the latter rules for the public good the former rules to aggrandize power, *Politics*, III, 7.

we must fall back upon a sporting analogy, I would suggest that rather than looking at the knockout competition of a football league we should inspect the organization of cricket. In this sport local, county and national teams and leagues exist with individual players holding membership of teams at all levels simultaneously, the national team being selected from the best county players who in their turn are selected from the best local players. The national team is not merely the best local team, and the emergence of national teams does not render local or county sides redundant. The social evolution that took place in early medieval Europe can be compared, in this analogy, to a shift in the focus of public support from local to national teams, statehood emerging when the public can be persuaded to supply the management with sufficient funds to buy in professional players, trainers and ancillary staff. Indeed, the difference between England and France in the eleventh century could be explained as the introduction of professionalism on a national scale in the former and at the county level in the latter. At all times, however, local, county and national sides continued to play, and public identification controlled their relative importance.

6 'Cockle amongst the Wheat': The Scandinavian Settlement of England[1]

Dawn Hadley

Studies of the Scandinavian settlement of England have been generally predicated on the belief that the settlers were, and long remained, recognizable as an ethnically and culturally distinctive people; the main point of dispute has been the *scale* of the settlement, and a solution to this problem has, in turn, commonly been used to resolve the debate about the *impact* of the Scandinavian settlers. In the light of more recent discussions of ethnicity and identity in the early medieval period I shall question a number of the assumptions inherent in previous studies of the Scandinavian settlement. I aim to demonstrate that the evidence of contemporary and later documentary sources, linguistics and onomastics, archaeology and sculpture will all sustain re-evaluation in the light of these ideas. I hope that this in turn will facilitate new insights into contemporary images and constructions of identity in the Danelaw in the period following the Scandinavian settlement.

The historiography of the Scandinavian settlement

We are told by the Anglo-Saxon Chronicle that Scandinavian raiding turned to settlement towards the end of the ninth century. In 876 the leader of a viking[2] army, Halfdan, 'shared out the land of the

---

1. I would like to thank the editors for their many helpful comments on this chapter.
2. I intend to use the term 'viking' rather than 'Viking' throughout. The term 'viking' is rarely used in contemporary sources, and seems best interpreted as a descriptive term for someone involved in raiding activities. My objection to the term 'Viking' stems from my belief that it represents the reification of a concept which, in fact, was rather nebulous. Moreover, the term is not as frequently used in contemporary documentary sources as are the terms 'pagan' or 'Dane'. See K. Eldjarn, 'The Viking myth', in *The Vikings*, ed. R.T. Farrell (1982), 262–73; D. O'Sullivan, 'Changing views of the viking age', *Medieval History* 2 (1) (1992), 3–13, at 4.

Northumbrians, and they proceeded to plough and to support themselves', and further divisions of land among members of other viking armies took place in parts of Mercia the following year and in East Anglia in 880.[3] In spite of the laconic nature of the documentary sources, the impact of the Scandinavian settlers has traditionally been believed to have been substantial. This supposition rests largely on a perception of the society of the regions in which the Scandinavians took control and settled in the late ninth and early tenth centuries as being quite distinctive. At a later date, the regions of Scandinavian settlement were characterized to varying degrees by Scandinavian place-names, by Scandinavian names for legal and administrative offices and institutions, by a distinctive legal and administrative organization, by large numbers of free peasants (sokemen), by the prevalence of large multi-vill estates (sokes), and by the survival of a range of artefactual evidence which displays iconographic influences from Scandinavia.[4] These aspects of the society of northern and eastern England were once directly attributed to the Scandinavian settlement, and used as an index of the scale of their settlement. Sir Frank Stenton, for example, argued for a massive settlement of Scandinavians, and proposed that it was no accident that 'a social organization to which there is no parallel elsewhere in England occurs in the one part of the country in which the regular development of native institutions had been interrupted by a foreign settlement'.[5] He also maintained that the regions in which the Scandinavians settled were characterized by the presence of two distinct ethnic groups – Danish and English – and that they long continued to be recognizable groups: 'all lines of investigation – linguistic, legal and economic – point to the reality of the difference between Danes and English in the tenth century'.[6] Henry Loyn later observed that the Scandinavians were 'an important recognizable element' in the population and 'a distinct community living under separate laws'.[7] For this group of scholars, the Scandinavian settlement was extensive; it was characterized by a transformation of legal and administrative institutions and of the social structure; and it resulted in a society typified by the distinctive and separate identity of the Danes and the English.

At the other extreme, a number of scholars have denied that the Scandinavian impact was so significant. Peter Sawyer, for example, has

3. *English Historical Documents, I, c.500–1042*, ed. D. Whitelock (2nd edn, 1979) no.1 (hereafter *EHD* I), s.a.876, 877, 880.
4. F.M. Stenton, *Anglo-Saxon England* (3rd edn, 1971), 502–25 [hereafter Stenton, *ASE*]; P.H. Sawyer, *The Age of the Vikings* (2nd edn, 1971), 152–76.
5. Stenton, *ASE*, 519; see also *idem, The Free Peasantry of the Northern Danelaw* (1925–6; repd 1969), 73–185; *idem*, 'The Danes in England', *Proceedings of the British Academy* 13 (1927); for a review see P. Stafford, 'The Danes and the Danelaw', *History Today* (Oct. 1986), 17–23, at 18–19.
6. Stenton, 'The Danes', 41, 46.
7. H. Loyn, *The Vikings in Britain* (1977), 113; D. Ó Corráin, *Ireland before the Normans* (1972).

argued that apart from their settlements and their influence on language, names and the terminology of law and administration, 'the Scandinavians do not seem to have made a distinctive mark on England'.[8] His argument rests on the opinion that the scale of the Scandinavian settlement was not as extensive as had traditionally been believed. For Sawyer, the viking armies were to be numbered in hundreds rather than thousands.[9] Linguists and some historians have, however, not accepted Sawyer's assessment of the small size of the viking armies, and have also argued that whatever the size of the armies, it is unlikely that they could have been responsible for the great impact made by the Scandinavian languages on the place-names, personal names and speech of Anglo-Saxon England. This linguistic impact has come to be accounted for by reference to a possible secondary peasant immigration; albeit an unrecorded event.[10] Although Sawyer's observations on the scale of the Scandinavian settlement have been questioned, his argument that the society and institutions of northern and eastern England owe little to the Scandinavians has, nonetheless, been very influential. Other scholars have demonstrated that many of the peculiarities of these regions can be attributed to differences of terminology. For example, recent studies have identified 'multiple estates' elsewhere in Britain comparable to the sokes of the region, and free peasants analogous to the sokemen; these characteristics of the regions settled by the Scandinavians can no longer be attributed directly to them.[11] This

---

8. Sawyer, *Age of the Vikings*, 172-3.
9. P.H. Sawyer, 'The density of the Danish Settlement in England', *University of Birmingham Journal* 6 (1) (1957), 1-17; *idem, Age of the Vikings*, 154-71.
10. K. Cameron, *Scandinavian Settlement in the Territory of the Five Boroughs: The Place-Name Evidence* (1965); *idem*, 'Scandinavian settlement in the territory of the Five Boroughs: the place-name evidence, part II, place-names in thorp', *Mediaeval Scandinavia* 3 (1970), 35-49; *idem*, 'Scandinavian settlement in the territory of the Five Boroughs: the place-name evidence, part III, the Grimston hybrids', in *England Before the Conquest*, ed. P. Clemoes and K. Hughes (1971), 147-63; Sawyer, *Age of the Vikings*, 154-71; N. Lund, 'The settlers: where do we get them from – and do we need them?', in *Proceedings of the Eighth Viking Congress*, ed. H. Bekker-Nielsen *et al.* (Odense, 1981), 147-71; N.P. Brooks, 'England in the ninth century: the crucible of defeat', *Transactions of the Royal Historical Society* (hereafter *TRHS*) 5th ser., 29 (1979), 1-20.
11. R.H.C. Davis, 'East Anglia and the Danelaw', *TRHS* 5th ser., 5 (1955), 23-39; G.R.J. Jones, 'Basic patterns of settlement distribution in northern England', *Advancement of Science*, 72 (1961), 192-200; *idem*, 'Early territorial organization in Gwynedd and Elmet', *Northern History* 10 (1975), 3-25; *idem*, 'Celts, Saxons and Scandinavians', in *An Historical Geography of England and Wales*, ed. R.A. Dodgshon and R.A. Butlin (1978), 57-79; C.D. Morris, 'Northumbria and the viking settlement: the evidence for land-holding', *Archaeologia Aeliana* 5th ser., 5 (1977), 81-103; *idem*, 'Viking and native in northern England: a case-study', in *Proceedings of the Eighth Viking Congress*, ed. Bekker-Nielsen, 223-44; A.K.G. Kristensen, 'Danelaw institutions and Danish society in the Viking Age: *sochemanni, liberi homines* and *königsfreie*', *Mediaeval Scandinavia* 8 (1975), 27-85; R.K. Morris, *Churches in the Landscape* (1989), 133-9; D.M. Hadley,

research has tended to be ambivalent about the scale of the settlement; it is not now necessary to grapple with that issue in order to demonstrate that the society and institutions of the region survived. Questions about the identities of the inhabitants of the regions where settlement occurred are now rarely posed. One recent account has gone as far as to ask what it was about the viking character that meant that in the Danelaw 'they disappeared'.[12] However, it is possible to go too far in minimizing the Scandinavian influence; the emphasis on continuity and the swift assimilation of the Scandinavians underplays the Scandinavian contribution to the society of the Danelaw and avoids dealing with the matter of why integration might have been so rapid. People do not integrate and adopt the social structures and belief systems of others by a process of unconscious osmosis; real and relevant decisions must be made, survival strategies adopted, and resistance encountered. A consideration of this has been lacking from recent work on the Danelaw.

Research on the impact of the Scandinavian settlement has foundered on the perceived incompatibility of the documentary sources and the place-name evidence; but the way forward lies not in a dismissal of the narrative sources as biased, nor in the generation of new place-name distribution maps nor in the refinement of place-name etymologies, but in the formulation of new questions and approaches. In short, a theorization of the subject is required. Much previous work on the Scandinavian settlement has been informed by a fairly limited understanding of the way in which social identity was constructed in the early medieval period. The traditional correlation of the scale of the Scandinavian settlement with the impact of the Scandinavians and the ethnicity of the inhabitants of the region is too simplistic to be useful. Many of the questions that have been asked of the available evidence are inappropriate – resting, as they do, on fundamental misconceptions about what it was to be 'Danish' or 'English' in the early Middle Ages.

The meaning and purpose of ethnic terminology

The existence of the term 'Danelaw' to describe the main areas of Scandinavian settlement in England has provided support for the argument that the Scandinavian settlers there retained a separate 'ethnic' identity after they settled. However, this assumption is flawed. We do not know when the term 'Danelaw' was coined, nor by whom;

---

contd.
'Conquest, colonization and the Church: ecclesiastical organization in the Danelaw', *Historical Research* 69 (1996), 109–28; Stafford, 'The Danes', 22.
12. J. Richards, *Viking Age England* (1991), 9; my apologies to Dr Richards for picking up on a comment that, while useful to my argument, does not in any way represent the content of his book!

the term is not recorded until a law-code compiled in 1008.[13] The idea of the Danelaw was most fully developed by twelfth-century jurists to define a region in which Danish as opposed to Mercian or West Saxon law was thought to prevail. As Pauline Stafford has observed, this may have been based on nothing more than a recognition that certain regional differences coincided with an area known to have once been under some form of Danish control.[14] Furthermore, it is not now thought that the law of the region exhibited anything more than a Scandinavian influence which may have been largely terminological.[15]

Nonetheless, an explanation is required for the perception of the legal personality of the law as Danish – certainly by the early eleventh century, and perhaps as early as the mid-tenth century when King Edgar legislated separately for 'the Danes'. It is arguable that the reasons for this lie less in the perceived social composition of the region and in the relative numbers of Danish descent, than in the *political* context of the tenth and eleventh centuries. When Edgar legislated (962–63, or possibly in the 970s) that 'there should be in force among the Danes such good laws as they best decide on', it may appear that the Scandinavian settlers were being legislated for separately.[16] It may also seem to offer support for the argument that society was divided into distinctive 'ethnic' groups which could be identified in objective, legal terms. However, this conclusion is problematic. We need to consider the background to Edgar's accession to understand his interest in the 'Danes' in his fourth law code.

Edgar succeeded to the former kingdoms of Mercia, Northumbria and East Anglia two years before he succeeded to southern England, on the death of his brother, Eadwig.[17] The charters issued by Edgar confirm the basis of his support between 957 and 959 as being north of the Thames, whereas Eadwig's support came from the bishops and ealdormen from south of the Thames. The context for Edgar's separate legal provision for northern England lies in the political circumstances of his accession: his accession to the north occurred when he was only fourteen, and just three years after the expulsion of Eric Bloodaxe from York. It has been argued that Edgar was set up by the northern magnates to protect their privileges against royal usurpation. Therefore, Edgar's fourth law code was arguably a measure designed to help a southern king handle the regionalism of the northern part of his kingdom, and a recognition of the support he had received from the

---

13. Literally, 'in the law of the Danes': O. Fenger, 'The Danelaw and the Danish law', *Scandinavian Studies in Law* 16 (1972), 85–96.
14. Stafford, 'The Danes', 19.
15. Fenger, 'The Danelaw'; J.M. Kaye, 'The Sacrabar', *English Historical Review* (hereafter *EHR*) 83 (1968), 744–58; Sawyer, *Age of the Vikings*, 153–4; Stafford, 'The Danes', 19.
16. *EHD* I, no.41.
17. Stenton, *ASE*, 364–72; N. Lund, 'King Edgar and the Danelaw', *Mediaeval Scandinavia* 9 (1976), 181–95.

magnates of those regions between 957 and 959; the law code was a confirmation of his intention to honour their privileges.[18] Edgar's legislation was the product of a specific political context, and may have little to reveal about ethnic relations and identities in northern England.

However, although Edgar's law code may find its context within a particular set of political circumstances, we do need to address the employment of ethnic terminology in this and other broadly contemporary documents. Patrick Amory has recently commented on the application of ethnic labels in legal contexts, noting that they commonly came to be used as territorial identifiers. Increasingly, ethnicity was defined by territorial origin and adherence to a particular law code rather than by blood or descent alone; he has commented that 'law was not so much a result as a major determining factor' of the new ethnic identities forged in the Carolingian period.[19] In other words, the use of an ethnic label may reveal something of the previous history of the region, the way in which it was perceived from an external perspective, and something of the common legal experience of the inhabitants of that region; but it may reveal little about the biological descent of the inhabitants of the region. Moreover, it is unlikely to reveal the ways in which the inhabitants of a region saw themselves. By analogy, the situation in northern England may be summed up thus: pre-existing regionalism was reinforced by successive conquests from Scandinavia and from Dublin; the circumstances of Edgar's accession in the mid-tenth century further emphasized the autonomy of the northern regions; Edgar's separate legislation for the region was a recognition of political reality; and the employment of ethnic terminology derives from a recognition of the regionalism within England as a whole, and is not primarily a reflection of a perceived binary division – between 'Danes' and 'English' – north of the Thames. The reason for the use of an ethnonym must derive in part from the recognition that there had recently been a conquest and settlement from Scandinavia, partly from the fact that some of leading magnates in the region were recognizably of Scandinavian origin, and partly from the prominence of Old Norse in legal and administrative contexts. Old English sources contain about 150 loans from Scandinavian languages, of which most are found in the technical vocabulary: legal, seafaring, and military terms, and words for ranks, measures and coinage.[20] It has, indeed, been argued that the technical nature of the Old English

---

18. Lund, 'King Edgar', 182.
19. P. Amory, 'The meaning and pupose of ethnic terminology in the Burgundian laws', *Early Medieval Europe* 2 (1) (1993), 1–28, at 23.
20. J. Geipel, *The Viking Legacy: The Scandinavian Influence on the English and Gaelic Languages* (1971), 70; B.H. Hansen, 'The historical implications of the Scandinavian element in English: a theoretical valuation', *Nowele* 4 (1984), 53–95; D. Kastovsky, 'Semantics and vocabulary', in *The Cambridge History of the English Language* vol. 1, ed. R.M. Hogg (1992), 290–408, at 320, 332–6.

borrowings marks them out as 'cultural loans',[21] which are 'compatible with a socially superior, more prestigious status of Scandinavian in the Danelaw'.[22] The ruling elite of northern England were not all of Scandinavian extraction in the tenth century, but the conquests of successive armies from Scandinavia when combined with pre-existing separate regional identities and a determination from the leading magnates (of whatever origin) to maintain regional autonomy, alongside the need of southern kings to 'deal with' the North, gave vent to expression of a regional political and legal identity which borrowed much from the newcomers. Thus, historical process in the tenth century saw new 'ethnic' identities formed and these informed the language of law and of territorial identification.[23] It is noteworthy that the region is not always identified as the Danelaw; geographical and other terms – such as East Anglia, Northumbria and *Norðleoda* – are more common. It suggests that the 'Danishness' of the region was only called into play at certain times: times of political conflict.[24]

Danishness might also be noticed in England in the context of the new threat from Scandinavia in the later tenth and early eleventh centuries. Yet, it is not the descendants of Danish immigrants of the late ninth century that are referred to as Danes in sources of this period, but rather recent arrivals, in particular merchants, nobles and political opportunists. It is notable that when Æthelred II ordered the massacre of Danes in 1002 the only place in which it can be shown to have taken effect – Oxford – was far from the regions in which earlier Danish settlement had taken place, and probably affected only recently-arrived urban merchants.[25] As far as the chroniclers were concerned the subjects of the kings of England were English; Danes were invaders and enemies – 'recent Danes' as Susan Reynolds has put it – people who had come recently from Denmark and who might be going back there.[26] If the better-documented situation after the Norman Conquest is in any way comparable, we can see that it was those great lords who maintained strong links with Normandy who – as far as the chroniclers were concerned – retained their Norman identity longest: lesser men with little or no property in Normandy quickly became known as 'English'.[27] Patrick Geary has recently remarked that in the early Middle Ages ethnicity tended to be invoked when an individual

21. L. Bloomfield, *Language* (1935), 461.
22. Kastovsky, 'Semantics and vocabulary', 324.
23. Amory, 'Ethnic terminology', 23; I.N. Wood, 'Ethnicity and ethnogenesis of the Burgundians', in *Typen der Ethnogenese unter besonderer Berücksichtigung der Bayern* 1, ed. H. Wolfram and W. Pohl (Vienna, 1990), 53–69, at 53–5, 63–4.
24. S. Reynolds, 'What do we mean by "Anglo-Saxon" and "Anglo-Saxons"?', *Journal of British Studies* 24 (1985), 395–414, at 408.
25. P. Stafford, *Unification and Conquest: A Political and Social History of England in the Tenth and Eleventh Centuries* (1989), 66.
26. Reynolds, '"Anglo-Saxon" and "Anglo-Saxons"', 409.
27. A. Williams, *The English and the Norman Conquest* (1995), 1–6, 187–219.

seemed 'out of place' in terms of geography or religion, and this observation may be of relevance to understanding some of the references to Danes in England in the tenth and eleventh centuries.[28] It is worth noting that in the early eleventh century Archbishop Wulfstan added to a panegyric on Edgar in the northern recension of the Anglo-Saxon Chronicle that 'he did one ill-deed too greatly. He loved evil foreign customs and brought too firmly heathen manners within the land, and attracted hither foreigners and enticed harmful people to this country'.[29] There was clearly a perception in the early eleventh century that foreigners – almost certainly including 'Danes' – had made their presence felt in English society and that some were not well-received. Yet although there were complaints about the disruptive effect of recent Danish arrivals 'who had sprung up in this island, sprouting like cockle amongst the wheat' (as is lamented in a charter of Æthelred II), there is little evidence to suggest that there was normally thought to have been anything markedly Scandinavian about eleventh-century society; inter-marriage was common and the descendants of these Danish immigrants quickly came to be identified as English.[30]

Recent studies of the construction of ethnic identity have rejected the notion that ethnicity was an objective phenomenon which invariably created antagonism, and instead have explored the extent to which ethnicity might be mobilized in the context of political conflict, as a means of moulding an identity and a sense of community in opposition to one's enemies.[31] Such reasoning may be applied to the political events of the tenth and early eleventh centuries, events that have frequently been adduced as further evidence for the reality of ethnic difference in the Danelaw. In the early tenth century, successive viking rulers captured York, and in 940 Olaf Guthfrithson used this as a base to expand control south of the Humber.[32] Although previous Scandinavian settlement may have aroused the ambitions of such rulers, in practice they relied upon native support, such as that provided by Archbishop Wulfstan, and there is little to support the claim that Olaf was attempting to unite 'Danish' England. If Olaf was capitalizing on any pre-existing sense of identity it was as likely to have been the claims of earlier Deiran kings of York who had sometimes ruled south of the Humber.[33] 'Ethnic' differences have also been seen behind the later activities of Swegn, who in 1013 acquired the

28. P. Geary, 'Ethnic identity as a situational construct in the early Middle Ages', *Mitteilungen der Anthropologischen Gesellschaft in Wien* 113 (1983), 15–26.
29. *EHD* I, no.1, s.a.959; Stenton, *ASC*, 371, n.2.
30. A. Williams, ' "Cockle amongst the wheat": Danes and English in the western Midlands in the first half of the eleventh century', *Midland History* 11 (1986), 1–22.
31. F. Barth, *Ethnic Groups and Boundaries: The Social Organisation of Cultural Difference* (Oslo, 1969); H. Wolfram, *History of the Goths* (Berkeley, 1980); Geary, 'Ethnic identity', 25.
32. Stenton, *ASE*, 323–43, 356–8.
33. Stafford, *Unification and Conquest*, 65.

submission of England north of Watling Street before ravaging southwards;[34] however, there are good reasons to question this assessment. It is certainly possible that the former area of Scandinavian settlement may have shaped the aspirations of Swegn, but there is no evidence that his support was anything other than regional. In fact, unlike Olaf, Swegn did not launch his assault from York, the focal point of earlier Scandinavian rule, but from Gainsborough on the river Trent; this decision may have been encouraged by knowledge of the disaffection of leading noble families in the North Midlands and by the presence of recently-arrived Danish merchants in the urban centres of the region.[35] Swegn may possibly have harboured notions of mobilizing ethnic support in the region, but if he did we should not suppose that he simply called on the descendants of earlier Scandinavian settlers. As we shall see, after a century and a half of intermarriage and social mixing the Scandinavian settlers, irrespective of their numbers, could barely have maintained a completely separate existence and identity, which could be readily mobilized by Swegn. It is improbable that one would have been able at that time to distinguish people of exclusively English or Danish descent; thus, if Swegn wanted to draw on 'Scandinavian' support, it would have to be from a people who had become firmly welded to native society.[36] Swegn's activities were, in any case, part of an attempt to capture the English kingdom from the north; there is no evidence that it was a movement to unite the 'Danish' parts of England. The areas that submitted to him did not do so in terms of 'ethnic' affiliation but as administrative units: the ealdormanries of Lindsey and Northumbria, and the Five Boroughs (Derby, Nottingham, Lincoln, Leicester and Stamford). Furthermore, it is noteworthy that there is an absence of what Pauline Stafford calls an 'ethnic voice' in the various recorded disputes of the late tenth and early eleventh centuries; regional grievances are more prominent.[37] While regional disputes and political manoeuvring may have revived memories of the diverse ancestry of inhabitants of parts of England in the tenth and eleventh centuries, they do not provide evidence for innate ethnic differences, nor do they prove that existing 'ethnic' differences were the cause of such antagonisms.

References to Danes in the tenth and eleventh centuries have more than one context: the political disunity of the English kingdom; and the

---

34. D. Whitelock, introduction to *EHD* I, 48; W.E. Kapelle, *The Norman Conquest of the North: A Region and Its Transformation 1000–1135* (1979), 14–15; Stenton, ASE, 384–5; Reynolds, ' "Anglo-Saxon" and "Anglo-Saxons" ', 410–11. Ethnic loyalties have been sought as an explanation for the conflicts of Edward the Confessor's reign and for the allegedly incomplete unity of England in 1066; F. Barlow, *Edward the Confessor* (1970), 89, 92–3, 102, 191–2; Kapelle, *The Norman Conquest of the North*, 12–15, 28–9, 47; R.A. Brown, 'The Norman Conquest', *TRHS* 5th ser., 17 (1967), 109–10, 116–20; cf. Reynolds, ' "Anglo-Saxon" and "Anglo-Saxons" ', 406–7.
35. Stafford, *Unification and Conquest*, 65–6.
36. Reynolds, ' "Anglo-Saxon" and "Anglo-Saxons" ', 407.

continuing arrival of merchants and political opportunists from Denmark. Irrespective of the scale of the Scandinavian settlement, there is little in the documentary evidence to suggest that the descendants of the Danish settlers of the late ninth century continued to be regarded as such. The use of ethnic terminology is generally related to specific situations of conflict in England, and substantiates Amory's observation that 'ethnic terminology could be the instrument of political agendas'.[38] The mere existence of the 'Danelaw' and references to 'Danes' in England is not a very sound basis for any argument concerning the ethnic affiliations of the majority of the inhabitants of northern and eastern England. That is not to say that individuals in the Danelaw never felt themselves to be 'English' or 'Danish', but rather that the documentary evidence we have for such feelings is less substantive than is sometimes supposed.[39]

The Scandinavian settlers

Before it is possible to discuss the relations forged between the Scandinavian settlers and the native population it is essential to consider whether the settlers shared a common identity with each other. There has been a tendency to emphasize the unity of the vikings and of the viking phenomenon, with insufficient emphasis being placed on the diversity of interests and identities which the raiders and settlers displayed; as Deirdre O'Sullivan has observed, 'by starting with a studyable commodity, a group of people or even peoples called the vikings, we are setting the terms of reference for our investigations, and we are setting them too narrowly'.[40] Even the smaller raiding parties may not have been composed exclusively of people who thought of themselves as Danes, or of people from the same region. Viking armies operated far and wide and had a great capacity to attract allies and followers from the regions they raided.[41] They were also prepared to change sides in a conflict, and to unite with their former victims if the prospects of booty were good.[42] The creation of a great army in the 860s – which drew together a number of viking leaders and their war bands – may have contributed to a sense of common interests, and it is precisely when peoples come into contact with other peoples that such common identities may be forged; and so the creation of a great army in the 860s may have created a

---

37. P. Stafford, 'The reign of Æthelred II: a study in the limitations on royal policy', in *Ethelred the Unready*, ed. D. Hill (1978), 17–21.
38. Amory, 'Ethnic terminology', 28.
39. Reynolds, ' "Anglo-Saxon" and "Anglo-Saxons" ', 411.
40. O'Sullivan, 'Changing views of the viking age', 4.
41. N. Lund, 'Allies of God or man? The viking expansion in a European context', *Viator* 29 (1989), 45–59.
42. *Ibid.*, 47.

common purpose. However, it is quite another matter to suggest that the participants in these events would have described these interests as 'Danish'.[43]

Settlement is a different proposition from raiding, at which point it is arguable that the ultimate origin of viking leaders and their followers became irrelevant, and political reality overlay any feelings of ethnic identity and military solidarity. Furthermore, once settlement began, the notionally divergent interests of the native population and the Scandinavian settlers must have been thrown into confusion by subsequent conquests of the region by the kings of Wessex and of Dublin, and by the vying for power of indigenous ruling families such as the Bernician earls of Bamburgh.[44] Although a simple distinction is sometimes made between 'Scandinavian' and 'English' interests in the tenth century it is not easy to see how, given the political and military context, such separate interest groups could have been maintained by the majority of people. That is not to deny that the kings of Wessex manipulated the concept of Englishness for political purposes, but it cannot be claimed that this was meaningful to the majority of the population; indeed, the main audience for such propaganda may have been Wessex itself rather than the whole of England.[45]

There is a tendency to depict the settlers as an undifferentiated mass.[46] However, it is arguable that, for the leaders of the Scandinavian settlers, political reality soon overlaid any common interest based on language or region of origin, which they may have felt with the peasant hordes who are supposed to have followed them. Men like Ivarr, Halfdan, Guthrum, Guthfrith or Ragnald relied upon and rewarded indigenous support, in addition to their own followers.[47] The elites, of whatever origin, manipulated landed estates, administrative units, strongholds, trading centres and the peasantry, whether native or from Scandinavia. Yet the power base of rulers in the Danelaw depended on commanding the support of, or subjugating, other powerful figures and had little to do with marshalling the support of peasants, and still less to do with maintaining divisions between 'Danish' and 'English' peasants. For the peasantry themselves issues of identity may have been rather different. Primarily their identities would have been forged in the communities and estates within which they lived and worked. Native peasants may well have reacted unfavourably to newcomers, although the details are hidden from

---

43. Brooks, 'The crucible of defeat', 8–11.
44. Stenton, *Anglo-Saxon England*, 323–63.
45. See, for example, David Rollason's argument that Athelstan promoted the cult of St Cuthbert (a Northumbrian saint) largely for its benefits to his rule in Wessex: D. Rollason, 'St Cuthbert and Wessex: the evidence of Cambridge, Corpus Christi College MS 183', in *St Cuthbert: His Cult and His Community to AD 1200*, ed. G. Bonner *et al.* (1989), 413–24.
46. Stenton, 'The Danes', 46.
47. Morris, 'Northumbria and the viking settlement', 83–4.

view in the documentary evidence. In order to explore further the ways in which the Scandinavian settlers of the late ninth and early tenth centuries were perceived, how they may have perceived themselves, and the ways in which they forged relationships with the native population, we need to consider linguistic and archaeological evidence.

Linguistic evidence

In addition to the vast corpus of Scandinavian place-names and personal names, Scandinavian influence is also manifest in lexical items of Old English and in its grammatical construction. Although the intensity of the influence is not in doubt, much less certain is its temporal deployment, the relationship between linguistic influence and the scale of the Scandinavian settlement, and its relevance to our understanding of relations between the Scandinavian settlers and the native population. Old English sources contain about 150 loans from Scandinavian languages – mostly in the technical vocabulary – but in Middle English sources there are many thousands.[48] The loans in Old English sources reflect social interaction only in the administrative and legal spheres, but many of the Middle English borrowings can, according to Dieter Kastovsky, only be accounted for by 'assuming the existence of a mixed speech community operating on the basis of social and cultural equality'.[49] One might express reservations about the appropriateness of the word 'equality', but the general point seems to be that the influence of the Scandinavian languages derives from the settlement of more than a few hundred aristocrats, and betokens social mixing across a much broader level of society.[50] The Scandinavian influence on English has been described by linguists in terms of 'eine Sprachmischung',[51] 'fusion'[52] or 'intimate mingling'.[53] More recently these relatively vague terms have been elucidated in detail, in particular by comparison with what is known of analogous situations of language contact. In such contexts, substantial influence requires a combination of mutual intelligibility, bilingualism and a period of coexistence of the two languages. Given that Scandinavian and English are part of the Germanic language family, some level of mutual comprehension can have been expected.[54] One linguist has recently

---

48. See n.20.
49. Kastovsky, 'Semantics and vocabulary', 324.
50. Hansen, 'The Scandinavian element in English', 79.
51. D. Hofmann, *Nordisch-Englische Lehnbeziehungen der Wikingerzeit* (Copenhagen, 1955), 175.
52. Geipel, *The Viking Legacy*, 14.
53. A.C. Baugh and T. Cable, *A History of the English Language* (3rd edn, 1978), 101.
54. Geipel, *The Viking Legacy*, 57; Baugh and Cable, *A History of the English Language*, 95 ; P. Poussa, 'The evolution of early Standard English: the creolization hypothesis', *Studia Anglica Posnaniensia* 14 (1982), 69–85, at 72.

observed that the mutual comprehension of English and Scandinavian speakers would have been sufficient to facilitate contact 'in everyday standard situations', but would have rendered a fluent conversation 'rather tiresome'.[55] Bilingualism may, then, have been an important vehicle for the influence of Scandinavian on English. An obvious immediate cause of this was intermarriage; that this occurred is indicated by the relatively slow rate at which Scandinavian female names filtered through into the naming stock of England, seemingly reflecting the low numbers of Scandinavian women who settled in England.[56] The requirements of trade and marketing must also have been important in fostering the emergence of mutual intelligibility of English and Scandinavian speakers.

It would be uncontroversial to state that Scandinavian remained a spoken language in the Danelaw for some time,[57] although the absence of any Scandinavian manuscripts from the Danelaw after 1200 must reflect that Old Norse was chiefly a spoken language and that it was replaced by English at some point before then.[58] Such a linguistic development is paralleled elsewhere; it is a situation in which the death of a language is concurrent with a language shift, in which speakers of the dying language switch to speaking a co-existent language. These processes offer a plausible explanation of the different effects on the English language: the loans into Old English stem from a period of bilingualism, from the influence of a small number of aristocrats and from the adoption of Scandinavian terms by English speakers during a period when Scandinavian was, even if temporally and geographically limited, the more prestigious language; the borrowings recorded in Middle English sources, however, derive from an influx of greater numbers of Scandinavian descent and their ultimate switch to speaking English, which eventually became the target language. The linguistic evidence, therefore, reflects related but distinct processes. Furthermore, what the linguistic evidence reveals is not the scale of the Scandinavian settlement, but the level of *contact* between Scandinavian and English speakers. These are separate propositions. Social contact and intermixing were required for this level of language change; and in this context the total usurpation of one community by another and the maintenance of separate social and cultural domains by the indigenous population and the Scandinavian settlers seem implausible. John Hines has described the impact of Old Norse in the following manner: 'The product [of Anglo-Scandinavian acculturation] is a mixed culture which is consciously articulated at the

---

55. Kastovsky, 'Semantics and vocabulary', 328–9.
56.   C. Clark, 'Clark's first three laws of applied anthroponymics', *Nomina* 3 (1979), 13–19, at 17–18.
57.   R.I. Page, 'How long did the Scandinavian language survive in England? The epigraphical evidence', in *England Before the Conquest*, ed. Clemoes and Hughes, 165–80.
58. Kastovsky, 'Semantics and vocabulary', 331.

highest social and most sophisticated artistic level, not simply the thoughtless confusion of cultures in contact ... [the] elaborate range of Scandinavian English was produced as a deliberate act and was part of the particular instances of acculturation. Culturally and linguistically these developments follow the sociolinguistic axiom that distinctive language forms ... are commonly used as "acts of identity" for individuals and groups, embodying an identity of speakers as members of a particular group, not just as classified by an analytical observer but as they wish to present themselves'.[59] This presents a challenge for future work, and suggests that linguistic evidence may be read in a similar manner to historical and archaeological evidence for an understanding of cultural change.

Do place-names have anything to reveal about the relationships between the settlers and the indigenous populations? On a technical level the infiltration of Scandinavian naming elements was facilitated by the similarity of the Old English and Scandinavian modes of place-name formation, and of place-name elements, although the Scandinavians certainly brought with them new elements; of which the most common is -*by*, 'farmstead/settlement'.[60] The Scandinavian influence also extended to pronunciation.[61] Yet although the Scandinavian influence on place-name forms was unquestionably great, the distribution of Scandinavian place-names is arguably surprising. Given the apparent dominance of Scandinavian in technical and administrative terminology, it seems incongruous that the major settlement and administrative centres should so conspicuously have Old English names. Furthermore, the bulk of the Scandinavian place-names are seemingly located away from the most densely settled regions, and on the periphery of estates.[62] This presents a dichotomy, which may reveal something about the context of place-name formation and transmission. On the one hand, the density of Scandinavian place-names and the impact of Scandinavian pronunciation on English place-names may reflect the density of their settlement and/or their cultural dominance in the districts concerned. On the other hand, the most prominent place-names in the region remained Old English, suggesting that in spite of the apparent social prestige of Scandinavian during the Old English period this did not, in the long term, impact on place-name formation. This may reflect the fact that some estates remained in

59. J. Hines, 'Scandinavian English: a creole in context', in *Language Contact in the British Isles*, ed. P. S. Ureland and G. Broderick (Tübingen, 1991), 403–27, at 417–18.
60. G. Fellows-Jensen, *Scandinavian Settlement Names in the East Midlands* (Copenhagen, 1978), 10–12.
61. C. Clark, 'Onomastics', in *The Cambridge History of the English Language* vol. 1, ed. Hogg, 452–89, at 483–4.
62. G.R.J. Jones, 'Early territorial organization in northern England and its bearing on the Scandinavian settlement', in *The Fourth Viking Congress*, ed. A. Small (1965), 67–84; C.D. Morris, 'Aspects of Scandinavian settlement in northern England: a review', *Northern History* 20 (1984), 1–22, at 5–9.

native hands.[63] However, another possible explanation is that in this aspect of naming strategies the Scandinavian rulers were concerned to adapt themselves to native practices. It is striking that the Scandinavian settlers for whom we have any details seem quickly to have adapted themselves to the native way of ruling and adopted pre-existing mediums of control. Perhaps the retention of Old English estate names was part of the same strategy as the issuing of coinage, the forging of relations with native lords and ecclesiastics, the adoption of Christianity, and the patronage of monumental stone sculpture (see pp. 131–35): it was a means to control and to legitimate their rule by reference to existing systems of power and social organization. It should be noted, however, that there is a difference between the coining of place-names and the recording of those names: nonetheless, our evidence reveals that whatever the cultural, social or political impact of the Scandinavian settlers in the Danelaw, the pre-existing names for the overwhelming majority of important places survived in use and remained in, or entered into, the written record.

Nevertheless, at some point there seems to have been a sizeable influx of settlers who influenced place-names to a much greater extent. The question arises of whether the distribution of Scandinavian place-names may be used as a guide to either the extent, chronology or nature of this settlement; and whether, in turn, this allows us to say anything about the nature of ethnic identity in the region. The partial or complete scandinavianization of existing place-names, and the foundation of new settlements following colonization, doubtless account for the great density of Scandinavian place-names,[64] but the implications of these divergent processes differ. Partial renaming necessitates a degree of interaction between the settlers and the incoming population, whereas colonization suggests a substantial influx of settlers which need not have involved very much contact between the two groups. Recent studies, however, have questioned the extent to which there was colonization of new land, suggesting instead that the proliferation of Scandinavian place-names may be plausibly attributed to the fragmentation of estates and to the emergence of a vigorous land market in the tenth century.[65] In other words, this is

63. P.H. Sawyer, *Kings and Vikings* (1982), 103–4.
64. Cameron, *Scandinavian Settlement*, 12; *idem*, 'Place-names in thorp'; *idem*, 'The Grimston hybrids'; Fellows Jensen, *Scandinavian Settlement Names in the East Midlands*, 12, 37, 43, 60, 67, 292–4; M. Gelling, *Signposts to the Past* (1978), 226; Morris, 'Aspects of Scandinavian Settlement', 8–9, 12–16; G. Fellows Jensen, 'Scandinavian settlement in Yorkshire – through the rear-view mirror', in *Scandinavian Settlement in Northern Britain*, ed. B.E. Crawford (1995), 170–86.
65. A. Everitt, 'River and wold: Reflections on the historical origin of regions and pays', *Journal of Historical Geography* 3 (1977), 1–19; *idem*, 'The wolds once more', *Journal of Historical Geography* 5 (1979), 67–78; H.S.A. Fox, 'The people of the wolds in English settlement history', in *The Rural Settlements of Medieval England*, ed. M. Aston, D. Austin and C. Dyer (1989), 77–101; Fellows Jensen,

more evidence to indicate that the creation of Scandinavian place-names owes much to contact and interaction between natives and settlers. We have to recognize that place-names were formed, retained and replaced in response to a complex series of circumstances; the chronology of place-name formation was not as simple nor as linear as many accounts have maintained. The distribution of Scandinavian place-names – as much as the evidence for the impact of Scandinavian languages on Old English – reveals a series of processes of interaction between the indigenous populations and the newcomers.

There are also reasons to doubt the commonly held relationship between the distribution of Scandinavian place-names and the areas of Scandinavian settlement. We know that newly arrived Scandinavian lords took over estates without causing the name of the estate centre to change, certainly in the long run.[66] Regions with a dearth of Scandinavian place-names may nevertheless have experienced a significant influx of Scandinavians, to judge from the occurrence in these same areas of large numbers of Scandinavian names for landscape features.[67] Furthermore, the location of stone sculpture displaying Scandinavian motifs at sites with Old English place-names similarly reveals problems in associating Scandinavian settlement with Scandinavian settlement names; the patrons of such sculpture were not necessarily of Scandinavian origin, but some surely were, and the adoption of Scandinavian motifs by native patrons must reflect some level of interaction with, and knowledge of, Scandinavian settlers. We cannot, conversely, assume that any settlement with a Scandinavian name ever contained only people of Scandinavian descent: the Scandinavian place-name Ingleby (farmstead/village of the English) is a reminder of the weaknesses of such assumptions. Place-names such as Ingleby, Danby (farmstead/village of the Danes) and Normanby/ Normanton (farmstead/village of the Northmen) may seem to reflect a degree of ethnic separateness, yet the picture was clearly more complex than that: for example, Ingleby (Derbs) is the site of a cremation cemetery at which Scandinavian-style artefacts have been

---

contd.

'Scandinavian settlement in Yorkshire', 181–3; Sawyer, *Kings and Vikings*, 103–4; *idem*, 'Some sources for the history of viking Northumbria', in *Viking Age York and the North*, ed. R.A. Hall (1976), 3–7, at 7 ; D. Roffe, 'An introduction to the Derbyshire Domesday', in *The Derbyshire Domesday*, Alecto Historical Editions (1990), 1–27, at 11.

66. F.M. Stenton, *Types of Manorial Structure in the Northern Danelaw* (1910), 74–5; Morris, 'Aspects of Scandinavian settlement', 6–10.

67. G. Fellows Jensen, *Scandinavian Settlement Names in Yorkshire* (Copenhagen, 1972), 118; K. Cameron, 'Early Field-Names in an English-Named Lincolnshire village' in *Otium et Negotium*, ed. F. Sandgren (Stockholm, 1973), 38–43, at 41; Lund, 'The Settlers', 156–67; V.E. Watts, 'Place-Names of the Darlington Area', in *Darlington: a Topographical Study*, ed. P.A.G. Clark and N.F. Pearson (1978), 40–3; C.D. Morris, 'The Pre-Norman Sculpture of the Darlington Area', in *ibid.*, 44–51; *idem*, 'Scandinavian Settlement', 8.

found.[68] Whoever lived there, and however they constructed their identity, one thing is certain: we cannot explore this by positing a simple binary opposition between 'Danish' and 'English'.

One final point to be made about Scandinavian place-names concerns the nature of land-holding in the Danelaw. Attitudes to land in the Scandinavian homelands were seemingly rather different from those that obtained in Anglo-Saxon England, and it is notable that place-names formed with -*by* in Scandinavia have a much lower incidence of personal names as their first element than is the case in England.[69] Consequently, the incidence of Scandinavian personal names in the place-names of the Danelaw suggests both contact with natives and adaptation to local attitudes to land. Together with the fact that a person bearing a Scandinavian name was not necessarily of Scandinavian origin, this dictates that this group of place-names cannot be taken in isolation as an index of exclusively Scandinavian activity. We also have to be more aware than is currently the case that, as has been said, the coining and the recording of place-names are not the same thing: the final record of names, several centuries after the initial phases of settlement, may be misleading when it comes to assessing the impact of the Scandinavian settlers. Even if we had a better understanding of the context in which place-names were coined their distribution cannot be used as a guide to the locations of peoples: we should not be tempted to divide the countryside into areas of English and Scandinavian settlements on the basis of place-name evidence alone, because this depends on assumptions about 'ethnic' separation and continuity that are difficult to sustain.

The Danelaw is also characterized by a plethora of Old Norse personal names.[70] However, personal names are not a reliable guide to descent and any conclusions drawn from them must be tempered by the knowledge that at a later date, the same family might have some members who bore Old English names, and others who bore Scandinavian names.[71] A more profitable line of enquiry would be to consider why native families began to employ the personal names of the newcomers; this process also occurred after the Norman Conquest

---

68. *The Place-Names of Derbyshire*, ed. K. Cameron, English Place-Names Society, vols 27–9 (1959), 639.
69. P. Wormald, 'Viking studies: whence and whither?', in *The Vikings*, ed. Farrell, 128–51, at 144–8; K. Hald, *Vore Stednavne* (Copenhagen, 1965), 109–13; Fellows Jensen, *East Midlands*, 15–17, 27–8.
70. Clark, 'Clark's first three laws', 13–19.
71. F.M. Stenton, *Documents Illustrative of the Social and Economic History of the Danelaw* (1920), cxiv–xv; O. von Feilitzen, *The Pre-Conquest Personal Names of Domesday Book* (Uppsala, 1937), 18–26; E. Ekwall, 'The proportion of Scandinavian settlers in the Danelaw', *Saga-Book of the Viking Society*, 12 (1937–45), 19–34; Davis, 'East Anglia', 29; D. Whitelock, 'Scandinavian personal names in the *Liber Vitae* of Thorney Abbey', *Saga-Book of the Viking Society*, 12 (1937–45), 127–53; G. Fellows Jensen, *Scandinavian Personal Names in Lincolnshire and Yorkshire* (Copenhagen, 1968).

and it appears that, as well as simply starting a new fashion in nomenclature, these conquests encouraged families to utilize naming strategies in order to align themselves – or, strictly, their children – self-consciously with their new overlords.[72] Naming processes may also have much to reveal about class and professional allegiances.[73]

In sum, the linguistic evidence from the Danelaw has much to reveal about *interaction* between the native population and the Scandinavian settlers, and if the linguistic evidence is to continue to dominate in Viking Studies we have to grasp this point. The evidence for this is manifold: the emergence of, effectively, an Anglo-Scandinavian language; hybrid place-names containing both Old Norse and Old English elements; the scandinavianization of pronunciation and spelling; the proliferation of Scandinavian personal names in place-names; the fragmentation of estates resulting in the creation of new Scandinavian place-names; the presence of Scandinavian settlement (evidenced in documentary sources and by sculpture) at places with Old English names; the presence of both Old English and Old Norse place-names in the same estate; the wealth of Old Norse words for landscape features alongside surviving Old English names. This evidence suggests that old notions about the separateness of the Scandinavians are unfounded; furthermore, as far as the subjective identities of the inhabitants of the regions are concerned, it indicates a period when language and naming processes became an arena for social interaction and the exercise of power, in which linguistic borrowings were made for divergent, and perhaps contradictory, purposes. Much work on place-names has presented a simplified version of events following the Scandinavian settlement; events which, as we shall see, can be shown from historical and archaeological evidence to have been temporally and culturally complex phenomena.[74]

Christianity and the Scandinavian settlers

It has traditionally been thought that the Scandinavian settlers were distinguishable from the native population on account of their paganism, but that nonetheless they quickly adopted Christianity and abandoned their pagan practices. Such an assessment is, however, inadequate. We need to consider the mechanisms by which the Scandinavian settlers and the native population adapted themselves to each other. Certainly viking armies were not prevented by their

---

72. Clark, 'Clark's first three laws', 15–17; Williams, *The English and the Norman Conquest*, 199–208.
73. Amory, 'Names, "ethnic identity" and community', *passim*.
74. For such observations about linguistic research in a different context see, M. Pluciennik, 'A perilous but necessary search: archaeology and European identities', in *Nationalism and Archaeology*, ed. J. Atkinson *et al.* (1996), 35–58, at 46–9.

paganism from finding allies among the peoples they were raiding.[75] What has always been seen as striking is the low incidence of evidence for 'active paganism' in the Danelaw: a number of burials accompanied by grave goods and cremation burials have been cited as examples of 'pagan' burial practice; and some of the motifs on the monumental sculpture of the region, including depictions of armed warriors and scenes from pagan mythology, have also sometimes been identified as further evidence for pagan practice. Yet this evidence is ambiguous. Many of the burials with grave goods were located within churchyards, and there are few examples of cremation which securely belong to this period: indeed, the corpus of what are in reality 'unusual' burials rather than certainly pagan or Scandinavian burials is limited to fewer than thirty sites in northern and eastern England.[76] This burial evidence, and especially its dearth, has given rise to various interpretations relating to the conversion of the vikings.[77] Yet, there is nothing inherently un-Christian about inhumation with grave goods, and cremation is rare in the region. Moreover, the supposedly pagan iconography on the stone sculpture may be interpreted in other ways, as we shall see. It is necessary, then, to set the burial and sculptural evidence in its wider social context.

First and foremost, grave goods are not evidence for pagan beliefs; grave goods within a Christian context are known across the Continent. Grave goods and funerary display have more to reveal about social stress and competition, and even if these burials did indicate the presence of Scandinavian settlers, they do not prove that they were created in antagonism to Christian beliefs.[78] Whatever the personal beliefs and practices of the leaders of the Scandinavians who settled in England, at a very early date they underwent a process of Christianization and were prepared to work with and accept the

---

75. Lund, 'Viking expansion', 50–1.
76. Richards, *Viking Age England*, 111; D.M. Wilson, 'Scandinavians in England', in *The Archaeology of Anglo-Saxon England*, ed. *idem* (1976), 393–403, at 396–7. Perhaps there were many more examples of accompanied burials which have not been discovered precisely because they were located at sites which continued to be used for burial long afterwards.
77. J. Graham-Campbell, 'The Scandinavian Viking-Age burials of England – some problems of interpretation', in *Anglo-Saxon Cemeteries*, ed. P. Rahtz (BAR Brit. Series, 82, 1980), 379–82; M. Biddle and B. Kjolbye-Biddle, *Repton 1986: An Interim Report* (1986); M. Biddle, 'A parcel of pennies from a mass-burial associated with the Viking wintering at Repton in 873–4', *British Numismatic Journal* 56 (1986), 25–30; Wilson, 'Scandinavians in England'; *idem*, 'Scandinavian settlement in the north and west of the British Isles: an archaeological point-of- view', *TRHS*, 5th ser., 26 (1976), 95–113; J. Graham-Campbell, 'Pagans and Christians', *History Today* 36 (1986), 24–8; M. Biddle and B. Kjolbye-Biddle, 'Repton and the Vikings', *Antiquity* 66 (1990), 36–51; R. Hodges, *The Anglo-Saxon Achievement* (1989), 153–4.
78. D. Bullough, 'Burial, community and belief in the early medieval West', in *Ideal and Reality in Frankish and Anglo-Saxon Society*, ed. P. Wormald *et al.* (1983), 177–201, at 185–6.

guidance of ecclesiastics. Well-known examples of this process include the mutually beneficial relationship between Archbishop Wulfstan and successive viking leaders at York, the promotion of the interests of the viking Guthfrith by the community of St Cuthbert, and the readiness with which Scandinavian rulers issued coinage in their name which also bore the names of Christian saints.[79] Yet this is not necessarily a reliable guide to the personal beliefs of those leaders, still less of the peasant settlers who apparently accompanied them. It is important to draw this distinction between private conversion and public Christianization; a distinction which may hold important clues for explaining the apparently contradictory nature of the documentary and archaeological evidence. It is not clear what the impact of the Church on the burial practices of the Scandinavian settlers would have been. By way of analogy, it is useful to note that following the Christianization of Scandinavia at a later date, there is archaeological evidence to suggest that the reception of Christianity was not even. Contemporary examples of churchyard burials, burials with grave goods and votive offerings in rivers have been discovered in the same locality, and this suggests that even near-neighbours responded to Christianity in different ways and that burial practices did not change uniformly, if at all.[80] It is as dangerous to deduce religious belief, as much as it is 'ethnic' origin, on the basis of burial practice alone.[81] It is also worth noting that the regions of Scandinavia were not characterized during the Viking Age by a single burial rite, and that there was some variation in burial rite and location in England, and therefore our attempts to identify the Scandinavian settlers on the basis of an intrusive burial rite may be misguided.[82] In the context of settlement, and of contact with new societies and belief systems, it would not be surprising to find that Scandinavian newcomers to England concerned themselves with a variety of burial practices. For evidence of 'Scandinavian' burial we have been encouraged to look for burials accompanied by grave goods and cremations, but this is only part of the story. We should scarcely need to be reminded that the dead do not bury themselves and that burial ritual portrays much about an identity

79. P. Grierson and M.A.S. Blackburn (ed.) *Medieval European Coinage* (1986), 319–23.

80. L. Ersgard, 'The change of religion and its artefacts: an example from Upper Dalarna', *Papers of the Archaeological Institute*, new ser., 10 (Lund, 1993–4), 79–94; I. Wood, 'Christians and pagans in ninth-century Scandinavia', in *The Christianization of Scandinavia*, ed. P. Sawyer, B. Sawyer and I. Wood (Alingsas, 1987), 36–67.

81. The problem concerning viking burial is reminiscent of the debate about Anglo-Saxon burial in the post-Conversion period: J. Blair, *Anglo-Saxon Oxfordshire* (1994), 70–3; D.M. Hadley, 'The historical context of the inhumation cemetery at Bromfield, Shropshire', *Transactions of the Shropshire Archaeological and Historical Society* 70 (1995), 146–55.

82. E. Roesdahl, 'The archaeological evidence for Conversion', in *The Christianization of Scandinavia*, ed. Sawyer, Sawyer and Wood, 2–3.

conceived by the extant members of the group; accordingly it is equally plausible that Scandinavian settlers, whatever their daily practices may have been, should have been tempted to adopt the burial practices and cemeteries of the native population when burying their dead, as well as to found their own cemeteries and to retain their own burial rites. We have to remain open to the likelihood that unaccompanied churchyard and non-churchyard burials, as much as accompanied burials and cremations, may have been a forum for the negotiation of social roles and relations, and that diverse burial practices were employed by both the indigenous population and the settlers. This is more nuanced interpretation than has traditionally been presented, and future discussions would profit from considering the wider social context of burial.

The sculptural evidence has also been hotly debated. Stone sculpture production was an ecclesiastical preserve in England on the eve of the Scandinavian settlement, and was known to only parts of Scandinavia. Most examples of the so-called Anglo-Scandinavian sculpture are located in and around churches, even those which seem to make explicit reference to 'pagan' symbolism. Our interpretation of this sculptural evidence is complicated by lack of evidence about its production and patronage. It is found in some locations which were continuously associated with surviving native lords or religious communities, at York and Chester-le-Street, for example, so the Scandinavian stylistic influence must have been embraced by indigenous lords.[83] It is important to note that the symbols generally regarded as being overtly 'pagan' – such as the heroic scenes involving Sigurd and Weland on sculptural fragments from Lancashire and Yorkshire[84] – occur on only a small percentage of the total corpus of Anglo-Scandinavian sculpture, and are depicted alongside traditional Christian iconography; even in those instances, Richard Bailey has urged us to think in terms of a 'fusion' of styles rather than the 'overwhelming of one by the other'.[85] More recently, Bailey has argued that many of the scenes commonly described as 'pagan' could be interpreted as Christian teaching and art 'being presented in Scandinavian terms'. Others could be indicative of aristocratic patronage and would be better described as 'secular'; they are a reflection of the 'martial ideals' of their patrons, and as compatible

---

83. R. Cramp, 'The Pre-Conquest sculptural tradition in Durham', in *Medieval Art and Architecture at Durham Cathedral*, Transactions of the British Archaeological Association (1980), 1–10; J. Lang, 'Recent studies in the Pre-Conquest sculpture of Northumbria' in *Studies in Medieval Sculpture*, ed. F.H. Thompson (1983), 177–89; R.N. Bailey, *Viking Age Sculpture in Northern England* (1980).
84. J. Lang, 'Sigurd and Weland in pre-Conquest carving from northern England', *Yorkshire Archaeological Journal*, 48 (1976), 83–94; cf. *idem*, 'Illustrative carving of the viking period at Sockburn on Tees', *Archaeologia Aeliana*, 4th ser., 1 (1972), 235–48.
85. Lang, 'Pre-Conquest sculpture', 187.

with 'Christian' values as was the poem *Beowulf*, which Patrick Wormald has observed reflects the 'aristocratic environment of early English Christianity'.[86] Although originally a 'monastic' preserve, monumental stone sculpture was 'enthusiastically taken up' in the tenth century by secular patrons, to judge from both the volume of sculpture produced and the increased secularization of iconography, including the depiction of secular lords on some pieces.[87] In the production of sculpture in the early tenth century we see a material manifestation of the processes of contact and integration of which I have already spoken. It must be noted, however, that not all sculpture production in this period adopted Scandinavian motifs, and it has recently been suggested by Phil Sidebottom that a reason for this may be the survival of regional polities with their own sense of regional identity, and the advance of West Saxon rule which made the adoption of Scandinavian iconography potentially dangerous.[88]

The stone sculpture of the Danelaw has much to reveal about regional responses to the circumstances of Scandinavian settlement and is not a straightforward index to the location of Scandinavian settlement. It is not surprising, then, that sculptures displaying Scandinavian motifs and Scandinavian place-names do not always coincide. Neither is a simple mirror of Scandinavian settlement. The sculptural evidence, as much as the coinage bearing Thor's hammer and the names of Christian saints, demonstrates the utilization of Christianity by Scandinavian lords as they took control of the region, and also reflects the fact that the Church was used by native lords in formulating their response to the new arrivals. With its mixture of traditional Christian motifs, Scandinavian ornamentation, secular figures and 'pagan' scenes, the stone sculpture produced in the tenth century represents a range of responses to new and changing political and cultural circumstances; ultimately it was the product of elite discourse, and the intended audience was social peers, not primarily the peasantry. It was the means by which newly arrived Scandinavian lords recorded their presence and sought to legitimate their authority by establishing links with the past and with native traditions; it was also the product of native patronage – perhaps from a lord seeking to express newly-formed allegiances and trying to understand something of the society of the newcomers. It was not essentially about being Scandinavian or English; it was about statements of authority which drew from a wide repertoire of symbols and motifs. The sculpture was produced at a time when two iconographic systems were equally

---

86. R.N. Bailey, *England's Earliest Sculptors*, Publications of the Dictionary of Old English, 5 (1996), 77–94; P. Wormald, 'Bede, Beowulf and the conversion of the Anglo-Saxon aristocracy', in *Bede and Anglo-Saxon England*, ed. R.T. Farrell (BAR Brit. Series, 46, 1978), 32–95.
87. Bailey, *Viking Age Sculpture*, 81.
88. P. Sidebottom, 'Monuments that mark out viking land', *British Archaeology* 23 (April, 1997), 7.

meaningful to those who produced it and to those who would observe it; it did not simply reflect social relations in a passive manner, it was actively involved in forming new identities and new legitimations of power. The use of two iconographic systems was deliberate, and perhaps deliberately ambiguous; allowing those who saw it to derive varied impressions from it.[89] In time it perhaps became simply the 'fashion' for sculptural design in parts of northern England; although it is worth noting that differences in sculptural style between northern and southern England continued well into the eleventh century (even following the second Scandinavian conquest and the reign of Cnut),[90] and perhaps formed part of the way in which northern lords – whatever their origins – continued to display their sense of separateness from southern rule. The stone sculpture, the coinage, changes to the corpus of personal- and place-names, and the adoption of particular burial practices were a product of their time; a period when two groups of peoples with different belief systems worked out a common means of existence.

Interaction and integration

It is difficult to uphold traditional ideas concerning the long-term binary division of society into Danish and English in the regions in which Scandinavians settled. Nor is it easy to identify very much about the society of those regions that can be said to have been especially Scandinavian. The outdated deployment of the ethnicity paradigm has diverted our attentions from what the native populations and the newcomers had, or quickly came to have, in common, and how they proceeded to forge a *modus vivendi*. Although they came as pagans, from a largely non-monetary and non-urban economy, with no extensive tradition of stone sculpture production, it is striking how quickly the Scandinavian leaders came to forge alliances with ecclesiastics, to issue coinage, to settle in and expand urban sites[91] and to influence the iconography of stone sculpture. Along with the evidence to suggest some basic level of continuity in the secular and ecclesiastical institutions of the region, this indicates that the Scandinavian rulers quickly adopted the forms of control utilized by those they had conquered, associated themselves with existing centres of power and replicated modes of behaviour. This is a common pattern across early medieval Europe when two societies come into contact.[92] Divorced from their Scandinavian background and seeking to establish

---

89. On the use of ambiguous symbols in material culture see, K. Greene, 'Gothic material culture', in *Archaeology as Long-Term History*, ed. I. Hodder (1987), 117–31.
90. Bailey, *England's Earliest Sculptors*, 95–104.
91. O'Sullivan, 'Changing views of the viking age', 4–9.
92. Amory, 'Names, ethnic identity and community', 3, 13–19.

themselves in an unstable environment, and in the face of great competition for power, it is not perhaps surprising that some Scandinavian leaders should have accepted aspects of Christianity, especially since the Church could offer models for kingship and the exercise of power.[93] By promoting the interests of a handful of Scandinavian rulers, the Church in the Danelaw echoed a well-worn policy for instilling order into a turbulent situation.[94] Individual ecclesiastics and religious communities had little to lose; the expansionist policies of the house of Wessex did not aim to restore the independent kingdoms of Northumbria, Mercia or East Anglia, and the West Saxon conquest was accompanied by the transfer of relics out of the region, the seizure of ecclesiastical land and isolated events such as Eadred's burning of the church at Ripon in 948.[95] It was not solely a Scandinavian problem that the West Saxons encountered. It was, rather, a series of regional problems, of which the most serious was a resurgent northern power reinforced from overseas. It was a complex political situation in the Danelaw, in which the distinction between neighbour and subject was blurred; it is perhaps not surprising that modern commentators are divided over the use of the words 'conquest' and 're-conquest' to describe the actions of the house of Wessex.[96] Cultural, ethnic, regional and local identities and concerns were fluid and the exercise of power in the Danelaw had to take account of and exploit these ever-changing allegiances and identities.

The forging of common interests between the settlers and the indigenous populations of northern and eastern England was doubtless fostered by such developments as urban expansion, the extension of trading networks, the striking increase in the quantity and quality of pottery production, the creation of a new silver currency, the proliferation of stone sculpture and transformations in the countryside which lead to the creation of nucleated villages and open-field systems in some regions in the decades following the Scandinavian settlement.[97] Indeed, it may be these developments as much as the

93. Wormald, 'Whence and whither', 144–8.
94. *Ibid.*, 145–6; see also I. Wood, 'The conversion of the barbarian peoples', in *The Christian World*, ed. G. Barraclough (1981), 85–98.
95. D.W. Rollason, 'Relic-cults as an instrument of royal policy c.900–1050', *Anglo-Saxon England* 15 (1987), 91–103, at 95–7; R. Fleming, 'Monastic lands and England's defence in the Viking Age', *EHR* 100 (1985), 247–65; D. Dumville, 'Ecclesiastical lands and the defence of Wessex in the first Viking-Age', in his *Wessex and England* (1992), 29–54; D. Whitelock, 'The dealings of the kings of England with Northumbria in the tenth and eleventh centuries' in *The Anglo-Saxons*, ed. P. Clemoes (1959), 70–88, at 70–78.
96. Stafford, *Unification and Conquest*, 114.
97. D. Hinton, *Archaeology, Economy and Society* (1990), 72–4, 82–97; Hodges, *The Anglo-Saxon Achievement*, 154–62, 166–77; J. Hurst, 'The Wharram research project: results to 1983', *Medieval Archaeology* 28 (1984), 77–111; P. Hayes, 'Relating fen edge sediments, stratigraphy and archaeology near Billingborough, South Lincolnshire', in *Palaeoenvironmental Investigations*, ed. N.R.J. Feiller

efforts of the Church which helped to bring to an end the pagan practices of the settlers, and contributed to the forging of a distinctive society which owed much to both pre-existing indigenous and Scandinavian culture.

Conclusion

Although Scandinavian settlers may for a time have been identifiable as 'cockles amongst the wheat', it is clear that we cannot continue to discuss the impact of the Scandinavian settlement in terms of a simple opposition between 'Danes' and 'English'. Traditional interpretations of the Scandinavian settlement have been fostered by a reductive, essentialist notion of Danish identity. I hope to have shown that such a view is unsustainable. The documented references to Danes in the tenth and eleventh centuries relate to specific political events and have little to reveal about the subjective identities of the settlers of the late ninth and early tenth centuries, and their descendants. The archaeological, linguistic, onomastic and sculptural evidence brings us closer to an understanding of those identities, and it betokens a whole series of levels of interaction between the native population and the Scandinavian settlers, which varied from region to region. During the course of the tenth century the Scandinavians did not simply 'disappear' but, rather, they forged a relationship with native culture and society which, in turn, adopted much from the new arrivals. The settlers cannot be said to have actively maintained a separate Danish ethnic identity; rather, the result of this settlement was, in part, to maintain the separate regional traditions of northern England, many – although not all – of which borrowed from the Scandinavians. Moreover, the settlement had the effect of defining the region as having something 'Danish' about it; but this was a Danishness that was not limited to the descendants of late ninth-century settlers, nor was it something that was directly related to the scale of the settlement, it was a malleable identity that was not consistently or invariably drawn upon.

---

contd.

(1985), 245–69; M. Harvey, 'Planned field systems in eastern Yorkshire: some thoughts on their origins', *Agricultural History Review* 31 (1983), 91–103; D. Roffe, 'The Lincolnshire hundred', *Landscape History* 3 (1981), 27–36; R.A. Hall, 'Vikings gone west? A summary review', in *Developments around the Baltic and North Sea in the Viking Age*, ed. B. Ambrosiani and H. Clarke (Stockholm, 1994), 32–49, at 33–8.

7 *Corpus Saxonum*: Early Medieval Bodies and Corporeal Identity[1]

Andrew Tyrrell

The body is confusing and sometimes awkward to discuss, since it can exist in both physical and imaginary forms. Individual bodies are able to traverse the boundary between these two states, offering the possibility of multiple interpretations by both a body's owner and all others that interact with that individual. The human body is bounded by various social, sexual and political codes enforced individually or by group, and it is these which enable it to be divorced conceptually from the physical or the 'natural'. In other words, although all humans occupy a corporeal body from conception until death they are not always physically constrained by this body, being able to use or adopt a selection of identities dependent on, among other things, their group affiliations – both biological and social – their sexual and gender orientations, age, kin and spiritual doctrine or belief systems.[2] Thus corporeal identity is possibly the most multi-faceted aspect of the identity mosaic. Its complexity is intimate to every aspect of human lives – nothing that humans do can be removed from the intervention of the body. It is the wide range of experiences which individual bodies can undergo, and which individual bodies can be used to effect on others, that makes the idea of the 'body' so powerful and desirable a tool in terms of our own understanding of past (and present) peoples.

Individuals interact and act through the vocabularies of their *body idiom*, defined as forms of non-verbal communication within groups of

---

1. I'd like to thank Bill Frazer for his comments on this chapter and for all his hard work while co-editing this volume with me. I'd also like to thank Andrew Chamberlain, my supervisor while I was undertaking this research. Various other helpful comments and suggestions were made by Kathryn Denning and for these I'm also extremely grateful. This research has been funded in part by a NERC studentship.
2. S. Kay and M. Rubin, 'Introduction', in *Framing Medieval Bodies*, eds S. Kay and M. Rubin (1996), 1–9.

people, including: dress, bearing and body language. The perception of bodily appearance provides a sense of the social boundaries within which a society operates.[3] Erving Goffman argues that body idiom provides a powerful demonstration of how classification systems affect our views of physicality.[4] To understand the body is therefore to understand the fabric of a society both in the literal sense that a society is composed of individual bodies and in the social sense of the body as metaphor for society[5] (and even *vice versa*). When we access this knowledge we intersect with a culture's display, its modification, ingestion, portrayal, diversity, its gender refractions and its sexual mores, its household rhythms and its group associations.[6]

Obviously a work comprising an investigation into all of these 'bodily functions' would be extensive and somewhat arduous; other chapters in this volume have explored more fully some of these aspects. Instead, I propose to concentrate on a part of the *corpus* which has been a perennial problem for early medieval scholars, ethnic identity. Targeting ethnicity as part of an inquiry into corporeality may seem like a contradiction, since I am eventually to argue that ethnicity *sensu stricto* is not predetermined by the body.[7] However, I envisage the body as having affected perceptions and portrayals of ethnic identity in the early medieval period as well as influencing our own views of ethnicity in that period.

The study of the relationship between corporeality and ethnicity is currently very confused.[8] Partly this is because of the inclination of modern scholars to associate the many previous mistreatments and occasional downright abuses of biological techniques with any studies which hope to approach a fuller understanding of the impact of human biological variation on identity.[9] This has led to a marginalization of such analyses. Discussions of past physicality and ethnicity now possess taboo status in some areas of the social sciences. The lack of a biological perspective in archaeological and historical discourses on identity in effect denies the study or existence of a fundamental constituent of corporeal identity: that which is the sum of the interplay between genome, environment and body idiom. A broad spectrum of confusion has resulted from this, oscillating wildly between the

---

3. C. Shilling, 'The body and difference', in *Identity and Difference*, ed. K. Woodward (1997), 63–121.
4. E. Goffman, *The Presentation of Self in Everyday Life* (1969), and also see E. Goffman, *Gender Advertisements* (1979).
5. See, for a pertinent example, J.B. Friedman, *The Monstrous Races in Medieval Art and Thought* (1981).
6. Kay and Rubin, 'Introduction', 1–2.
7. See also I. Banks, 'Archaeology, nationalism and ethnicity', in *Nationalism and Archaeology*, eds J.A. Atkinson, I. Banks and J. O'Sullivan (1996), 1–12.
8. S. Jones, *The Archaeology of Ethnicity: Constructing Identities in the Past and Present* (1997), 1–10.
9. See S.J. Gould, *The Mismeasure of Man* (New York and London, 1981), for the many past mistreatments of human variation.

extremes of the determinist 'genes equals people' arguments and inadequate culture-history approaches,[10] to ignorant and prejudicial dismissals of any investigation into the topic.[11] It is well established that deterministic readings of the results of previous studies, whether based in bio-molecular, morphometric (the use of quantitative measurements to determine the evolutionary relationship between organisms) or material culture remains, have tended to overlook the complexity of past peoples' histories and effectively have acted as a negation of such narratives by ignoring or de-emphasizing all the other histories which contribute to peoples' notions of their past. Some would say that this is especially true of those studies of past peoples based in molecular biology.[12] The traditional culture–history approach identifying changes in material culture (and mainly change in distribution and type of grave goods) during the early medieval period as equivalent to a gene-flow map of the period is probably grossly mistaken in terms of actual events and certainly flawed in its initial theoretical premise.[13] A distribution of skeletal traits or allele frequencies[14] does not make an Anglo-Saxon any more than does a disc brooch and a cloisonné belt buckle. Yet, the literature is filled with such associations, both explicit and implicit.[15] However, these failings should not be reason to dismiss or ignore study into past ethnicities.

---

10. See for example H. Härke, '"Warrior graves?" The background of the Anglo-Saxon weapon burial rite', *Past and Present* 126 (1990), 22–43; H. Härke, 'Changing symbols in a changing society: The Anglo-Saxon burial rite in the seventh century', in *The Age of Sutton Hoo: The Seventh Century in North-Western Europe*, ed. M.O.H. Carver (1992), 149–65, and H. Härke, 'Finding Britons in Anglo-Saxon graves', *British Archaeology* 10 (1995), 7.
11. E.g. N.J. Higham, *Rome, Britain and the Anglo-Saxons* (1992), 187–8. Higham indicates that all analysis of skeletal remains to determine genetic penetration within this period is worthless. Unless genetic penetration is what one is interested in, I would tend to agree with Higham's conclusions, but perhaps not his sentiment. As illustrated below, skeletal analyses of affiliation are possible, but not to determine 'genetic' relatedness.
12. E.g. M. Pluciennik, 'A perilous but necessary search: archaeology and European identity', in *Nationalism and Archaeology*, eds J.A. Atkinson, I. Banks and J. O'Sullivan (1996), 35–59 esp. at 35–48.
13. See I. Hodder, *Reading the Past* (1992), 11–12 and B. Trigger, *A History of Archaeological Thought* (1989), 173, 206, 235, 244–7 and 275–6 for a fuller explanation of arguments against culture history.
14. An allele is defined as a pair (but sometimes more) of dissimilar genes responsible for a set of alternating characters. Alleles hold corresponding positions, or 'loci', in corresponding chromosomes.
15. For a ceramic example see R.G. Collingwood and J.N.L. Myres, *Roman Britain and the English Settlements* (Second Edition, 1937), 331. Although Myres's writings are as much influenced by the theories of his contemporaries as anyone else's, and therefore a product of his times, the strongly culture-historical ideas expressed in his work are repeated again and again in more up-to-date literature, e.g. J. Campbell, E. John and P. Wormald, *The Anglo-Saxons* (1982), 9–19; M. Welch, *Anglo-Saxon England* (1992), 11 and M. Welch, 'The kingdom of the South Saxons: the origins', in *The Origins of Anglo-Saxon Kingdoms*, ed. S. Bassett (1989), 75–84.

This is particularly pertinent for the study of the early medieval past where issues of 'who's who' seem to be a large preoccupation for most scholars concerned with the transition between the end of Roman military occupation and the appearance of new cultural horizons usually associated with the 'Anglo-Saxons'.

This chapter attempts to advance current ideas about ethnic identity in the early medieval period by deconstructing previous arguments and then attempting to incorporate concepts of body idiom and my understanding of its relationship to early medieval identity. To do this I have taken a previous study[16] and illustrated where I think improvements to both our current methodology and our interpretations might be made in the hope that these suggestions may be taken up in future studies concerned with identity and human physical variation.

Moving towards sophistication

To advance we need to inquire deeper to discover more than just what being an Anglo-Saxon was, or means to us.[17] We should also be enquiring 'what does and did it mean to be ethnic and to have an ethnicity?' These are difficult questions to deal with, especially when there is no contemporary (i.e. late twentieth-century) consensus on definitions of the term 'ethnicity'.[18] In recent times the term has become a nebulous catch-all for media and political commentators and manipulators in reference to minority groups, whether the groups themselves are consciously 'ethnic' or not. People are still likely to associate ethnicity with a series of phenotypic traits,[19] and worse still, are prepared to kill in the name of 'ethnic cleansing'. Yet for some groups and individuals, ethnicity is a source of pride, no doubt occasionally as a reaction to the semi-colonial behaviour of the previously mentioned media and political operators. The situation is yet more complex for the investigator of past ethnicity when faced with the filters, inadequacies and obscurities of source material and archaeological record.

---

16. H. Härke, ' "Warrior graves?" '.
17. For example see S. Reynolds, 'What do we mean by "Anglo-Saxon" and "Anglo-Saxons"?', *Journal of British Studies* 24 (1985), 395–414 at 396–9.
18. Steven Shennan defines it as 'self-conscious identification with a particular social group at least partly based on a specific locality or origin'. S. Shennan, 'Introduction: archaeological approaches to cultural identity' in *Archaeological Approaches to Cultural Identity* ed. S. Shennan (1989), 1–32 at 14. See also B. R. Penner, 'Old World traditions, New World landscapes: ethnicity and archaeology of Swiss-Appenzellers in the colonial South Carolina backcountry', *International Journal of Historical Archaeology* 1(4) (1997), 257–321 especially at pages 258–69 for an excellent discussion of definitions of ethnicity.
19. See J. Marks, 'Replaying the race card', *American Anthropological Association Anthropology Newsletter* 39(5) (1998), 1–5.

The interpretation of the term ethnicity for scholars is, naturally enough, mediated by their own histories as well as by their personal understanding of group and inter-group dynamics – ethnicity is after all a product of contact rather than of isolation.[20] It is through the guilt of the racist tradition, which is still unfortunately all too apparent in academic as well as popular literature,[21] that modern scholarship has failed to treat the subject of human variation with the fairness that it deserves. For the most part, the term *race* is now retracted from the discourse of human genetics,[22] and this is almost certainly 'a good thing', but unfortunately by removing the concept of race from discussions of human identity we are left with an empty space: there are now no new ways of discussing human variation and its effect on identity without apparently condemning oneself by association – accessory after the misconception.

> This is not the same as saying race doesn't exist or has no meaning, which one commonly hears. It has plenty of meaning and existence to the extent that it widely confers identity. What has no existence is a natural subspecies of humans.[23]

Jonathan Marks's point is made to illustrate that while racial differences are consistently stereotyped, they must not be immediately assigned to the different biological natures of two groups. The burden of proof should lie with the claimant to show the biological origin of such differences. Instead of innate biological origins it might be more appropriate to incorporate the notion of physical 'difference' into Pierre Bourdieu's concept of 'doxa', whereby bodily attributes and their meaning are established as a 'pre-verbal taking-for-granted of the world that flows from practical sense'.[24] Hence attributes of the body, whether dress, hair colour, jewelry, badges of office, and so on, which may be considered as identifiers of certain groups are learned by others as symbols of those groups, through the conceptualization of 'doxa'. These symbols become incorporated into a 'body idiom'. Body idiom is highly plastic in terms of its construction and its perception, but it is potentially capable of being used to determine 'ethnic groups'. It is pertinent that at this point we distinguish between ethnicity as a euphemism for 'race' or other sub-divisions of humanity based primarily on biological data, and other socially determined groups.

---

20. T.H. Eriksen, *Ethnicity and Nationalism: Anthropological Perspectives* (Boulder, 1993).
21. Prime modern examples of the use of 'biology' to legitimize racist policy and ideology are: R.J. Hernstein, *The Bell Curve: Intelligence and Class Structure in American Life* (New York, 1994) and also J. Philippe Rushton, *Race, Evolution, and Behaviour: A Life History Perspective* (New Brunswick, NJ, 1995). For critiques of these see R. Jacoby and N. Glauberman, eds, *The Bell-Curve Debate* (New York, 1995).
22. Although exceptions can still be found. See note 21.
23. Marks, 'Replaying the race card', 4.
24. P. Bourdieu, *The Logic of Practice* (1992), 68.

Ethnic groups are socially defined groups of self-reflexive belonging, consistently being created and recreated, with a potential basis in objective reality through their use of material symbols. Ethnicity has no determined basis in any aspect of biology.

If we are to accept that display and portrayal of bodies are means by which the group differentiates itself from the other – and if we don't, then the idea that any material culture signifies and mediates identities of any kind seems to be on a distinctly shaky foundation – then we must accept that visible and distinctive phenotypic variation as part of the body idiom may have had a bearing on the construction of group identity. To be sure, there is the possibility of modification – the symbols which can adorn, or can be fashioned from, the body are many and varied – but as indicated above there can be no escaping the sheer physicality of the body. It is how we intercede with the rest of the world, and that includes other people and other groups. It would be a mistake to assume that by this I mean that group identity is defined solely by physical appearance or that the perception of a person's physical appearance is determined by his or her biological history and make-up. It would be even worse to propose that physical appearance predetermines an individual's group identity, but humanity is framed by its body and this, by definition, includes the way it looks, smells, sounds and is perceived.

Current favour with the construction of moral histories where archaeologists and historians have an interest to 'do the right thing' provides investigators with a paradox: when there is a clash of interest between two modern groups – consciously ethnic or not – whatever the history or histories of those peoples that archaeologists and historians provide, it *will* be offensive or amoral to somebody. This is Shennan's 'double edged weapon'.[25] With respect to past ethnicity the sheer complexity of the multiple forms of evidence, let alone of the presentation of that evidence in a meaningful and balanced interpolated form, soon becomes apparent. When issues of conflicting morality are added into this equation, the scale and difficulty of the task are obvious. This is a pressing issue in studies of the early medieval period. For those with any doubt whether studies of the early medieval occupation of a relatively small ex-Roman north-western continental province should provide reason for concern, they should look at the reaction of the English (and I use the term advisedly) media, and of some academics, to a short article in *British Archaeology*.[26]

25. S. Shennan. 'Archaeological approaches', 10.
26. The original article: M. Evison, 'Lo the conquering hero comes (or not)', *British Archaeology* 26 (1997), 8–9 and its response: S. Wavell, 'No Saxon please we're British', *Sunday Times* (20 April 1997).

Investigating early medieval bodies

Erving Goffman defined the three main characteristics of the physical body when used in social relations as:

1. The body is used as a means by which interaction occurs in a physical sense between individuals.
2. Meanings attached to the body by groups and individuals are a product of socially constructed vocabularies of body idiom.
3. Bodies are thus the properties of individuals, but are also categorized by society. The body mediates the relationship between self-identity and social identity.[27]

So physical bodies are potentially ethnic in the sense that they can be used as mediators in the construction of social identities. However, as Frederik Barth says, ethnicity only works as a concept with internal consistency and social effectiveness when the peoples concerned acknowledge the expression of ethnicity as a cultural phenomenon.[28] So following from Goffman's tri-partite definition above, we can see that when individuals choose – whether consciously or not – to express ethnicity, the physical body is likely to be one channel through which this is achieved. Unfortunately for archaeologists, historians and all others interested in the early medieval past, the physicality of early medieval bodies is a subject with which we cannot directly participate. On the other hand, the way groups and individuals portrayed themselves and imagined their origins *is* accessible to us, as is the use of symbols to advertise and mediate identity through the study of texts, artwork, the use of dress, burial furniture and so on. Since we cannot now view the people of the early medieval past or interact with them directly we must take another, more circuitous route in our investigation.

Bodies and bias

Giles Deleuze and Felix Guattari[29] have shown the importance of the fragmented body, the culmination of various non-hierarchical interacting machines. Such a conceptualization has been extended to the assignation of various bodies to the individual by the realms of science, politics, religion and so on.[30] The fragmented body also provides a useful corporeal metaphor for social identity, illustrating social

---

27. Quoted in Shilling, 'The body and difference', 63–121.
28. F. Barth, *Ethnic Groups and Boundaries: The Social Organization of Culture Differences* (Boston, 1969).
29. G. Deleuze and F. Guattari, *Anti-Oedipus: Capitalism and Schizophrenia*, trans. R. Hurley, M. Seem and H. Lane (Minneapolis, 1990).
30. See for instance a brief discussion of this in D. Olkowski, 'Bodies in the light', in *Thinking Bodies*, eds J.F. MacCannell and L. Zakarin (1994), especially 177–9.

interaction and the continual renegotiation of power relations as the operation of interrelated but recognizable social 'machines'. In short it sums up succinctly the theme of this book: that social identity can be fragmented when subject to analysis and investigation, but that for individuals the heuristic is subject to a conscious and occasionally subconscious manipulation, highlighting various aspects of an individual's persona according to his or her circumstance and context.

However, the interpretation of bodies is not without its difficulties. 'A *corpus* is not a discourse: however what we need here is a corpus.'[31] Jean Luc-Nancy makes this point in reference to all bodies, but especially to those with which the reader is contemporary. To illustrate further:

> We need a passive recording ... a seismograph of bodies, of senses, and again of the entries of these bodies: access, orifices, pores of all types of skin, and 'the portals of your body' (Apollinaire). We need to recite, to blazon, body after body, place after place, entry by entry ... All this would be possible only if we had access to bodies.[32]

Luc-Nancy's argument centres around the intractable difficulty that humans have when dealing with issues of the body, namely that inhabiting a body precludes an objective understanding of the nature of physicality.

Early medieval bodies are now almost impenetrable to us in any investigation. What we have been left with are a select sample of the lifeless skeletal remains of the inhumed and the cremated. Such physical reminders of the previous inhabitants of these islands are rich in the information which they divulge to us, but in terms of Luc-Nancy's corpus they leave us with barely a fraction of the full volume which we wish to access. Roberta Gilchrist puts it succinctly when she says: 'eloquent as these sources [human bones] are for reconstructing the flesh and blood of medieval bodies, they do not directly reflect contemporary perceptions of the body'.[33] Various different methodologies have traditionally been adopted to interpret the physicality of existence – the textual and spatial metaphors of the structuralist and structural-functionalist traditions being among the most familiar to archaeologists. In trying to understand the imaging and imagining of physical identity by early medieval peoples we are confronted by the quagmire of associations with which we conceptualize our own existence and physicality. In trying to approach early medieval ethnicity we are again confronted with the inescapability of our own

---

31. J. Luc-Nancy, 'Corpus' in *Thinking Bodies*, eds J.F. MacCannell and L. Zakarin (1994), 17.
32. *Ibid.*, 17.
33. R. Gilchrist, 'Medieval bodies in the material world: gender stigma and the body', in *Framing Medieval Bodies*, eds S. Kay and M. Rubin (1996), 43–59 at 43.

bodies. Thus in attempting to read Luc-Nancy's 'seismograph' we encounter within the data a bias of our own making.

Early medieval images of ethnic bodies

> Who is there living in Europe who does not know the loftiness of her forebears, their names and habitats and the places they owned?[34]

This somewhat cavalier quotation from the seventh-century *Life of Saint Gertrude* adequately illustrates not only an emerging Eurocentrism, but also the importance of an individual's ancestors and the ties believed by individuals to be shared with ancestral names and property. Reynolds has shown that most studies of early medieval ethnic identity start from the premise that

> medieval people seem to have envisaged their world as divided into 'peoples' (*gentes, nationes, populi*) of common biological descent and culture who normally and 'naturally' formed separate political units[35]

As Reynolds goes on to say:
> a great deal of our picture of the age of migration or *Völkerwanderung* is based on myths of origin and descent of a very conventionally mythical kind that have not gained credibility by being adapted to philological nationalism.[36]

Origin myths from the early medieval period – such as those related by Nennius in the *Historia Britonnum*,[37] which describe Europe as Japheth's share of the world and thus consequently all the greater peoples (sic) of Europe including the Franks, Latins, Alemans and Britons as descendants from Japheth and his immediate progeny – were also utilized or modified by other early medieval authors. A case in point can be found in the writings of Paul the Deacon, historian of the Lombards, who maintained that Germany was the homeland of all the *gentes* that had afflicted Europe.[38] These origin myths, particularly those which isolate the 'Germanic' nature of European peoples, have become further incorporated in modern contexts by later nationalist groups. Ironically, some modern scholarly interpretations of the early medieval past in the British Isles appear to owe much to the view

---

34. 'Vita Santae Gertrudis', prologue, in *Scriptores rerum Merovingicarum*, ed. B. Krusch, 454.
35. Reynolds, 'What do we mean?', 399. My emphasis.
36. *Ibid.*, 401.
37. F. Lot, *Nennius et l'historia Brittonum: une étude critique*, (Paris, 1934), 160–1; also see Isidore of Seville, *Etymologiarum Libri*, ed. W.M. Lindsay (1911), ix.11, 26–9, 89–90.
38. 'Pauli Historia Langobardorum', i.2, in *Scriptores Langobardicarum*, ed. G. Waitz (Hanover, 1878).

proposed in the *Life of Saint Gertrude*, as scholars continually offer nationalist and legitimizing hypotheses as to the 'origin' and 'ethnicity' of the peoples who inhabited these islands during the early medieval period.[39] This mistaken emphasis on 'ethnicity' and more particularly ethnic labels as synonyms for 'origin' was iterated by Patrick Geary when he indicated that many of the problems which are faced by early medieval scholars have their root cause in the origin myths of the migration period:

> Early medieval authors stress origin, customs, languages and law, as the most significant characteristics by which ethnicity is determined ... When one examines the actual uses of ethnic *labels*, one finds that these articulated criteria in fact had a very limited role in determining the vocabulary of ethnicity.[40]

This is crucial to an understanding of our own misrepresentation of early medieval ethnic identities. Our predilection for labels, along with the idea that ethnicity is something which can be identified as a separate entity reflected solely in either biological or material cultural remains is misguided.[41] It is the matters of 'perceived' origin, custom and law which we need to consider, for example when Boniface in 738, as a rhetorical tactic to propagandize for the 'English Missions', cries for all 'Englishmen' to help in converting Saxons who were of the same *'blood and bone'*.[42] Boniface puts great belief by the common origin of the eighth century 'English' and the continental Saxons, which presumably he owes in part to the origin myths and occasional ecclesiastic misrepresentations of his period. Boniface demands that his fellow Englishmen take part in the mission not for reasons of missionary zeal – although this is presumably what Boniface himself is consciously interested in – but because he is addressing the wealthier classes of 'English' society who share a perceived physicality with populations identified as continental pagan Saxons. Boniface obviously sees this as a powerful motivation for certain types of social behaviours. Barbara Yorke in this volume sees this 'motivator' as a consequence of shared conceptions of Roman Christianity. This type of received essentialism seems to be typical of early medieval views of identity and the body. Norbert Elias has characterized such a perspective on identity as the beginning of the socialization of the body, whereby the body and physical identity become a location for, and an expression of, codes of

---

39. M. Welch, *Anglo-Saxon England*.
40. P.J. Geary, 'Ethnic identity as a situational construct in the early middle ages', *Mitteilungen der Anthropologischen Gesellschaft in Wien* 113 (1983), 15–26, at 16, my italics.
41. *Ibid.*, 16.
42. *Bon. Ep.*, 74–5, 150–1, 156, 169, 171 quoted in P. Wormald, 'Bede, the Bretwaldas and the origins of the Gens Anglorum' in *Ideal and Reality in Anglo-Saxon Society*, ed. P. Wormald (1983), 99–129 at 122.

behaviour.[43] Whether this physicality lies in the substance of the physical body in terms of actual genetic relatedness is totally irrelevant in terms of the effect it has on those who perceive an imagined common origin, common law and common language.

Investigating early medieval ethnicity from other sources: material culture

Although it is becoming increasingly clear that the expression of identity is imbued in all aspects of early medieval material culture, and particularly that of the fifth and early sixth centuries,[44] there are nevertheless some stumbling blocks over which scholars frequently trip.[45] In the assignation of symbolic value – perhaps identifying or expressing an ethnic affiliation – to a type or form of artefact, architectural style and so on, archaeologists tend to adopt methodologies founded on both obscurity and assumption: cultures tend to be treated as isolated items equivalent to 'tribes', 'states' or 'ethnic groups'. Richard Bradley was commenting as far back as 1979 that much more needed to be made of 'how and why an ethnic group will use artefacts to symbolise its identity' in archaeological explanations of ethnicity in the early medieval period.[46] Problematically, most approaches which have attempted to study ethnicity have extracted from the symbolic identity of an individual or group *in toto* those aspects which seem to represent 'ethnicity'. For the early medieval period, if not for all of human existence, this is misguided and barely more sophisticated than the essentialist approach of original early medieval authors. Inevitably scholars end up comparing contemporaneous archaeological material, again usually grave goods, from different geographical regions and calling identified geographical variation 'ethnic symbolism'. We establish 'patterns' and 'links' which are as much an artefact of the way in which we study as they are of the material that we are studying.

The first procedure undertaken in an archaeological interpretation of ethnic symbolism is usually the selection of those parts of material culture which are assumed to be reflections of the ethnicity of an individual or group. So for example, for J.N.L. Myres these artefacts are pots,[47] for others they may be dress, or weapons or

---

43. N. Elias, *The Civilizing Process, Volume 1: The History of Manners* (New York, 1978).
44. H. Geake, *The Use of Grave Goods in Conversion-Period England, c.600–c.850*, British Archaeological Reports, British Series 261 (1997).
45. See also S. Jones, *Archaeology of Ethnicity*.
46. R. Bradley, 'Anglo-Saxon cemeteries: some suggestions for research', in *Anglo-Saxon Cemeteries*, eds P. Rahtz, T. Dickinson and L. Watts, British Archaeological Reports, British Series 82 (1980), 171–8, at 172.
47. J.N.L. Myres, *Corpus of Anglo-Saxon Pottery* (1977), 114–18.

brooches.[48] This may seem banal at first glance but it reveals the extent of the circularity within which we currently find ourselves. If we were to propose a hypothesis that 'all individuals buried with disc brooches are Anglian', one which isn't too unlikely,[49] based perhaps on a long-standing typological link between two north-western European regions, then we only have to wait for the consequent emergence in the literature of Anglian cemeteries and by association Anglian settlements and then further the Anglian grave furniture set and so on and so forth.[50] This rather glib hypothetical example is easily recognizable to most workers operating with the period – it is the result of a modern artificial division of a (less) modern artificial typology. Typologies are not reflections of early medieval ethnicity.[51] They are the reflections of our need to classify and separate the enormous data set of artefactual evidence from archaeological excavation and recovery.

One of the mistakes that such studies have fallen into is that of identifying cultural boundaries as ethnic boundaries. Ethnic boundaries are among some of the most important aspects of expressions of group identity, but:

> The boundary itself is a social product that may have variable importance and may change through time. The ethnic group's 'culture', as well as forms of social organization, may change without removing the ethnic boundary: however in some cases, groups may actually become more culturally similar at the same time that their boundaries are strengthened.[52]

This provides obvious problems for the typological approach to ethnic identity. Groups who have similar material cultures may view each other as being ethnically diverse. Archaeologists must be more careful to understand that 'ethnic boundaries do not contain "cultures" as such'.[53]

---

48. For use of dress as an ethnic identifier see Welch, *Anglo-Saxon England*, 62–63. For use of weapons as an ethnic identifier see H. Härke, 'Warrior graves'.
49. See, for example, C.J. Arnold, *An Archaeology of the Early Anglo-Saxon Kingdoms* (1988), especially 150–3 or J. Campbell (ed.) *The Anglo-Saxons* (1982), 30.
50. Welch, *Anglo-Saxon England*, 62, and H. Härke, 'Changing symbols in a changing society: The Anglo-Saxon burial rite in the seventh century', in *The Age of Sutton Hoo: The Seventh Century in North-Western Europe*, ed. M.O.H. Carver (1992), 149–65.
51. Although to be fair some scholars have realized this for a while; for example: J. Hines, 'The Scandinavian character of Anglian England', in *The Age of Sutton Hoo: The Seventh Century in North-Western Europe*, ed. M.O.H. Carver (1992), 315–31; and C. Scull, 'Approaches to material culture and social dynamics of the migration period in eastern England', in *Europe Between Late Antiquity and the Middle Ages: Recent Archaeological and Historical Research in Western and Southern Europe*, eds J. Bintliff and H. Hamerow (1995), 71–82.
52. Penner, 'Old World Traditions', 261.
53. *Ibid.*

Ellen Pader has attempted to use the distribution of grave goods within individual Anglo-Saxon graves in order to determine a more nuanced approach to grave-good study. Although ethnicity was not a subject considered in depth in her thesis, the study illustrates that very often the sheer complexity of symbolic meaning attributed to material culture (more specifically grave inclusions) from the time of deposition to excavation can be difficult to interpret in terms which we can assimilate.[54] Compounding our interpretative problems are the filters which are imposed by the people who buried the individual, the individual's influence on how he or she was buried and the particular circumstances which surrounded that individual's death. Amid the usual gamut of archaeological inconsistencies, such as variation between individual burials, inverted symbolism, taphonomy and diagenesis, as well as all our current interpretative filters, one could be forgiven for thinking that interpretations of ethnicity based on material culture which have any resemblance to the early medieval understanding of this concept are going to be very difficult indeed.[55]

Relations between artefact and region, while important for the interpretation of other information, are unlikely to bear much relation to an early medieval understanding of ethnic groups. This becomes increasingly apparent when we again consider that early medieval aspects of identity are more firmly based in aspects of perceived origin, custom, language and law. If material culture in terms of burial goods is in part the reflection of an aspect of identity which we might term ethnicity, then these divisions are likely to be infinitely more subtle and nuanced than the reinforcement of the 'three most warlike tribes'.[56] The ludicrousness of the situation is made more clear when we realize that geographic patterning of artefacts is used to determine ethnic groups; small wonder then that we find particular regions associated with ethnic groups defined by the selfsame geographic patterning of artefacts.

---

54. E.J. Pader, *Symbolism, Social Relations and the Interpretation of Mortuary Remains*, British Archaeological Reports, International Series 130, (1982), and 'Material symbolism and social relations in mortuary studies', in *Anglo-Saxon Cemeteries*, eds P. Rahtz *et. al.* 143–60. Unfortunately, Pader's work also stumbles over the problem of normative patterning. While Pader accepts complexity, she also argues that this remains uniform for social behaviour within groups. While individuals seem to operate in socially defined patterns of behaviour when communicating and interacting, these patterns are not totally proscriptive, for transgressions act as powerful social communications in themselves. (For an early medieval example see Knüsel and Ripley, Chapter 8.)
55. Ethnicity, as we understand it, may simply have not been an issue in the early medieval period. Susan Reynolds suggests that we should be restructuring our ideas on this, in S. Reynolds, 'Medieval Origines Gentium and the community of the realm', *History* 68 (1993), 375–90.
56. Bede, *HE*, I.15.

An archaeological reconstruction of early medieval ethnicity: some problems and some suggestions

One of the fundamental errors which has plagued the study of ethnicity in early medieval studies is the equation of biology or material culture directly with an ethnic identity. Let us look closely at one example which has used skeletal remains in conjunction with documentary and material cultural evidence to reconstruct ethnicity as part of a wider study.

Heinrich Härke has proposed that certain individuals in the Anglo-Saxon cemetery of Berinsfield, Wally Corner are of Germanic origin. This hypothesis is based on the distribution of grave goods in the individual graves of that cemetery.[57] To add a 'biological' dimension to his argument, Härke has used the correlation of non-metric trait frequency and stature variation with those individuals buried with and without weapons. In part, Härke's arguments are a justifiable reaction to functionalist proposals that those buried with weapons are more likely to have been warriors in their lifetimes, or that weapon burials could be used to infer standard weapon sets.[58] Härke's arguments in his 1990 paper about the frequency of weapon burials in relation to the dating of battles in *The Anglo-Saxon Chronicle* seem to me to be powerful enough on their own to make the point that individuals buried with weapons are not automatically to be defined as warriors.[59]

However, the 'correlation' between the occurrence of weapon burials with the stature of individuals and the occurrence of non-metric traits on their skeleton is erroneous on at least two accounts: those relating to the misuse of biological methods and concepts, and those relating to inappropriate archaeological assumptions. First let us look at the biological misconceptions. Non-metric traits are normal anatomical variants which have a probable basis in genetic polymorphisms. Härke uses six variants (which in itself could be considered a highly inadequate number[60]) including a sixth lumbar vertebra, metopic suture (a sutural division of the frontal bone which persists after the first year post-partum), olecranon foramen (a small foraminal opening in the olecranon fossa of the humerus), an un-named dental 'anomaly', wormian bones (which are small ossicles in the sutures of the skull – most frequently the lambdoid – possibly related to

---

57. Härke, 'Warrior graves', 'Finding Britons' and, 'Weapon burials and knives', in *Berinsfield and Didcot*, eds A. Boyle, A. Dodd, D. Miles and A. Mudd, Thames Valley Landscapes Monograph, No.8 (1995), 67–74.

58. L. Alcock, 'Quantity or quality: the Anglian graves of Bernicia', in *Angles, Saxons and Jutes*, ed. V.I. Evison (1981), 168–83.

59. The periods with the highest frequency of battles seem to have coincided with the periods of least frequent weapon burials. See Härke, 'Warrior graves', 30–2.

60. See M. Finnegan and K. Cooprider, 'Empirical comparison of distance equations using discrete traits', *American Journal of Physical Anthropology* 49 (1978), 39–46.

continued periods of skull growth after suture closure) and spina bifida occulta (a neural tube defect leading to non-fusion of the sacral and occasionally lumbar vertebrae with no discernible pathological effect). All of these examples are typical of the type of skeletal variation which constitutes non-metric traits; however, not many of them are good choices for inclusion in a study of this type. This is because, like all phenotypic traits, non-metrics can be affected by the interplay between environmental fluctuations and the genomic basis for the traits. Some traits are more likely to be affected by environment than others, but in the main, traits which are associated with highly canalized structures (or those which are given a high priority during development; e.g. the brain is highly canalized because it is an extremely important organ, and the development of the toe bones or the floating ribs is likely to be canalized to a much lesser extent) will or should reflect the underlying genetic variance better than those that aren't. Härke's trait list consists of post-cranial traits which are hardly buffered against environmental effects at all and traits which are strongly affected by post-partum growth patterns (metopic suture and wormian bones). The only trait which is part of a highly canalized complex is the 'dental anomaly' but this remains unnamed and is thus difficult to analyse.

There are further reasons for questioning this particular use of non-metrics. Polymorphisms are those traits which occur in various forms throughout a population.[61] An example of a stable polymorphism would be biological sex, i.e. the presence of male and female forms. Other examples of polymorphisms of varying stability include those which affect blood group and serum proteins. The fact that skeletal traits have some genetic basis is presumably why Härke uses non-metrics as the premise for identifying individuals of either Germanic or British decent. Although it is possible to determine relative associations between groups by using non-metrics, the identification of individual 'ethnicities' from the occurrence of the six traits which Härke isolates is an oversimplification of what is in fact quite a complex area of physical anthropology. To measure the relative distance between groups of skeletons based on the frequency of non-metric traits within those groups requires the use of a non-Euclidean distance measure, rather than just a simple comparison of frequency. This is because non-metrics are quasi-continuous – in other words they occur phenotypically as either present or absent, but their underlying genetic expression is continuous. Thus the data which result from their observation is in binomial form, as a series of ones (for present) and

---

61. E.B. Ford has defined polymorphism as 'the occurrence together in the same habitat of two or more discontinuous forms of a species in such proportions that the rarest of them cannot be maintained merely by recurrent mutation'. Quoted in G.A. Harrison, J.M. Tanner, D.R. Pilbeam and P.T. Baker, eds, *Human Biology: An Introduction To Human Evolution, Variation Growth, and Adaptability* (1988), 212.

zeros (for absent).[62] A metric trait, such as the length of a bone, has a continuous expression as well as a continuous underlying genetic basis. Bone length as a trait can potentially express anywhere along the infinitely divisible metric scale from zero to the maximum possible length for a particular bone. By contrast, either a non-metric trait, such as say a particular cusp on a particular tooth crown, will be there, or it won't.

Additionally, as seen above, the expression of non-metric traits is mediated by the developmental environment of an individual from conception through to death. So, while the heritability of non-metrics plays a part in the determination of their expression, the localized environment of the osteogenic cells (those cells responsible for the production of the skeleton) – which is in turn determined by the environment of the organism and so on – is another, and potentially greater, part of the basis of non-metric trait expression. Unfortunately, this issue is probably further compounded by the threshold nature of non-metric traits; in other words, trait expression is achieved when sufficient loci from the polymorphisms contribute.[63] The threshold is achieved when sufficient weighting (which consists of the number of loci contributing as well as all environmental effects) contributes to the expression of a trait. The effect of environment is such that the same individual who expresses a trait in one environment may not express it under different developmental environments. Varying contributions of the constituents of an individual's weighting mean that comparing individuals within a population is meaningless in terms of determining genetic relationship, especially when one considers that even tiny fluctuations in the environment can alter the expression of a trait, so potentially even identical twins may vary in their trait expression.[64]

---

62. Non-Euclidean distances are those which measure distance in non-Euclidean space. That is, in any space which cannot be mapped using three-dimensional co-ordinates. The usual measure for non-metrical skeletal traits is the Mean Measure of Divergence developed by C.A.B. Smith; C.A.B. Smith, 'A note on genetic distance', *Annual of Human Genetics* 40 (1977), 463–79. This measures the distance between two populations based on the frequency of a suite of presence/absence traits. The variance of the binomial (presence/absence) distribution is at its highest when the frequency of a trait is at fifty per cent within a population and at its lowest when it is expressed in all or none of the population. The use of a transformation to standardize the variance of these traits means that quantifying the divergence between two frequencies has to be done in multidimensional space (a hypersphere). For further details see: A.W.F. Edwards and L.L. Cavalli-Sforza, 'Affinity as revealed by differences in gene frequencies', in *The Assessment of Population Affinities in Man*, eds J.S. Weiner and J. Huizinga (1972), 37–47; also see Finnegan and Cooprider, 'Empirical comparison of distance equations', 39–46.
63. Polymorphisms have variable numbers of loci (locations on the genes of an individual) contributing to their expressions. The average number for skeletal non-metrics is supposed to be approximately thirty loci per trait, according to R.J. Berry; R.J. Berry, 'Genes and skeletons, ancient and modern', *Journal of Human Evolution* 8 (1979), 669–77 at 674.
64. See, for example, B.S. Kraus and R.E. Jordan, *The Human Dentition Before Birth* (Philadelphia, 1965), 200–18.

Comparing individual relatedness by simple frequency of non-metric trait expression is as facile as walking into a party and assuming you are related to everyone who shares your eye or hair colour. Ultimately we all share large portions of our genome with large segments of our ancestral population, but this does not mean that we are all family relatives.

However all is not lost. Comparative measures of relatedness based on non-metrics have been formulated for use between groups, but they are complex and have several underlying assumptions. The first and most obvious to make is that they do not elucidate genetic relatedness *per se*. Their function is to demonstrate a measure of total similarity of interaction between the genome and the environment within which the genetic material was expressed. Secondly, the measures associate groups: this has the convenient effect of partially bypassing the difficult problem of variation between individuals' trait thresholds, by assuming a population average. Using methods illustrated elsewhere,[65] this author undertook a comprehensive study of the Berinsfield Anglo-Saxon period cemetery population, which Härke uses in his own studies. All adults were selected. (The possible correlation between age and trait expression and the varied relative contributions of environment and genome mean that juveniles were not included in this investigation.[66]) The adults were then divided according to grave inclusions.[67] Thus, 35 adults made up the group with grave inclusions of 'Germanic' type, consisting of 17 male or male?, 17 female or female? and one unsexed adult.[68] The group without any grave inclusions consisted of 31 adults – the no-grave-inclusions group contained those individuals with only single sherds of pottery or other non-identifiable artefacts – consisting of 10 male or male?, 16 female

65. Smith, 'A note on genetic distance', 463–79, T. Sjøvold, 'Non-metrical divergence between skeletal populations', *Ossa* 4 Supplement (1977), 1–117; J.E. Buikstra and C.A. Peters, 'Non-metrical skeletal variants as indicators of biological distance in Macaca mulatta', *American Journal of Physical Anthropology* 41 (1974), at 498; and A. Tyrrell, *Biodistance: An Anglo-Saxon Case Study* (Unpublished MSc dissertation, University of Sheffield, 1993) and *Skeletal Non-metric Traits and the Assessment of Inter- and Intra-population Diversity: An Analysis of Early Medieval Population Dynamics* (PhD thesis, University of Sheffield, 1999).
66. See J.E. Buikstra, 'Techniques for coping with the age regressive nature of non-metric traits', *American Journal of Physical Anthropology*, 37 (1972), 431–2 (abstract).
67. The divisions were formulated following Härke's criteria for 'males', with all individuals buried with weapons considered hypothetically as 'Germanic'. Knives were not considered as weapons (following Härke, 'Warrior graves'). All 'females' with brooches, and or amber beads were also included in the hypothetical 'Germanic' group, although Härke does not include female skeletons in his study.
68. The individuals from the Berinsfield cemetery were divided by skeletal sexing criteria into definite males, definite females, probable males, probable females and adults of unknown sex.

or female? and 9 unsexed individuals. Thirty-five cranial traits were recorded for each individual and then these were subjected to the mean measure of divergence test.[69] This test, which measures the relative dissimilarity between two groups, runs on a theoretical scale of zero (total similarity) to one (total divergence).

The results for the MMD test between the two groups showed no divergence between them (value −0.12861).[70] Thus, on the basis of these thirty-five traits no difference can be determined between the group with 'Germanic-style' grave goods and those without. Thus on biological grounds the hypothesis that the two groups are biologically divergent is, at least on the basis of cranial non-metric trait evidence, invalidated.

This brings us to the second problematic area: that of the theoretical premise for calling those buried with certain grave-good types 'Germanic'. As others have indicated,[71] weapon burials are likely to have been more to do with status than descent. The payment of weapons, or heriot, was most likely conferred as a sign of service to a lord. While it may have been a tradition started by continental warbands in the fifth century to bury their deceased members with weapons, it can hardly have been an exclusive right of those of actual Germanic descent by the time of the sixth to eighth centuries. The accurate identification of an individual's biological descent has only been available to humanity in the latter quarter of the twentieth century. Perceived descent may be another matter altogether, and here we once again return to issues of common origin, common law and common language. Again the actual presence of 'Germanic' or continental genes is likely to have been totally irrelevant. Härke's work has unfortunately replaced one causal relationship, that of 'weapons equals warriors', with another, 'weapons and traits equals Germans'. If descent or ethnic identity was an issue in the inclusion of certain types of grave goods in the early medieval period, it is the shared body idiom and imagined origin which mediated the self-reflexive sense of belonging to a kin group, whether or not shared genes were really present.

Final thoughts

During the writing of this chapter it has become apparent that ethnicity as a concept used by scholars in relation to the early medieval period is largely inapplicable. Traditional associations between grave goods and kin groups offer little more than typological reinforcements

---

69. Sjøvold 'Non-Metrical Divergence'.
70. The standard deviation was valued at 0.080193.
71. N.P. Brooks, 'Arms, status and warfare in late-Saxon England', in *Ethelred the Unready*, ed. D. Hill, British Archaeological Reports, British Series 59, (1978), 81–104.

of old labels which were unlikely to have been accurate even when they were first coined by early medieval historians in the late sixth and seventh centuries. It is also plain that biology used as further evidence to reinforce these ideas is just as misguided and dangerous. This is especially true when the biological premise for analysis is misunderstood, whether accidentally or wilfully, since its relations to ethnic expression are largely immaterial. The tensions between the essentialist approaches of biological determinism and the constructionism of social archaeology and history have produced an antagonism which is not at present easily resolved. Determinism is easy to refute, but the idea that people in the past were not influenced by variation between their physical bodies is also ludicrous. As Shilling has reminded us: '"biology" and "culture" are interrelated processes central to the constitution of embodied social relations, identities and differences'.[72] The use of biology to investigate issues of identity is not as pointless or hopeless as some might consider; we are constrained and moulded by the physical aspect of our existence as much as we are by the limits, or lack of them, in our social environments. However, as stated at the beginning of this chapter, it is our ability to manipulate and transcend our basic physicality through concepts such as body idiom that allows us to understand the complexity of the relationship between the genome and our environment to the point of realizing that they are two polarities of a false dichotomy. Human biology cannot exist outside of human social relations any more than can human relations without humans.

---

72. C. Shilling, 'The body and difference', in *Identity and Difference*, ed. K. Woodward (1997), 102.

8 The *Berdache* or Man–woman in Anglo-Saxon England and Early Medieval Europe[1]

Christopher Knüsel and Kathryn Ripley

The archaeological problem

Archaeologists have noted discrepancies between the gender of inhumed individuals, as determined by grave goods associations, and their biological sex (see below for a definition) as determined from osteological studies. These gender and sex disagreements have often resulted in a dismissal of the biological sex determination and, subsequently, the attribution of the discrepancies to the well-known overlapping sexual dimorphism characteristic of human populations. Alternatively, the *sex* of inhumed skeletal remains is often determined from associated grave goods, a method which assumes a close correspondence between sex and gender. In those reports that distinguish the osteologically determined sex from the gender implied by the grave inclusions, there is a practice of opting for a female designation in the case of apparently male skeletons associated with female grave inclusions.[2] The origins of these practices can be found

1. The authors would like to thank Robin Coningham for commenting on an early version of this chapter, and the editors of this volume, Andrew Tyrrell and Bill Frazer, for their many comments and suggestions. Discussions with Robin Coningham, Helen Geake, Carol Palmer and Tim Taylor, as well as with two successive years of MSc students on the Osteology, Palaeopathology and Funerary Archaeology course, contributed to the development of this chapter Carol Palmer helped with the preparation of figures 4 to 7. These colleagues, of course, bear no responsibility for the chapter's final content and appearance. A version of this chapter was previously presented as a paper at the 'Gender and Material Culture from Prehistory to the Present' conference held at the University of Exeter in July 1994.
2. K.M. Ripley, 'The man-woman or "berdache" and the woman-man in Anglo-Saxon England' (unpublished BSc dissertation, University of Bradford, 1994).

among nineteenth-century antiquarian perceptions which have been adopted in some more recent studies.[3] The application of such practices has contributed to the view that gender roles have remained unchanged from the fifth to the nineteenth centuries.[4] The result has been an apparent lack of gender variation in early medieval society, despite considerable documented variation in modern societies,[5] and age-related changes in gender identity within others, for example among post-menopausal women.[6] The apparent absence of individuals of alternative gender in early medieval society may be due more to an historical precedent which denied their existence rather than to an absence of the phenomenon. Later medieval society appears to have been ill-disposed to such gender-ambiguous individuals. The emasculated ecclesiastic and philosopher, Abelard, wrote in the following way about the social stigma attached to his condition:

> I thought how my rivals would exult over my fitting punishment, how this bitter blow would bring lasting grief and misery to my friends and parents, and how fast the news of this unheard-of disgrace would spread over the whole world. What road could I take now? How could I show my face in public, to be pointed at by every finger, derided by every tongue, a monstrous spectacle to all I met? I was appalled to remember that according to the cruel letter of the Law, a eunuch is such an abomination to the Lord that men made eunuchs by the amputation or mutilation of their members are forbidden to enter a church as if they were stinking and unclean, and even animals in that state are rejected for sacrifice.[7]

Similar precedent likely governed the external expression of gender:

> No garb of an able-bodied man should be put upon a woman, neither should an able-bodied man wear the mantle of a woman; for anybody doing these things is something detestable to Jehovah your God.[8]

From an archaeological perspective, however, Ellen-Jane Pader[9] and

---

3. S.J. Lucy, 'Housewives, warriors and slaves? sex and gender in Anglo-Saxon burials', *Invisible People and Processes: Writing Gender and Childhood into European Archaeology*, eds J. Moore and E. Scott (1997), 150–68.
4. K.A. Brush, 'Gender and mortuary analysis in pagan Anglo-Saxon archaeology', *Archaeological Review from Cambridge* 7(1) (1988), 76–89.
5. P. Drucker, '"In the tropics there is no sin": sexuality and gay–lesbian movements in the Third World', *New Left Review* 218 (1996), 75–101.
6. N. Barley, *Dancing on the Grave: Encounters with Death* (1995), 88.
7. P. Abelard, 'Historia Calamitatum', in *The Letters of Abelard and Heloise*, trans. B. Radice (1985), 75–6.
8. Deuteronomy 22:5, *The Holy Bible* (New World translation).
9. E.J. Pader, 'Material symbolism and social relations in mortuary studies', in *Anglo-Saxon Cemeteries 1979*, eds P.A. Rahtz, T. Dickinson, and L. Watts, British Archaeological Reports, British Series 82 (1980), 143–59; E.J. Pader, *Symbolism, Social Relations and the Interpretation of Mortuary Remains*, British Archaeological Reports, British Series 130 (1982).

Janet Henderson[10] have noted that there is an incomplete correlation between grave goods and the sex determination of skeletal remains. John Shephard writes: 'Although some separation could be detected between types normally considered to be male and female, shared items were not clearly distinguished and it would have been necessary to combine pairs and sets of clusters in a rather arbitrary way.'[11] He attributes this difficulty to chronological and social variation. At the Portway site in Andover, Hampshire, Alison Cook and Maxwell Dacre suggest another interpretation when they write that the osteologists

> were convinced, when examining the skeleton in grave 9, that it was male. The objects associated with the burial are those one would expect to find accompanying a female and it is tempting to dismiss the osteological evidence. Nevertheless, we may be dealing with a complex burial ritual involving the deposition of a male body in female apparel.[12]

Another explanation may relate to the presence of more than two genders in early medieval society.[13] In this chapter, we will argue that individuals of an intermediate or mixed sex and gender were likely to have contributed to the social structure of early medieval Europe and, among these, there may have been a type of pre-Christian ritual specialist, a *sacerdos*.

The biological basis of sex and gender

Sex is part of the genetic make-up (genotype) of an individual that is determined by the presence of a single male Y-chromosome inherited from the father at conception.[14] This Y-chromosome contributes to a series of hormonal changes that normally produce a phenotypic male (e.g. an individual with male external genitalia). It is the Y-chromosome that has been connected with the sexual dimorphism in size noted in humans.[15] Modern humans are moderately sexually

10. J. Henderson, 'Pagan Saxon cemeteries: a study of the problems of sexing by grave goods and bones', in *Burial Archaeology: Current Research, Methods, and Developments*, eds C.A. Roberts, F. Lee, and J. Bintliff (1989), 77–83.
11. J. Shephard, 'The social identity of the individual in isolated barrows and barrow cemeteries in Anglo-Saxon England', in *Space, Hierarchy, and Society*, eds B.C. Burnham and J. Kingsbury, British Archaeological Reports, International Series 59 (1979), 52.
12. A.M. Cook and M.W. Dacre, *Excavations at Portway, Andover 1973–1975* (1985), 56.
13. C.J. Knüsel, 'Pagan charm and the place of anthropological theory', *Journal of European Archaeology* 1(2) (1993), 205–8.
14. M.F. Lyon, 'Evolution of mammalian sex-chromosomes', in *The Difference Between the Sexes*, eds R.V. Short and E. Balaban (1994), 381–96.
15. J. Varrela and L. Alvesalo, 'Effects of the Y chromosome on quantitative growth: an anthropometric study of 47, XXY males', *American Journal of Physical Anthropology* 68 (1985), 239–45.

dimorphic when compared with living apes, which means that males are, on average, about 20 per cent heavier than females.[16] The degree of sexual dimorphism, however, varies among modern human populations and through time, hominids having become less dimorphic during prehistory.[17] Therefore, accurate assessment of sex from skeletal remains relies on having a sound understanding of population variation. Sex assessment is based on both differential body proportions and on features associated with the onset of sexual maturity – *the secondary sexual characteristics* – such as the broader pelvis of females. Features of the pelvis and cranium are most often used to determine the sex of skeletal remains, with those of the pelvis being accorded more accuracy.[18] Because secondary sexual characteristics develop only after puberty, sex assessment of prepubescent individuals remains problematic.[19] Sex characters are altered by the ageing process such that older females often develop male features and younger males may possess those of females;[20] this tends to produce an over-representation of males in skeletal populations.[21]

The appearance of secondary sexual characteristics at puberty, upon which sex determination relies in skeletonized individuals, is under the influence of testicular hormones which are secreted during intra-uterine development by the fetal gonads.[22] Differential hormonal levels of mother or child at this early stage can often confuse the external expression (the phenotype) of the sex chromosomes and produce intersex individuals, those possessing both male and female traits in variable combinations.[23] The gender of such individuals can be either

16. R.D. Martin, L.A. Willner and A. Dettling, 'The evolution of sexual size dimorphism in primates', in *The Difference Between the Sexes*, eds R.V. Short and E. Balaban (1994), 159–200.
17. For the evolutionary changes in sexual dimorphism see: D.W. Frayer, 'Sexual dimorphism and cultural evolution in the Late Pleistocene and Holocene of Europe', *Journal of Human Evolution* 9 (1980), 309–415; F.H. Smith, 'Sexual differences in European Neanderthal crania with special reference to the Krapina remains', *Journal of Human Evolution* 9 (1980), 359–75; H.M. McHenry, 'Body size and proportions in early hominids', *American Journal of Physical Anthropology* 87 (1992), 407–31.
18. W.M. Krogman and M.Y. Iscan, *The Human Skeleton in Forensic Medicine* (1986); L.E. St Hoyme and M.Y. Iscan, 'Determination of sex and race: accuracy and assumptions', in *Reconstruction of Life from the Skeleton*, eds M.Y. Iscan and K.A.R. Kennedy (1989).
19. H. Schutkowski, 'Sex determination of infant and juvenile skeletons: I morphological features', *American Journal of Physical Anthropology* 90 (1993), 199–205.
20. P.L. Walker, 'Problems of preservation and sexism in sexing: some lessons from historical collections for paleodemographers', in *Grave Reflections: Portraying the Past Through Cemetery Studies*, eds S.R. Saunders and A. Herring (1995).
21. K.M. Weiss 'Demographic models for anthropology', *Memoirs of the Society of American Archeology* 27 (1973).
22. J.D. Wilson, 'Translating gonadal sex into phenotypic sex', in *The Differences Between the Sexes*, eds R.V. Short and E. Balaban (1994).
23. J.J. Roslyn, E.W. Fonkalsrud and B. Lippe, 'Intersex disorders in adolescents and adults', *American Journal of Surgery* 146 (1983), 138–44; J.L. Rutgers,

male or female or a combination of both, depending on the social and cultural circumstances. Modern Western medicine views such abnormalities as an 'acute medical emergency', requiring reconstructive surgery and psychological therapy.[24] In other societies, a similar congenital abnormality evokes a very different response. Garry Warne *et al.* report on one such case from a Tiwi community on Bathurst Island, Australia, where an XY boy with androgen (a predominately male hormone) insensitivity developed genital abnormalities that were also present in other men from the same place. Doctors advised *reversing* the two-year-old boy's *sex*. The boy's mother refused such a course of action, saying that if the boy were altered, the child would 'be put to the spear', and she would face spearing through the leg. The authors note: 'It was clear that this traditional Aboriginal society could tolerate a number of its members having naturally occurring physical malformations, but could perhaps cope less well with any dramatic change perceived to be unnatural.'[25]

Through the mediation of sex hormones, then, genotypic sex contributes to the make-up of an individual's gender. Thus gender is defined as an element of human social relations based on culturally perceived and culturally inscribed differences and similarities between and among males and females.[26] A gender opposite to that of one's sexual anatomy can be assumed at the discretion of the individual and with the active or passive acceptance of the social group.

Although tests to detect the sex chromosomes in cells only became available in 1949,[27] it is likely that people in the past recognized variable sexual behaviours and their anatomical attributes because intersex is relatively common (two to fifteen per cent of dairy goats are affected, for example) and problematic in domesticated animals.[28] In the later medieval period, Geoffrey Chaucer seems to be aware of the existence of such individuals. Of his Pardoner he writes:

> This pardoner hadde heer as yelow as wex,
> But smothe it heng, as dooth a strike of flex; ...
> Swiche galringge eyen hadde he as an hare ...

contd.

'Advances in the pathology of intersex conditions', *Human Pathology* 22(9) (1991), 884–91; P.C. Sen Gupta, 'Atypical female intersex', *British Journal of Obstetrics and Gynaecology* 99 (1992), 689–96.

24. D. Muram and J. Dewhurst, 'Inheritance of intersex disorders', *Canadian Medical Association Journal* 130 (1984), 121–5.

25. G.L. Warne, H.E. MacLean and J.D. Zajac, 'Genetic disorders of human sex differentiation', in *Sex Chromosomes and Sex Determining Genes*, eds K.C. Reed and J.A. Marshall Graves (1993), 57–67.

26. J.M. Gero and M.W. Conkey (eds), *Engendering Archaeology: Women and Prehistory* (1991).

27. H. Sheldon, *Boyd's Introduction to the Study of Disease* (1984), 40.

28. W.T.K. Bosu and P.K. Basrur, 'Morphological and hormonal features of an ovine and a caprine intersex', *Canadian Journal of Comparative Medicine* 48(4) (1984), 402–9.

> A voys he hadde as smal as hath a goot.
> No berd hadde he, ne never sholde have
> As smothe it was as it were late y-shave; I trowe
> he were a gelding or a mare.[29]

In modern human clinical samples the number of intersex individuals (those of an ambiguous sex) varies from one or two per thousand[30] through to as many as 1 in 850 births – the most common, in cases of Klinefelter's syndrome (47, XXY)[31] – to as few as 1 in 62,000 for complete testicular feminization.[32] One should expect interments from the past to include such individuals, perhaps in frequencies not unlike these more recent examples, as most of these disorders do not affect individual survival, although the individual may be rendered infertile. The perceived gender of such individuals, culturally prescribed or individually assumed, may be signified by grave-good deposition which differs from the biological sex inferred from skeletal remains. It is also possible that true intersex (hermaphroditism) was recognized on anatomical or behavioural grounds and the ambivalence recognized in burial rites. Individuals may also have assumed the dress and accoutrements of the 'opposite' gender for socially and culturally prescribed reasons in the past, thus blurring distinctions understood to exist in recent Western societies.

The mixed sex and gender Germanic *sacerdos*

Tacitus provides a unique description of a Germanic *sacerdos* when he writes:

> The Naharvali proudly point out the grove associated with an ancient worship. The presiding priest dresses like a woman but

---

29. G. Chaucer, *The Canterbury Tales*, The Great Books Series, Encyclopaedia Britannica (1979), Ll. 675–91 *passim*. The transliteration of these lines is as follows: 'This Pardoner had hair as yellow as wax/ But lank it hung as does a strike of flax … /As shiny eyes he had as has a hare … /A voice he had that bleated like a goat. / No beard had he, nor ever should he have, /For Smooth his face as he'd just had a shave; /I think he was a gelding or a mare.' – G. Chaucer, *The Canterbury Tales*, ed. B. Radice, trans. N. Cowgill, Penguin Revised Edition (1958), 37–8. The absence of a beard, a high voice, and thin hair is similar to the description of more recent eunuchs among the eastern European Skoptzy religious sect – E. Pittard, *La Castration chez l'homme et les modifications morphologiques qu'elle entraine: recherche sur les adeptes d'une secte d'eunuques mystiques, les Skoptzy* (Paris, 1934), 21.
30. J. Glatzl, 'Intersexformen im Kindesalter (Pathogenese-Klinik-Diagnose Therapie)', *Wiener Klinische Wochenschrift* 99(9) (1987), 295–306.
31. M.A. Parsons, 'Disorders of growth, differentiation, and morphogenesis', in *General Systematic Pathology*, ed. J.C.E. Underwood (1992), 41–69.
32. J. Varrela, L. Alvesalo and H. Vinkka, 'Body size and shape in 46, XY females with complete testicular feminisation', *Annals of Human Biology* 11 (1984), 291–301.

the deity is said to be the counterpart of our Castor and Pollux. This indicates their character, but their name is the Alci.[33]

Rudolph Simek equates the *Alci* with horse worship.[34] Tacitus also mentions the importance of horses in rituals involving divination and the consultations of 'kings and priests', noting that the animals were husbanded especially for such use in sacred groves.[35] Proselytizing ecclesiastics among the northern and eastern peoples of Europe from as early as the seventh and eighth centuries through to the later medieval period continually inveighed against ceremonial rites involving sacrifice, mutilation, and consumption of horse-flesh.[36] In Hungary, the *táltos* or horse sacrificer was a feature of Hungarian ceremonies into the Middle Ages; horse-flesh was consumed in Denmark until the tenth century[37] and in Siberia at least until the eighteenth century.[38] Pope Gregory III wrote to the missionary Boniface, in AD 732, advising 'that some [*of the Bavarians*] eat wild horses and many tame horses. By no means allow this to happen in the future, but suppress it in every way possible with the help of Christ and impose a suitable penance upon offenders.'[39] Horses, it seems, and rites associated with them involving divination and perhaps social display, made such practices a target in the struggle for both souls and socio-political allegiance. Rituals involving the interment of horses or parts of horses appear to have been a common and widespread practice among the Eurasian peoples in later prehistory and is found in the modern period in some areas.[40] From this information it appears

---

33. C. Tacitus, *The Agricola and Germania*, trans. H. Mattingley (1979), 43.
34. R. Simek, *Dictionary of Northern Mythology* (1993).
35. C. Tacitus, *Germania* (1979), 10.
36. A. Meaney, *Anglo-Saxon Amulets and Curing Stones*, British Archaeological Reports, British Series 96 (1981); T. Dömötör, 'The problem of the Hungarian Female *Táltos*', in *Shamanism in Eurasia* 2, ed. M. Hoppál (Budapest, 1984), 423–9; Simek, *Dictionary* (1993), 157–8.
37. P. Sawyer, 'The process of Scandinavian Christianization in the tenth and eleventh centuries', in *The Christianization of Scandinavia: Report of a Symposium Held at Kungälv, Sweden 4–9 August 1985*, eds B. Sawyer, P. Sawyer and I. Wood (1987), 80.
38. Z.P. Sokolova, 'A survey of the Ob-Ugrian shamanism', in *Shamanism: Past and Present*, eds M. Hoppál and O.J. Sadovszky (Budapest, 1989), 155–64.
39. J.N. Hillgarth (ed.), *Christianity and Paganism, 350–750: The Conversion of Western Europe* (1986), 174.
40. Archaeological contexts that include horses or parts of horses from across Eurasia have frequently been recovered, stretching in time from later prehistoric periods through to the modern period in eastern Europe and parts of the Far East. See S. Piggott, 'Heads and hoofs', *Antiquity* 36 (1962), 110–18; T.P. O'Connor, 'A horse skeleton from Sutton Hoo, Suffolk, U.K.', *Archaeozoologia* 7(1) (1994), 29–37; J.M. Bond, 'Burnt offerings: animal bone in Anglo-Saxon cremations', *World Archaeology* 28 (1) (1996), 76–88; N. Roymans, *Tribal Societies in Northern Gaul: An Anthropological Perspective* (Amsterdam, 1990), 78–80; E. Crubézy, H. Martin, P.-H. Giscard, Z. Batsaikan, S. Erdenebaatar, J.P. Verdier and B. Maureille, 'Funeral practices and animal sacrifices in Mongolia at the Uigur period: archaeological and ethno-historical study of a *kurgan* in the Egyin Gol valley (Baikal region)', *Antiquity* 70 (1996), 891–9.

that a type of *sacerdos* wearing certain gender-female garments or accoutrements may have been implicated in rites involving horses, divination, and sacrifice. The cross-dressing priest of Tacitus' description suggests parallels with individuals encountered in ethnographic sources worldwide, one of whom is the ethnographically recorded *berdache* or man–woman.

Ethnographic descriptions of the man–woman

A man–woman is defined as 'a person, usually male, who was anatomically normal but assumed the dress, occupations, and behavior of the other sex to effect a change in gender status. This shift was not complete; rather it was a movement toward a somewhat intermediate status that combined social attributes of males and females.'[41] In other words, certain aspects of female dress might be adopted, but the person affecting the role did not become gender female. Previously, these individuals were referred to by the term *berdache* derived from the Arabic word *bardag* and the Persian *bardaj*, which connote the passive partner in male-male sexual intercourse.[42] This pejorative use results from misunderstandings of American indigenous cultures by contact-period Europeans; the term 'man–woman' better represents the intermediate gender of such individuals.[43] The man–woman is a widespread phenomenon with examples known not only from North America,[44] but also from Central Asia,[45] Indonesia, Korea, South America,[46] and China up to at least the fourteenth century.[47] It has been suggested that similar individuals may be identifiable in Herodotus' description of the ancient Scythian 'Enarees' of southeastern Europe.[48] It is argued below that the negative reaction to such individuals in recent contact situations may have a considerable antiquity in Europe itself and have contributed to inimical attitudes

---

41. C. Callender and L.M. Kochems, 'The North American berdache', *Current Anthropology* 24 (4) (1983), 443–70.
42. W.L. Williams, *The Spirit and the Flesh: Sexual Diversity in American Indian Culture* (1992), 9.
43. R. Fulton and S.W. Anderson, 'The Amerindian "man-woman": gender, liminality, and cultural continuity', *Current Anthropology*, 33(5) (1992), 603–10.
44. Callender and Kochems, 'The North American berdache', 443–70; Fulton and Anderson 'The Amerindian "man-woman"', 603–10.
45. V.N. Basilov, 'Vestiges of transvestism in Central-Asian shamanism', in *Shamanism in Siberia*, eds V. Diószegi, V. and M. Hoppál, trans. S. Simon (Budapest, 1978), 281–9; M. Eliade, *Shamanism: Archaic Techniques of Ecstasy* (1964).
46. J.M. Atkinson, 'Shamanisms today', *Annual Review of Anthropology* 21 (1992), 307–30; Eliade, *Shamanism* (1964).
47. C. Humphrey, 'Shamanic practices and the state in northern Asia: views from the centre and periphery', in *Shamanism, History, and the State*, eds N. Thomas and C. Humphrey (1994), 207.
48. T. Taylor, 'The Gundesrup cauldron', *Scientific American* 166 (1992), 66–71.

levelled against such individuals more recently. It is suggested, therefore, that the memory of the existence of such individuals was almost completely suppressed in historical sources.

Robert Fulton and Steven Anderson argue that the man–woman possessed a sacerdotal role in indigenous North American society that is commensurate with roles identified as those of a *shaman*, a term deriving from the central Siberian Tungusian word *saman* or *hammas*, meaning one who is excited, moved or raised, or who knows in an ecstatic manner.[49] The term refers to rites performed while in a trance-state (a ritualized death) during which totemic helping-spirits are consulted. The ubiquity of ritual specialists, cross-culturally, many of whom have been called *shamans*, suggests that, although the word may be related to a specific type of Siberian specialist, the concepts which it represents are likely to have applicability outside this particular region. It is this use of the word that is employed here, although variations in such practices no doubt existed through time and across geographic space. It has previously been suggested that shamanic individuals and rites were present in the early medieval period, from considerations of early medieval literature,[50] iconography and myths,[51] archaeological remains,[52] and from anthropological treatments, especially centred on the god Odin.[53]

Although Mary Beard divorces the Near Eastern-inspired Roman eunuch priests of *Cybele* or *Magna Mater* from shamanic associations,[54] it seems that their appearance (long hair, extravagant jewellery, long yellow silken robes), their penchant for ecstatic dancing, frenetic self-flagellation, and trance-induced self-emasculation, as well as their sexual practices, clashed with Roman mores in the way similar attributes of the man–woman clashed with more recent precepts of decorum. The stories surrounding Cybele, who gave birth to a bisexual monster called *Agdistis*, as well as the eunuch *Attis*, seem to suggest an association with deviation from sexual norms.[55] Beard writes:

> The double edge of the transgression is clear. The 'galli' [*priests of Cybele*] are portrayed as breaking the laws of nature by becoming 'women', or at least 'half-men' (castrated, dressed in women's clothes, long-haired, the apt sexual partner ... for a man). But they compound that crime by not obeying the rules of

49. J.A. Grim, *The Shaman: Patterns of Religious Healing among the Ojibway Indians* (1983); Eliade, *Shamanism* (1964), 4.
50. S.O. Glosecki, *Shamanism and Old English Poetry* (1989).
51. H.R. Ellis Davidson, *The Lost Beliefs of Northern Europe* (1993).
52. T.C. Lethbridge, *A Cemetery at Lackford Suffolk: Report of the Excavation of a Cemetery of the Pagan Anglo-Saxon Period in 1947* (1951).
53. A.-L. Siikala and M. Hoppál, *Studies on Shamanism* (Budapest, 1992), 81; Eliade, *Shamanism* (1964), 379–87.
54. M. Beard, 'The Roman and the foreign: the cult of the "Great Mother" in Imperial Rome', in *Shamanism, History, and the State*, 164–90.
55. J. Ferguson, *The Religions of the Roman Empire* (1970), 26.

either their old or new gender. . . . In the Roman imagination, the eunuch *gallus* was both a non-man and a man who broke the rules of proper male behaviour.[56]

According to Dionysius of Halicarnassus (late first century BC) the feminine and 'Phrygian' demeanour of these individuals was accompanied by 'wearing figures upon their breasts and striking their timbrels while their followers play tunes upon their flutes in honour of the Mother of the Gods.'[57] Having such attributes, these priests resemble ritual specialists from eighteenth- and nineteenth-century Hungary, of whom similar attributes were also noted.[58] It could be that the late survival in eastern Europe of such individuals and practices may represent a remnant of what was originally a much more widespread phenomenon.

The roles filled by the man–woman were among the most important for social cohesion. They included the production of crafted objects of high value, officiation at children's naming ceremonies, accompaniment of warriors into battle and care for the wounded, supervision of ceremonies, participation in councils, and orchestration of events at the time of death, during mourning, and at funerary ceremonies.[59] They were also renowned for their ability as teachers and story-tellers; many of these stories were often sung.[60] This feature is shared with shamans who are often keepers of oral tradition and in this capacity exert a profound influence on maintaining cultural identity.[61] Much like shamans, the man–woman also acted as mediator between deities and humans, especially during burial, and between men and women in courtship and ritual, as part of their liminal social identity.[62] Peter Metcalf and Richard Huntingdon characterize liminality as a state of transition, a case of 'betwixt and between' normal social roles and intimately involved with sacred and moral codes.[63] Liminal individuals are sometimes referred to as 'threshold' people in that such persons are said to

> elude or slip through the network of classifications that normally locate states and positions in cultural space. Liminal entities are

---

56. Beard, 'The Roman and the foreign', 175.
57. T. Dömötör, 'The problem of the Hungarian Female *Táltos*', in *Shamanism in Eurasia* 2, 423–9.
58. J. Fazekas, 'Hungarian shamanism: material and history of research', in *Studies in Shamanism*, ed. C.M. Edsman (Budapest, 1984), 97–119; Callender and Kochems, 'The North American berdache'.
59. Fulton and Anderson, 'The Amerindian "man–woman"; Williams, *Spirit and the Flesh*, 33.
60. A.-L. Siikala and M. Hoppál, *Studies on Shamanism* (Budapest, 1992), 128.
61. Callender and Kochems, 'The North American berdache'.
62. Fulton and Anderson, 'The Amerindian "man–woman"; Williams, *Spirit and the Flesh*, 70–1.
63. P. Metcalf and R. Huntington, *Celebrations of Death: The anthropology of mortuary ritual* (2nd edn, 1991).

assigned and arrayed by law, custom, convention, and ceremonial. As such, their ambiguous and indeterminate attributes are expressed by a rich variety of symbols in many societies that ritualize social and cultural transitions. Thus, liminality is frequently likened to death, to being in the womb, to invisibility, to darkness, to bisexuality, to the wilderness, and to the eclipse of the sun and moon.[64]

The social identity of the man–woman in archaeological contexts

In analyses of social organization, archaeologists have concentrated on differences in the quality and number of grave goods, the place of burial, the orientation of the burial, and the type and size of burial monuments to provide data relating to social distinctions between individuals and groups within a burial sample.[65] Combinations of such features have been used to identify paramounts or socio-political leaders. Such analyses have not been employed until recently to identify other socially distinctive individuals. Following the precept that a person's social identity, an amalgam of statuses, is reflected in the grave goods, burial place, and the manner of burial,[66] it is in the funerary context that one would expect to find distinctive material objects associated with the man–woman identity. Since no descriptions of the burials of pre-Christian ritual specialists exist from western Europe, any potential ability to identify them from archaeological contexts requires predictions developed from ethnographic accounts of such individuals and their burials, where they exist. Those believed to have a sacerdotal role in many societies are often accorded burial rites consonant with a liminal status.[67] Many are often buried apart and the place hidden due to the fear such individuals evoke, as in the case

64. V. Turner, *The Ritual Process* (1969), 94.
65. See, for example, L.R. Binford, 'Mortuary practices: their study and their potential', in *An Archaeological Perspective*, ed. L.R. Binford (1972), 108–243; M. Parker Pearson, 'Mortuary practices, society, and ideology: an ethnoarchaeological case study', in *Symbolic and Structural Archaeology*, ed. I. Hodder (1982), 99–113; K. Randsborg, 'Burial, succession and early state formation in Denmark', in *The Archaeology of Death*, eds R. Chapman, I. Kinnes, and K. Randsborg (1981), 105–21; E.J. Pader, 'Material Symbolism and social relations', (1980), 143–59.
66. C.J. Arnold, 'Territories and leadership: frameworks for the study of emergent polities in early Anglo-Saxon southern England', in *Power and Politics in Early Medieval Britain and Ireland*, eds S.T. Driscoll and M.R. Nieke (1988), 111–27.
67. M. Barbeau, *Medicine Men on the North Pacific Coast*, National Museum of Canada Bulletin No. 152 (1958); M.B. Kenin-Lopsan, 'The funeral rites of the Tuva shamans', in *Shamanism in Siberia*, eds V. Diószegi, V. and M. Hoppál, trans. S. Simon (Budapest, 1978), 291–8. V.P. Djakonova, 'The vestments and paraphernalia of a Tuva shamaness', in *ibid.*, 325–39; J.C. McGregor, 'Burial of an early American magician', *American Anthropologist* 86 (2) (1941), 270–98.

of the Yakutian shaman, Tokoyeu, perhaps because his helping spirit was a raven, an associate of death.[68] Among the Sioux, the man–woman or *Winkte* was interred on a special hill and considered to be both man and woman in the spirit land.[69] Sacerdotal status is often indicated, therefore, by unusual interments: those distinguished from others in their form and content.

The famous Zuni man–woman, *We'wha*, was dressed for burial in female attire but then a pair of white trousers was pulled over her legs, which were the first male clothes she had worn since assuming her man–woman role.[70] Similarly, one of the last transvestite priests among the Uzbeks, *Tasmat Kholmatov*, wore 'a knee-length shirt-dress of light-blue flowered crêpe with buttoned "upstanding" collar, characteristic of traditional Uzbek women's wear ... [under which he wore] trousers of dark-blue material with white dots – a colour combination not used in men's clothing.'[71] In addition, Kholmatov refused to wear a girdle (belt) associated with men's attire, even when encouraged to do so by members of his family. Since early medieval peoples appear to have interred the dead fully clothed,[72] we may hope to find objects of personal adornment that might relate to a similar status distinction.

Because such individuals could have accumulated considerable wealth, the man–woman may be expected to be accompanied by numerous grave goods. Ethnographically, success among ritual specialists was recognized through more elaborate costumes[73] and increased payment for services in the form of prestige goods such as a blanket on the north-west coast of North America[74] or a horse among the Tetons of the Great Plains.[75] The burial of the man–woman could include prestige objects shared by other high-status individuals, which would be expected to vary with group access to such goods. Due to the liminal status of the man–woman, facets of the burial might reflect a symbolic association, including a particular type of burial or interment with various symbolic objects. Mihàly Hoppál has noted the importance of these objects to the shaman, writing: 'The shaman as a mediator is a specialist in ritual communication and in maintaining the fragile state of social/psychological equilibrium by symbolic mediation between worlds of ordinary and non-ordinary realities. He

---

68. M.M. Balzer, 'Flights of the sacred', *American Anthropologist* 98 (2) (1996), 305–18.
69. Williams, *Spirit and the Flesh*, 84.
70. M.T. Stevenson, 'The Zuni Indians', *Bureau of American Ethnology*, Report 23 (1901-1902), 313, cited in Williams, *Spirit and the Flesh*, 83.
71. Basilov, 'Vestiges of transvestism' (1978), 285.
72. B.K. Young, 'Paganisme, christianisation et rites funéraires mérovingiens', *Médiévale* 7 (1977), 5–81. M. Welch, *Anglo-Saxon England* (1992).
73. Djakonova, 'The vestments and paraphernalia'.
74. Barbeau, *Medicine Men* (1958).
75. J. Fire, *Lame Deer, Seeker of Visions* (1972), cited in Callender and Kochems, 'The North American Berdache' (1983).

has special symbols which give him power, and in all shaman ceremonies symbolize the process of eliminating ordinary reality in order to gain access to another state of consciousness, or, to put it even more briefly: symbols make the shaman.'[76] To summarize: the man–woman may be identified from a mixed sex and gender interment with a potential for many grave goods, some of which may be those associated with prestige, objects of symbolic significance, and a burial type and placement different from those of the majority of the group.

Archaeological application

The site reports from Buckland, Dover, Kent;[77] Sewerby, East Yorkshire;[78] Norton, Cleveland;[79] and Portway, Andover, Hampshire[80] were selected for analysis because they included separate recording of biological sex and gender as represented by grave inclusions. Comparisons were made between the types of grave goods found and their relative position in relation to the sex attribution of the skeleton. In this way male/female (M/F), male (M/M?), and female (F/F?) were identified. Male/female graves refer to individuals who were considered male on the basis of osteological criteria but which contained 'female' grave inclusions. M/M? and F/F? refer to those inhumations in which the sex determination matched the gender suggested by the grave inclusions, but where the sex determination was questionable due to incompleteness of the skeletal remains or due to disagreement among the skeletal indicators of biological sex. Because no two burials were completely identical at any of the sites, these comparisons consisted of lists of the frequencies of grave good associations for each type of burial (Figure 1). The type of burial and its placement were also considered. In a cross-cultural survey, Christopher Carr maintains that grave goods are most often associated with the deceased's gender and vertical social position, that body orientation, body position, and the spatial arrangement of furniture in the grave reflect aspects of belief, and that the location of the interment is linked with the beliefs and worldview of past societies.[81] Bettina Arnold makes a similar case for distinguishing genders, noting that the factors which are of most use are the quantity of each category

---

76. Siikala and Hoppál, *Studies on Shamanism*, 127.
77. V.I. Evison, *Dover: The Buckland Anglo-Saxon Cemetery* (1987).
78. S.M. Hirst, *An Anglo-Saxon Inhumation Cemetery at Sewerby, East Yorkshire* (1985).
79. S.J. Sherlock and M.G. Welch, *An Anglo-Saxon Cemetery at Norton, Cleveland*, Council for British Archaeology report no. 82 (1992).
80. A.M. Cook and M.W. Dacre, *Excavations at Portway, Andover 1973–1975* (1985).
81. C. Carr, 'Mortuary practices: their social, philosophical-religious, circumstantial, and physical determinants', *Journal of Archaeological Method and Theory* 2 (2) (1995), 105–200.

Site name	Male	Female	Male/Female
Sewerby	10	24	13
Buckland	28	38	34
Norton	14	24	14
Portway	11	20	6

Figure 1 The number of major types of grave goods associated with each sex/gender category.

with the burial and the placement of those objects on the body.[82] Therefore, in addition to the types of grave goods present in burials, the placement of objects, relative to anatomical areas of the skeleton, was also considered in order to compensate for variable burial positions (Figure 2).

The numbers and percentages of adult individuals identified as of male sex but with grave goods normally associated with females were as follows: Sewerby, 6 per cent; Buckland, 8 per cent (4 per cent for those of a 'definite' disagreement); Norton, 10 per cent; and Portway, 3 per cent (Figure 3). Juvenile burials were not included due to difficulties in assessing sex for these individuals.

Comparisons between burials were made difficult by variations in terminology and identification among these reports. For example, 'keys' at Buckland take variable shapes, which might suggest that the single term does not sufficiently account for the variation; and 'tweezers' and 'workboxes' presuppose a specific function without reference to some external criterion. Similarly, 'keys', 'latchlifters' and 'girdlehangers' do not appear to be completely discrete categories in that these names subsume a variety of different-shaped objects. At Norton latchlifters, keys and girdlehangers form a single category, while the t-shaped 'key' in burial 160 at Buckland (item 5b) looks little different from the girdlehanger (item 11) found with burial 49 at Sewerby.

---

82. B. Arnold, 'The deposed princess of Vix: the need for an engendered European prehistory', in *The Archaeology of Gender: Proceedings of the 22nd Annual Chacmool Conference*, eds D. Walde and N. Willows (1991), 366–74.

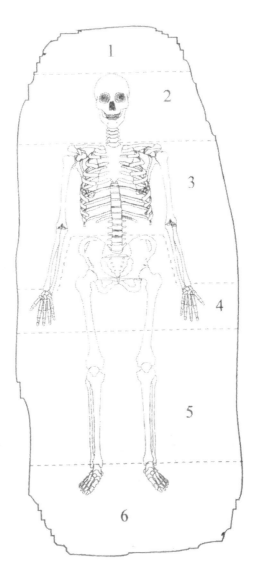

Figure 2   Object placement relative to anatomical areas of the skeleton.
Areas are defined as:

    1 = the area above the cranium

    2 = the area of the cranium, mandible, and cervical vertebrae

    3 = the area of the pectoral girdle, thoracic and lumbar vertebral column (to the vicinity of the fourth lumbar vertebra), arm, and forearm, inferiorly to the carpals

    4 = the hands and pelvic girdle to the mid-femoral area (including the area of the fourth and fifth lumbar vertebrae)

    5 = the mid-femoral area to the tibio-talar joint

    6 = the feet and lowermost portion of the grave.

Site name	Male/Female interments	Total interments	Percentage
Sewerby	3	55	6
Buckland	13 (7*)	169	8 (4*)
Norton	12	120	10
Portway	2	69	3

Figure 3   The number of mixed sex and gender interments at the sites under discussion.
(Asterisk refers to 'definite' observations from those of less certain association from Buckland.)

Graves goods and sex/gender categories

The number of types of each grave good was tabulated for each sex and gender category (Figures 4–7). At all sites under study the female graves contain a greater number of grave-good types. The male/female burials contain more than the male burials at Buckland and Sewerby, the same number at Norton, and fewer at Portway. The male/female graves, then, are generally not impoverished ones. In general, there is a variation in the number of grave goods per individual with some of the male/female graves containing an abundance of goods (see p. 179).

From the diagrams of the grave goods recovered from the Buckland site, it is clear that weapons – including swords, spearheads, ferrules, seaxes, and shields – are found only within the graves of males and female/males. (Eight of this latter category were recorded from Buckland, the only site that produced such a group, discussion of which is beyond the scope of this chapter.) The only other objects that are found exclusively with males are silver buckles, lace tags, coffins, sharpening steels, awls, a possible mattock, copper balances, and a possible lyre. The only objects that appear to be exclusively female are square-headed brooches, Frankish disc-brooches, gold bracteates, garnet pendants, buckets, bone lids, fire-steels, weaving battens, silver needles, and spindle whorls. This group of objects, therefore, distinguishes the female/males from females. Male/Females share objects with males and females, although they occur with no weapons and the previously identified male associates. They do, however, share objects with males exclusively, including belt/strap mounts, bone boxes, and tweezers. In addition, though, they share some objects only with females. These include Kentish disc brooches, coin pendants, silver disc pendants, other miscellaneous pendants, beads, bracelets, finger rings, glass objects, wooden boxes, silver workboxes, shears, keys, girdlehangers, spoons, iron diamonds, and silver rings. The only unique objects are weaving picks and annular brooches. Female/Males possess no unique objects which distinguish them from the male/females. Only pottery and miscellaneous iron objects were found in all but the male/female graves.

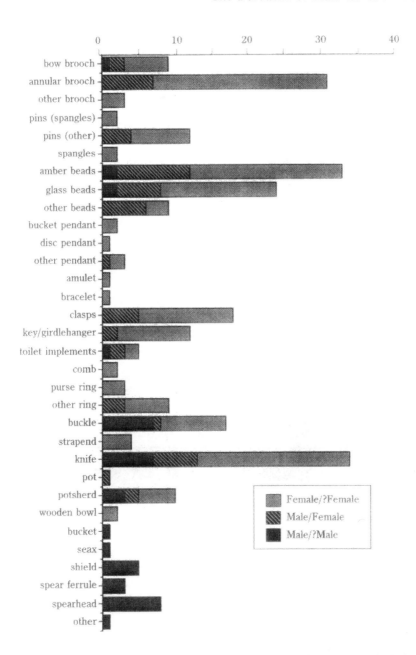

Figure 4 The distribution of burial goods at Norton by sex/gender category.

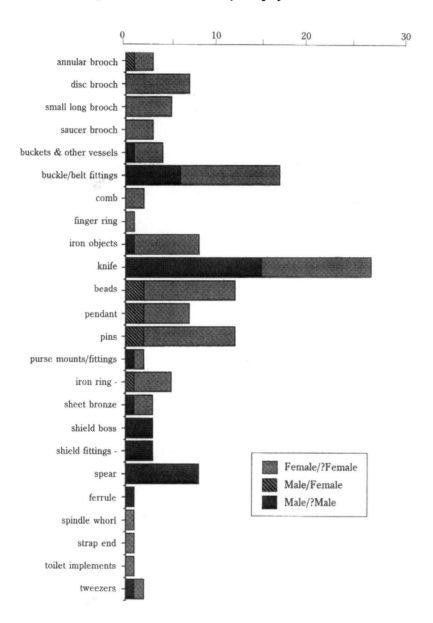

Figure 5   The distribution of burial goods at Portway by sex/gender category.

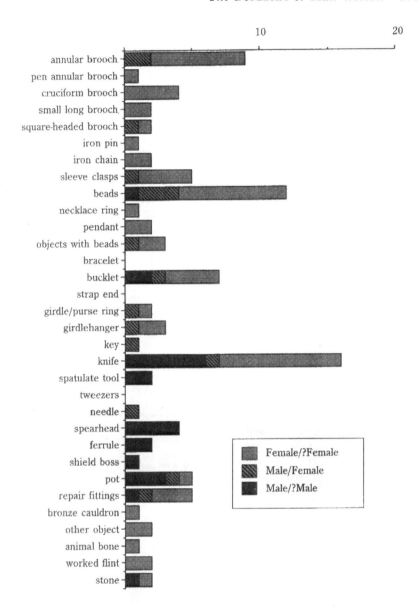

Figure 6 The distribution of burial goods at Sewerby by sex/gender category.

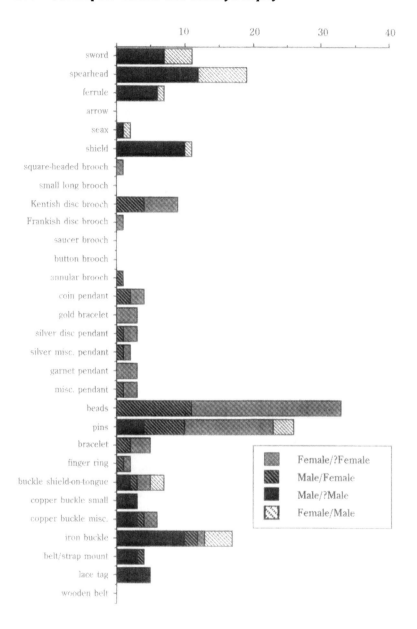

Figure 7   The distribution of burial goods at Buckland by sex/gender category.

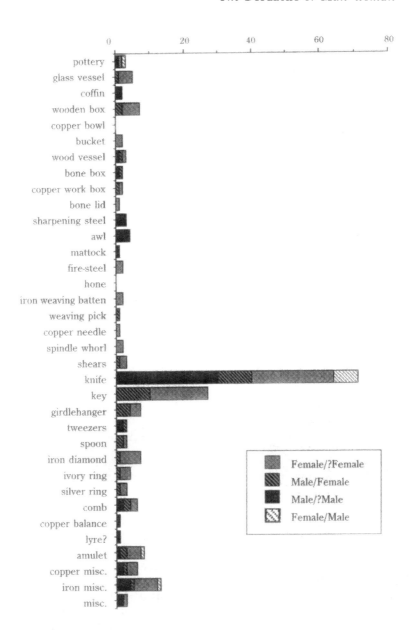

Figure 7   cont'd

Some objects seem not to have any specific association with the biological sex of the interred – that is, they are found with all four sex/gender groups. These include pins, silver shield-on-tongue buckles, iron buckles, knives, amulets, and miscellaneous iron objects. The amulets found in female graves include the tooth of a large horse, a lump of iron ore, a pebble, a disc-shaped pebble (perhaps a playing piece), a possible bone playing piece and a Roman coin. Male graves contained a lump of iron ore and small spherical pebbles; whereas one male/female in grave 15 contained a Roman coin.

The Portway population produced far fewer grave goods and only two individuals, burials 9 and 19, appear to be of male/female status. The burials of males are again exclusively characterized by the inclusion of weapons, which include shield bosses, shield fittings, spears, and ferrules. Both male and female graves possess buckets or vessels, knives, purse mounts or fittings, and tweezers. Females possess exclusively disc, small-long, and saucer brooches, as well as combs, finger rings, spindle whorls, strap ends and toilet implements. The burials of male/females possess no unique grave inclusions of the main types (see p. 174), although they are found without knives, iron objects, purse mounts or fittings, sheet bronze and tweezers, which both male and female burials contain. Their graves contain annular brooches, beads, pendants, pins, iron rings and iron buckles, all of which are shared with female burials.

At Sewerby male burials are again identified as having weapons to the exclusion of other sex/gender categories. These include spearheads, ferrules and shield bosses, as well as spatulate tools. Female burials are distinctive in that they include pendants, penannular, cruciform and small-long brooches, iron pins and chains, necklace rings, bronze cauldrons, animal bones, worked flint and boxes. Male/Female burials share objects with both male and female burials at the site, although they are uniquely distinguished by the inclusion of a key and needle. These burials share annular and square-headed brooches, sleeve clasps, objects found with beads, girdle/purse rings, and girdlehangers with female burials, and no objects exclusively with male burials. All three sex/gender categories possess beads, buckles, knives, pots and repair fittings. Essentially, the male/female interments at Sewerby look like males that have been interred with grave goods usually associated with female interments.

The same situation obtains at Norton – the male/female burials at this site share no objects exclusively with males, although they are uniquely identified by the inclusion of a pot with burial 107. They share a number of objects with the interments of females at the site, including bow brooches, amber and glass beads, toilet implements, buckles and knives. The burials of males are again distinguished by weapons, which include seaxes, shields, spear ferrules and spearheads, as well as buckets and strap ends. Female burials are exclusively associated with brooches other than the major types, pins, spangles, buckets and disc pendants, amulets, bracelets, combs, purse rings, strap ends and wooden bowls.

Although the discussion to this point has emphasized the similarities between burials deemed male/female and those deemed female, there are also notable differences. Although male/female burials are found with annular brooches and square-headed brooches, keys, beads, sleeve clasps and girdlehangers, they are not found with the majority of brooch types at these sites, including penannular, cruciform, saucer and disc brooches – objects which may then be argued to be female markers. They are also not found with items associated with weaving, spindle whorls or weaving battens, except for the single instance of a bone weaving pick found with individual 75 at Buckland.

The meaning of graves goods associated with male/female interments

In a cross-cultural analysis of mortuary behaviour Carr has noted that factors associated with social organization and belief systems have a nearly equal influence on mortuary behaviour.[83] Circumstantial or physical (i.e. functional) factors are five to ten times less likely to influence such behaviour. Furthermore, the latter two more frequently influenced mortuary behaviour than did ecological determinants. This assessment provides support for Peter Ucko's notion that the richness or poverty of grave offerings may represent the imposition of 'social and ritual sanctions' imposed on the dead by and for the living, rather than being related to the wealth of the individual.[84] Many of the objects shared between the male/female and female categories are objects that have previously been suggested by Audrey Meaney to have amuletic importance.[85] Among these she includes staves, crystal beads and balls, sieve spoons, cowrie shells, animal teeth and claws, antlers and horns, girdle-rings, 'toilet implements' such as earscoops, model implements, 'Hercules Club' (cone-shaped) and bucket-shaped pendants, keys, girdlehangers, Roman coins and workboxes. Meaney identifies the following as being most common and connected with women in archaeological contexts: crystal balls, usually in metal slings; cylindrical bronze boxes hung on chatelaine chains with inclusions of fabric and herbs; and a group of artefacts found beside the left side of the body, perhaps remnants of a bag, which contained broken glass, rings of bronze and iron, curated heirlooms and animal remains.[86] The contents of these containers seem to suggest some of the same types of inclusions that Gregory of Tours found so deviant during the visit of

---

83. Carr, 'Mortuary practices'.
84. P.J. Ucko, 'Ethnography and archaeological interpretation of funerary remains', *World Archaeology* 1 (1969), 266.
85. Meaney, *Anglo-Saxon Amulets*.
86. *Idem*, 'Women, witchcraft and magic in Anglo-Saxon England', in *Superstition and Popular Medicine in Anglo-Saxon England*, ed. D.G. Scragg (1989), 9–10.

an 'imposter' to Tours who was found to possess 'a big bag filled with
the roots of various plants ... mole's teeth, the bones of mice, bear's
claws and bear's fat ... recognized ... as witchcraft'.[87] Among the many
meanings these objects likely had, there may have been a symbolic,
medicinal or apotropaic purpose above and beyond a purely functional
one. From the extent of Meaney's list, early medieval society appears
to have been suffused with ritualistic symbolism in burial rites. In
addition to these objects, abstract masks have previously been noted in
early medieval metalwork, most notably on brooches. David Leigh
argues that the repeated use of profile masks with juxtaposed human
and animal images is meant to be representational.[88] Such representations may be akin to an apotropaic spirit associated with a particular
individual, perhaps a helping spirit or transformed deity.

In general, the types of grave goods associated with these male/
female individuals are similar to those found among female burials at
the same site. There is also a suggestion that some of the associated
objects, many of apparent amuletic inspiration, were in some way
associated with the left side of the body, usually the hip and thigh
region (Appendix 1, p. 188). The occurrence of antler fragments,
bucket pendants, and other metallic objects found in the vicinity of the
head suggests a head-covering of some sort. The occurrence of square-
headed brooches with some of these male/female individuals and a
large number of inclusions suggest both the richness of such burials
and a potential association with masked figures and ritual participation.

Location and type of burial

All of the male/female burials reviewed in this chapter are found within
the confines of burial grounds amid other interments. In no case do they
appear to be separated from the interments of others, nor are they
apparently singled out by special above-ground markers such as cairns
or mounds. The occurrence of male/female burials in multiple burials,
either vertically placed one above another or horizontally within the
same grave is, however, a repeated pattern at these sites. (See Appendix
2, p. 190) Not all of these burials are accorded such treatment and some
others do not include a male/female interment, however.

Although Siberian and North American ritual specialists were often
separated from others when interred, the individuals reviewed here do
not appear to have been. There are other, more isolated burials in bogs
and other locations that would suggest that some individuals were
separated in death in early medieval Europe. That the individuals

---

87. Gregory of Tours, *The History of the Franks*, trans. L. Thorpe (1983), 9.6: 485.
88. D. Leigh, 'Aspects of early brooch design', in *Anglo-Saxon Cemeteries: A
     Reappraisal*, ed. E. Southworth (1990), 107–24.

discussed here are interred among others and often with other individuals suggests a closer intimacy in death that might reflect the situation in life. This pattern holds as well for other individuals thought to be of a sacerdotal status such as the female from Bidford-on-Avon[89] and Burial AX at Yeavering.[90]

Discussion

How can we explain these male skeletons with what appear to be grave goods normally associated with females? The numbers of these individuals seem to mitigate against a suggestion that they are all chance anomalies. Assuming that no archaeological mishaps have occurred, the following hypotheses may be levelled to explain the occurrence of males interred with ostensibly female grave inclusions:

1. The lack of skeletal completeness, especially of the pelvis, has hampered sex determination. Crania are somewhat less reliable than the pelvis in sex determination. There are times when the two regions provide mixed assessments.
2. As noted above, the expression of sexual traits is affected by the ageing process. Older females may often possess what may be identified as male features, while younger males may be mistaken for females.[91] These individuals would then be observed to concentrate in those age categories.
3. Multiple burials have caused mixing of the grave goods.
4. Some grave goods, thought to be female, are not in fact discretely associated with females. Therefore, they are not so much associated with the sex of the interred individual as with some other aspect of an individual's social identity. This hypothesis is similar to that previously levelled by Pader, which relates gender female artefacts to the clothing interred with the deceased.[92]
5. Some males were interred with these grave goods because of some character trait, perhaps because they were associated with an otherwise predominately female activity or role that required them to take up some, but not necessarily all, female accoutrements.
6. There was some spiritualistic or ritualistic association that was female and this provided the motivation for burial with predominately female accoutrements. Such a person may have been like the cross-dressing Tasmat Kholmatov or the man–woman, *Whe'wa*, described on p. 168.

---

89. T.M. Dickinson, 'An Anglo-Saxon "cunning woman" from Bidford-on-Avon', in *In Search of Cult*, ed. M.O.H. Carver (1992).
90. B. Hope-Taylor, *Yeavering: An Anglo-British Centre of Early Northumbria* (1977), fig. 25; 67–9, 200–3.
91. Walker, 'Problems of preservation and sexing'.
92. Pader, *Symbolism, Social Relations*, 101.

All of these could be the case for different individuals. The first of these may especially apply to the Sewerby and Buckland burials 15, 30, 58, and the 'indefinite' individuals from this site as their pelvic remains are fragmentary. It is difficult to ascertain how well-preserved the Norton remains are, as only descriptions of a few are provided, but the ones that are described appear to be generally well-preserved. Portway burials 9 and 19 appear to be generally well-preserved. Not all of these individuals are multiple burials, which indicates that the third explanation cannot apply to all of these interments. The male/female individuals cut across all age categories, so their identification is not dependent upon the age assessment for the entire group (Figures 8 and 9). It is possible, however, that the morphology of these individuals falls within the overlap that exists between males and females in all human populations. We know that the 'Angel of Death' in Ibn Fadlan's account of a *Rus* funerary ceremony was described as 'dark, thick-set' or 'heavy-featured'[93] and as a 'strapping old woman, fat and louring'.[94] This description would seem to be of an androgynous, possibly elderly, female.

Sewerby	*Buckland**	*Norton*	*Portway*
G19 (35–45)	14 (20–30)	4 (21–25)	9 (50+)
G33 (elderly)	15 (30–45)	7 (45–61)	19 (25–35)
G38 (17–25)	30 (30–45)	36 (15–21)	
	54 (30–45)	57 (17–25)	
	58 (20–30)	59 (35–45)	
	66 (30–45)	63 (25–35)	
	94a (old)	71 (15–21)	
		76 (mature)	
		86 (35–45)	
		90 (25–30)	
		98 (20–30)	
		107 (15–21)	
		113 (32–38)	

Figure 8   Interments identified as male, but with female grave goods at the sites under study, with estimated age-at-death in parentheses.
*   Burials F, 32, 75, 107, 141 and 142 were identified as possibly being of the same type, but it was decided that they were of a disturbed or otherwise incomplete nature.

93.   A.S. Cook, 'Ibn Fadlan's account of Scandinavian merchants on the Volga in 922', *Journal of English and Germanic Philology* 22 (1923), 60.
94.   H.M. Smyser, 'Ibn Fadlan's account of the Rus with some commentary and some allusions to *Beowulf*, *Medieval and Linguistic Studies in Honour of Francis Peabody Magoun, Jr.*, eds J.B. Bessinger, Jr and R.P. Creed (1965), 92–119.

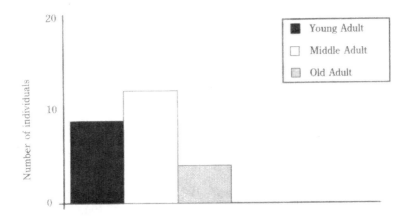

Figure 9   The number of individuals of 'male/female' status by age category.

The last three of these hypotheses are related and all are predicated upon the equally plausible explanation that the presence of female accoutrements in the graves of males may signify something about some males in early medieval society. Such an interpretation echoes Hodder's recommendation that

> reference should be made to a second type of meaning – the content of ideas and symbols. This involves more than saying, 'this fibula functions to symbolize women' or 'this sword symbolizes men'. Rather the question becomes 'what is the view of womanhood represented in the link between female skeletons and fibulae in graves?'[95]

If certain objects were not gender female, what might they have represented, perhaps in addition to gender? In addition to animals having spirits in many traditional societies, many inanimate objects also have them. Among the Siberian peoples and many others, objects, including household utensils, are considered to have a spirit. Therefore, boats and horses, as well as the drum and drumstick, have such attributions in that they aid the ritual specialist in attaining access to the spirit-world. A leather sieve or sifter was used by Hungarian shamans, similar to a drum in shape and having the same function in healing rituals as a means to attain the spirit-world. Wooden spoons and knives could be used to beat the drum.[96] The metal objects which adorn a shaman's costume, bells and pendants of metal, bone, and cloth are associated with the supernatural world. They often depict

95. I. Hodder, *Reading the Past* (1986), 121.
96. Siikala and Hoppál, *Studies of Shamanism*, 162–4.

spirits in animal or human form, the costume itself often being associated with some kind of animal helping spirit.

A consideration such as this has the potential to answer how gender ambiguous individuals were integrated within society. From their burial location among other individuals, the male/females considered here do not appear to have been segregated in death. This may mean that they were accorded a similar treatment in life. The majority of grave goods found in male/female burials are those found also with females. There are few distinctive grave goods found with the male/females. These may actually be a reflection of sample bias as many of the objects may have been in perishable materials. Only at the Buckland site do male/female interments share some objects uniquely with male interments. At Portway, the objects associated with the male/female interments completely overlap with those found in association with females. At Norton and Sewerby, the objects associated with the male/females are in the majority found only with females and a few found with the burials of males. In none of these burials, however, are there the weapon inclusions associated with male interments. There are also some objects which are found in the burials of females that are not found in those of male/females. Whatever this role entailed it was not associated with weapons of any type, nor apparently with weaving implements. These latter objects may suggest an occupation identified with females at these sites or with a particular deity, perhaps with the 'goddess who weaves' as discussed by Enright.[97] Like the man–woman, Bede's high priest Coifi may have come under special prohibitions in warfare,[98] being allowed to participate, if at all, without normal male weapons.[99] In his defamation of the temple, Coifi used a 'spear', a weapon normally associated with male burials in early medieval Europe.[100]

From the foregoing discussion, it seems that we have some archaeological evidence to support the ethnographic and literary references to the existence of males wearing elements of female attire. Like Tacitus's *sacerdos* (see p. 162), some of these may have been sacerdotal figures from among a group of such individuals sharing a similar status on a more local, residential, or lineage-based level. Some of the objects that have been associated with the burials of women may, in fact, not be gender-specific objects but those associated with ritual participation. Due to the vagaries interjected into the discussion

---

97. M.J. Enright, 'The goddess who weaves', *Frühmittelalterliche Studien* (University of Münster), 24 (1990), 54–70.
98. Bede, *A History of the English Church and People*, trans. L. Shirley-Price (1968), 2:13.
99. Callender and Kochems, 'The North American berdache'; Fulton and Anderson, 'The Amerindian "man–woman"'.
100. Pader, 'Material symbolism and social relations'; H. Härke, ' "Warrior graves"? the Background to the Anglo-Saxon weapon burial rite', *Past and Present* 126 (1990), 22–43.

by the relatively low level of human sexual dimorphism, some of these individuals may be better understood as androgynous females, some of whom may have had a role similar to the one indicated in Ibn Fadlan's account.

Charles Callender and Lee Kochems, in their review of the North American man–woman, note that this identity appears to be more common among these peoples than are shamans.[101] This assessment seems to accord with the archaeological evidence presented above for early medieval England, which suggests that no more than a maximum of 10 per cent (and in most cases a far smaller percentage) of the buried individuals could have been of this status. The potential male/females identified in this study are often recorded as high-status female burials due to their association with abundant grave goods. The man–woman, by assuming a gender female role, may also be involved in the manufacture of high status goods, some of which have a ritual function.[102] The relationship between grave-good contents, biological sex and incised (sometimes stamped and sometimes hand-drawn) decoration and its repetition on cinerary urns at Spong Hill,[103] rather than being the result of ' "a potter with a commercial eye for the heathen cremation market" deciding "dispassionately [*to*] copy and develop traditional shapes ... because they were aesthetically pleasing" ',[104] may relate to a single individual in a long lineage of such individuals making the pot and determining its decoration.

Ethnographic accounts document how the man–woman identity has come into conflict with the precepts of state-level societies and their formation. Due to the associations of the man–woman with traditional healing practices, government bans on such practices impacted strongly on the man–woman in North America.[105] The Cybelline priests of Rome were disbarred from inheritance because they were neither men nor women, and because of their claim to have received calling directly from the gods transgressed the traditional prerogative of the priests of the state cults.[106] In this unsanctioned link to the deities, these priests drew scorn and proscription from the state much like the man–woman and other ritual specialists in later interactions with states and their institutionalized religions. Many North American peoples rejected the man–woman identity after enculturation by Euro-Americans, informants often denying their former existence in response to the identification of such individuals with Western views

---

101. Callender and Kochems,'The North American Berdache'.
102. *Ibid.*, 456. Fulton and Anderson, 'The Amerindian "man–woman" ', 606.
103. J.D. Richards, *The Significance of Form and Decoration of Anglo-Saxon Cremation Urns*, British Archaeological Reports, British Series 166 (1987).
104. G.R. Owen, *Rites and Religions of the Anglo-Saxons* (1981), cited in D. Wilson, *Anglo-Saxon Paganism* (1992), 143.
105. Williams, *Spirit and the Flesh*, 178.
106. Beard, 'The Roman and the foreign', 178.

of sexual and psychological deviancy.[107] When the Spanish enforced a ban on the man–woman and, thereby, their ritual activities, so strong was the association of the feminine role with spirituality that native Chileans turned to shamanesses.[108] Hamayon observes that 'shamanism in any hierarchical system, let alone a state, becomes marginalised, feminised, and fragmented'.[109] Early medieval Europe is dominated by the process of state formation, first in Merovingian Gaul and then in more northerly regions.[110] The attested association between the cross-dressing *sacerdos* of Tacitus' description and omens interpreted from horses affirms a link between such individuals and decision-making and authority. Such a link would have made such individuals and their rites an obstruction to the hegemonic structures of the state. The rapid loss of ritual knowledge and oral history due to the death of the man–woman ritualist has been suspected of bringing about the demise of the man–woman identity in Eastern North America, where the role has been argued not to have existed.[111] A similar phenomenon may explain why there is so little mention of such individuals in the writings of the Roman and early medieval periods. As noted more recently in many parts of the world,[112] religious belief is bound up with state formation, writings and teachings which inspire this process,[113] and aristocratic political aspirations.[114] Such a process marginalizes, excludes, undermines, and suppresses even the memory of many of those previously exercising social and political control. The man–woman, then, was likely a prime target in the enculturation process.

107. W.W. Hill, 'The status of the hermaphrodite and transvestite in Navajo culture', *American Anthropologist* 37 (1935), 273–9; Callender and Kochems, 'The North American berdache', 443ff.
108. Williams, *Spirit and the Flesh*, 141.
109. R. Hamayon, *La Chasse à l'âme: Esquisse d'une théorie du chamanisme sibérien*. Nanterre: Société d'ethnologie, cited in *Shamanism, History and the State* (1994), 193–4.
110. R. Hodges, 'Peer polity interaction and socio-political change in Anglo-Saxon England', in *Peer Polity Interaction and Socio-political Change*, eds C. Renfrew and J. Cherry (1986), 69–78; J. Moreland, J. and R. van de Noort, 'Integration and social reproduction in the Carolingian Empire', *World Archaeology* 23(3) (1992), 320–34.
111. Fulton and Anderson, 'The Amerindian "man–woman"'.
112. See essays in R.W. Hefner (ed.), *Conversion to Christianity: Historical and Anthropological Perspectives on a Great Transformation* (1993).
113. Sawyer, 'The process of Scandinavian Christianization'; J.C. Russell, *The Germanization of Early Medieval Christianity: A Sociohistorical Approach to Religious Transformation* (1994).
114. P. Wormald, 'Bede, "Beowulf", and the conversion of the Anglo-Saxon aristocracy', in ed. R.T. Farrell, *Bede and Anglo-Saxon England*, British Archaeological Reports, British Series 46 (1978), 32–95.

Conclusion

Timothy Taylor notes that

> ethnicity, gender, and mythology may all have been more
> complex than previously supposed [in prehistory and protohis-
> tory]. Firm cultural boundaries may not have existed, humanity
> and its gods may have been viewed as having more than simply
> male and female genders, and religious beliefs may have been
> flexible and multifaceted.[115]

In the light of this comment, it is instructive to entertain the notion
that there may have been more than two genders in early medieval
society; some individuals may have been considered to be of the
opposite or even a third gender, despite being anatomically and
perhaps genetically male or female. Some, too, may have been truly
intersex or transgendered and were attired in female items at death in
recognition of their anatomical ambiguity and possible sacerdotal
connection.

Although the man–woman has been demonstrated to occur in many
parts of the world for considerable periods of time, archaeological
research has rarely identified them. There are, however, some notable
exceptions. Taylor has interpreted the horned figure on the
Gundestrup cauldron from northern Jutland as a ritual specialist of
ambiguous gender.[116] He notes that 'the figure is partly levitated,
balancing on one toe, and it has a round torc, a ram-headed snake and
antlers. These attributes make sense in terms of a shamanic extension
of power over three usually separate domains: female, male, and
animal.' Sharisse and Geoffrey McCafferty have also commented upon
an individual of indeterminate sex accorded a unique burial in Tomb 7
at Monte Albán, Mexico, accompanied by weaving instruments, as
possibly representing 'a berdache-like' male acting as a woman in
ritual.[117] Similar presentments concerning gender attributions have
been made concerning the high-status, sixth-century BC 'Princess of
Vix' burial.[118] These individuals may have attained an extremely
exalted, liminal position that precipitated elaborate depictions and
interments.

Since age and sex categories form the basis of much of social
distinction,[119] the bioanthropological study of the remains to discern

---

115. Taylor, 'The Gundesrup cauldron', 84.
116. *Ibid.*, 71.
117. S.D. McCafferty and G.C. McCafferty, 'Engendering tomb 7 at Monte Albán:
     respinning an old yarn', *Current Anthropology* 35(2) (1994), 161.
118. K. Spindler, *Die Frühen Kelten* (Stuttgart, 1983), cited in Arnold, 'Deposed
     princess of Vix' (1991), 370.
119. A.A. Saxe, 'Social dimensions or mortuary practices in a Mesolithic population
     from Wadi Halfa, Sudan', *Memoirs of the Society for American Archaeology* 25
     (1971), 39–57; Carr, 'Mortuary practices'.

sex and to identify physical evidence of funerary treatment or the motivation for certain types of funerary treatment is essential. The separation of this determination from that associated with gender, implicit in the grave goods, is important because it may allow us to discern changes in social structure through time. Work involving the development of extractive techniques for the sex chromosomes from ancient DNA would greatly aid this endeavour. Recently, Anne Stone *et al.* have been able to determine the sex of archaeological skeletal material based on use of the amelogenin gene which is located on the X and Y chromosomes (the gametes or sex chromosomes).[120] The application of this type of procedure would provide a complement to the morphological study of sex in past human societies. Such individuals may also be identified by proportional changes in the body's elements.[121] These assessments can be easily made by most practitioners. It is likely that few have looked for such differences in skeletal assemblages.

The importance of the man–woman to society was great. In Navajo society the man–woman (*Nadle*) was said to:

> know everything. They can do the work of a man and a woman ... If there were no *Nadle* (man–woman), the country would change. They are responsible for the wealth in the country. If there were no more left, the horse, sheep, and Navajo would all go. They are leaders ... A *Nadle* around the hogan will bring good luck and riches ... They are, somehow, sacred and holy.[122]

Given the importance attributed to the man–woman and the ubiquity of such an identity worldwide, it seems that their archaeological identification and context, rather than being anomalous or enigmatic, may allow us to view early medieval social transitions from a new perspective. It may be that Abelard's twelfth-century social tribulations might have been eased substantially had he lived in Western Europe a thousand years or so before.

Appendix 1

At Buckland all the male/female burials, except 94a, a very incomplete individual, contained at least one of the amulets discussed by Meaney[123] and many contained several. At Sewerby only G38 contained such objects, a key and girdlehanger. At Norton ten of the thirteen

120. A.C Stone, G.R. Milner, S. Pääbo, S. and M. Stoneking, 'Sex determination of ancient human skeletons using DNA', *American Journal of Physical Anthropology* 99 (1996), 231–8.
121. W.U. Gardner and C.A. Pfeiffer, 'Influence of estrogens and androgens on the skeletal system', *Physiological Review* 23 (1943), 139–65; E. Pittard, *La Castration* (1934), 21.
122. Hill, 'The status of the hermaphrodite', 278.
123. Meaney, *Anglo-Saxon Amulets*.

individuals contained such objects; only 76, 107, and 113 did not. At Portway both burials 9 and 19 contained amuletic objects.

All of the male/female burials but 15 and 94a at Buckland contained at least one key found on the left side of the skeleton in the waist and/ or thigh region. Nineteen female/female? burials contained multiple keys. Burial 75, a possible male/female, shares an iron spoon of a type also found with two female burials, 110 and 127. These are located on the left side in the pelvic and thigh region. Burial 75 is unique in having a bone weaving pick located near the right tibia and a line of metal objects, including multiple keys and a spoon, which end above the weaving pick and an associated 12.7 cm-diameter ivory ring. These objects descend from the left hip region where a pair of shears is located. A similar pattern is shared by burials 107 and 110, although the former has a bronze workbox and antler fragments between the lower limbs, while the latter is associated with keys, a large L-shaped key, a pair of shears, two coin pendants, an iron spoon, and beads in the same location. Burial 107 also has a tweezers, an object usually associated with male burials at this site and the others considered. Burial 110 had an unborn infant in the pelvis, a unique occurrence. Burials 32 and 75 also contain earscoops, an object shared by burial 127, a female buried on her own. Burials 14, 15, and 141 share Roman coins, and burial 141 was found with the remains of a possible box of black oak and antler above the cranium in the grave, the placement of which is unique on this site. Grave 54 possesses several keys aligned along the left femur and two objects of a similar shape to, though smaller than, the girdlehanger associated with burial 13. Objects either referred to as girdlehangers or of a similar shape are identified with nine female burials. A large key with a suspension ring also accompanied the burial of an old female in Grave 13, which also contained two square-headed brooches, both decorated with masks, number 1 with a mask with two eye-slits at one end similar in composition to one from Sewerby, discussed on p. 178.

The individuals of male/female status at Norton have grave goods which are similar and, again, are normally indicative of female burials, including wrist clasps in 4, 7, 57, 59, and 63. 'Latchlifters' (keys) are found with 63 and 86 on the left side of the pelvis and thigh region, while 4 has an earscoop found in the head region. Burial 7 possesses a Roman coin of Constantine I, dated to AD 341-6 . Burial 71 has bucket pendants arrayed around the head region. Burials 4, 7, 63, 86, 90, and 107 all contain brooches, 63 a square-headed brooch with a mask motif. Burial 57 also has a square-headed brooch decorated with a mask motif. Burial 59 was accompanied by wrist clasps, an iron ring and a knife on the left side of the body. The grave goods of three well-furnished female burials, 29, 35, and 52, all aged 25–35, possess grave inclusions similar to those associated with these male/female burials, including wrist clasps, knives, large metal rings and latchlifters (keys) on the left side of the body at this site. The only other burial associated with multiple bucket pendants is the individual interred in burial 35;

here nine such pendants are located above the cranium and two others scattered in the grave fill. This individual also has multiple latchlifters (keys) located on the left side of the pelvis and thigh region.

The individuals G19, G33 and G38 from Sewerby are poorly preserved, but their apparent male/female status and grave goods, especially of the better furnished and less disturbed G19 and G38, are of interest. G38 was interred with two girdlehangers and a small (less than 5 cm in diameter), heavy bronze girdle-ring, located on the left side of the skeleton in the pelvic and thigh region. Also on this side of the skeleton were the only keys (three) accompanying a burial at this site. Burial G19 has the only needle recorded from the site and a 'bronze rim binding' in the frontal region of the cranium, plus a large square-headed brooch, complete with a masked-face design. A comparison with the only other individual from Sewerby found with an (unmatched) pair of girdlehangers and a square-headed brooch, G49, 'by far the most lavish in the part of the cemetery dug' (see Hirst, *Cemetery at Sewerby*, 39) shares similarities with both G19 and G38. This burial possesses a girdlehanger decorated with a horse's head, a mask-bearing square-headed brooch, crystal beads, a knife, wrist clasps, and a shale box containing ungulate ribs and a bronze cauldron in the head region. In both G38 and G49 the girdlehangers are found in the vicinity of the left pelvic and thigh region, and a split-iron purse ring is located close to the left femur.

Neither of burials 9 and 19 at Portway was interred with what the report calls 'girdle groups', which are found in seven female burials at the site. Burial 9 also had a large flint nodule placed on the right pectoral region, a feature it shared with burial 12 nearby in the same alignment, the burial of a male of 40–55 years. The finding of bread wheat grains (*Triticum aestivum*) beneath the pelvis in burial 9 is unique among the sites studied. At Portway burial 9 had beads to the left side of the pelvic area and thigh, and burial 19 also had beads located in the area of the waist and near the hands where they may have been held.

Appendix 2

There are two multiple burials at the Buckland site and both involve individuals within the male/female group. Grave 58, a young adult, occurs above grave 59, another young adult, and 94a, an old individual, is above 94b, an adult male; these are the only such burials at the site. The other male/female burials are not singled out in this manner and do not appear to provide any easily identifiable pattern that is unique to them.

Burial 36 at Norton forms part of a triple burial with burials 37 and 38, a middle-aged adult female and another female aged 20–30. Burials 57 and 59 form two-thirds of a triple burial with burial 58, a young female 17–25 years of age. Burial 59 may have been interred before the other two. Burial 98 was part of a double burial with 99, a young female, buried in a prone position beneath. This individual possesses robust cranial features that are rare in a young individual and that would have given her a rather masculine facial appearance.[124] A prone position for burial is unusual at these sites.

Burial 19 at Portway appears to have been a member of a triple burial, although the excavators could not discern whether or not the burials were made separately in individual graves or together in a large pit. This assessment is based entirely on an inability to distinguish individual grave cuts, but would be in keeping with a pattern of such groups containing a male/female. The other multiple burials at this site are 7 and 17, of a female 35–45 years of age and a 7–8-year-old child and, burial 2A, which is on top of burial 2, a female of 45–55 and male of 30–35, respectively. The lower burial, 2, is in supine and crouched position with possibly bound hands. This unusual elaboration is unique at these sites.

The only multiple interment at Sewerby was that of G41 and G49, the former being interred above the latter beneath a cairn. Both of these individuals are females. The association is unusual and the G49 interment the most elaborate at the site, which is in keeping with the notion that multiple interments may designate some unusual identity.

In fact, the only burial of two or more individuals, a male and female, that was not of an individual possessing objects thought to be of amuletic significance were burials 2 and 2A at Portway. It may be, then, that this distinctive mortuary treatment was reserved for at least two types of individuals. Double or multiple burials suggest an unusual mortuary rite and perhaps a liminal status.

---

124. S. Robinson, 'Barbarous superstitions: an investigation of human sacrifice through deviant burials' (unpublished MSc thesis, University of Bradford, 1997).

9 Posthumous Obligation and Family Identity[1]

Julia C. Crick

> Too much scholarly attention to the facts makes one blind; too much listening to the rhythms of theory and world history makes one deaf.[2]

Of all those involved in the study of early medieval Britain, students of history have particular reason to resist the notion of social identity. On the one hand, the history of their own discipline encourages them to consider ideas and questions developed within the disciplines of others.[3] Professional history notoriously lacks a technical vocabulary of its own; much of the language used by historians has been imported, notably from the social sciences.[4] On the other hand, early medieval historians can sustain an illusion of linguistic self-sufficiency to a greater extent than their colleagues in cognate disciplines because they work on texts (in the old-fashioned sense) which supply them with terms, vocabulary and a narrative agenda. Each item evokes a reasonably coherent, if deficient, story. Every charter, for example, purports to describe in contemporary language a transaction between named individuals, however little is known of the context. In such a situation, the arrival of a concept such as social identity – which comes crashing out of the late twentieth century, clearly bearing the marks of current political and intellectual trends[5] – may be viewed as an

---

1. This chapter owes much to John Critchley, Tia DeNora, Christopher Holdsworth and Julia Smith who generously shared with me their expertise, discussed all or parts of the chapter in draft and offered bibliographical guidance.
2. M. Mann, *The Sources of Social Power, Vol. 1, A History of Power from the Beginning to AD 1760* (1986), viii.
3. See the discussion by Eric Hobsbawm, 'An historian's comments', in *Space, Hierarchy, and Society: Interdisciplinary Studies in Social Area Analysis*, eds B.C. Burnham and J. Kingsbury (1979), 247–52, especially at 247–8.
4. C. Wickham, 'Problems of comparing rural societies in early medieval Western Europe', *Transactions of the Royal Historical Society*, 6th ser., 2 (1992), 221–46, at 228.
5. On identity politics, 'a politics that eschews such terms as groups, rights, value, and society in favour of terms such as places, spaces, alterity and subject

unwarranted intrusion. It is an intrusion, certainly. Whether or not it is warranted remains to be seen.

The concept of social identity was developed by social scientists writing specifically about the industrialized world,[6] and very useful it has proved. Psychologists, sociologists, and social anthropologists for more than two decades have used it to modify well-established polarities in their respective disciplines.[7] Crudely speaking, social identity provides a model for locating the individual in society which makes allowance both for the action of competing collective influences such as predetermined roles, status and membership of groups and for the response, conscious and unconscious, of the individual. By positing this reflexive interaction between the social environment and the individuals who comprise it, commentators can escape some of the determinism inherent in previous descriptions of the social world. Social identity thus offers a way of connecting the individual to society,[8] of allowing for the effects of both human action and structural restraints,[9] and of examining how groups are the product of conscious and unconscious forces.[10]

Applying a concept of such evident contemporaneity to the pre-modern world presents considerable difficulties. Not only does the early medieval West constitute a social, political and economic landscape radically different from that in which the concept was formulated, but this landscape is recorded in writings whose preoccupations and assumptions are more radically different still. For example, some commentators on social identity place at its heart the motivation and consciousness of individuals. To Bourdieu, social identity means *'the work of representation ...* that they [individuals] constantly perform in order to impose their view of the world or the view of their own position in this world';[11] for Sarbin and Scheibe:

---

contd.

   positions', see E. Zaretsky, 'Identity theory, identity politics: psychoanalysis, Marxism and post-structuralism', in *Social Theory and the Politics of Identity*, ed. C. Calhoun (1994), 199–215 and at 200.

6. C. Calhoun, 'Social theory and the politics of identity', in *Social Theory*, ed. Calhoun, 9–36, at 9–11; V.L. Allen, D.A. Wilder, M.L. Atkinson, 'Multiple group membership and social identity', in *Studies in Social Identity*, eds T.R. Sarbin and K.E. Scheibe (1983), 92–115, at 96.

7. For older examples see for example Sarbin and Scheibe, *Studies in Social Identity*, who report that their interest began as early as 1965 (at 3); B. Misra and J. Preston, *Community, Self, and Identity* (1978); also P. Bourdieu, 'The social space and the genesis of groups', *Theory and Society*, 14 (1985), 723–44, at 727.

8. T.R. Sarbin and K.E. Scheibe, 'A model of social identity', in *Studies in Social Identity*, eds Sarbin and Scheibe, 5–28, at 5–6; Zaretsky, 'Identity theory', 202.

9. M.R. Somers and G.D. Gibson, 'Reclaiming the epistemological "other": narrative and the social constitution of identity', in *Social Theory*, ed. Calhoun, 37–99, at 39–40.

10. Bourdieu, 'The social space', 728–9.

11. *Ibid.*, 727, his emphasis.

'One's social identity is defined as the multiple product of attempts to locate oneself in the role system.'[12] Such definitions presuppose both that the individual can select paths to follow and that the commentator can review the process of reflexion or even gain access to the individual's thoughts. Few working on early medieval texts would claim to be able to glimpse such insights.

However, although the term 'social identity' has remained outside the vocabulary of most early medieval historians,[13] the discussion of certain aspects of identity has not been overlooked. The rash of recent work on national identity shows medievalists coming to terms with a concept formulated in a modern time-frame, this time borrowed ultimately from political science.[14] Moreover, despite the conceptual problems inherent in the term 'identity', it is the applicability to pre-modern history not of identity but of the term 'national' that has attracted most comment:[15] the problems of identity – the difficulty of questions of reflexivity, reception and response, the impossibility of documenting the inner thoughts of individuals – have not hampered the debate.[16] Historians have simply taken identity to mean something like sentiment, consciousness, or even solidarity. Indeed, the term has already entered historical parlance.[17]

Thus, we can bring to the study of early medieval Britain a ready-customized definition of identity. Not only that, social and political scientists have already hinted at how identity might work in pre-

---

12. Sarbin and Scheibe, 'A model', 8.
13. With the precocious exception of Eric John: 'In pre-literate societies, such a matter as the calculation of Easter can be also an expression of social identity': 'The social and political problems of the early English church', in *Land, Church and People: Essays Presented to Professor H.P.R. Finberg*, ed. J. Thirsk (1970), 39–63 at 52. For another early use of the term, this time meaning the identification of an individual's rank, see J.F. Shephard, 'The social identity of the individual in isolated barrows and barrow cemeteries in Anglo-Saxon England', in *Space, Hierarchy and Society*, eds Burnham and Kingsbury, 47–79.
14. For example, R.R. Davies, 'The Peoples of Britain and Ireland 1100–1400: 1. Identities', *Transactions of the Royal Historical Society*, 6th ser., 4 (1994), 1–20; P. Wormald, '*Engla Lond*: the making of an allegiance', *Journal of Historical Sociology* 7(1) (1994) and 'The making of England', *History Today* 45.2 (1995), 26–32. On origins, see A.D. Smith, *The Ethnic Origins of Nations* (1986), 14–16 and also 'National identity and myths of ethnic descent', *Research in Social Movements, Conflict and Change* 7 (1984), 95–130.
15. For example, E. Gellner, *Nations and nationalism* (1983), 9, *Encounters with Nationalism* (1994), 36, 62, 65. Discussed by Smith, *The Ethnic Origins of Nations*, 8–13. See also 14–15 on identity. On medieval concepts of *natio*, see S. Reynolds, 'Medieval *Origines gentium* and the community of the realm', *History* 68 (1983), 375–90, at 375, 383–4, 388.
16. The problem of intention and motivation is scarcely easier in the study of more fully documented periods.
17. Two reviews by historians in the *Times Literary Supplement* 9 August 1996: Colin Jones, at 14: 'Bread lay at the heart of the most basic of Parisians' daily routines, their sense of collective identity'; Alexander Murray, at 30 'The identity of "those who prayed" was eroded by other distinctions – virgins and married, monastic and non-monastic, monks and friars.'

modern situations: through kinship. So, for Norbert Elias, 'the extended family and the native village are the older focal points of the personal we-identity of the individual',[18] while Craig Calhoun reflected that: 'Kinship no longer offers us an overall template of social and personal identities.'[19] Even Ernest Gellner, writing in a different tradition altogether, appears to have shared these sentiments: 'In a sense, ethnicity has replaced kinship as the principal method of identity-conferment.'[20] These statements all set up kinship as little more than a foil for modern developments. Commentators may agree that kinship structured the economic and social life of pre-industrial societies, families being centres of production, consumption, social reproduction,[21] but how it operated more subtly in determining social location remains to be worked out. Here we can apply the concept of social identity more directly. Its focus on the social categories within which men and women were located and located themselves – 'role, status and group memberships', to borrow the terminology of a group of psychologists working on modern social identity[22] – has clear relevance to early medieval kinship.

In the remainder of this chapter, I look at family and social identity in the context of the *post obit* arrangements made by certain members of the elite in pre-conquest England. These provisions promise to reveal social location in several ways. At the time of death, group pressures operated in the form of conventions, norms and obligations, to which the dying individual and his or her bereaved relatives variously responded, whether by compliance or by rejection.[23] Arrangements for the soul of the deceased, therefore, can be expected to show social aspirations and assumptions alongside more concrete provisions for the transmission of property.

Death and social identity

> Human beings create a special cosmos of their own within the natural cosmos ... what shapes and binds the individual within this human cosmos, and what gives him the whole scope of his life, is not the reflexes of his animal nature but the ineradicable

18. N. Elias, *The Society of Individuals*, ed. M. Schröter, trans. E. Jephcott (1991), 178.
19. Calhoun (ed.) 'Social theory', 11.
20. Gellner, *Encounters with Nationalism*, 45.
21. Described, for example, by P. Crone, *Pre-industrial Societies* (1989), 108.
22. Allen, Wilder and Atkinson, 'Multiple group membership', 94.
23. Compare N.Z. Davis, 'Ghosts, kin and progeny: some features of family life in early modern France', *Daedalus,* 106.2 (1977), 87–114, at 92–4 and H. Wimberley and J. Savishinsky, 'Ancestor memorialism: a comparison of Jews and Japanese', in *Community, Self and Identity*, eds Misra and Preston, 115–31. See also G. Halsall, 'Female status and power in early Merovingian central Austrasia: the burial evidence', *Early Medieval Europe*, 5.1 (1996), 1–24, at 13.

connection between his desire and behaviour and those of other people, of the living, the dead, and even, in a certain sense, the unborn.[24]

Burial occasioned many different displays of social status, both individual and collective, in the medieval West. Peter Brown noted years ago how the socially privileged of late antique Italy sought burial in prominent positions near to the altars where relics were housed.[25] Robert Dinn has documented how the wealthier citizens of late medieval Bury St Edmunds displayed their rank by choosing to be buried in certain prime locations and so after death could still 'assert their status to the living'.[26] The feasting and singing at burials condemned by the Carolingian Church have been interpreted by Donald Bullough as a clear expression of 'the cohesive identity of the bereaved family and of the wider community'.[27] Burials in barrows in sixth- and seventh-century Anglo-Saxon cemeteries functioned as advertisements of social status by the bereaved.[28] The diversity of such social statements conceals an underlying problem. Elaborate burials may have satisfied the social aspirations of individuals and their families, but any such conspicuous consumption took wealth out of the hands of prospective heirs.[29]

The material to be considered here, taken from wills, charters, and dispute-settlements from the 250 years before the Norman Conquest, illustrates a further complication: the stress placed by the Church on individual salvation.[30] When the deceased had made arrangements on his own behalf, the possibilities for a clash of interests with heirs increased. Elias, whose work has influenced recent writers on social identity, stressed the comparative modernity of concern with the individual, tracing its origin to the seventeenth century.[31] In so doing, he overlooked the pervasive influence of the medieval Church, which placed on individuals responsibility for influencing their own fate by their actions, including attempts through death-bed bequests to

24. Elias, *The Society of Individuals*, 43.
25. P. Brown, *The Cult of the Saints* (1981), 32–8.
26. R. Dinn, '"Monuments answerable to men's worth": burial patterns, social status and gender in late medieval Bury St Edmunds', *Journal of Ecclesiastical History* 46(2) (1995), 237–55, at 241.
27. D. Bullough, 'Burial, community and belief in the early medieval West', in *Ideal and Reality in Frankish and Anglo-Saxon Society: Studies Presented to J. M. Wallace-Hadrill* (1983), eds P. Wormald *et al.*, 177–201, at 199.
28. M. Carver, 'Kingship and material culture in early Anglo-Saxon East Anglia', in *The Origins of Anglo-Saxon Kingdoms*, ed. S. Bassett (1989), 141–58, at 149–52.
29. On the effectiveness of such investments as symbolic capital see P. Bourdieu, *Outline of a Theory of Practice* (1977). Compare M. McLaughlin, *Consorting with Saints: Prayer for the Dead in Early Medieval France* (1994), 138–45, 165. On the social value of individuals, Halsall, 'Female status', 13–17.
30. Compare the remarks of Crone, *Pre-Industrial Societies*, 109.
31. Elias, *The Society of Individuals*, 155–66. See also S. Mennell, 'The formation of We-images: a process theory', in *Social Theory*, ed. Calhoun, 175–97.

compensate for deficient behaviour during life.[32] At the moment of death propertied Anglo-Saxons, in common with other groups under the influence of the pre-Reformation Church,[33] faced obligations to provide not just for the material needs of their survivors and dependents but for their own souls. However, individual salvation did not rest solely on the actions of the individual. It required the cooperation of his or her heirs. One cautionary tale, recounted AD 716/ 719 in a letter by St Boniface to a religious woman, Eadburh, tells how a monk of Wenlock who died and visited hell witnessed the torments of the trapped soul of a man whose brother had ignored his death-bed wish to free a slave.[34] The doctrine of purgatory had not reached its fullest development, but Boniface's letter and other eighth-century texts attest belief in the existence of a place where the soul rested before Judgement Day and where its destiny and well-being could be influenced by the prayers and offerings of the living.[35] In other words, death did not sever the dead from the living; the individual may have ceased to be a visible part of the collective but he or she continued as an invisible part, one which could impose obligations and economic demands on the living.

By the early ninth century, Anglo-Saxon documents start to mention provision for masses to be held to commemorate the donor's anniversary.[36] This relief was often secured at some cost to heirs who were required either to provide food-rents from their estates or to ensure that gifts of property passed to specified religious houses in return for intercessions. The imposition of these obligations and the response of the family to the resulting responsibilities reveal assumptions about social aspirations, family cohesion and the role of individuals.

---

32. McLaughlin, *Consorting with Saints*, 186–94; M.M. Sheehan, *The Will in Medieval England from the Conversion of the Anglo-Saxons to the End of the Thirteenth Century* (1963), 11–12.
33. Compare C. Burgess, ' "By quick and by dead": wills and pious provision in late medieval Bristol', *EHR*, 102 (1987), 837–58.
34. Boniface, Letter 10, 'Die Briefe des heiligen Bonifatius und Lullius', ed. M. Tangl, *Monumenta Germaniae historica Epistolae Selectae* (1955), 7–15, trans. E. Kylie, *The English Correspondence of Saint Boniface* (1924), 45–6. Discussed in P.P. Sims-Williams, *Religion and Literature in Western England, 600–800* (1990), 243–72. For other accounts see B. Colgrave (ed.), *Felix's Life of Saint Guthlac* (1956), 31, 100–7; B. Colgrave and R.A.B. Mynors (eds), *Bede's Ecclesiastical History of the English People* (1969), III.19, at 270–5.
35. Bullough, 'Burial', 177–8, and 178 n. 2; J. Le Goff, *The Birth of Purgatory*, trans. A. Goldhammer (1984), 96–124 and the comments of P. Aries, 'Le purgatoire et la cosmologie de l'au-delà...', *Annales Economie Société Culture* 38 (1983), 151–7.
36. For example, the arrangements made by Oswulf and Beornthryth, AD 805 x 810: H 1 (S 1188).

Expectations

Donors could record their expectations in various forms. The most common, the will, gives every outward impression of being a direct expression of the donor's wishes. Relatives and friends reportedly gathered to witness the testator's declaration: an ecclesiastic, invited for the purpose, produced a record, usually in the vernacular in direct or reported speech, which was often preserved in triplicate, the donor or his immediate family beneficiary retaining a copy.[37] The final document cannot be regarded as a verbatim report – it will reflect the turns of phrase of the ecclesiastical draftsman and even, at an earlier stage, the moral influence of a clerical adviser[38] – but whatever the origin of the sentiments expressed in wills, it is clear that laymen sometimes took the initiative to provide for their own souls and those of their ancestors. Earl Ælfred and his wife Werburg, for example, presented to the community of Christ Church a gospel-book ransomed from the Vikings, with the stipulation that 'they [the gospels] are read every month for Ælfred and for Werburg and for Alhthryth, to the eternal salvation of their souls', apparently with immediate effect.[39]

Post obit arrangements show that past, present, and future generations were linked in mutual obligation. Ælfgar gave estates to his daughter to grant to religious houses 'for the sake of our ancestors' souls' and 'on condition that she be the more zealous for the welfare of my soul and of her mother's soul and of her brother's soul and of her own'.[40] Wulfgar made grants of an annual food-rent and the reversion of an estate to pass to the monastery at Kintbury for the sake of his soul, that of his father and that of his grandfather (both named).[41] Sometimes, as in Wulfgar's case, it is clear that the donor inherited the land from the persons named. (His grandfather had 'first acquired it'.) Thus Wulfwaru made a grant to St Peter's Bath 'for my poor soul and for the souls of my ancestors from whom my property and my possessions came to me'.[42] Likewise, Brihtric and Ælfswith reserved for their relative, Brihtwaru, a life interest in three estates which they gave to Rochester 'for her husband Ælfric and his ancestors, in accordance with their will'.[43] Of course, these donors' ancestors may themselves have imposed duties of remembrance on their heirs.

37. Sheehan, *The Will*, 54–9. See also *Liber Eliensis*, ed. E.O. Blake (1962), 157–8; A. Campbell, *Charters of Rochester*, Anglo-Saxon Charters, i (1973), no. 34, at 47–8; R 41 (S 1458).
38. See, for example, N. Brooks, *The Early History of the Church of Canterbury: Christ Church from 597 to 1066* (1984), 147; see also 167–74 on the monastic archive.
39. Harmer, *SEHD* 9. Ælfred later remembered Christ Church in his will: H 10 (S 1508).
40. Whitelock, *Wills* 2, at 6–9 (S 1483).
41. Robertson, *Charters* 26, at 52–3 (S 1533).
42. Whitelock, *Wills* 21, at 62–3 (S 1538).
43. Whitelock, *Wills* 11, at 28–9 (S 1511).

200 Julia C. Crick

Certainly, many documents record the practice. In a joint grant, Ealhburg required from Eadweald, her kinsman and heir, and his heirs an annual offering to Christ Church for her soul, 'so long as Christianity endures',[44] while Ealhhere gave land to his daughter on condition of an annual payment to the monastery.[45] Thus, in one step, members of the present generation imposed obligations on the yet-to-be born and acquitted those inherited from the long dead.

However, the imagined community of the dead, the living, and even those to come was not solely defined by blood. Commemoration was strictly reciprocal: possession of the land, not filiation to the donor, triggered the obligation to satisfy posthumous obligations. Thus non-relatives were included within the circle of obligation. So Ælfgifu sought from Bishop Æthelwold intercession for herself and her mother, giving him an estate.[46] A clutch of documents from ninth-century Kent provides further examples.[47] Thus Ealhhere, whom we have just encountered, is made to say 'And whosoever has possession of this land is to give this money in the sight of God and of all His saints, and whosoever fails to perform this, be it on his soul, and not on the soul of him who has commanded it to be done.'[48] Abba's land will ultimately revert to Christ Church, Canterbury, but meanwhile 'Whosoever may have this land of mine' should pay an annual food-rent to his place of burial, Folkestone.[49] Ealdred and Ealhburg imposed an annual food-rent for their souls on 'whoever has the estate'.[50] Badanoth Beotting made his property over to Christ Church Canterbury after the deaths of his wife and children, with the proviso: 'And I entreat the community, for the love of God, *that the man to whom the community grants the usufruct of the estate* carry out the same arrangements with regard to a feast at my anniversary, as my heirs shall have appointed it, and so obtain the divine reward for my soul.'[51] Oswulf and Beornthryth grant land to the same monastery, requesting inclusion 'in the fellowship of those who are God's servants there, and of those who have been lords there, *and of those who have given lands to the church*: and that our anniversary may be celebrated every year with

---

44. Harmer, *SEHD* 5 (S 1195). On the family see Brooks, *The Early History*, 148-9.
45. Harmer, *SEHD* 5.
46. As diocesan of Winchester he had jurisdiction over the Old Minster to which she left property. Whitelock, *Wills* 8, at 20-1 (S 1484).
47. It has not been possible here to investigate how the corpus of evidence changes over time. My initial impressions of the English material differ from McLaughlin's observations about France: *Consorting with Saints*, 165-70.
48. Harmer, *SEHD* 5.
49. Harmer, *SEHD* 2 (S 1482).
50. Harmer, *SEHD* 6. *Charters of St Augustine's Abbey Canterbury and Minster-in-Thanet*, ed. S.E. Kelly, Anglo-Saxon Charters, iv (1995), no. 24, at 95-7; S 1198.
51. My emphasis; R 6, at 10-11 (S 1510), AD 845 x 853: see Brooks, *The Early History*, 148. On anniversary feasts, see McLaughlin, *Consorting with Saints*, 150-2.

religious offices, and also with the distribution of alms, as theirs are'.[52] In these last two documents we are observing the evocation of a non-familial social group with whom individuals wish to identify: the patrons of the monastery.[53] As both sets of donors have direct descendants – they mention the existence of children – this association appears to be voluntary, not an attempt to substitute for the lack of direct descendants.

These documents show expectations of future action from family members past and present, the specified never extending beyond the generation of the subject's grandparents and grandchildren, the unnamed stretching further into the past and future.[54] However, they also suggest the existence of a wider community of heirs, past and future owners of the property, who were unrelated to the donor but whose possession of a particular estate placed them in a reciprocal arrangement with the living. This community comprised not only people who might come into possession of the property at some remote point in the future when the family line eventually failed; the donor could also make grants to living non-kin in return for specified services: intercession from a bishop,[55] assistance in implementing the will from the king or queen.[56] Property-holders as well as family were treated as potential channels for the aspirations of testators.

Outcome

The arrangements for commemoration made by testators suggest something of the ties which bound the present to past and future generations. Occasionally it is also possible to gauge the reactions of subsequent generations to obligations imposed on them by their ancestors, although the documentary assemblage offers only highly

---

52. My emphasis; Harmer, *SEHD* 1 (S 1188). Brooks, *The Early History*, 138. R. Fleming, 'Christchurch's sisters and brothers: an edition and discussion of Canterbury obituary lists', in *The Culture of Christendom: Essays in Medieval History in Commemoration of Denis L.T. Bethell*, ed. M.A. Meyer (1983), 115–53, at 115–16. See also J. Crick, 'Church, land, and local nobility in early ninth-century Kent: the case of Ealdorman Oswulf', *Historical Research* 61 (1988), 251–69.
53. Not the saint *per se* as in equivalent continental examples: McLaughlin, *Consorting with Saints*, 153; B.H. Rosenwein, *To Be the Neighbor of St Peter: The Social Meaning of Cluny's Property, 909–1049* (1989), 202–7.
54. For equivalent three-generation limits see Wimberley and Savishinsky, 'Ancestor memorialism', 118 and for a narrower group still, R.P. Saller and B.D. Shaw, 'Tombstones and Roman family relations in the principate: civilians, soldiers and slaves', *Journal of Roman Studies* 74 (1984), 124–56, at 134–8. These limits fail to correlate with those defined by the Church in consanguinity regulations: D. Herlihy, *Medieval Households* (1985), 84–5, J. Goody, *The Development of the Family and Marriage in Europe* (1983), 56.
55. See note 46.
56. Whitelock, *Wills* 15 (S 1486: king); Whitelock, *Wills* 11 (S 1511: queen); S 1497 ('royal lord').

arbitrary glimpses of the process. Only a handful of cases can be traced from their beginnings through to completion.

Successful completion

As I have already suggested, testators who mentioned the souls of ancestors may sometimes have been carrying out the wishes of previous testators. When Ælfflæd 'for God's sake and for the sake of my lord's soul and for the sake of my sister's soul' listed the grants of land granted by her ancestors to their burial place of Stoke, eleven of thirteen can be traced in the wills of her sister and father.[57] Certainly, in this and other cases, we can observe the property passing down the family line as requested.[58] In rare documents the fulfilment of pious obligations (whether reversionary grants or commemoration arrangements) is made explicit. Most of the evidence concerns adoptive and not natal family: wives and widows.

Ceolwynn, for example, granted to the community at Winchester an estate inherited from her husband, 'on condition that they remember her and Osmod's soul as seems right and fitting to them, on his commemoration day which is seven days before the Rogation Days'.[59] Ælfhild granted an estate to Ramsey just as her husband had granted it.[60] Tole obtained royal permission to satisfy the terms of an earlier agreement and grant property to St Peter's Abbotsbury for her soul and that of her husband.[61] There are other indications that wives were particularly concerned with the relief of their late husbands' souls. Abba's will carries a contemporary addition in his wife's name recording an annual food-rent to be paid to Christ Church for her soul and Abba's.[62] Florence Harmer suggested that the estate named might have been part of her own property.[63] If so, it may suggest that the actions of a widow in a later case may have been less mercenary than they might first appear. Æthelric's will gave his wife usufruct of all his lands, with reversion to several religious houses. The will was revoked and the property forfeited to the king after Æthelric was convicted of treachery.[64] His widow, however, paid his heriot and gave up her marriage gift to have the will restored, 'that is ... the estate at Bocking to Christchurch, and his other landed property to other holy places as

---

57. All except Wiston, Freston: Whitelock, *Wills* 15, 14, 2.
58. Whitelock, *Wills* 14, 15, 32, 34.
59. Robertson, *Charters* 17, at 30–1 (S 1513).
60. *Codex Diplomaticus Aevi Saxonici*, ed. J.M. Kemble (6 vols, 1839–48), no. 968, iv, 301–2.
61. F. Harmer, *Anglo-Saxon Writs* (1952), no. 2, 121–2 (S 1064).
62. Harmer, *SEHD* 2, at 5, 42.
63. Harmer, *SEHD* 2, at 76.
64. See S. Keynes, 'Crime and punishment in the reign of King Æthelred the Unready', in *People and Places in Northern Europe 500–1600: Essays in Honour of Peter Hayes Sawyer*, eds I. Wood and N. Lund (Woodbridge, 1991), 67–81, at 80.

his will specifies'.[65] The basis of her calculation remains a mystery: was it anxiety to obtain relief for Æthelric's soul or the realization that she thus obtained usufruct of more valuable estates than the one which she sacrificed?

Subversion and alteration

How frequently were the pious requests expressed in wills simply vain hopes? The written record certainly preserves numerous examples of disputes but we should be wary of seeing these as representative. Michael Sheehan, in his book on English wills, cautions against assuming too readily that the wishes of testators occasioned opposition among family heirs: 'In all likelihood, there were strong pressures in the society of the time that tended to aid the execution of the desire of the deceased.'[66] His warning should be heeded, although a more prosaic explanation looks possible. When a will reached fruition and estates passed to individuals or a religious house, new documentation was not necessarily called for: thefts of charters show that even out-of-date documents could serve as title.[67] If, however, the bequest had occasioned a dispute and arbitration had been necessary, a permanent record of the resolution would have proved useful, especially to any monastic landowner involved.[68] Thus difficult cases are more likely to leave a trace in the written record than straightforward ones. For the same reason we should be wary of reading too much into the cases of conjugal piety just discussed. Wives may have had more need than other heirs to resort to writing to implement their wishes.[69]

On many occasions, wills were not followed to the letter. Ketel, for example, satisfied the terms of his mother's will by granting an estate at Stisted to Christ Church Canterbury, but omitted mention of her soul when he did so, despite her specific request.[70] Reversionary gifts to religious houses (which would presumably have secured religious advantages for the donor) were frequently delayed by one generation or more. Thus, the elder daughter of Ælfgar, who otherwise carried out her father's will faithfully, postponed the granting of two estates to

---

65. Whitelock, *Wills* 16.2, at 44–5 (S 939); Whitelock, *Wills* 16.1 (S 1501).
66. Sheehan, *The Will*, 36.
67. In the late tenth century priests stole and sold charters relating to Rochester estates: Robertson, *Charters* 59 (S 1457). Discussed by P. Wormald, 'Charters, law and the settlement of disputes in Anglo-Saxon England', in *The Settlement of Disputes in Early Medieval Europe*, eds W. Davies and P. Fouracre (1986), 149–68, at 157–61.
68. Compare Wormald, 'Charters', 151.
69. See below.
70. Whitelock, *Wills* 34, 32, at 88–9 and 84–5 (S 1519, S 1535). Thus Wulfgyth originally granted it 'for my soul and for my lord Ælfwine's and for the souls of all my children' but Ketel remembered only the soul of his father and of Sæflæd, his wife.

Stoke by making over usufruct to her sister for her lifetime.[71] Grants to religious houses were often postponed not by the blood relatives of the original donor but by relatives by marriage. Two husbands negotiated to retain usufruct of grants of property to religious houses after the deaths of their wives; in both cases the women had acquired the land through an earlier marriage and their second husbands should have had no claim on it.[72] In both cases, therefore, the donors' pious intentions (and arrangements to secure relief for the soul) were delayed or even subverted by relatives by marriage.

Widows could be used by male relatives or a new husband to appropriate reversionary grants made to religious houses by her late husband or his relatives. Leofsunu, having married Eadric's widow, laid claim to lands which were leased by Eadric from a relative but whose ultimate destination appears to have been the Church.[73] Likewise, a dispute over lands which one Ælfhere had bequeathed to Rochester was rekindled when a relative of his son's widow claimed the estates on her behalf. The relative not only secured for his kinswoman usufruct of lands over which he had no personal claim, but used his will to record the fact and to mention Ælfhere's original grant.[74] The consequence of his actions seems to have been a temporary postponement of the bequest. A similar set of circumstances perhaps lies behind the story of the widow of Æthelstan Mannesune, who, at the instigation of her natal family (*parentum inducta suggestione*), negotiated to retain rights of disposal over land promised to Ramsey by her husband.[75] Æthelstan's widow may in fact have been asserting rightful claims to the land: monastic accounts offer a highly selective and partisan view of such cases. Alternatively, if the terms of her husband's will had placed the estates which had formerly supported her in the hands of religious houses, her natal kin may have been unwilling to take on the burden of a widowed relative and have preferred to press for usufruct of the estates for her lifetime.

Women, whether donors or heirs, were enmeshed in many disputes. The cause often stemmed from cross-family claims: for example when a bequest to a widow was undermined by a member of the husband's family. Sometimes the inheritance itself was at stake – the stepmother disinherited by her stepson or the widow whose inheritance from her husband was contested by his relatives[76] – sometimes the right to dispose of it for the care of the late husband's soul. Cynethryth's late

---

71. Peldon and Mersea: Whitelock, *Wills* 2 and 14, at 8–9 and 36–7.
72. Robertson, *Charters* 80 (S 1464). Kemble, *Codex Diplomaticus*, no. 927, iv, 265 (S 1481).
73. Robertson, *Charters* 41 (S 1458).
74. Robertson, *Charters* 59 (S 1457); Campbell, *Charters of Rochester*, no. 36; Whitelock, *Wills* 11. Wormald, 'Charters', 157–61.
75. W. D. Macray (ed.) *Chronicon Abbatiæ Rameseiensis*, Rolls ser., 83 (1886), 59–61.
76. Robertson, *Charters* 63 (S 877): see Keynes, 'Crime', 78–9. *The Will of Æthelgifu*, ed. D. Whitelock *et al.* (1968) S 1497.

husband, Ealdorman Æthelmod, had given her freedom to dispose of property in Kent 'after their time, as might be for them most just and most charitable' but had allowed that it might pass to Osberht, his nephew, if he survived Cynethryth 'but afterwards to no other member of the family'.[77] In other words, Cynethryth seems to have been entrusted with the disposal of the land to a religious house, reserving the usufruct for one relative only. When Osberht predeceased Cynethryth, Æthelmod's will was contravened by a great-nephew, who obliged Cynethryth to forfeit the land and her rights to dispose of it charitably. The consequence was immediate family advantage. The new owner of the land had secured it for his children.

Conclusions

Elias, Gellner and Calhoun have all looked to family and kinship as means of conferring identity in pre-modern situations,[78] but in these examples of the honouring and avoidance of posthumous obligations in Anglo-Saxon England kinship proves an insubstantial, even self-contradictory, basis for determining social location. One problem lies in the torque between the putative kin-group and the individuals or groups of individuals which comprise it. Thirty years ago, Sheehan, commenting on the wills, formulated the problem thus: 'The notion that man continued to live and to have needs after death was the most important force in Germanic society, impelling towards *the assertion of the rights of the individual against the rights of the family*'.[79] The tension between the claims of the ancestor (donor) and the heirs (relatives and future holders of property) clearly lies at the heart of the material discussed. However, the opposition between individual and family should not be over-simplified. Individuals behave as members of groups; the interests of groups are upheld by the actions of individuals. A donor, in providing for his own soul, will often provide for that of his wife and so act as part of a conjugal unit; when bequests meet opposition, they are challenged not by the family *en masse* but by individuals pursuing their own set of interests. Æthelmod provided not just for his soul but for that of his wife by instructing her to dispose of the land 'as might be for them both most just and most charitable'; when his great-nephew claimed the estate for himself he did so in the interests of his own immediate family group: 'it is most natural that he should have the land, and his children after him'.[80]

Thus families constantly fragment into multiple groups. Sometimes the tension lies along an obvious fault line as between a woman's natal

---

77. Harmer, *SEHD* 7 (S 1200): see Brooks, 'The Early History', 147–8.
78. See notes 18–20.
79. My emphasis: Sheehan, *The Will*, 17.
80. Harmer, *SEHD* 7.

kin and her husband's family. So a husband's bequest may be contested by his widow's kin or by her second husband on her behalf. Sometimes we see the widow on the other side of the conjugal divide, attempting to honour her late husband's will by arranging for the alienation of estates to religious houses but so precipating a dispute with his family. The widow could find that her family loyalties fell in two or even three directions: towards her natal family, her husband's family and the now-dissolved conjugal unit. We could argue, perhaps, that the extant evidence over-represents such strains. The assertion of non-standard rights may have occasioned the use of writing more frequently than did the transmission of land from father to son (little recorded in surviving documentation); many conjugal wills, in response to established Christian practice, show married couples providing for their souls by making pious grants, including reversionary grants from husbands to wives entrusted with the care of both their souls,[81] which will have left the widow particularly vulnerable to her husband's disputacious kin.[82] However, the cases discussed here, although not necessarily representative in any way, attest a tension inherent within the family at the most basic level. Even within the donor's natal family clear interest groups could emerge. When Æthelmod arranged for an estate to pass to a religious house his bequest was blocked by a descendant who claimed the estate for himself and his children.[83] The interests of past and future members of the family were clearly at variance. Thus family cohesion could break down not only horizontally – between different collateral groups – but vertically as well, within one direct line of the family.[84]

Besides the complex and competing interests within the kin-group, these cases of posthumous obligation show the extension of ostensibly familial obligations outside it, beyond the circle of relatives. Several grants, without stipulating a family connection – indeed, where none is likely – mention that obligations fall on the future owner of an estate. Even in more usual grants within a family, it is made clear that donors placed requirements on their kin not by virtue of kinship but by virtue of property-holding. The system of pious obligations turned not on blood but on land, not on belonging but on ownership.

Such conclusions should occasion little surprise. Working on different material from different perspectives, Robin Fox and Alexander Murray have both stressed the insubstantiality of the kin-

---

81. See J. Crick, 'Women, posthumous benefaction and family strategy in pre-Conquest England', *Journal of British Studies* 38 (1999), 399–422.
82. Some of these testators may have been childless; *ibid.*
83. See note 76.
84. For the spatial analogy see P. Guichard and J.-P. Cuvillier, 'Barbarian Europe', in *A History of the Family, Volume I: Distant Worlds, Ancient Worlds*, eds A. Burgiere *et al.* (1996), 318–78, at 371.

group.[85] Not only does its composition change constantly with the passage of time through birth, marriage and death, but even at a given moment, from the point of view of an individual member, its boundaries remain indistinct. Fox goes no further in defining 'the essence of the kindred' than that 'all ego's cognates up to a certain degree are recognized as having some duties towards him and some claims on him'. Relatives can be mobilized on certain occasions but kin is no more than 'a category out of which a group can be recruited by ego for some purposes'.[86] In other words no gulf separates individual and family: the individual recruits members of his wider family for specific purposes but that group 'only comes to life, as it were, when the purpose for which it exists arises'.[87] The group may not even be restricted to relatives. As we have found in the case of pious duties associated with the ownership of land, on certain occasions obligations associated with family membership were extended beyond it. Murray, looking specifically at early medieval kinship, noted that when the group was mustered for the particularly important purpose of extracting compensation-payments for injury, the recruitment could be extended to included interested non-kin.[88] Indeed, Murray has revised traditional thinking about the early medieval family in such a way that he has undermined the view of the Middle Ages offered by certain writers on identity. Elias appealed to 'The extended family' as a focus for 'the personal we-identity of the individual', but Murray has challenged not only the role of the extended family in early medieval society but the notion 'that early kinship was fundamentally different in structure from the prevalent forms of well-documented periods'.[89] Kinship, as we have seen, does not provide the individual with a stable, free-standing social framework. If Fox and Murray are to be believed, we should consider it as a product of the social milieu as much as a cause.

When, as in the cases examined here, the personal and the collective intersect in peculiarly complicated ways, the *individual* and *family* or *kin* appealed to by Sheehan and Elias in very different ways fail to provide an adequate description of the forces at work. Individual nobles provided for their own souls and those of their wives by placing burdens on those who survived them and inherited their property; however, at the same time, they could remember the souls of ancestors, especially previous owners of the property, and include them in the obligations imposed on future heirs. In doing so they promoted individual and collective interests simultaneously. Familiar

85. R. Fox, *Kinship and Marriage: An Anthropological Perspective* (1967), at 167; A.C. Murray, *Germanic Kinship Structure: Studies in Law and Society in Antiquity and the Early Middle Ages* (Toronto, 1983), 11–32, 177, 224.
86. Fox, *Kinship*, 167.
87. *Ibid.*, 167.
88. Murray, *Germanic Kinship Structure*, 136.
89. *Ibid.*, 222.

categories having fallen short on this occasion, there is an opportunity for experimentation with the language of social identity. Instead of providing a stark choice between a limited number of fixed terms, social identity, as a description of a process not a category, allows for plurality and mobility.[90] It describes the adoption of multiple roles, both collective and individual (we- and I-identities), without limiting their number, duration or simultaneity. Thus social identity has built into it allowance for the kind of complicated and unexpected outcomes observed here, when Christian conventions, social status and the expectations of spouses and direct descendants compete and sometimes collide. Donors can act out a complicated series of roles and at the same time fulfil and dash multiple expectations. Terms like family, community, and individual, however familiar and central to the vocabulary of historians, are no less alien and assumption-laden than social identity; it remains to be seen when they will be dislodged.[91]

---

90. On kinship as a category, see Fox, *Kinship*, 167.
91. On the problems of terminology see A. Guerreau-Jalabert, 'Sur les structures de parent dans l'Europe médiévale', *Annales* 36 (1981), 1028–49, at 1030–1.

10 Class, Space and 'Feudal' Identities in Early Medieval England

Tom Saunders

It is rather surprising that the concept of class has been so poorly received in British archaeology. Although the present dominance of postmodernism means that such perceived 'objectivist' categories are now treated with derision or irrelevance, class has played a central role in the neighbouring disciplines of history, anthropology and sociology. In particular, class has been one of the core subjects of analysis in the work of the British Marxist historians. Not only has it been employed in the analysis of the early modern period, but it has also been used with great success in the study of medieval and ancient societies.[1] Regrettably, this rich tradition of historical scholarship has seldom been taken up by British archaeologists.

It is not in the scope of this chapter to dwell upon the reasons for the absence of a class debate. My main intention is to examine how some of the recent Marxist discussions on class can be applied in an analysis of identity in the material culture of early medieval England. Exploring class and identity, however, can be a rather ambiguous task. The term identity has become a fashionable buzzword of postmodernism, with its appeal largely derived from a critique of the Marxist concept of class, particularly in the realm of politics and political practice.[2] Instead of treating class and identity as mutually antagonistic categories, here I will attempt to explore the *active* relationship between the development of classes and the construction of social identities. The central theme will be an analysis of the ways in which class formation in the early medieval period was structured by a specific organization of social space, and how this use of space became a means of expressing social identities.

---

1. See H.J. Kay, *The British Marxist Historians: An Introductory Analysis* (1984).
2. See for example S. Smith, 'Mistaken identity – or can identity politics liberate the oppressed?', *International Socialism*, 62 (1994), 3–50, and A. Callinicos, *Theories and Narratives: Reflections on the Philosophy of History* (1995), 179–203.

This discussion of the connections between class, space and identity will be prefaced by two short sections defining the terms class and feudalism. Unfortunately, *class* and *feudalism* remain highly controversial concepts and have been the subject of much caricature and abuse. They necessarily require clarification as a prerequisite for their use. In outlining these two terms I hope to draw out some archaeological implications in regards to the link between social order and spatial order. These will then form the basis of an analysis of two major processes underlying the 'making' of the English landscape, namely the rise of the manorial village and the origins of the town.

Class and identity

One of the impressive achievements of the British Marxist historians has been the careful integration of theory and data, of combining a close scrutiny of Marxist analytical concepts with detailed empirical studies. The work of Geoffrey de Ste Croix, especially his seminal book *The Class Struggle in the Ancient Greek World*, stands out as an excellent example of such an approach.[3] De Ste Croix manages to combine an extensive analysis of ancient history with a rigorous reconstruction of the concepts of class and class struggle. In following the logic of Marx's method, he provides one of the most theoretically coherent definitions of class:

> *Class* (essentially a relationship) is the collective expression of the fact of exploitation, the way in which exploitation is embodied in a social structure. By *exploitation* I mean the appropriation of part of the product of the labour of others ...
>
> A *class* (a particular class) is a group of persons in a community identified by their position in the whole system of social production. Defined above all by their relationship (primarily in terms of the degree of ownership or control) to the conditions of production (that is to say, the means and labour of production) and to other classes.[4]

In the parlance of postmodernism this quote may seem desperately dry and reductive, but it succinctly summarizes the distinctive features of a Marxist theory of class which I wish to develop. In contrast to the more prevalent approaches, inspired by Max Weber, which describe social stratification in a static manner according to status, this definition provides an explanation of class in terms of a dynamic social relationship.

Three key elements can be highlighted from de Ste Croix's discussion of class. First, class is defined objectively as a *structural*

---

3. For an excellent critical assessment of the work of Geoffrey de Ste Croix, see P. Anderson, *A Zone of Engagement* (1992), 1–24.
4. G.E.M. de Ste Croix, *The Class Struggle and the Ancient Greek World* (1983), 43.

relationship, more precisely as a relationship of production. It is not dependent on subjective attitudes and behaviour, or perceived individual status, but upon a social relationship formed in the process of production. Second, this structural relationship is an inherently *antagonistic relationship*. Unlike Weberian-type status groups which can be graded independently, classes for Marxists are organically related to each other in mutual opposition.[5] Classes are forged in the processes of production and the mechanisms of exploitation. Classes are thus inseparable from class struggle, the social conflicts and tensions generated by the realization of, and resistance to, exploitation. Third, class and class struggle must be understood as a *historical process*. The Marxist approach to class does not aim to simply label groups within a static conception of social hierarchy. Rather, class is part of a broader theory of the social processes through which human beings make history.[6] The structural and antagonistic relationships at the heart of the Marxist definition of class provide the means to understand the processes by which 'real' people, as a result of their shared experiences and capacities, shape and transform society.

E.P. Thompson, in particular, has been at the forefront of exploring the historical processes of class formation and the workings of class experience.[7] His emphasis on class as an active process has successfully drawn out the complex and often contradictory processes by which materially-structured conditions give rise to class consciousness, how class experiences are 'handled in cultural terms: embodied in traditions, value-systems, ideas, and institutional forms'.[8] Class is not just a theoretical construction imposed upon the evidence 'but something which in fact happens (and can be shown to have happened) in human relationships'.[9] The class experience can be observed in history: it can be observed in the visible patterns of social and cultural relationships, institutions, values and ideas which have shaped our past. As Ellen Meiksins Wood neatly puts it, 'Class ... is a phenomenon visible only in process'.[10]

This chapter consequently aims to render visible the making of early medieval class formations in the patterns of material culture evident in the archaeological record. Its main aim will be to examine some of the ways in which the developing relations of production and exploitation during this period gave rise to a specific 'feudal' identity: in short, how the

5. For a sharp critique of the Weberian concept of status see *Ibid.*, 85–96.
6. See for example A. Callinicos, *Making History: Agency, Structure and Change in Social Theory* (1989), 39–95, for a discussion of class and Marxist theories of history.
7. For a detailed discussion of E.P. Thompson's theory of class, see E. Meiksins Wood, *Democracy Against Capitalism: Renewing Historical Materialism* (1995), 76–107.
8. E.P. Thompson, *The Making of the English Working Class* (1968), 9–10.
9. *Ibid.*, 10.
10. Meiksins Wood, *Democracy Against Capitalism*, 81.

'feudal' class experience became expressed through the cultural landscape of the period, mediated within certain patterns of social space.

The question of identity is then firmly linked to the issue of 'lived' class relations. It is the logic of shared material conditions, rooted in antagonistic structural relations, which frames the articulation of certain collective interests and social identities. This is not to say, as it is often caricatured, that all social identities or even all social conflicts can somehow be reduced to the theoretical concept of class. What will be argued, however, is that the inherent conflicts at the centre of social production in early medieval England played a powerful role in the cultural expression of social relations and collective identities. Class is visible, embodied in the diverse patterns of material culture, and should not be written out of history by a mere shift of intellectual fashion.

Feudalism and Anglo-Saxons

The use of inverted commas around the word 'feudal' in the title of this chapter denotes the problematic nature of the term. Of all the concepts discussed within English medieval history, feudalism probably remains the most controversial. Traditionally this term has been closely linked to the dual notions of fiefs and vassals to describe a highly specialized relationship within the medieval ruling class. This orthodoxy has recently been challenged in a comprehensive manner by Susan Reynolds. In a wide-ranging survey exploring the evidence of property law and of social and political relations in medieval Europe, Reynolds reveals how 'fiefs and vassalage, as they are generally defined by medieval historians today, are post-medieval constructs',[11] and consequently inappropriate for understanding the realities of medieval society. However, Reynolds draws a favourable distinction between feudalism in its traditional, narrow sense and feudalism in its Marxist sense, as the latter examines 'the whole economic structure of society and the reasons for economic and social change'.[12] Hence the concept of feudalism, defined as a *mode of production*, can still be usefully used as a heuristic category on which to base an analysis of medieval social relations.

Rodney Hilton, more than any other historian, has become associated with the integration of Marxism in the study of the Middle Ages and with developing a Marxist concept of feudalism in terms of class and class struggle.[13] Hilton has described the essence of the feudal mode of production as 'the exploitative relationship between landowners and subordinated peasants, in which the surplus beyond subsistence of the latter, whether in direct labour or in rent in kind or

---

11. S. Reynolds, *Fiefs and Vassals: The Medieval Evidence Reinterpreted* (1994), 2.
12. *Ibid.*, 3.
13. See Kay, *The British Marxist Historians*, 70–98.

in money, is transferred under coercive sanctions to the former'.[14] The principal motive force within feudalism was therefore the social conflict between landlord and tenant. It was this class relationship which defined the general characteristics of feudal society. Hilton has further defined feudalism in medieval Europe as a specific social formation, in which the essential character of the mode of production was the fragmented, or decentralized, nature of economic and political relations.[15] Social production was based on separate household units with peasant families in effective control over their own holdings, while the landlords themselves were split up and divided from each other by the private ownership of estates. Consequently, feudal exploitation was expressed through private jurisdiction. It was *direct* and *individual*, being articulated through various systems of rent extraction.

Retaining the concept of feudalism by defining it as a mode of production has the added advantage of cutting through the traditional cultural historical categories which have structured early medieval studies. Both historical and archaeological research has tended to be organized within a framework of ethnic divisions – Britons, Anglo-Saxons, Vikings, Normans – which, while important, can obscure rather than highlight patterns of social change.[16] This has especially been the case with debates over the origins of feudalism, focused as they have been on the Anglo-Saxon/Norman divide. However, when viewed as a specific class relationship between landlords and peasants, feudalism can be seen to have emerged long before 1066, during the Anglo-Saxon period.

The rise of lordship in early medieval England was a historical process which can be traced back to the seventh century, if not earlier.[17] Developments in the political economy of rights and obligations connected to the ownership of land underpin the social change which occurred in the following centuries. This was the period when the basic institutional structures of medieval power took shape with the rise of Church and state, trade and towns, and above all in the establishment of a manorial landscape. Furthermore, these developments in England were clearly part of a European-wide phenomenon, which has recently been described by some as a 'feudal revolution'.[18]

It is not the intention of this chapter to directly enter the historical

---

14. R. Hilton, 'Introduction', in *The Transition from Feudalism to Capitalism* (1978), 30.
15. R. Hilton, *Class Conflict and the Crisis of Feudalism* (1990), 1–11.
16. See B. Wailes and A.L. Zoll, 'Civilization, barbarism and nationalism in European archaeology', in *Nationalism, Politics and the Practice of Archaeology*, eds P.L. Kohl and C. Fawcett (1995), 21–38.
17. For discussions of the rise of lordship in early medieval England, see E. John, *Land Tenure in Early England* (1960); P. Abels, *Lordship and Military Obligation in Anglo-Saxon England* (1988); and Reynolds, *Fiefs and Vassals*, 323–95.
18. T.N. Bisson, 'The "Feudal Revolution"', *Past and Present* 142 (1994), 6–42.

debate on lordship and tenure, focused as it has been upon the legal meanings and ambiguous usage of the words *bookland, folkland* and *loanland*. Rather, it is to stress that a new and perhaps more fruitful approach to considering the growth of feudal class relations is to examine changing patterns of landscape and settlement. The developing structures of power in early medieval England may have been expressed in forms of judicial terminology, but they were also physically mapped out in material and spatial patterns of everyday life. It is here that an archaeology of feudalism is of relevance.

Feudal relations and spatial order

Exploring the relationship between class, identity and social space in early medieval England requires a clear statement of the spatial implications of the previous discussions, in order that they might guide empirical investigations. The key to understanding feudal class relationships lies in the nature of exploitation, 'the specific economic form in which surplus-labour is pumped out of the direct producers' as Marx himself put it.[19] If, as argued above, exploitation was mediated through individual and direct systems of rent extraction, with peasants in possession of their means of subsistence through their family holdings, then it follows that all feudal rents were ultimately 'extorted from them by *extra-economic compulsion* [emphasis added]'.[20] That is, the maintenance of exploitation by the landowning class rested upon methods of *political coercion* and ultimately by means of *physical force*.

This essential character of feudal class relations is of great significance. Primarily it provides the means to locate 'the shifting place of the economy' in medieval societies.[21] Feudal exploitation was not an open economic relationship, but embedded and enmeshed in other social institutions. Law, politics and religion structured the form of integration between economy and society. Robert Brenner, in his studies of economic development in agrarian societies, has argued that landowners' reliance on forms of 'extra-economic compulsion'

> meant they had to deploy their resources toward building up their *means of coercion* – by investment in military men and equipment. Speaking broadly, they were obliged to invest in their politico-military apparatuses ... Indeed, we can say the drive to *political accumulation*, to *state-building*, is the *pre-capitalist* analogue to the capitalist drive to *accumulate capital*.[22]

---

19. K. Marx, *Capital* (3 vols, 1981), 3, 927.
20. *Ibid.*, 926.
21. For Marxist appraisal of this Karl Polanyi concept, see M. Godelier, *The Mental and the Material* (1988), 179–207.
22. R. Brenner, 'The social basis of economic development', in *Analytical Marxism*, ed. J. Roemer (1986), 31–2.

This logic can help explain, in a materialist way, how feudal class relations and identities were present in numerous and diverse forms of 'non-economic' cultural practices. The 'drive to political accumulation' fashioned the medieval image of the conqueror, the sword, the castle, and all the military symbols of power. It conditioned the patterns of conspicuous consumption, the constant feasting, the demand for luxury and prestige goods. Above all, the intrinsic political and physical character of feudal class relations was inscribed into the primary basis of social power – the land. Place, space and architecture were laden with class meanings. As Marx argued, under feudalism landed property 'appears as the inorganic body of its lord'.[23]

The way in which the feudal class experience was mediated in patterns of social space has been explored, albeit from a slightly different perspective, by the historical geographer Robert Dodgshon. In *The European Past*, Dodgshon shows how the rise of state and class societies was marked by a 'revolution in spatial order'.[24] With the breakdown of kinship ties, social relationships became defined by landed property, constituted in fixed and bounded territories. The feudal landscape was therefore set apart from earlier and later landscapes by the particular way in which medieval social relations became firmly set within a distinctive spatial order.

Critical to Dodgshon's argument is the notion of regulated space. Under feudalism the class relationships between lords and peasants were 'anchored to specific territories and specific spaces'.[25] Far from being an unintended consequence of the rise of lordship, a passive reflection of social change, Dodgshon sees 'this structuring of relations in space as part of the very essence of feudalism'.[26] It was the territorialization of power which allowed the build-up of the state, through the integration of landed estates. This meant that the hierarchy of social order in medieval society existed through a hierarchy of land rights. Control over land became part of the means by which class relationships were structured and regulated. For the lord and peasant the landscape was divided into bounded units of land, rigorously defined by measures of rents, services, renders and dues. It was a 'chequerboard on which occupation was legitimised in some spaces but not in others'.[27]

There is much to be gained from Dodgshon's geographical interpretation of feudalism. His notions of bounded and regulated space have far-reaching implications for an archaeological study of medieval landscape and settlement. Social space was organically part

23. K. Marx, 'Economic and philosophical manuscripts', in *Marx: Early Writings* (1975), 318.
24. R.A. Dodgshon, *The European Past: Social Evolution and Spatial Order* (1987), 135.
25. *Ibid.*, 186.
26. *Ibid.*, 186.
27. *Ibid.*, 192.

of the political and physical character of feudal class relations. Bounded and regulated space was one of the key structuring principles behind the construction of class identities. I shall now move on to explore this argument by considering an archaeology of early medieval feudalism.

The making of the feudal landscape: from dispersed to nucleated settlements

There can be little doubt that the period between the seventh and eleventh centuries was one of the most formative periods in the development of the landscapes and settlements of medieval England. Although the documentary and archaeological evidence is sparse, it is clear that some regions of the country experienced massive changes. A pattern of nucleated villages and open arable fields began to emerge which came to characterize the medieval landscape in the 'champion' regions of the country (the broad belt of lowlands running from the north-east, through the Midlands to the south of England). These changes reflect developments in land use, and directly relate to the imposition and growth of new forms of social relationships. In particular, the nucleation of settlements was rooted in the physical bounding and regulation of feudal class relations.[28]

The nucleated village arose within a cultural landscape predominantly occupied by scattered farmsteads. Numerous excavations and field surveys around the country have revealed that many rural settlements from the early medieval period were dispersed in character, with no formal plan or layout. The typical settlement consisted of a fluctuating arrangement of wooden post-built halls and sunken-floored buildings set within an open landscape. The settlements of Mucking in Essex and West Stow in Suffolk are probably the best examples (Figure 10).[29] Both sites consisted of several phases of farmsteads, dating between the fifth and seventh centuries, which were periodically abandoned and re-established in different places.

This type of settlement dispersal evidently persisted throughout the early medieval period. However, from the seventh century onwards, with the establishment of kingdoms and the growth of the Church, more clearly planned settlements began to emerge. So-called 'high-ranking' sites have been identified, such as the famous royal *vill* at Yeavering in Northumbria, and the settlements at Chalton and

---

28. This argument is developed more fully in my unpublished PhD thesis, 'Marxism and Archaeology: The Origins of Feudalism in Early Medieval England' (University of York, 1991).
29. See S. West, *West Stow: The Anglo-Saxon Village* (1985), and H. Hamerow, *The Excavations at Mucking: The Anglo-Saxon Settlement* (1993). Also, for a general overview of the archaeology of early medieval settlements, see for example M. Welch, *Anglo-Saxon England* (1992).

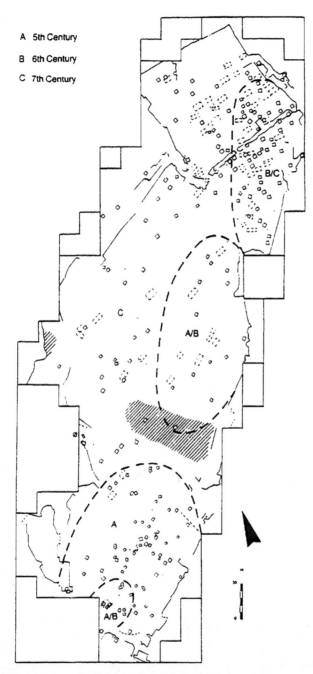

A 5th Century

B 6th Century

C 7th Century

Figure 10 Plan of the dispersed and fluid settlement at Mucking, Essex
Source: H. Hamerow, *The Excavations at Mucking: The Anglo-Saxon Settlement* (1993) © English Heritage

Cowdery's Down in Hampshire, in which hall complexes were carefully organized with rectilinear enclosures.[30] Although these settlements were not nucleated in the conventional sense, they illustrate the increasing prominence that bounded space began to play in the spatial organization of rural sites.

The use of enclosures and bounded units became a defining characteristic in the formation of nucleated villages. Arguably, from the late ninth and tenth centuries a qualitative change in the character of many landscapes and settlements occurred. Excavations and field-walking projects in parts of central and eastern areas of England have demonstrated that the pattern of dispersed and fluctuating farmsteads of the earlier period was abandoned, and replaced by a network of fewer, large-scale and more permanent settlements.[31] Such re-organization of the landscape marked the initial stages in the long, drawn-out process of settlement nucleation and the adoption of open-field farming practices.

The Raunds Area Project in Northamptonshire has produced some of the most convincing evidence for this dramatic change in the rural landscape, revealing that planned villages and hamlets were established during the tenth and eleventh centuries.[32] Significantly, bounded space played a key structural role in the organization of this new settlement morphology. At Raunds itself, for example, two ditched and banked rectilinear enclosures, surrounding a stone-built church and an aisled hall, were placed on the higher ground to the north of the village (Figure 11). Immediately to the south of this possible manorial complex, rows of tenements were laid out in a series of rectilinear ditched enclosures, fronting a central street which ran the length of the village. This bounded spatial pattern of manorial complex, rows of tenements and street was repeated at the neighbouring hamlet of West Cotton (Figure 12).[33] Here the whole site was divided up by a row of rectangular plots of standard width on either side of a central road. At the northern end of the settlement was a double plot which enclosed a large hall that straddled the central road, as well as a water mill. Further, accompanying these developments there is evidence that

---

30. See T. Champion, 'Chalton', *Current Archaeology*, 59 (1977), 364–9; B. Hope-Taylor, *Yeavering: An Anglo-British Centre of Early Northumbria* (1977); and M. Millet and S. Jones, 'Excavations at Cowdery's Down, Basingstoke, 1978–81', *Archaeological Journal* 140 (1983), 151–279.

31. See D. Hooke, 'The mid–late Anglo-Saxon period: settlement and land use', in *Landscape and Settlement in Britain AD 400–1066*, eds D. Hooke and S. Burnell (1995), 95–116; 107–24, for a recent summary of the archaeological and historical evidence.

32. M. Audouy, 'Raunds: Saxon and medieval village and manor from 6th to 16th centuries', unpublished paper from the conference *The Raunds Area Project: The Archaeology of Northamptonshire*, held by the Society of Antiquaries at Burlington House, London, Summer 1990.

33. D. Windell, *From Barrows to Bypass: Excavations at West Cotton, Raunds, Northamptonshire 1985–1989* (1992).

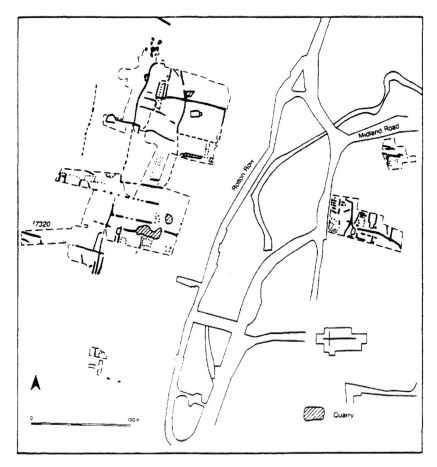

Figure 11 Plan of the planned nucleated village at Raunds, Northants
Source: B. Dix, 'The Raunds Area Project: second interim report', *North-amptonshire Archaeology*, 21 (1987) © Brian Dix

the surrounding landscape of Raunds and Northamptonshire was laid out into open-fields.[34]

These processes of change in the early medieval landscape, specifically the movement towards bounded patterns of rural settlement morphology, are of great significance for the exploration of the emergence of feudal relations and the expression of class identities. The origins of the nucleated village cannot be explained simply as a functional response to technical changes in farming practices in the

---

34. D. Hall, 'The late Saxon countryside: villages and their fields', in *Anglo-Saxon Settlements*, ed. D. Hooke (1988), 61–9.

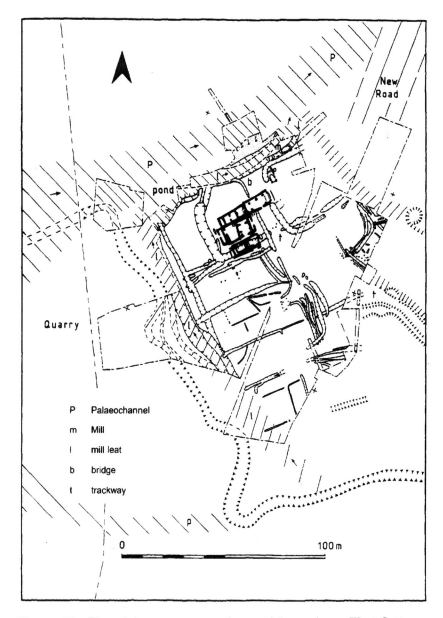

Figure 12   Plan of the tenements and manorial complex at West Cotton, Raunds
Source: D. Windell, *From Barrows to Bypass: Excavations at West Cotton, Raunds, Northamptonshire 1985–1989* (1992) © Northampton City Council

early medieval period. Of course, the move towards more intensive and communal forms of arable cultivation would have affected rural settlement organization. The use of heavy ploughs and a three-field system of farming was best administered through a village community. But these technological and economic developments cannot be separated from the intricate web of social relations in which they were embedded. The complex processes of class formation, the rise of lords and peasants, are embodied in the visible shift from dispersed and fluctuating rural settlements to stable nucleated villages in the 'champion' regions of early medieval England.[35]

Della Hooke has argued that 'some of the earliest signs of settlement planning seem to appear on royal estates or those of powerful bodies such as the Church'.[36] This is illustrated in the arrangement of seventh-century halls and enclosures at 'high-ranking' royal and ecclesiastical sites. The expansion of lordship during the tenth century, the creation of a class of individual landowners, would have accelerated this process. Early medieval settlement nucleation appears to have been focused upon manor houses or halls and churches, suggesting that local lords, on gaining rights of jurisdiction over private estates, were the principal organizing force behind settlement planning. The parcelling up of sovereignty led to the physical breaking down of the ties of kinship which previously dominated the social relationship between early medieval farmers and the land. The dispersed farmsteads which had moved across a relatively undivided landscape were abandoned, replaced by fixed and bounded villages with new feudal relations oriented around the manorial hall.

At Raunds and West Cotton, tenements were planned and laid out in respect to the manorial enclosure prior to occupation with only some, if any, of the plots subsequently filled. The aggregation of peasants around central settlements clearly facilitated greater efficiency in agricultural production, achieved through the adoption of more communal and intensive forms of farming. The generation of increased agriculture surpluses, however, was directed towards the political and economic interests of the local lord. Feudal exploitation was inscribed in the spatial patterning of the nucleated village; the establishment of rows of tenement plots marked the imposition of feudal relations of exploitation. Land was held in return for feudal rent, with the village divided into a fixed number of land measures, and with the size of each tenement being the basis of rent assessment. Thus the class relationship between lord and peasant became constituted within bounded space. This physical organization of class relations was more

35. T. Saunders, 'The feudal construction of space: power and domination in the nucleated village', in *The Social Archaeology of Houses*, ed. R. Samson (1990), 181–96.
36. D. Hooke, 'Introduction', in Hooke and Burnell (eds), *Landscape and Settlement*, 7.

than just a spatial reflection of feudal rent; it was integral to the way in which a lord subordinated a peasantry and maintained his dominant class position.

Feudal class formation, defined as a structural relationship of exploitation, inherently generated conflicts. The re-organization of parts of the early medieval landscape may have been initiated by a growing class of local landowners, but in the breaking down of dispersed kinship relations a class of peasants was created with material interests to resist feudal exploitation. With the development of more collective systems of farming, a village community emerged whose cohesion, at least at a local level, cast definite limits on the powers of lordship. These social tensions at the heart of medieval society have often been explored as an opposition between the customs and traditions of peasant communities and the ideas of hierarchy and obedience expressed and imposed by a ruling aristocracy.[37] They are also tangibly present in the opposition between tenements and manor in the spatial organization of nucleated settlements.

The pattern of hall and church placed at the top of the village with peasant plots aligned along a street below is a common arrangement in the champion regions of medieval England. It is a pattern which actively mediated the class conflict generated by feudal exploitation. In terms of lordship the feudal construction of space became one of the instruments of 'extra-economic compulsion'. Potentially, the nucleated village enabled the lord to discipline the peasants. The rigorous demarcation of space at villages and hamlets, such as Raunds and West Cotton, allowed for social regulation and supervision by the local landlord. Movement in the village could be observed and restricted with the bounding of space defining legitimate and illegitimate places, communal and private property. Access to key resources – woodland, pasture and mills, for example – could be checked and monopolized by the bounding and regulation of space.

However, there was no total monopoly of power within the rural landscape. As Christopher Dyer and others have argued, 'lords exercised an intermittent and imperfect control over their subordinates'.[38] With peasants in effective possession of their own holdings there were real constraints to seigneurial exploitation. Feudal strategies of surveillance could always be circumvented in the day-to-day management of production. The fact that many of the tenements laid out at Raunds and West Cotton were not initially occupied does suggest that the logic of bounded space was challenged. But even

---

37. See for example Reynolds, *Fiefs and Vassals*, 34–56.
38. C.C. Dyer, 'Power and conflict in the medieval English village', in *Medieval Villages: A Review of Current Work*, ed. D. Hooke (1985), 27. See also M. Mann, *The Sources of Social Power: A History of Power from the Beginning to AD 1760* (1986), 394–7, and Hilton, *Class Conflict and the Crisis of Feudalism*, 49–65.

within the defined boundaries of the village and open-field, peasants had control over their own plots and holdings. Thus the organization of fields and use of space within tenements was also an expression of peasant interests and mentalities.

The construction of the feudal landscape, it needs to be emphasized, must be understood as a historical process. The shift from dispersed farmsteads to nucleated villages was not an even development nor one which occurred throughout the whole country. It was likewise a reflection of conflicts embedded in the structuring of social space within early medieval society. Patterns of land use remained varied, with dispersed forms of settlements continuing within many regions such as East Anglia and south-west England.[39] This diversity reflects real differences in systems of land tenure. Brian Roberts, for example, suggests that it is possible 'to see in the landscape the contrast between "closed" estate villages, under the control of a single landowner, and "open" villages usually dominated by freehold farmers'.[40] These varied patterns relate to both the historical complexity of class formation and the strength of peasant communities *vis-à-vis* the powers of lordship. The social construction of space embodied class conflict and class struggle. The constant changes and transformation of medieval settlements, on both regional and local bases, was an expression of how feudal relations were continually being imposed, negotiated and resisted in the making of the past. In this sense social space was not fixed, but subject to an on-going historical process.

The bounded and regulated nature of feudal space, however, remained a fundamental feature of the medieval landscape. As such it played a prominent role in the construction of social identities. Aristocratic property is a good illustration of this. As described above, the pattern of halls planned in association with enclosures can be traced back to the royal *vills* of the seventh century. It was a pattern emulated across the country in the building of early medieval manorial sites. The examples of Raunds and West Cotton are certainly not the only ones. In particular, the excavations at Goltho in Lincolnshire and Sulgrave in Northamptonshire have revealed the importance of ditched and banked enclosures surrounding hall complexes.[41] Such constructions clearly expressed the physical presence of lordship, identifying the owners as part of the ruling elite. The ramparts, ditches and ringworks at these sites defined the lord as a military power and

---

39. See for example T. Williamson, 'Settlement chronology and regional landscapes: the evidence from the claylands of East Anglia', in Hooke (ed.), *Anglo-Saxon Settlements*, 153–75; and P.R. and A. Preston-Jones, 'Changes in the Cornish countryside', in Hooke and Burnell (eds), *Landscapes and Settlement*, 51–68.
40. B. Roberts, *Landscapes of Settlements: Prehistory to the Present* (1996), 57.
41. See B. Davison, 'Excavations at Sulgrave, Northamptonshire 1960–76', *Archaeological Journal* 134 (1977), 105–14, and G. Beresford, *The Development of an Early Medieval Manor c. 850–1150* (1987).

symbolized his dominant position in relation to the village as well as his status among other lords. The deliberate investment of resources in manorial complexes of this kind reflected the underlying 'drive to political accumulation' in feudal society.

In this respect, the conspicuous consumption of wealth in building programmes was an important means of displaying class identities. The construction of churches in nucleated villages and their close spatial association with manor complexes is highly indicative of feudal power. Richard Morris has convincingly argued that the tenth and eleventh centuries comprised the period in which the parochial system rapidly took shape; he evocatively describes the process of church establishment as akin to the arrival of 'mushrooms in the night'.[42] Instrumental in this development was the growing class of local landowners. Churches became symbols of feudal power situated, as they usually were, upon prominent ground within enclosures, adjacent to manorial halls. They were the first stone buildings to be erected in early medieval England, and gave a sense of permanence and stability to the new feudal landscape. Their physical presence signified the dominance of lordship, and the integration of economic and ideological legitimization. Christianity formed a dominant ideology in feudal society, not in the sense of enforcing peasant subordination (this was achieved through non-ideological means), but in the integration of a fragmented ruling class behind a set of common beliefs.[43] The Church, more than any other early medieval institution, exemplified the socially embedded nature of feudal class relations. As a powerful force in the construction of feudal identities it is not surprising that local churches, as revealed by many excavations, were continually modified or enlarged through new building programmes.

Class identity for feudal lords was thus as much directed towards each other as towards the peasants. The fragmented nature of economic and political relations, structured by the private control over individual landed estates, led to conflicts between feudal lords at all levels of the social hierarchy. These tensions consequently influenced the cultural expression of social identities, most vividly in forms of conspicuous consumption. They are also evident in the patterns of landscape and settlement. The movement towards nucleated villages may have marked the imposition of feudalism, but it also embodied the fragmentation and individualization of class power through which this process unfolded. Despite the common features of nucleation, there were significant variations and differences between villages. Each has a distinctive organization of space and particular architectural styles which characterize the social identities of individual lords. Simon James, Ann Marshall and Martin Millet, for example, have drawn

42. R. Morris, *Churches in the Landscape* (1989), 140–67, 227–74.
43. For a development of this argument, see N. Abercrombie, S. Hill, and B. Turner, *The Dominant Ideology Thesis* (1980).

attention to the way in which a highly characteristic building tradition within England during the fifth to eighth centuries became less unified during the course of the ninth century, with buildings tending to be less precisely laid-out and with different plan forms and varying construction techniques.[44] This growth of architectural diversity, I suggest, relates to the way in which landed estates under feudalism became individualized with their lord.

The making of the feudal town: from ports of trade to regional markets

The movement from dispersed to nucleated rural settlements between the seventh and eleventh centuries coincided with another major transformation which altered the basic fabric of the early medieval landscape – the birth of the medieval town. This development was just as dramatic as those changes affecting rural settlements and was likewise intertwined with the articulation of new class relations and the construction of feudal identities.

In the seventh and eighth centuries, large trading and manufacturing centres known as *wics* were established on coastal sites and along the major waterways of England. These *wics* are commonly thought to have been royal foundations, serving as emporia in the administration of craft production and the regulation of trade within the emerging kingdoms of England. During the ninth and tenth centuries these sites appear to have been abandoned or in decline, replaced by an expanding network of more insular regional centres, *burhs*. This change marked a distinct break in settlement patterns, not simply in site location but in terms of the character of occupation. In essence, these new centres represented the establishment of towns. Their rapid proliferation meant that, by the end of the eleventh century, the primary elements of the urban system of medieval England had been established.[45]

Traditionally, the process of urbanization has been perceived as being organically connected to the evolution of trade, with medieval towns understood as 'non-feudal islands in the feudal seas'.[46] The movement from coastal trading settlements, *wics*, to regional towns, *burhs*, for instance, has often been described as a shift from a gift-

44. S. James, A. Marshall and M. Millet, 'An early medieval building tradition', *Archaeological Journal* 141 (1984), 182–215.
45. For an overview of the archaeological evidence and review of the current interpretations of early medieval towns, see P. Otterway, *The Archaeology of British Towns: From Emperor Claudius to the Black Death* (1992), 120–61, G. Astill, 'Archaeological theory and the origins of English towns – a review', *Archaeologia Polana* 32 (1994), 27–71, and S. Roskams, 'Urban transition in early medieval Britain: the case of York', in *Towns in Transition: Urban Evolution in Late Antiquity and the Early Middle Ages*, eds N. Christie and S. Loseby (1996), 262–88.
46. M.M. Postan, *The Medieval Economy and Society* (1975), 239.

exchange economy, administrated at ports-of-trade, to a market-orientated economy, with trade the dynamic of social development.[47] This orthodoxy, however, has been challenged by a number of Marxist historians. Hilton, in particular, has extensively shown how the medieval town was a thoroughly feudal institution, shaped by the class forces of lords, Church and state.[48] Far from being an independent process separate from rural society, early medieval urbanization was an integral product of the growth of new landed social relations, an expression of the 'feudal revolution'. Economically, towns acted as key nodal points in an essentially fragmented feudal structure. They operated as centres in the administration of agricultural surpluses and regulated markets for the exchange of petty commodities and luxury goods. Critically, in the framework of a decentralized political system, early medieval towns were fundamental institutions in the formation and projection of state power.[49]

Placing the phenomena of medieval urbanism firmly in the context of feudalism holds important implications for an archaeology of class and identity. As nodal points in the emerging feudal political economy, towns became a focus for the enforcement and display of class relations. In town, as well as country, the construction of elite power was grounded in forms of political coercion and physical force. This reality of class relations permeated the social organization of urban space and architecture. Thus, in a more concentrated form than in the manorial village, patterns of bounded and regulated space structured urban life.

The use of bounded and regulated space in early medieval towns was not necessarily a new development. The seventh- and eighth-century *wic* settlement exhibited a similar degree of conscious planning. For example, excavations at Southampton (Hamwic) have revealed the settlement to be well organized, delineated by a boundary ditch and laid out in a fairly regular manner with a rectilinear pattern of gravelled roads.[50] What was new in late ninth- and tenth-century towns was the extent to which bounded and regulated space became intrinsically built into the organization and functioning of these settlements. This was not simply a quantitative development, but more of a qualitative change. *Burhs* were essentially defined by their enclosed bounded space, their walls and ramparts. The typical rectilinear-based plans of early medieval towns, illustrated by the classic Alfredian street plan at Winchester, conditioned their internal

---

47. See for example R. Hodges, *Dark Age Economics* (1982).
48. R. Hilton, *English and French Towns in Feudal Society: A Comparative Study* (1992).
49. For a further elaboration of this argument, see for example G. Bois, *The Transformation of the Year One Thousand: The Village of Lournand from Antiquity to Feudalism* (1992), 70–93, and T. Saunders, 'Trade, towns and states: a reconsideration of early medieval economics', *Norwegian Archaeological Review* 28 (1995), 31–53.
50. A.D. Morton, *Excavations at Hamwic* (1992).

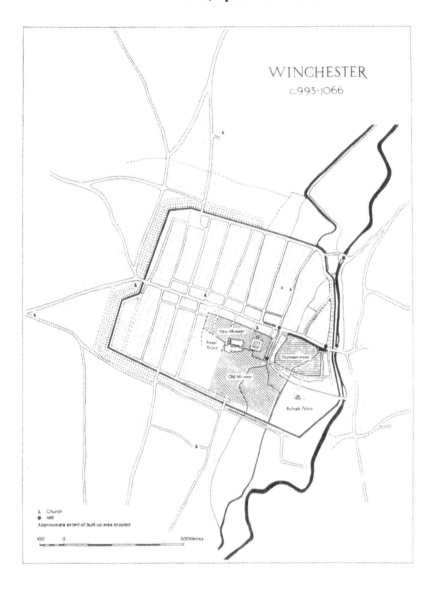

Figure 13 The bounded and regulated town plan of late Anglo-Saxon
Winchester
Source: M. Biddle, 'Towns', in *The Archaeology of Anglo-Saxon England*, ed.
D.M. Wilson (1976) © Methuen & Co

arrangement of regularly spaced grids of parallel streets and perpendicular central thoroughfares (Figure 13).[51] It was onto this layout that urban plots and tenements were carefully set out with deliberate regularity – churches and palaces were erected in ordered enclosures, and urban activities were confined to discrete zones.

The physical morphology of early medieval towns was a vital part of the means by which urban relations were constituted. Of course *burhs*, surrounded by walls, ramparts and ditches, were clearly intended to be major defences. However, these evident military aspects cannot be separated from the role of these settlements as political and economic central places. The functioning of early medieval towns as nodal points in the administration of rural surpluses, tax collection, and trade and exchange depended upon their privileged position within the rural hinterland. These were not competitive commercial enterprises. Towns were socially regulated institutions based on powers of monopoly and exclusion.[52] Walls and gates, planned street systems and zoned occupation were all mechanisms in the maintenance of control. Walls certainly possessed defensive functions, but they also restricted access in and out of towns, channelling traffic through selected gateways where it could be checked and monitored. Street networks guided and directed movement in the town, breaking up internal space into specific units and fixed blocks. Consequently, urban tenements could be highly organized, with the size and width of each plot the basis of rent assessments, and with certain activities potentially confined to particular streets and areas. Thus the physical arrangement of towns facilitated the ordering and control of occupation.

It was in this urban arena of bounded and regulated space that feudal elites acted out and displayed their class power. Towns were primarily institutions established for and by the landed aristocracy, lords as well as monarch and state. Documentary evidence reveals the prominence of 'urban manors' in towns such as Winchester, where it is possible to link tenements and property to the rural estates of individual lords within the surrounding hinterland.[53] Early medieval towns were important meeting places for a fragmented feudal aristocracy, specialized centres where dispersed agricultural surpluses could be collected and redistributed, and administrated markets for the

---

51. See M. Biddle and D. Hill, 'Late Saxon planned towns', *Antiquaries Journal* 51 (1971), 70–85; P. Crummy, 'The system of measurements used in town planning from the ninth to the thirteenth centuries', in *Anglo-Saxon Studies in Archaeology and History*, eds S.C. Hawkes, D. Brown and J. Cambell (1979), 149–63; and M. Biddle, 'The study of Winchester, archaeology and history in a British town', *Proceedings of the British Academy* 69 (1983), 93–135.
52. D. Hill, 'Towns as structure and functioning communities through time: the development of central places from 600 to 1066', in Hooke (ed.), *Anglo-Saxon Settlements*, 197–212.
53. See S. Reynolds, 'Towns in Domesday Book', in *Domesday Studies*, ed. J.C. Holt (1987), 295–309, and R. Fleming, 'Rural elites and urban communities in late Saxon England', *Past and Present* 141 (1993), 3–37.

production and exchange of prestigious items. Urban space, therefore, was highly charged in class terms. It was a place for the projection of powerful imagery, the promotion of rival ideologies and competing symbols of power. In the words of Martin Carver, a town was the focus of a 'war of images',[54] with architecture and space invested with class meanings and identities.

Towns were centres for conspicuous consumption. It was through the open expenditure of wealth that the feudal presence within towns was clearly felt. Perhaps this is most vividly expressed in the unfolding pattern of church-building. Alongside the founding of towns around cathedrals and minsters, one of the most striking characteristics of early medieval urbanization was the proliferation of other ecclesiastical provisions. In contrast to *wics*, which were marked by a paucity of churches, tenth- and eleventh-century towns were swarming with churches. For example, by the end of the twelfth century the number of parish churches in Winchester had grown to fifty-seven, and similar numbers of churches were present in the other major towns of England.[55] These urban churches, like their rural counterparts, were largely founded by lay people and were initially treated as pieces of private property. The pattern of multiplication can be seen as a guide to the size and wealth of particular towns in the early medieval period, but also as an expression of the heterogeneous nature of feudal interests which were focused upon urban centres. The church was a monument to conspicuous consumption and competitive emulation between feudal elites. It became a symbol of the status and identities of individual lords. The positioning of churches within towns was therefore of great significance. Morris has examined in detail the relation of churches to other components of urban topography and shown how they were situated in prominent and potentially prestigious places.[56] Churches tended to be concentrated along the principal thoroughfares of towns and sometimes within the main street itself. Market places, gates, and crossroads were also favoured positions for church-building. The spatial patterning of churches in towns was thus one highly conspicuous element in the 'war' of feudal images.

The active involvement of royalty in the establishment of urban foundations also left its physical mark on urban development. It should not be forgotten that the defended *burh* lay at the heart of the military campaigns with which the early medieval state of England was created. The emphasis on walls and defence, and the centralized planning and organization of space, were all signatures of royal authority. Towns operated as political and economic focal points in the administration of the realm; they were a key means to extend and maintain state power. The central position of towns in the dynamic process of state formation

---

54. M. Carver, *Arguments in Stone* (1993), 63–77.
55. Morris, *Churches in the Landscape*, 178.
56. *Ibid.*, 168–226.

meant they were an important focus of inter-class conflict. This is probably best expressed in the development of urban castles in England after 1066. The deliberate siting of royal castles in towns was one of the main tools in the consolidation of Norman control of the country. Castles introduced a highly specialized element in the bounded and regulated space of urban topography.[57] The distinctive motte and bailey type constructions were typically inserted in one corner of pre-existing towns, overlooking the main gates, thorough-fares, and markets (Figure 14). From such an imposing position, the castle formed an intrinsic component in the royal surveillance and control of urban relations. Furthermore, the erection of castles in towns, together with the large-scale rebuilding of cathedrals, formed a

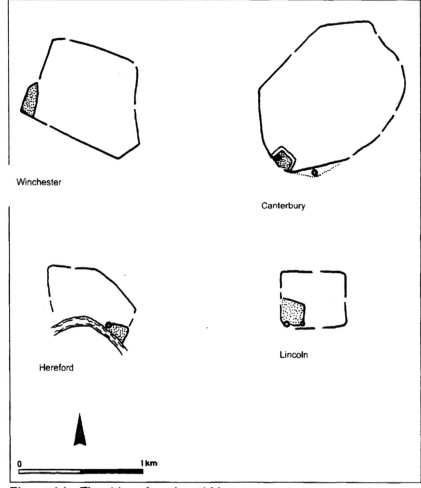

Figure 14   The siting of castles within towns
Source: C. Drage, 'Urban castles', in *Urban Archaeology in Britain*, eds J. Schofield and R. Leech (1987)

blatant ideological statement in the promotion of Norman state power, signalling the imposition of a new politico-religious regime. As such, the castle can be seen as the archetypal symbol of state power and identity. Castles were the most potent manifestation of the feudal need for 'extra-economic compulsion', a physical embodiment of the 'drive towards political accumulation'.

The changes and developments in the urban landscape indicate that early medieval urbanization was part of a historical process. Towns evolved in time as well as in space. Archaeological research in recent years has pointed towards the growing diversity in the character of English urban sequences. The evidence for more intensive industrial production in towns in the north and east of the country such as Lincoln, Stamford and York, for example, suggests qualitative differences were emerging between urban experiences during the course of the tenth century. This development is also reflected in the unfolding picture of an urban hierarchy – of regional county and small towns.[58]

These patterns of diversity relate to the real complexity of the social construction of urban entities. However, they also allude to the active and transformative nature of the urbanizing process. Early medieval towns were a product of feudalism, but also a *producer* of new social relations and conditions. The dynamics of these settlements are reflected in the rise of particular urban material culture.[59] For example, new house-types, based upon the dug-out cellar, were built upon the confined, bounded space of urban tenements. Activities and occupations diversified with the growth of special urban crafts and industries. And, as towns expanded, less organized and regulated space grew up in the back streets and behind fronts of tenements. It was outside the limits of feudal surveillance that structures of power were resisted and defied.[60] In particular, it was on the fringes of bounded space, beyond the walls and ramparts, that the poor and socially marginalized congregated. The irregular suburbs that evolved outside early medieval towns reflected the growth of new communities which were not so constrained by the rigid framework of feudal space.[61] The medieval town, therefore, was not simply the arena for the display of feudal elite identities, aristocrats, Church and state, but was also the cradle within which new, distinctively *urban* identities were born.

---

57. C. Drage, 'Urban castles', in *Urban Archaeology in Britain*, eds J. Schofield and R. Leech (1987), 117–32.
58. See G. Astill, 'Towns and town hierarchies in Saxon England', *Oxford Journal of Archaeology* 10 (1991), 95–117.
59. See for example J. Schofield and A. Vince, *Medieval Towns* (1994), for an overview of the developing material culture of medieval urban life.
60. For a discussion of urban conflict, see Hilton, *English and French Towns*, 127–51.
61. See, D.J. Keene, 'Suburban growth' in *The Medieval Town: A Reader in English Urban History 1200–1540*, eds R. Holt and G. Rosser, (1990) 97–119.

Conclusion

This chapter has been concerned with the concept of class in the early medieval period. Understood as a structural relationship and historical process, class has been used to trace the development of feudal relations in the changing landscapes and settlements between the seventh and eleventh centuries. The specific character of feudal exploitation, underpinned as it was by physical force and coercion, and locked into forms of political accumulation and consumption, became embedded in the social construction of space. The bounding and regulation of space lies at the heart of an archaeology of feudalism. It was this distinct 'revolution of spatial order' which can be seen in the movement towards a fixed and ordered cultural landscape during the tenth and eleventh centuries. Bounded and regulated space was present in the nucleation of villages, as well as being a defining attribute of town foundations where it took a more concentrated form.

This archaeology of feudal class formation has been the framework within which the issue of social identity, particularly the construction of feudal elite identities, has been addressed. Lords, monarchs and Church were the principal agents of the transformations which occurred in the early medieval period, and are arguably at their most visible in the development of villages and town. One key element of this process was the way in which the structure of feudal class formation influenced the construction of certain feudal identities. Bounded and regulated space played such an intrinsic part in feudal class experience that it became a central medium for the cultural expression of social identity. The classic symbols of feudal power – manor, church and castle – were all shaped by the bounded space of tenement, enclosure, walls and ramparts. The fragmented character of lordship meant that feudal identity was as much a display of social status and position *within* this class as *between* classes, if not more so. The overtly military symbols of power were certainly a vivid reflection of the basis of feudal exploitation, but these symbols were essentially directed towards the feudal elites themselves. This development took its most concentrated form in the process of early medieval urbanization, with the town becoming the focus for the war of feudal images.

Finally, in making these arguments about the connections between the feudal class formation and the construction of social identity, I am not suggesting that social identity can be reduced to class. The point is that classes *were* present in the making of the early medieval period and that there was a relationship between economy and society, class and identity. These connections, unfortunately, are all too frequently lost in the current celebration of fragments within academic circles. Explicit in this chapter, therefore, is a defence of Marxism and an attempt to demonstrate the relevance of a Marxist analysis. To this extent, I hope that I have shown that the British Marxist historians still have a great deal to offer to both the theoretical and empirical debates and the discussions within medieval archaeology.

11 Christian Monumental Sculpture and Ethnic Expression in Early Scotland[1]

Stephen T. Driscoll

From the chronicles and books of the ancients we find that among other famous nations our own, the Scots, has been graced with widespread renown ... Thence they came, twelve hundred years after the peoples of Israel crossed the Red Sea, to their home in the west where they still live today. The Britons they first drove out, the Picts they utterly destroyed, and, even though very often assailed by the Norwegians, the Danes and the English, they took possession of that home with many victories and untold efforts: and, as the historians of old time bear witness, they have held it free of all bondage ever since.

Declaration of Arbroath, 1320[2]

In the fourteenth century Scottish ethnicity was understood as a straightforward history of conflict and triumph. There is no sense of ambiguity or intermingling in this view of Scottish origins, much less is there any sense that Scottish identity was constructed. In recent years notions of race and ethnicity have proved integral to our understanding of how the Scottish nation developed, and still colour our understanding of contemporary Scottish society. Rather less attention has been paid to how ethnic differences were expressed during the

---

1. The research upon which this chapter is based has been largely funded by the H.F. Guggenheim Foundation. Versions of this discussion have been presented previously at the Society for American Archaeology Annual Conference in Minnesota 1995 (with support from the British Academy) and at the Early Medieval Research Group annual conference in Edinburgh 1996. I am grateful to many people who provided me with critical comment, especially Katherine Forsyth.
2. Translation by Sir James Fergusson of the letter by the barons of Scotland to Pope John XXII arguing for Scottish independence during the Wars of Independence (1297–1328), *The Declaration of Arbroath* (1970), 7.

formative centuries from the sixth to eleventh centuries. This chapter reviews the categories of evidence which provide access to ethnicity in early medieval Scotland and examines the social context of such ethnic expressions. Archaeology contributes a significant component of the evidence,[3] but historical and linguistic sources are equally important. Overall, I hope to demonstrate that the Church provided an important setting for the display of ethnicity, because it was a focus for the display of political power.

From an archaeological perspective the most conspicuous elements of this religious display consist of sculptured stone monuments – crosses, gravestones and decorated architectural features. This sculpture is especially significant because it survives so well. Although this sculpture was devotionally inspired, it is possible to examine how the different peoples who inhabited Scotland identified themselves and constructed their identities through it. Indeed, the religious sculpture is such an important archaeological resource for this question of ethnic identity, that this chapter will also consider why the Church was so influential in this process and whether it is appropriate to give monumental sculpture ethnic labels.

One of our few points of certainty in early medieval Scottish history is that its early development was competitive and violent.[4] However, despite the fact that scarcely any of the early Scottish kings died in their beds, we must allow that war was not the only means of competition. Off the battlefield, other resources were mobilized to achieve political objectives. This chapter will focus on these other non-militarized arenas of political discourse, which embrace religion and economics. In many instances these discourses were expressed in material form and in such cases archaeology often provides our only insight into the represented social processes.[5] Ethnicity is a case in point. Regional variation in the material record is not a constant feature of medieval Scotland. So where regional variations can be identified as ethnic distinctions, they assume an historical importance, which may be indicative of a particularly abrupt social change. Of course, the attribution of ethnic meanings to stylistic differences, whether by ourselves or by the Scottish barons, may be a misreading of the evidence.[6]

---

3. The problematic nature of the relationship between ethnicity and archaeology is a point to which we will return.
4. Two of the most respected overviews of recent years make this explicit in their titles: L. Alcock, *Economy, Society and Warfare* (1987) and A. Smyth, *Warlords and Holy Men* (1984).
5. For a general discussion of the material component of socially situated practices see J. Barrett, 'Fields of discourse: reconstituting a social archaeology', *Critique of Anthropology* 7 (1987/1988), 5–16.
6. Ethnicity, like any social construct which has a meaning beyond the confines of academic debate, is a difficult concept to employ without being glib or superficial. My understanding of ethnicity derives from anthropological and sociological studies which regard ethnicity entirely as a social construct that

Modern historic knowledge of early medieval Scotland was largely mapped out at the end of the nineteenth century,[7] but current understanding depends upon the critical advances made by historians and archaeologists since the Second World War.[8] Accomplished though this history is, we appear to have entered a new era of critical scholarship in which work on familiar materials is producing startling new insights.[9] Among the most important developments in political history has been Dauvit Broun's work on the origins of the Pictish provinces and the significance of the kingdom of Alba (or Scotia), the kingdom ruled by Gaels (Dalriadic Scots) but largely based in Pictish territory.[10] One theme underpinning these advances is a concern to see ethnic identity as a cultural construct rather than to accept that it is biologically determined.

The social picture in early Scotland was extremely complex, so it is not surprising that there has been a tendency to accept medieval statements about population shift and ethnic origins at face value, particularly when making up maps (Figure 15). The prevailing orthodox history of northern Britain during the sixth to tenth centuries recounts the emergence of regional ethnic identities (Pictish, Dalriadic, British, Anglian and Norse) and their eventual suppression by the Scottish state.[11] Rather than see ethnicity as an epiphenomenon of little lasting significance, I would like to suggest that ethnicity in early medieval

contd.
    owes nothing to genetics and everything to specific historical circumstances. From this perspective ethnicity is composed of a variety of cultural components including the conceptual (e.g. language, myth and kinship system) and the physical (e.g. subsistence method, clothing and shelter), all of which are open to modification, manipulation and conflicting interpretations. Following Marshall Sahlins's *Historical Metaphors and Mythical Realities* (Ann Arbor, 1981), the process of reproducing ethnicity is also the process by which it is transformed.

7. W.F. Skene, *Celtic Scotland* (3 vols, 1876–80); A.O. Anderson, *Early Sources of Scottish History* (2 vols, 1922).

8. A.M.M. Duncan, *Scotland: The Making of the Kingdom* (1975) is still the best single volume on the Middle Ages. F.T. Wainwright (ed.), *The Problem of the Picts* (1955) serves as the model for interdisciplinary historical investigation and despite recent advances contains much useful information. P. McNeill and R. Nicholson (eds), *An Historical Atlas of Scotland c. 400–c.1600* (1975) provides an indispensable geographic perspective. The *Scottish Historical Review*, 73 (1994), on the theme 'Whither Scottish history?' contains a series of important historiographical articles which provide useful perspectives on the advances of Scottish history in recent years.

9. The two recent volumes edited by Barbara Crawford – *Scotland in Dark Age Europe* (1994) and *Scotland in Dark Age Britain* (1996) – illustrate the vitality of some of this work.

10. D. Broun, 'The origins of Scottish identity', in *Nations, Nationalism and Patriotism in the European Past*, eds C. Bjørn, A. Grant and K.J. Stringer (Copenhagen, 1994), 35–55.

11. Straight historical accounts can be found in Duncan, *Scotland: The Making of the Kingdom*; Smyth, *Warlords and Holymen*; and B. Crawford, *Scandinavian Scotland* (1987). S. Foster, *Picts, Gaels and Scots* (1996) is a reliable, well-illustrated archaeological introduction.

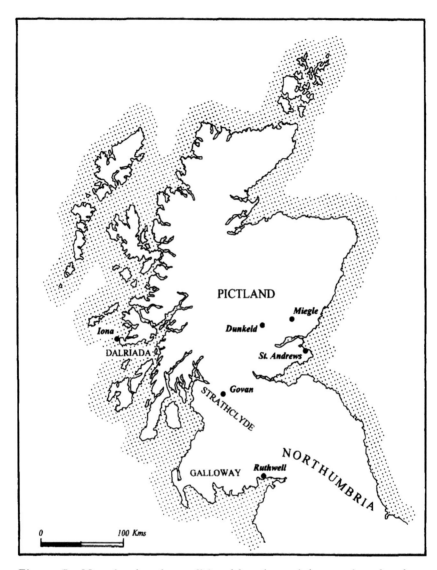

Figure 5   Map showing the traditional locations of the peoples of early Scotland. These areas are broadly conceived as representing political and ethnic groupings.

Scotland provides one of the clearest guides to the arenas where political struggles were taking place. One of these arenas focused on religion and centres of Christian worship.

In some respects the modern Scottish preoccupation with ethnicity is not surprising.[12] More widely, the past decade has seen a huge growth of archaeological interest in ethnicity and national identity and a corresponding growth in the number of books on the subject. Much of this energy has been focused on identifying how recent and contemporary politics have influenced our understanding of the past.[13] An almost equal amount of energy has been expended searching for ways of recognizing ethnic and national identities in prehistoric societies.[14] These efforts have certainly led to a much greater awareness of the influences of nationalist politics on our work and of the potential for reconstructing identity latent within the archaeological record.

As archaeologists we must establish that differences observed in the archaeological record in, for example, pottery styles or dress were meaningful to contemporaries and understood as expressions of ethnic difference. However, one of the key problems which prehistorians have come up against is the lack of independent validation of their identifications of ethnicity. For instance in concluding a study of prehistoric ethnicity, Siân Jones writes that even if one follows a non-normative programme of stylistic analysis, 'it will be necessary to employ independent contextual evidence in the interpretation of ethnicity, as the significance of material culture in terms of ethnicity is culturally and historically specific'.[15] In observation of the early medieval period, archaeologists have primarily used notions of ethnicity which allowed them to chart the movements of populations, by and large without questioning whether these distinctions mattered to contemporary peoples and without critically examining the ethnic labels they use.

As medievalists we are fortunate to have contextual evidence in the form of contemporary writings, like the *Declaration of Arbroath* or Bede's *Ecclesiastical History*, which make it clear that ethnicity was socially meaningful. The significance of ethnicity is one of the dominant themes of Robert Bartlett's *The Making of Europe*,[16] a survey which not only recognizes ethnicity as a cultural construct, but

---

12. In 1997, Scots voted for devolution from the United Kingdom and a parliament of their own.
13. For example, J.A. Atkinson, I. Banks and J. O'Sullivan (eds), *Nationalism and Archaeology* (1996) and P.L. Kohl and C. Fawcett (eds), *Nationalism, Politics and the Practice of Archaeology* (1995).
14. For example, P. Graves-Brown, S. Jones and C.S. Gamble (eds), *Cultural Identity and Archaeology* (1995).
15. S. Jones, 'Discourses of identity in the interpretation of the past', in (eds) Graves-Brown *et al.*, *Cultural Identity and Archaeology*, 73.
16. R. Bartlett, *The Making of Europe* (1993).

uses it as an analytical tool in discussing the social transformation of medieval Europe. According to Bartlett, in the tenth century, the primary badges of ethnicity were customs, language and law.[17] Interestingly he argues that the vulgar criterion usually used today to define ethnicity, i.e. race, was perceived as being less important than it is now. This is not because kinship and bloodstock were unimportant, but because the outward signs of race were not sufficiently obvious to serve as useful markers. Within medieval Europe gradual changes in skin tone and physical attributes were commonplace – Germans could look French, Nordic or Slavic – and therefore were far less significant in determining identity and social standing than were the cultural criteria. From an analytical perspective one feature which cuts across customs, language and law is that they are all malleable: granddaughters of Picts could become Scots by changing their speech and their clothes.

Bartlett's three media of ethnic identity – language, law and custom – provide a valid structure for reviewing the evidence for ethnicity in early medieval Scotland. In theory all should provide us with access to contemporary perspectives on the question of how peoples in northern Britain distinguished themselves from one another, but the evidence for each category does not survive equally well.

Language history is a topic which requires more detailed consideration than I am able to provide here, so I will be brief. It is clear, in contemporary texts from the time of Columba in the sixth century to that of Macbeth in the eleventh, that language was seen as a natural index of social affiliation. Bede, for example, uses language groups, not political divisions or kingdoms, to underpin his geography of eighth-century Britain. Dramatic changes in the geography of language are obvious in texts and place-names.[18] From the place-name evidence it is possible to identify areas with distinctive linguistic histories. In areas of Pictish and Cumbric speech, the native languages were overlain and eventually displaced by Gaelic, English and Norse and this gave rise to complex patterns of overlapping language use. In the absence of more direct documentary evidence, place-name studies have become the backbone of Dark Age political geography. But at present the process of language change is only understood at a broad-brush level; we are only beginning to see the potential for fine-grained analyses of particular locales or name types, exemplified in the work of Taylor on Fife[19] and by Clancy on *annatt* places.[20]

---

17. *Ibid.*, 198–9.
18. W.J. Watson, *Celtic Place-Names of Scotland* (1926, reprinted 1986); K.H. Jackson, *Language and History in Early Britain* (1953); W. F. Nicholison, *Scottish Place-Names* (1976).
19. S. Taylor, *Settlement-Names of Fife* (PhD Thesis, University of St Andrews, 1995); and 'Place-names and the early Church in eastern Scotland', in Crawford (ed.), *Scotland in Dark Age Britain*, 93–110.
20. T. Clancy, 'Annat place-names in Scotland and the origins of the parish', *Innes Review* 46 (1995), 91–115.

Despite the difficulties of providing precise chronological control, these analyses can reveal the dynamic relationship which existed between language use, military fortunes and regional politics. We will return to place-names, because they provide crucial evidence for the growth of religious centres and the propagation of devotions to specific saints.

Early medieval Celtic law provides good insights into questions of ethnicity, because the kin-based principles upon which it was constructed required careful definition of family and group membership. In Ireland, the impact of both the Vikings and the Anglo-Normans is apparent.[21] The similarities between Scotland and Ireland might lead one to expect an equally rich legal history for Scotland; this is not the case. David Sellar has surveyed the early survivals within Scottish legal traditions of the modern era and has shown that while their influence is interesting, the legacy is not great.[22] Although Patrick Wormald has recently reminded us of the political and ethnic overtones of the few bits of evidence pertaining to the ninth-century proclamations of law in Scotland,[23] too little survives to provide a well-rounded view of the different legal traditions.[24] The absence of this potentially revealing category of evidence is all the more annoying, given the ubiquity of open-air court sites as reflected in place-names, folk traditions and archaeology.[25] Clearly such places, whether based at ancient prehistoric barrows or on purpose-built mounds, served as a key element in the administrative apparatus of early medieval lordship.[26]

The notion of custom is the most difficult of the three ethnic criteria to focus on, because any description of an anthropological culture must embrace multiple aspects of learned behaviour and meaningfully-constituted social practices. Here I will limit myself to three social fields where custom resides that can be studied archaeologically: housing, attire and religious practice. Each has a potential for revealing ethnicity, but each has intrinsic archaeological limitations in Scotland.

Domestic architecture and settlement form are the stock-in-trade of most archaeologists interested in social questions. Anthropologically we know that houses are one of the most significant repositories of

---

21. F. Kelly, *A Guide to Early Irish Law* (1988).
22. D. Sellar, 'Celtic law and Scots law: survival and integration', *Scottish Studies* 29 (1989), 1–27.
23. 'The emergence of the *Regnum Scottorum*: a Carolingian hegemony?', in Crawford (ed.), *Scotland in Dark Age Britain*, 140–2.
24. 'Leges inter Brettos et Scotos', *The Acts of the Parliament of Scotland, vol. 1 (1126–1423)* (1844), 663–5, stands alone as a legal testament to the interrelationships between different legal traditions.
25. G.W.S. Barrow, *'Popular Courts' in Scotland and its Neighbours in the Middle Ages* (1992), 217–46, examines the evidence for the north and east of Scotland; the potential of detailed local historical study to fill the gaps in the west is illustrated by A. Campbell of Airds, 'Hangman's Hill', *West Highland Notes and Queries* ser. 2, no. 13 (1995), 3–9.
26. S.T. Driscoll, 'The archaeology of state formation in Scotland', in *Scottish Archaeology: New Perceptions* (1991), eds W.S. Hanson and E.A. Slater, 81–111, especially 93ff.

learned behaviour, because they structure activity both within and without the dwelling.[27] Where the evidence is available, the lived-in environment provides solid grounds for detecting and analysing significant social practices, including those we might categorize as 'ethnic'. In spite of recent advances in the settlement archaeology including attempts to distinguish cultural traditions,[28] significant obstacles remain to be overcome. Superficially we appear to be able to identify regional differences in settlement forms which roughly accord to those areas occupied by the different peoples as indicated by historical and place-name evidence. For instance, the dry-stone fortified homesteads known as duns are predominately a phenomenon of Argyll, the area of Dalriadic settlement and Gaelic speech,[29] while classic bow-sided Scandinavian long houses are found in those areas of Norse settlement as evidenced by burials, hoards, small finds and place-names.[30] When looked at in more detail, however, it appears that geographic and climatic influences may override cultural ones. Critically examined, there is not much to link the 'Pictish' house from Buckquoy, Orkney with that from Easter Kinnear, Fife, apart from radiocarbon dates.[31] In the case of these two sites, it can clearly be agreed that raw materials and landscape have been more important in determining the form of these houses than has any notion of a 'Pictish' architectural template.

Not only does the variable geography of Scotland introduce problems, but the main obstacle to using architecture for our purposes is that lack of modern excavations which allow detailed comparisons, let alone more complex spatial analysis. In the case of the Pictish province, there is little on the mainland with which to compare the

27. H. Glassie, *Folk Housing in Middle Virginia: A Structural Analysis of Historic Artifacts* (Knoxville, 1975); P. Bourdieu, *Outline of a Theory of Practice* (1977).
28. L. Alcock, 'A survey of Pictish settlement archaeology', in *Pictish Studies Settlement: Burial and Art in Dark Age Northern Britain*, eds G. Watson and G. Friell (1984), 7–42; I. Armit (ed.) *Beyond the Brochs* (1990); and S. Foster, 'The state of Pictland in the age of Sutton Hoo', *The Age of Sutton Hoo: The Seventh Century in North-Western Europe*, ed. M. Carver (1992), 217–34.
29. Royal Commission on Ancient and Historical Monuments of Scotland (hereafter RCAHMS), *Argyll: An Inventory of the Monuments* (7 vols, 1980–92); L. and E. Alcock, 'Reconnaissance excavations in Scotland 1974–84: 2, excavations at Dunollie Castle, Oban, Argyll, 1978', *Proceedings of the Society of Antiquaries of Scotland* 117 (1987), 119–47.
30. A. Fenton and H. Palsson (eds), *The Northern and Western Isles in the Viking World: Survival, Continuity and Change* (1984); C.D. Morris and D.J. Rackham (eds), *Norse and Later Settlement and Subsistence in the North Atlantic* (1992); and B. Scott, 'The Viking move west: houses and continuity in the Northern Isles', in *Meaningful Architecture: Social Interpretations of Buildings*, ed. M. Locock (1994), 132–46.
31. A. Ritchie, 'Excavation of Pictish and Viking-age farmsteads at Buckquoy, Orkney', *Proceedings of the Society of Antiquaries of Scotland* 108 (1976–77), 174–227; S.T. Driscoll, 'A Pictish settlement in north-east Fife: the Scottish Field School of Archaeology excavations at Easter Kinnear', *Tayside and Fife Archaeological Journal* 3 (1997), 74–118.

middle-ranking site of Buckquoy. We cannot say how it might have differed from socially analogous settlements in Moray or Angus. At a more exalted level, in the architecture of the elite, we would be justified in expecting self-conscious expressions of social status; unfortunately, sites of the highest status have been excavated either badly or on a small scale. The Northumbrian *villa regalis* of Yeavering stands alone in having been both extensively excavated and published.[32] Faced with such archaeological gaps, the settlement evidence remains a field to be exploited in the future, but is not yet particularly useful in our search for ethnic identity.

Clothing and articles of personal adornment have been shown to be some of the most revealing artefacts we have from the early Middle Ages. Despite the sometimes coarse and racist analyses by archaeologists, dress remains a fertile field for ethnic analysis. Sensitively used, Migration Period funerary practices constitute one of the best avenues through which we may study the negotiation of status in small-scale political groups.[33]

Apart from the first generation or so of Norse settlers, the residents of Scotland more or less stopped putting things in graves after the Bronze Age, thereby depriving us of the best contexts for reconstructing dress and interpreting how transferable objects of personal adornment might have been used to express identity. From the perspective of ethnic identification, this is most unfortunate because the objects of dress we *do* have (pins, brooches and their manufacturing waste), which might have provided signs of regional social and political developments, are too mobile. They can and do turn up anywhere in the country. Even where manufacturing sites have been examined, it is clear that the styles which art historians had confidently assigned to particular groups were swapped around, thus 'Anglo-Saxon' motifs were present at the Mote of Mark in the Wigton peninsula, while 'Pictish' and 'Germanic' motifs are mixed with 'Dalriadic' at Dunadd in the heart of Argyll.[34] What the metalwork shows is that by the seventh century, there were common decorative styles which were available throughout northern Britain and were also current in Ireland and Anglo-Saxon England. Elements of this common vocabulary were put together in subtle ways to convey information about social position and affiliation which we are only beginning to understand.[35] The subtlety of the positioning and selection of articles included in Anglo-Saxon burials would seem to suggest that without

---

32. B. Hope-Taylor, *Yeavering: An Anglo-British Centre of Early Northumbria* (1977).
33. R. Samson, 'Social structures from Reihengräber: mirror or image', *Scottish Archaeological Revue*, 4 (1987), 116–26.
34. E. Campbell and A. Lane, 'Celtic and Germanic interaction in Dalriata: the 7th-century metalworking site at Dunadd', in *The Age of Migrating Ideas*, eds J. Hugget and M. Spearman (1993), 52–63.
35. Margaret Nieke, 'Penannular and related brooches: secular ornament or symbol in action?', in Hugget and Spearman (eds), *The Age of Migrating Ideas*, 128–34.

similarly precise information, a detailed social analysis of the ethnic dimension in Celtic metalwork may be beyond us.[36]

These deficiencies in the documentary and material records are compensated for by the quality and quantity of early medieval monumental sculpture with which Scotland is blessed. This most remarkable collection, known as the *Early Christian Monuments of Scotland* (*ECMS*) after the title of the nineteenth-century corpus,[37] is explicitly ecclesiastical and was erected in public contexts.

The findspots and the imagery of this sculpture indicate that the Church provided the setting for the most informative material displays of ethnicity. Before asking why churches provided especially potent places for such displays, we must look to the coherence of the Church itself.

In northern Britain, unlike England and northern Europe, the key religious distinctions of the early Middle Ages were not between Christians and pagans, but between competing authorities within the Church. We are shown by Bede that the path to conversion could lead to spectacular disputes, such as that unleashed at the Synod of Whitby in the mid-seventh century, in which the source of religious authority and the path to belief seemed more important than belief itself. There are hints that similarly deep religious fault lines were present throughout northern Britain. It is unfortunate that we can say so little about the progress of conversion in the North, because the source of evangelization was clearly an important factor in establishing communities of belief. Even without detailed knowledge of the coming of Christianity, it seems that neither the process of conversion nor later variations in organization and practice can be adequately explained by the traditional dichotomy of a Roman party and a Celtic one.

There are two categories of evidence which appear to reflect a complex structure in which politics and religious practices were interconnected. First, the propagation of saints' cults which exhibit a connection between local political and ethnic concerns. Second, the large numbers of Christian monuments erected between the seventh and tenth centuries suggest, through their stylistic differences, that 'schools' of sculpture might reflect secular patronage. Before returning to the saints let us consider the sculpture at greater length.

These monuments exhibit stylistic characteristics which allow us to recognize regional distinctions with confidence since they are geographically stable. Moreover, as has been long recognized, the broad distinctions in the distributions seem to correspond to the various ethnic regions, which have been constructed through historical and place-name studies. This is not the place to argue about stylistic

---

36. As for instance has been outlined by E.J. Pader, *Symbolism, Social Relations and the Interpretation of Mortuary Remains* (1982).
37. R. Allen and J. Anderson, *The Early Christian Monuments of Scotland* (3 vols, 1903, reprinted 1993).

origins, to fret about dates or speculate about patrons of particular stones. For this discussion, it is enough to recognize the broad distinctions apparent in the sculptural traditions. Since the nineteenth century, these differences have been seen as expressing ethnic distinctions.

The regional distinctions can be appreciated by reference to monumental crosses from Iona, Govan, Meigle and Ruthwell. With the exception of Ruthwell, the crosses are part of larger collections of sculpture from major religious establishments, probably with connections to the local royal houses. Iona, without question the most significant religious centre in Argyll, had clear royal associations and is widely regarded as a centre from which the classic ring-headed cross form (Figure 16) developed in the seventh and eighth centuries.[38] Although Meigle in Angus has almost no contemporary documentation, the sculpture there is presumed to derive from a Pictish monastery, perhaps under royal patronage.[39] Among the huge collection of eighth- to tenth-century sculpture are several monumental crosses (Figure 17) which assume the typical Pictish cross-slabs form. Govan, in Strathclyde, possesses another large, but ahistoric, collection of sculpture which includes a range of monumental crosses of both free-standing and slab form (Figure 18). The sculpture[40] has been used to propose that the site was linked to the Strathclyde royal house of the tenth and eleventh centuries. Anglian royal patronage is harder to detect north of the Tweed (the modern Scottish border), but the cross (Figure 19) which survives at Ruthwell, Dumfriesshire testifies to a period of Anglian dominance of the Solway region.[41] These examples demonstrate a widespread interest in monumental religious sculpture and illustrate the distinctive regional preferences in monument form. Naturally, when one looks closer there is ample evidence for artistic cross-fertilization throughout northern Britain and Ireland. Moreover, the distributions of these stones exhibit large gaps. While this does not undermine the general point about regional preferences it does suggest that the appropriate scale of analysis should be finer than the typical culture area maps, such as that reproduced in Figure 15.

---

38. RCAHMS, *Argyll: An Inventory of the Monuments, vol. 4 Iona* (1982), 17–19; R.B.K. Stevenson, 'The chronology and relationships of some Irish and Scottish crosses', *Journal of the Royal Society of Antiquaries of Ireland* 86 (1956), 84–96; and D. Kelly, 'The relationship of the crosses of Argyll', in Hugget and Spearman (eds), *The Age of Migrating Ideas*, 219–29.
39. A. Ritchie, 'Meigle and lay patronage in Tayside in the 9th and 10th centuries AD', *Tayside and Fife Archaeological Journal* 1, 1–10; RCAHMS, *South-East Perth* (1994).
40. A. Ritchie (ed.), *Govan and Its Early Medieval Sculpture* (1994) is an up-to-date survey and discussion of the artistic and historical context of the collection. On the royal connection see W. Davies, 'Ecclesiastical centres and secular society in the Brittonic world in the tenth and eleventh centuries', in *ibid.*, 92–102.
41. B. Cassidy (ed.), *The Ruthwell Cross* (Princeton, 1992).

Figure 16   St Martin's Cross, Iona
The sculpture features snake-boss ornament on one side with a sequence of biblical scenes, some of which, like the musicians, had a clear secular resonance. (By courtesy of the RCAHMS, Crown Copyright.)

Figure 17   Meigle Cross no. 1
The slab has been made from a cup-marked standing stone. Opposite
the cross are Pictish symbols: above a scene of mounted hunters,
intermingled with fantastic beasts. (By courtesy of the RCAHMS, Crown
Copyright.)

Although the stylistic treatment and skill of the sculptors varies
considerably, one of the most consistent features is the tendency to
draw upon decorative motifs found in secular and ecclesiastical
metalwork, making full use of the broadly available repertoire. Such
treatment establishes an implicit link with the aristocracy who owned
and used such precious objects. In Pictland, the identity of the
sponsors of many of the stones is even more obvious. There are
frequent representations of the elite as warriors and hunters. Such
images are integral to the iconographic schemes of Pictish stones,
although not unique to them. Hunting is represented in some way in
the sculpture of all parts of early medieval Scotland, but the warrior
motif is largely confined to Pictish and British sculpture.

The ECMS were certainly linked to religious observance but they
seem to indicate more than religious enthusiasm. I would argue that
they were consciously used to help define the political landscape. As
public statements of devotion they carry considerable ideological
weight, especially in those areas of Pictland and Strathclyde where the
aristocracy feature prominently on the sculpture. Nevertheless,

Figure 18   Govan, the 'Sun-Stone'
Note the snake-boss swastika on one side of the roughly-shaped slab; on
the opposite a mounted warrior, much eroded, is surmounted by an
interlace cross. (© T.E. Grey)

surprisingly little attention has been directed towards the analysis of
the social and political content of the sculptures. One way of assessing
this is to consider their wider context within the bounds of religious
observance. As far as we can tell the Church had its own political
dimension, linked to patterns of patronage, internal organization and
doctrine. Competition between various saints' cults is the clearest sign
of this political dimension, but this dimension is likely to go deeper.

The regional character of certain Scottish saintly cults, as evidenced
by dedications, has long been recognized, even if we are only
beginning to see modern critical scholarship brought to bear on the
problem.[42] At a macro-scale, the four major cults which survived into
the later Middle Ages – dedicated to Andrew, Columba, Kentigern and

---

42. S. Taylor, 'Place-names and the early Church in eastern Scotland', in Crawford
(ed.), *Scotland in Dark Age Britain*, 93–110.

Ninian – all have early medieval origins, distinctive spheres of popularity, and clear ethnic associations. The *vita* of our best known saint, Columba, leaves little doubt as to why his cult was promoted by the kings of Dalriada – not only did he come from the royal lineage of Dalriata but he was also successfully involved in royal politics.[43] However, it is not the large cults which I want to focus on; rather, I wish to draw attention to the cohesion of some of the lesser saints' cults. The case of St Serf, who is found predominantly in southern Perthshire and western Fife, is a representative example.

Serf's principal centre of devotion was at Culross, in south-west Fife. Although we can only speculate as to Serf's particular appeal for the region, the dedications indicate active patronage extending across Fife into Southern Perthshire. The concentration of dedications cuts across the Pictish kingdoms of Fortriu and Fothrif and the later medieval earldoms of Strathearn and Fife. Thomas Clancy has identified similar concentrations of dedications to St Drostan in Badenoch and Strathspey, to St Uinniau in Renfrewshire and Ayrshire and to St Mael Rubha in Wester Ross, Skye and Lorn.[44] If we impute a political motive to the patronage and sponsorship of saints' cults, then these lesser cults may represent the eroded footprints of ancient polities, perhaps petty kingdoms. The point here is that we have traces of religious activity which operated on a scale which corresponds to that occupied by different groups ('schools') of stylistically linked sculpture.[45] Broun's recent demolition of the framework of Pictish political geography requires that we discover more complexity within the political landscape.[46] The spread of cults is one way of exploring these obscure polities.

If we had *vitae* for some of these less exalted saints, with their tightly clustered dedications, we would find that they had been selected for two reasons; first, that they were credited with the evangelization of a people or petty kingdom, and second, that they had kin-links with the ruling dynasties. What I would like to suggest is that the politics associated with the development of small kingdoms

43. R. Sharp (ed.), *Adomnan of Iona: Life of St Columba* (1995), 355; M. Herbert, *Iona, Kells and Derry: The History and Hagiography of the Monastic Familia of Columba* (1988).
44. J. MacQueen, 'Myth and legend of the Scottish Lowland saints', *Scottish Studies* 24 (1981), 1–22, draws attention to the geographical focus of some of the lesser saints. Thomas Clancy is engaged in a more detailed investigation of some of the other lesser Scottish saints and I am grateful to him for showing me a draft of his work in progress – T.O. Clancy, 'Scottish saints: national identities in the early middle ages', in R. Sharpe and A. Thacker (eds), *Local Saints and Local Churches* (forthcoming). He documents the evidence in detail and shows more restraint in using this material than I have.
45. Ritchie, 'Meigle and lay patronage' is a recent study of one such Pictish group.
46. D. Broun, 'The origins of Scottish identity in its European context', in Crawford (ed.), *Scotland in Dark Age Europe*, 21–32.

Figure 19   The Ruthwell Cross
One of the most complex pieces of early medieval sculpture to survive;
its obelisk shaft contains biblical scenes framed by Anglo-Saxon runic
and Latin inscriptions. (J. Stuart, *Sculptured Stones of Scotland* (1856),
plates xix and xx.)

provided the contexts for mobilizing the ethnic components which we see in both the ECMS and saints' cults.

Power in early medieval Britain was not exercised simply through the sword, but through a complex interplay of kin-relations, bonds of lordship and effective control of material and ideological resources.[47] Elsewhere I have argued that the monumental sculpture of early Scotland shares many qualities of early texts such as charters, sagas and saints' lives which not only recorded events or beliefs, but were actively used to mediate social relations.[48] One social transformation in which monumental sculpture appears to have been active was in the development of estates. This process of estate formation can be charted across northern Britain as it ultimately led to the shift away from military conquest (the dominant mode of political control), to be replaced by a system in which power was more clearly associated with the control of agricultural wealth. Here I wish to draw attention to the role of monumental sculpture in the development of estates. Among the earliest of the ECMS is a unique set of stones, the Class I Pictish Symbol Stones,[49] which use an abstract symbolic code carved on rude stone pillars to establish a link between the best land, burials and the Pictish nobility. The stones are part of the enabling technology by which prominent individuals were presenced in the landscape and were one of the means through which large estates were first defined. These early estates appear to survive into the twelfth century, when documentation of landholding becomes more common and they are recorded as *thanages* – places held by officials of the king or of regional magnates (earls or *mormaers*).[50]

The point of this digression is that Symbol Stones help to identify an important strategy for gaining control of and maintaining landed resources which would otherwise be lost to us. These monuments therefore represent evidence for the early exercise of power which was not explicitly military, although the raising of fighting men must have been an important duty of those holding the estates, whatever

47. This territory has been charted by a number of influential scholars including L. Alcock, *Arthur's Britain* (1971); W. Davies, *Patterns of Power in Early Wales* (1990); C.P. Wormald, 'Celtic and Anglo-Saxon kingship: some further thoughts', in *Proceedings of the First Symposium on Anglo-Saxon Studies at Kalamazoo*, ed. P. Szarmach (Binghampton, 1985), 151–81.
48. S. T. Driscoll, 'Power and authority in early historic Scotland: Pictish symbol stones and other documents', in *State and Society: The Emergence and Development of Social Hierarchy and Political Centralisation*, ed. J. Gledhill (1988), 215–36.
49. E.A. Alcock, 'Pictish Class I Stones: where and how?' *Glasgow Archaeological Journal* 15 (1989), K. Forsyth, 'Language in Pictland, spoken and written' in *A Pictish Panorama*, ed. E.H. Nicoll (1995), 7–10.
50. G.W.S. Barrow, 'Prefeudal shires and thanes', in *The Kingdom of the Scots* (1973), 1–68; A. Grant, 'Thanes and thanages from the eleventh to the fourteenth centuries', in *Medieval Scotland: Crown, lordship and community*, eds A. Grant and K. Stringer (1993), 39–81; and Driscoll, 'The archaeology of state formation in Scotland'.

their title. Moreover, they are regionally quite restricted and imply that such changes in lordship followed separate histories of development in different areas.

The later ECMS represented by the monumental crosses also exhibit an uneven distribution, which fits well with this idea of separate histories and the use of sculpture as part of a particular strategy followed by some of the petty kingdoms. The monumental crosses represent a distinct stage in the development of lordship and the formation of hereditary aristocracy. The explosion of sculpture was part of a strategy to define and secure new positions of privilege. The strength of this proposition can be appreciated by considering who erected the sculptures and why, and by thinking about who saw them and how they were influenced by the carved images.

We must presume from their findspots, predominantly in church-yards, that these stones were erected at places of worship. Moreover, in the absence of stone architecture, such monuments were among the most permanent statements that could be made. As I have mentioned, the secular imagery on the Pictish and British stones may have been intended to commemorate particular patrons and certainly implies elite sponsorship. Beyond the actual moment of erection, which *might* commemorate specific grants of lands or privileges, the monuments contributed to establishing a setting which was used to reinforce the position of the patrons.

The ECMS would have provided the backdrop against which key ceremonial events were conducted, such as baptisms, marriages and funerals. Given what we know about the social dynamics of early medieval society, such ceremonies were critical for the development and propagation of aristocratic authority. Such events could be politically charged insofar as they related to issues of heirship and inheritance and of dynastic networks and lordship. This political aspect is self-evident for those stones which clearly show secular patronage, but even where the patrons were not secular, we should remember that major religious houses worked much like the rest of the aristocracy in restricting access to high office to a noble elite. The overarching message of the ECMS proclaims divine support for the lives (and souls) of the patrons, their families and their political enterprises.

If we are to allow these monuments any active social influence, then we must also consider who saw them and what they thought. These stones are found in and around churches, but also may have been located along prominent routes, as for instance with the Maiden Stone, Chapel of Gairoch. These were of course public monuments, executed in the most spectacular visual form available. Perhaps such sculptures were paralleled by tapestries, paintings and other perishable media, but these stones were certainly more accessible than the internal fittings of lordly residences would have been. We can surmise that the primary audience was composed of other nobles, branches of the kindred and other members of the aristocracy. The non-noble locals constituted an important secondary audience. Few of them might have witnessed the ceremonial activities, like a marriage, first-hand, but all would have nevertheless appreciated the association with the events. People from further afield would have been a less critically-appreciative audience, but would have recognized the monuments for what they were: emblems of legitimate lordship. Not the least because similar monuments using some of the same imagery and decorative motifs were being erected all around northern Britain and Ireland.

To summarize, our most reliable material evidence of ethnic expression in early medieval Scotland is found on monumental sculpture erected at places of worship. These monuments appear to be manifestations of local aristocratic support for the Church. In these monuments we see the mobilization of selected stylistic traits directed primarily towards an audience composed of noble peers and local subjects. From their distribution and locations, these monuments seem to indicate a relatively localized political discourse. If they were all about local politics, why do they appear to be drawn along 'ethnic' lines?

I believe that the answer relates to the role which Christianity assumed in centralizing religious activity and identifying it with the secular land-owning elite. In the past, archaeological interest in early medieval ethnicity has been concerned with the reconstruction of the boundaries of the petty kingdoms in North Britain. I regard this as misguided, insofar as it is impossible to locate ethnic groups by collecting and sifting traits. We need to recall that ethnicity is not an inherent quality but a cultural construct, fashioned from the available cultural resources and influenced by contemporary political concerns. Particular groups may have been signified by selected traits for only a short period of time. On the other hand, if we focus on transient expressions specifically in order to identify moments of significant discourse, when political and religious modes of expression were united to make authoritative social statements, then we have made some progress in understanding the processes at work here.

Both the appearance and decline of ECMS can be understood with reference to their political context. Initially they serve to provide a new means of legitimizing an emerging aristocracy. The consequences of this activity, which probably reached its peak in the ninth century, was to create a nation of small regions, which accentuated the natural topographical distinctions. Regional identities were created based around places and monuments intended to bolster the legitimacy of local elites, and this included creating a bond between a local community and the ruler. The Church provided a particularly effective setting since it too sought to establish communities which embraced all but were dominated by a few.

In this chapter, the sculptural decoration that I have been labelling as 'ethnic' can be seen to have its origins in the *aristocratic* and the *Christian*. It marks social distinction within groups rather than serving as an intentional marker of cultural difference between groups such as the Picts and the Scots. While it remains convenient to describe the sculpture using terms such as Pictish (as I have here), we should recognize that the sculpture only acquired its ethnic significance through its political associations. The danger is that in labelling a particular style as Pictish or Scottish we are making the same sort of retrospective attribution of ethnicity as did the authors of the *Declaration of Arbroath*. Where they saw the march of warriors, we see migrating sculptors. While these visions are simple and convenient for descriptive purposes, neither is particularly helpful in understanding the development of early medieval Scotland.

Ironically, a desire to avoid the ethnic character of this sculptural tradition may have been one of the factors responsible for the end of the monumental sculpture. By AD 1000, monumental sculpture had all but ceased to be carved, except for tombstones. The monumental crosses were replaced by an even more effective medium for social expression, church building. As Scotland moved towards statehood, its society became increasingly stratified and the distances between classes became more marked, despite the continued importance of the agricultural economy and local kin networks. Resources were redirected away from carving and into the construction of the earliest surviving stone-built churches,[51] which provided a setting for more elaborate ceremonial events to which access could be restricted. The architectural language which was employed was firmly European in its conception and execution, leaving less space for local expression.

51. G. Donaldson, *Scottish Church History* (1985), 1–10.

12 Monastic Memory and Identity in Early Anglo-Saxon England[1]

Catherine Cubitt

Memories hold a formative place in the creation of identities. Communities create a shared identity through the negotiation and exploration of memories.[2] This is true no less of early medieval societies than of modern, but the study of memory and identity in the Middle Ages is hampered by the loss of the voices, artefacts and texts which created and preserved them. For this reason, lay memories from the early Middle Ages are particularly elusive but the comparative wealth of surviving evidence for the Church, and particularly for early medieval monasteries, can be used to give insights into the workings of memory and its role in the formation of group identities.[3] This chapter examines how early medieval monastic communities remembered, investigating the means by which memories were passed from one generation to another and what persons, events or objects were particularly important in the transmission of a monastery's memories.

Janet Coleman has already made an important case for the distinctive nature of memory within early medieval monasteries, drawing chiefly upon the *Regula Benedicti*. Coleman emphasizes how the communal discipline of the monastic life, which sought to obtain individual salvation for its members through their subordination to

1. I am most grateful to Geoff Cubitt, Bill Frazer and Andy Tyrrell for encouraging me to write this chapter and for their comments on it, and to Monica Coutts for hospitality while the bulk of the work was completed.
2. D. Thelen, 'Introduction: memory and American history', *Memory and American History*, ed. D. Thelen (1990).
3. For recent studies of medieval collective memory see for example J. Fentress and C. Wickham, *Social Memory* (1992); P.J. Geary, *Phantoms of Remembrance: Memory and Oblivion at the End of the First Millennium* (Princeton, 1994); and A.G. Remensnyder, 'Legendary treasure at Conques: reliquiaries and imaginative memory', *Speculum* 71 (1996), 884–906. This chapter is intended as a companion piece to my 'Memory and narrative in the cult of early Anglo-Saxon saints', in *Using the Past in Early Medieval Europe*, eds Y. Hen and M. Innes (2000, forthcoming).

community life and its strict self-denial, transformed the understanding of the self. The individual, she suggests, was refashioned through the practice of obedience and humility; the goal of eternal life demanded the rejection of a man's experience outside the monastery. Monastic memory was aimed at the obliteration of personal memory and its replacement by spiritual ideals derived from the study of the Scriptures and Fathers. The memory of spiritual texts and images and events derived from them were substitutes for experiential recollection:

> ...what [the monk] remembers is not the past or events in the extramural world. Rather he remembers the commandments of God and how hell will burn for their sins those who despise God. The monk's memory is filled only with the images of the eternal life which is prepared for those that fear God.[4]

Coleman portrays a monastic world isolated from that of the secular sphere, cut off so radically that its inmates did not even share the same ways of measuring time as the laity. Instead of following the rhythms of the seasons and the natural world, monastic time was reckoned by the liturgy which punctuated the monk's day and ordered the year through its feasts and fasts.[5] Thus the community possessed its own time scheme which united all its members, whereas in the outside world individuals participated in the different chronologies of the different groups to which they belonged. Monastic time was therefore not only radically different from that of the lay sphere but also, unusually, a unifying feature of the community.

If memory has its source and its content in the thought of the diverse groups to which secular man is attached, then the monk's memory has its source and content in the thought of his enclosed and singular group. Beyond the movement of the collective social time of the monastery there is nothing. A day so structured and time so filled ensure that before the monk's mind is the presence of God and his works as described in the Scripture. After several years of such an experience the monk would be a walking thesaurus of biblical history expressed in words shared by the whole community.[6]

Coleman's evocation of an idealized early medieval monastery is both stimulating and provocative. The impact of monastic discipline with its emphasis on the internalization of texts as part of its regime of self-improvement can be seen in a number of texts, for example the writings of Bede. The autobiographical sketch with which Bede closed his *Historia ecclesiastica* describes his life purely in terms of the monastic and priestly life which was made up almost entirely of study

---

4. J. Coleman, *Ancient and Medieval Memories: Studies in the Reconstruction of the the Past* (1992), 129–36, quotation from 131.
5. *Ibid.*, 131–2, 'One need not be sensitive physically to the changes in the season and the weather. The liturgy would tell a monk where he was in the year.'
6. *Ibid.*, 134–5.

and learning – from his entry into the monastery at the age of seven, his life consisted of 'applying myself entirely to the study of the Scriptures; and, amidst the observance of monastic discipline and the daily task of singing in church, it has always been my delight to learn or to teach or write'.[7] This outline of his life forms a brief preface to his real and much lengthier *curriculum vitae*, his list of scholarly publications which is completed by a short salvificatory prayer to Jesus. Bede's own telling of his life history agrees with Coleman's characterization of the monastic life, and in his homilies addressed to his monastic brothers, he advocated the use of liturgy and Scripture to imprint monastic values. In one homily, he urges the brothers to meditate on the Gospels in imitation of the Virgin Mary:

> The virgin mother very carefully retained in her heart everything which she found out about the Lord ... Let us too, my brothers, imitate the Lord's holy mother; and by keeping all of our Lord and Savior's words and deeds in a steadfast heart, let us also, by meditating on them day and night, drive away the troublesome assaults of empty and harmful thoughts. And by frequent discussion of these words, let us take care to rebuke ourselves and our neighbors about our pointless tales, and chatter filled with the wicked sweetness of slander, and to enkindle the frequent offering of divine praises.[8]

While Bede's words affirm the role of the internalization of texts in monastic discipline, they also hint at a world at variance with this ideal, occupied in gossip and slander. Coleman's characterization of the monastic life fails to encompass its variety; the world she describes is curiously monochrome, filled only with textual symbols and experiences. Even the liturgy – that most sensual of all religious experiences – is seen only as a chronological marker and a substitute for the physically-experienced world of nature. She raises many questions: What shaped and structured monastic memory? Could early medieval monks and nuns recall their pre-monastic experiences? This chapter is a response to Coleman's analysis of early medieval monastic memory, intended to explore the workings of memory in a monastic community more fully. Coleman concentrated on prescriptive texts, chiefly the *Regula Benedicti*, and upon the way in which these changed individual experience. Here, I shall use descriptive accounts from early Anglo-Saxon England – monastic histories like Bede's *Historia abbatum* or the poet Æthelwulf's *De abbatibus* – and concentrate upon the ways in

7. *Bede's Ecclesiastical History of the English People*, eds B. Colgrave and R.A.B. Mynors (rev. edn, 1991), (hereafter *HE*), V.24, 566–7.
8. Bede, *Homiliarum evangelici Libri II.*, ed. D. Hurst, *Bedae Venerabilis Opera III: Opera homilectica, Corpus Christianorum Series Latina* (hereafter *CCSL*) 122 (Turnholt, 1955), I.19, 139 (translation from *Bede the Venerable: Homilies on the Gospels*, translated by L.T. Martin and D. Hurst, Cistercian Studies Series, 110 (Kalamazoo, 1991), 193).

which the monastic communities portrayed in these works preserved and transmitted their memories.[9]

The image created by Coleman of the early medieval monastery as a placid collection of individuals, striving in unison for spiritual perfection, absorbed in the study of books, fits ill with what other texts tell us about it. It could not be more different, for example, from Gregory of Tours' description of the nunnery of the Holy Cross in Poitiers where the nuns revolted against their abbess because of *inter alia* the hardships of their way of life, including poor food and the enforced sharing of the bathroom, and who indulged in prolonged armed insurrection during which a number of the sisters managed to get pregnant.[10] Early medieval monasteries were not the harmonious and homogeneous communities represented by their rules – these tell us one story while monastic histories and hagiographies another. They consisted of a number of groups which could be in conflict with one another; the untrammelled power of the abbot or abbess, for example, particularly if he or she was brought in from outside the community, could provoke the ire of the longstanding rank and file of the monastery. One thinks of the monks of Fulda who complained to the Emperor Charlemagne of the excessive building projects of their abbot or of the assassination of Abbo of Fleury and attempted murder of John the Old Saxon by their communities.[11]

Monastic memory must have been diversified between different groups within the house, all possessing their own chronologies but brought together by the dominant and insistent rhythm of the community's liturgical life. The groups of *pueri* and those who had entered as child oblates possessed a very different sense of identity from that of the older monks and those who had come late to the

---

9. For an overview of an early Anglo-Saxon monastery, see S. Foot, 'What was an early Anglo-Saxon monastery?' in *Monastic Studies: The Continuity of Tradition*, ed. J. Loades (1990), 48–57.

10. Gregory of Tours, *Libri Historiarum X, Monumenta Germaniae Historica* (hereafter *MGH*), *Scriptores Rerum Merovingicarum* I.i, eds B. Krusch and W. Levison (Hanover, 1951), IX.39–44 and X.15–17, 460–75, 501–17.

11. *Supplex Libellus Monachorum Fuldensium Carolo Imperatori Porrectus*, printed in *Epistolae variorum Carolo Magno regnante scriptae*, ed. E. Dümmler, *MGH, Epistolae* IV, *Epistolae Karolini Aevi* II (Berlin, 1895), no. 33, 548–51; and see J. Semmler, 'Studien zum Supplex Libellus und zur anianischen Reform in Fulda', *Zeitschrift für Kirchengeschichte*, 69 (1958), 268–98. *Asser's Life of King Alfred, together with the Annals of St Neots erroneously ascribed to Asser*, ed. W.H. Stevenson (1904), cc. 92–7, 79–85. Haimo, *Vita s. Abbonis, Patrologia Latina* 139, 410–14; P. Cousin, *Abbon de Fleury-sur-Loire. Un savant, un pasteur, un martyr à la fin du Xe siècle* (Paris, 1954), 172–88. For later medieval monastic insurrections A. Dimier, 'Violence, rixes et homicides chez les Cisterciens', *Revue des Sciences Religieuses* 46 (1972), 38–57, who notes that the majority of outbreaks of violence concerned the abbot, perhaps resulting from his disciplinary powers. J. Leclercq, 'Violence and devotion to St Benedict in the Middle Ages', *Downside Review* 88 (1970), 344–60, provides an account of violent incidents concerning Fleury recorded in the *Miracula St Benedicti*.

monastic life.[12] Bede, for example, often makes careful note of whether a brother at Wearmouth-Jarrow began his monkish life as an oblate – as Abbot Hwaetberht did – or whether, like Abbot Eosterwine, a former thegn of King Ecgfrith, he joined later in life.[13] Bede's account in the *Historia ecclesiastica* of Owine, a member of Chad's community at Lastingham and former *minister* of Æthelfrith in East Anglia, makes clear the significant differences between the two types of entrant. Because of his age, Owine was 'less capable of the study of the Scriptures' and so 'applied himself more earnestly to manual labour'. His spiritual merits were so outstanding that he became a member of Chad's intimate group of companions, 'yet when they were engaged in reading inside the house, he used to work outside at whatever seemed necessary'. Owine's religious devotion outweighed the impediments to his intellectual developments.[14] Bede's pointed praise for this man seems intended to ward off criticism of his poor scholastic attainments and one senses behind it an environment in which the less accomplished devotional life of the mature entrant was scorned by the religious proficiency of those trained from earliest youth in the exacting disciplines of the monastery. Alcuin's exhortation to the monks of Wearmouth-Jarrow that the rule of St Benedict should be read and translated for all to understand during the monastic meal indicates that not all brothers even at such a learned institution could comprehend Latin.[15] The spiritual life of a child oblate must have differed greatly from that of a former king's thegn, and the balance between such members must have greatly affected a community's sense of its religious identity and traditions.

Monasteries contained a diversity of ways of life and of memories. Life within the community was measured not only by the liturgy but also by the different stages of clerical ordination, the highest rank being that of the priest, a respected status which ecclesiastical sources are usually careful to indicate. Priest-monks were distinguished by their higher calling and each grade of the ecclesiastical hierarchy – acolyte, lector, deacon, and priest – carried out different roles within the community's liturgical life.[16] Priests were not the only members of a community to have superior status – the elders of the community

---

12. My discussion of the importance of child oblation within Anglo-Saxon monasteries is deeply indebted to the excellent study by M. de Jong, *In Samuel's Image: Child Oblation in the Early Medieval West* (Leiden, New York, Köln, 1996).

13. Bede, *Historia abbatum*, in *Venerabilis Baedae, Opera Historica*, ed. C. Plummer (1896) (hereafter *HA*), cc.18, 8, 383, 371.

14. Bede, *HE*, IV.3, 338–41.

15. Alcuin, *Epistolae, MGH, Epistolae Karolini Aevi* II, ed. E. Dümmler (Berlin, 1895), no. 19, 54: 'Saepiusque regula sancti Benedicti legatur in conventu fratrum et propria exponatur lingua, ut intellegi possit ab omnibus. Ad cuius institutionem unusquisque suam corrigat vitam . . .'.

16. See, for example, Bede's autobiography where progression through the clerical grades at the appropriate ages marks the passage of time (*HE*, V.24).

were accorded respect and authority, in the chapter for example, and were required to set an example of virtuous living.[17] They also must have played an important role in the transmission of a community's history, seen in Bede's account of how he consulted the elders at Lindisfarne when writing his *Vita Sancti Cuthberti*.[18]

The practical organization of the monastery – the provision of food and clothing or the responsibility for the school or the divine services – also allocated to individuals special roles and responsibilities.[19] The anonymous author of the *Vita Ceolfrithi* extols his hero's accomplishments as monastic baker while Eosterwine was praised by Bede for his diligence and humility in all the demands of monastic life – in agricultural activities like threshing or milking, in the bakehouse, garden and kitchen.[20] The work of the smith and other industrial activities also contributed to the monastic economy and must have involved individuals with special training. In Æthelwulf's description, the smith, Cwicwine, appears to have spent his day in metalworking when not participating in the divine services or personal spiritual exercises.[21] These specialized activities may have led to the formation of different groups within the monastery; the daily routine of food preparation and the seasonal timetable of farming all contributed to the monastic sense of time and those involved may very well have

---

17. For example Alcuin, *Epistolae*, no. 19, 54, to the brothers of Wearmouth-Jarrow: 'Vos vero, qui estis patres et pastores sanctae congregationis, docete diligentissime fraterno amore familiam, quam acceptistis regendam; omneque bonitatis exemplum in vobismetipsis ostendite. Seniores ut patres cum honore ammonete, iuniores ut filios cum omni dilectione castigate, omnes in spiritu mansuetudinis et verborum honestate instruite', or to Jarrow, no. 286, 445: 'seniores adulescentulos bonis erudiant exemplis'.
18. Bede, *Vita Sancti Cuthberti prosa*, ed. B. Colgrave, in *Two Lives of Saint Cuthbert: A Life by an Anonymous Monk of Lindisfarne and Bede's Prose Life* (1940), 143–5, preface where Bede's *vita* was read to the 'senioribus ac doctoribus' of the community for their vetting. According to the anonymous author (*Vita Sancti Cuthberti*, ed. B. Colgrave, in *Two Lives of Saint Cuthbert*, IV.14, 130) the translation of Cuthbert's body was agreed after a council of the 'decani'.
19. See for example Boniface's disposition of the house at Fritzlar, in his *Epistolae* (*Die Briefe des Heiligen Bonifatius und Lullus*, ed. M. Tangl, MGH, Epistolae Selectae (Berlin, 1916)), no. 40, which distributes positions and responsibilities among the brothers.
20. Anon., *Vita Ceolfrithi*, c. 4, 389 (*Baedae Opera Historica*, ed. Plummer); Bede, *HA*, c. 8, 371–2.
21. Æthelwulf, *De abbatibus*, ed. A. Campbell (1967), c. 10, 24–7. M. Lapidge ('Aediluulf and the school of York', in his collected essays, *Anglo-Latin Literature 600–899* (London and Rio Grande, 1996), 381–98 (reprinted from *Lateinische Kultur im VIII. Jahrhundert. Traube-Gedenkschrift*, ed. A. Lehner and W. Berschin (St Ottolien, 1990), 161–78), suggests that Æthelwulf's house may be identified with Crayke in Yorkshire, citing *inter alia* the archaeological remains of iron workings. See also for example the evidence of industrial activities at Jarrow, R. Cramp, 'Monkwearmouth and Jarrow: the archaeological evidence', in *Famulus Christi: Essays in the Commemoration of the Thirteenth Centenary of the Birth of the Venerable Bede*, ed. G. Bonner (1976), 14–15.

shared memories. The kitchen and the guesthouse are common settings for miracle stories.[22] The diversity of life within the community must have been richly reflected in its memories.

Although physically separated from the secular world by some sort of enclosure, monasteries were by no means divorced from it.[23] Coleman argues that monastic memory was aimed at substituting a spiritual and textual memory for that of the secular world; she points out that since memory is bound up with the groups within which events were experienced and with their sense of time, the memories of the former secular life of new entrants would have been weakened within the monastic sphere.[24] But the constant interchange between monastic and secular, and the close bonds deliberately forged between the two, must have lead to the retention of some contacts, affinities and memories. Coleman's idealized view of an isolated monastic community is supported by Æthelwulf's *De abbatibus* which, apart from its foundation narrative, is oblivious to political chronology and events. This contrasts with the histories of Wearmouth-Jarrow where royal intervention regularly punctuates their narratives, usually with generous endowments. Where Æthelwulf's community owed its origins to a political outcast – Eanmund forced into monastic life by King Osred of Northumbria – Wearmouth-Jarrow was, as Ian Wood has recently pointed out, a royal *Eigenkloster*, a fact which may explain the discrepancy between the two houses' memories. The inclusion of Ecgfrith's regnal dating on the Jarrow foundation stone is emblematic of its close political connections.[25]

Wearmouth-Jarrow's founder, Benedict Biscop, was much in demand at the royal court for counsel. The worlds of monastery and court overlapped: Aldfrith of Northumbria exchanged land with Wearmouth-Jarrow in return for two sumptuous silken cloaks and for a copy of a volume on cosmography which Benedict Biscop had purchased in Rome.[26] The *Historia abbatum* describes Aldfrith as 'very learned in the Scriptures' and elsewhere Bede tells of his devotion to the holy man Dryhthelm at Melrose.[27] While I remain unconvinced that all monasteries participated in the work of pastoral care, none were

---

22. For example Anon., *Vita Sancti Cuthberti*, II.2, 76–9; Bede, *Vita Sancti Cuthberti prosa*, c. 7, 174–9.
23. J. Blair, 'Anglo-Saxon minsters: a topographical review', *Pastoral Care before the Parish*, eds J. Blair and R. Sharpe (1992), 231–5.
24. Coleman, *Ancient and Medieval Memories*, 133–4.
25. I.N. Wood, *The Most Holy Abbot Ceolfrid*, Jarrow Lecture 1995, 3–4. E. Okasha, *Handlist of Anglo-Saxon Non-Runic Inscriptions* (1971), no. 61, 85–6.
26. Bede, *HA*, cc. 9, 15, 373, 380.
27. *Ibid.*, c. 15, 380; Bede, *HE*, V.12, 496–8; Aldfrith was also the godson of Aldhelm and the recipient of a long work, the *Epistola ad Acircium*, on *inter alia* biblical typology and Latin metrics (*Aldhelmi Opera*, ed. R. Ehwald, *MGH*, *Auctores Antiquissimi* XV (Berlin, 1919), 33–204). A useful summary of Aldfrith's career and intellectual interests can be found in *Adomnán of Iona, Life of St Columba*, trans. R. Sharpe (Harmondsworth, 1995), n. 349, pp. 350–1.

oblivious to the physical and spiritual needs of the surrounding laity, whether of their estate workers or of the destitute in need of sustenance or the local nobility anxious to win credit with God through their association with a holy community.[28] Monasteries had material interests which they needed to pursue within the secular realm and the laity spiritual needs for which they resorted to monasteries. Disputes over property ownership were the source of much less harmonious interactions between monastery and laity but the need to safeguard property and rights was a major impetus to the cultivation of monastic archival memory, as Patrick Geary has shown.[29] Interactions with the secular world were an important prompt to monastic memory.

How the secular world was remembered and interpreted within a monastic community is a difficult question. The texts we have both support and refute Coleman's arguments: Bede's slight autobiography in the *Historia ecclesiastica* recalls his kindred only as the agents through whom he entered the monastery; he 'even records his birth place in terms of a monastery which was not yet founded'.[30] In the histories of Wearmouth-Jarrow, while the noble origins of Benedict Biscop and Eosterwine are recorded and remembered, the texts are (deliberately) silent about the names of their secular kindred; they are concerned to note that one was a thegn of Oswiu and the other of Ecgfrith.[31] This status may have been important not only for its prestige but also because it was linked to Wearmouth-Jarrow's own

---

28. For the debate over the pastoral role of monasteries and full references to the literature, see my 'Pastoral care and conciliar canons: the provisions of the 747 Council of *Clofesho*', in *Pastoral Care*, eds Blair and Sharpe, 193–211, also E. Cambridge and D. Rollason, 'Debate: the pastoral organization of the Anglo-Saxon church: a review of the "Minster hypothesis"', and J. Blair, 'Debate: ecclesiastical organization and pastoral care in Anglo-Saxon England', *Early Medieval Europe*, 4(1) (1995), 87–104 and 4(2) (1995), 193–212. For a monastery's concern for its estate workers, A. Thacker, 'Monks, preaching and pastoral care in early Anglo-Saxon England', in *Pastoral Care*, eds Blair and Sharpe, 140–2; on the care for the poor, see Æthelwulf, *De abbatibus*, cc. 7, 15, 18–19, 38–9.
29. Geary, *Phantoms of Remembrance*, 81–144.
30. Bede, *HE*, V.24; quotation from M.T.A. Carroll, *The Venerable Bede: His Spiritual Teachings*, Catholic University of Washington Studies in Mediaeval History New Series 9 (Washington, 1946), 2. Bede records at a number of points the family networks of the religious – brother and sister partnerships like Eorcenwald and Æthelburh (*HE*, IV.6) or the brothers Cedd, Chad and Caelin (*HE*, III.23) – but rarely mentions the secular members of their kindred. At Wearmouth-Jarrow, Benedict Biscop's relationship with Eosterwine is recorded but his wicked brother, against whose possible claims to the abbacy Benedict warns the brothers in a deathbed speech, is not even named although many within the community must have been sufficiently conscious of him to require this warning (Bede, *HA*, 8, 11). The portrayal of family relations in hagiography relating to the continental missions is discussed by L. Padberg, *Heilige und Familie. Studien zur Bedeutung familiengebundener Aspekte in den Viten des Verwandten- und Schülerkreises um Willibrord, Bonifatius und Liudger* (Münster, 1980).
31. Bede, *HA*, c. 1, 8, 364, 371.

place as a royal house, owing its foundation to Ecgfrith's munificence and generously endowed through kingly bounty. Henry Mayr-Harting has pointed out that Bede is at pains to attack the presumption of privilege on the part of noble monastic inmates and to demolish the claims of Benedict's kindred over his house and abbacy.[32] The strength of his endeavour emphasizes the power retained by noble birth in the monastery: the anonymous biographer of Ceolfrith records how the abbot was driven out of Wearmouth through the attacks by nobles, probably angered by Ceolfrith's superior authority but inferior aristocratic status.[33] The memory of secular identity certainly remained strong.

What of events? It is true that early Anglo-Saxon texts tell us very little about the secular careers and actions of Anglo-Saxon monks. Coleman argues that where such memories survived, they would be interpreted according to the new spiritual values of the community.[34] The *Vita Ceolfrithi* records a story about Ceolfrith's father, who was left unexpectedly with a feast prepared for a royal visit upon his hands, and followed the biblical model of inviting the poor and destitute to it.[35] This episode and another from the *De abbatibus* suggest Coleman is correct. The poet Æthelwulf describes how one monk of his house experienced an out-of-the-body vision in which his children plead with his first wife to absolve the monk of the damning consequences of his failure to honour their pre-marital agreement never to remarry after her death. The wife finally relents and he is allowed to alleviate his punishment by renewed penance upon earth. While this certainly recounts memories before the monk's entry into the house, they are decontextualized and selected according to their relevance to the monk's spiritual welfare.[36] Maurice Halbwachs observed that within dreams images drawn from memory are fragmented and divorced from their context.[37] Æthelwulf's vision sequence is dreamlike in this way and the memories are only invoked in relation to the monk's need to pursue the spiritual life with renewed efforts and urgency.

Although our modern understanding of early medieval monasteries is necessarily dominated by texts, life inside them was not and nor were its memories. A monk's life could be both sensory and sensual – early medieval texts abound with lush descriptions of the splendour of church interiors, particularly during the night office – which shone with gold and silver ornaments, resounded with music and were filled with the smell of incense.[38] The unexpected departure of Abbot

32. H. Mayr-Harting, *The Venerable Bede: The Rule of St Benedict and Social Class*, Jarrow Lecture 1976, esp. 10–12.
33. Anon., *Vita Ceolfrithi*, c. 8, 390–1.
34. Coleman, *Ancient and Medieval Memories*, 134.
35. Anon., *Vita Ceolfrithi*, c. 34, 401.
36. Æthelwulf, *De abbatibus*, c. 11, 26–33.
37. M. Halbwachs, *Les cadres sociaux de la mémoire* (Paris, 1925), 28–9, 48–53.
38. This chapter limits itself to the use of literary texts for the study of monastic memory and has not tried to include or interpret the growing body of

Ceolfrith from Wearmouth-Jarrow left behind extremely vivid memories. It is recounted with close attention to chronology – according to the liturgy over a number of days – and located very precisely in the different churches and oratories of the two monasteries. The anonymous author describes how, after mass on the morning of his departure, Ceolfrith assembled the brothers in St Peter's and, standing on the gradual steps of the church, censing thurible in hand, kissed the brothers farewell. His progression, again with censer in hand, to the oratory of St Lawrence and thence to his boat on the river is described in detail, recalling particularly the liturgy sung at each point and his farewell address. The final frame, his departure in a boat, accompanied by two deacons holding a gold cross and candles, is recalled with almost photographic vividness.[39] Ceolfrith's leavetaking was remembered by Bede and his anonymous biographer for an audience at Wearmouth-Jarrow familiar with its setting in terms of sound, gesture, smell and objects, its emotional charge carried through the density of its recollection. The trauma caused by Ceolfrith's sudden removal was great – Bede remarks in his commentary on Samuel that its composition had been interrupted as a result of the news and ensuing disturbance – and its remembrance carries the hallmarks of the type of snapshot memory experienced by victims of shock.[40]

Even a community's educational endeavours cannot be understood purely in terms of the internalization of the Scriptures and patristic commentaries but must be set in the context of the moral and physical training of brothers for the monastic routine, all mediated through the personal example of the teacher. Monks were introduced to the study of texts which facilitated their internalization as masters through the monastic schools, where the minute study of certain prescribed texts was expounded word by word and line by line to them as pupils who had to learn them by heart.[41] Lessons on texts were preceded in the

contd.

archaeological evidence for early Anglo-Saxon monasticism. For literary descriptions of church interiors see for example *Alcuin: The Bishops, Kings and Saints of York*, ed. P. Godman (1982), 1490-1514; Aldhelm, *Carmen ecclesiastica* no. 3, in *Aldhelmi Opera*, ed. Ehwald, 17-18 (translation from *Aldhelm: The Poetic Works*, trans. M. Lapidge and J.L. Rosier (Woodbridge, 1985), 47-9); Æthelwulf, *De abbatibus*, c. 14, 15, 20, 21, 22, 34-41, 49-63.

39.   Bede, *HA*, cc. 16-23, 380-7; Anon., *Vita Ceolfrithi*, cc. 21-39, 395-403.

40.   Bede, *In primam partem Samuhelis Libri III*, ed. D. Hurst, *Bedae Venerabilis Opera II: Opera Exegetica* II.2, CCSL 119 (Turnholt, 1962), IV.212; he also gives an account of Ceolfrith's pilgrimage in his *Chronica Maiora*, ed. C.W. Jones, *Bedae Venerabilis Opera VI, Opera Didascalia 2*, CCSL 123B (Turnholt, 1977), 534. These references were collected by Plummer (ed.), *Venerabilis Baedae Opera Historica*, 366-7.

41.   On monastic education see P. Riché, *Education and Culture in the Barbarian West from the Sixth through the Eighth Century* translated by J.J. Contreni (University of South Carolina, 1976; French edition, 1962), and P. Riché, *Écoles et Enseignement dans l'Occident chrétien de la fin du siècle* (Paris, 1979); P. Riché, 'La vie quotidienne dans les écoles monastiques d'après les colloques

curriculum by those on grammar and although monastic education imparted both practical and technical knowledge (such as the ability to speak Latin, facility in verse or a mastery of computus) the whole was aimed at the moral and spiritual self, intended, as Coleman says, to refashion the individual according to textual and spiritual ideas. However, it would be wrong to represent the world of monastic education as purely textual. An oblate would begin his education by taking part in the daily services of the monastery, memorizing the psalter, the backbone of the daily office. His initiation, therefore, into Latin learning was through music and ritual and his training would affect not only his intellectual habits but also his physical, forming his stance and walk, for example. Children offered to a monastery as oblates were subject to a strict regime of personal discipline and supervision aimed at the Christian formation of their mental and physical conduct.[42]

Moreover, monastic education in the early Middle Ages was as much personal as textual. The role of the master in teaching was paramount and the close study of texts could be a powerful personal encounter. It is recounted how both Bede and Boisil of Melrose passed their last days in study with their pupils; their devotion of their final days on earth to an educational exercise indicates the importance which was attached to the transmission of learning and to the spiritual benefits it could bring to both master and pupil.[43] Scholars and teachers like Archbishop Theodore of Canterbury were famous, and attracted pupils through their personal reputations.[44] Their knowledge

---

contd.

scolaires', in *Sous la Règle du Saint Benoît: Structures monastiques et sociétés en France au moyen à l'époque moderne* (Geneva and Paris, 1981), 417–26. For Anglo-Saxon education see D. Bullough, 'The educational tradition in England from Alfred to Ælfric: teaching *utriusque linguae*', reprinted in his collected essays, *Carolingian Renewal: Sources and Heritage*, ed. D.A. Bullough (1991), 297–34 reprinted from *Settimane di Studio del Centro italiano di studi sull'alto mediovo* (hereafter *Settimane*), 19 (1972), 453–94; M. Lapidge, 'Anglo-Latin literature' in his *Anglo-Latin Literature*, 1–35, reprinted from S.B. Greenfield and D.G. Calder, *A New Critical History of Old English Literature* (New York and London, 1986), 5–37. My account of monastic education in this paragraph is largely derived from Lapidge, 'Anglo-Latin literature', 1–5.

42. M. de Jong, *In Samuel's Image*, 153–5, '[the oblates'] long education under *custodia* aimed at a gradual interiorisation of the claustral "techniques du corps"'; M. de Jong, 'Growing up in a Carolingian monastery: Magister Hildemar and his oblates', *Journal of Medieval History* 9 (1983), 99–128. See here also the discussion of T. Asad, 'Notes on body pain and truth in medieval Christian ritual', and 'On ritual and discipline in medieval Christian monasticism', in *Economy and Society* 12 (1983), 287–327 and 16 (1987), 159–203.

43. Cuthbert, *Epistola de obitu Bedae*, printed in Bede, *HE*, 581–7; Bede, *Vita Sancti Cuthberti prosa*, c. 8. 182–3. On Bede as teacher, see G.H. Brown, *Bede the Educator*, Jarrow Lecture 1996.

44. On the attraction of Theodore and Hadrian as teachers see Bede, *HE*, IV.2 and Aldhelm's letter to Heahfrith, *Aldhelmi Opera*, ed. Ehwald, no. 5, 486–94 (translated by M. Lapidge and M. Herren, *Aldhelm: The Prose Works* (1979), 160–3, with commentary, 143–6).

communicated was not simply the fruits of bookish study and erudition but could be personal – John of Beverley recalled in a crisis the medical teaching of Theodore on the dangers of bleeding in the wrong season. The Archbishop himself plainly taught from his own experience since, when expounding the meaning of 'cucumeres et pepones' (cucumbers and melons) in a passage from the Pentateuch, he commented that the melons in Edessa grew so large that a camel was barely able to carry two of them.[45] Bede recorded an anecdote about St Chad which had been told to him by his teacher at Jarrow, Trumberht, who had been a monk at Lastingham. This described how the saint would beseech God's mercy during storms. The saint explained his eccentric behaviour by reference to the psalm 17, 'The Lord also thundered in the heavens'. Was this story passed on during the study of the same verse?[46]

Just as personal experience was intimately bound up with the exposition of texts, so too was the actual conduct of the teacher with the lessons to be learnt. The master provided not simply the knowledge which could unlock the spiritual understanding of texts but also a model of holy living which his students were to imbibe. The vital link between living and teaching well is a persistent theme in writings of Bede and Alcuin.[47] Alcuin, for example, wrote to a former pupil of his own with advice on how to teach – 'Be careful, therefore, that [the young men] should see in you good examples together with holy words of admonition.' In the same letter, Alcuin's advice makes clear that teaching was more than a matter of book-learning; he urges his former pupil to admonish the 'adulescentulos' 'concerning bodily chastity, the confession of their sins, diligence in learning, fitting behaviour, the avoidance of drunkenness, the shunning of excess and the rejection of the vanities of this world'.[48] Indeed, Alcuin's correspondence with his students gives greater emphasis to the moral education of pupils than to the imparting of Latin grammar or

---

45. Bede, *HE*, V.3; B. Bischoff and M. Lapidge, *Biblical Commentaries from the Canterbury School of Theodore and Hadrian* (1994), 375, n. 413. And see D. Whitelock, 'Bede and his teachers and friends', in *Famulus Christi*, ed. Bonner, 27–8 which collects Bede's references to information derived from personal contacts in his commentaries.

46. Bede, *HE*, IV.3, 342–5; Plummer (*Baedae Venerabilis Opera Historica*, II, 209) noted that a passage in Bede's commentary on Ezra suggested that his own beliefs on the weather were similar (Bede, *In Ezram et Neemiam Libri III, Bedae Venerabilis Opera II, Opera Exegetica IIa*, ed. D. Hurst, CCSL 119a (Turnholt, 1969), 332–3).

47. A. Thacker, 'Bede's ideal of reform', in *Ideal and Reality in Frankish and Anglo-Saxon Society. Studies presented to J.M. Wallace-Hadrill*, eds P. Wormald with D. Bullough and R. Collins (1983), 130–53, esp. 131 (with references cited there – see for example *De Templo, Bedae Venerabilis Opera, Opera exegetica IIa*, ed. D. Hurst, CCSL 119A (Turnholt, 1969), 194.)

48. Alcuin, *Epistolae*, no. 19, 54 and see the passage from the same letter quoted in n.59.

Scriptural exegesis, reiterating the need for rejection of secular vanities, steadfastness in spiritual discipline and attendance at the daily office. In actuality, mental attitudes, bodily abstinence, attentive reading and participation in the liturgy were the combined means through which monks and clerks sought spiritual perfection.[49]

Intense and enduring personal links were created by the all-encompassing responsibility of the master which often began in the pupil's earliest childhood, from the age of seven or earlier.[50] In a letter of advice and exhortation, Alcuin reminded one former and now renegade student of the family intimacy of their relationship; Alcuin had 'given birth to him, nourished and nurtured him, bringing him to manhood ...'.[51] His own numerous letters to former pupils, especially to those who had gone morally astray, expressing concern for their spiritual and physical well-being, testify to the powerful emotions created by the teacher–pupil relationship.[52] This relationship also carried with it the duty of the student to pass on the wisdom learnt from his master when he himself became a teacher – 'whatsoever you have received from your teacher or you may understand through the inspiration of the Holy Spirit, hand on and teach with the greatest care'.[53]

---

49. See, for example, Alcuin, *Epistolae*, no. 88, 132: 'Tu vero, fili carissime, in caritate te ipsum exerce, et in ecclesiasticis officis ornare vitam tuam memento; vigilias et orationes frequentans, et in lectionis studio die noctuque desudans quaere Christum in litteris prophetarum praedictum, et in evangelica ostensum auctoritate.' See also J. Leclercq, 'Pédagogie et formation spirituelle du VIe au IXe siècle', *Settimane*, 19, I, (1972) 285–6.
50. Alcuin compared the role of the community of York Minster to both father and mother, 'Vos fragiles infantiae meae annos materno fovistis affectu; et lascivum puericiae tempus pia sustinuistis patientia et paternae castigationis disciplinis ad perfectam viri edocuistis aetatem et sacrarum eruditione disciplinarium roborastis.' (*Epistolae*, no. 42, 85).
51. *Ibid.*, no. 294, 451, 'Olim te genui, nutrivi, alui, et ad perfectum virum usque Deo donante perduxi, artibus studiose eruditum, sapientiae sole inluminatum, moribus adprime ornatum ...'. And see no. 295, 452, 'Quare dimisisti patrem, qui te ab infantia erudivit, qui te disciplinis liberalibus inbuit, moribus instruxit, perpetuae vitae praeceptis munivit?'
52. Alcuin's letters give many examples of this; see for example no. 25 to his pupil Riculf, an intimate letter, refering to their father–son relationship and offering anxious prayers for Riculf, and also commenting on the dispersal of Alcuin's pupils between many lands: 'Ego pene quasi orbatus filiis remaneo domi' (*ibid.*, 66). Aldhelm's letters also illustrate this theme; see his letter to his own teacher, Hadrian, no. 2 (*Aldhelmi Opera*, ed. Ehwald, 478), and those to and from his pupils Wihtfrith and Aethilwald which betray a moral concern for them (nos 3, 7, 11, pp. 479–80, 495–7, 499–500). Aethilwald (no. 7, p. 496) refers to Aldhelm as rearing him 'from the very cradles of tenderest infancy, by nourishing, loving and gradually restoring me ...'. (Translated in *Aldhelm: The Prose Works*, eds Lapidge and Herren, 153–5, 164–6, 168 with commentary 138–40, 147–8). See also de Jong's account of the bitter conflict between the former child oblate Gottschalk and his teacher, Hrabanus Maurus, *In Samuel's Image*, 77–91, esp. 89–90.
53. Alcuin, *Epistolae*, no. 88, 132.

The vertical bond between master and pupil was not the only lasting relationship formed by the educational process; close affiliations were forged between pupils in the camaraderie and competition of the schoolroom, glimpsed in Aldhelm's description of Theodore's intellectual defence of himself against his Irish pupils like a wild boar surrounded by hounds.[54] The strength of the bonds established between both masters and pupils and among pupils can be seen in the poems of Alcuin and Æthelwulf which commemorate their communities. Alcuin's long and loving account of his former teacher, Archbishop Ælberht is followed by the vision and death of a young member of the York community whose life, Alcuin tells us, deeply influenced his own.[55] In a vivid dream narrated at the end of Æthelwulf's poem, the *De abbatibus*, the poet's teachers and early mentor – the 'doctores' Hyglac and Eadfrith, and 'magister' Wulfsig – reappear to him, visualized in a resplendent church.[56] Alcuin and Æthelwulf remembered their early training and education through their teachers and it was these personal memories which they chose to perpetuate in their texts.

The role of the master as not only an expert in erudition but also as a model of the holy life was one strand in a tradition that cast all the senior members of a religious house as examples for younger monks. Alcuin wrote to the brothers at Wearmouth-Jarrow, 'You truly, who are the fathers and shepherds of the holy company, teach with brotherly love and with the greatest zeal the community which you have received for ruling; and show in yourselves the complete model of goodness'.[57] This custom extended beyond current members of the community to past figures whose memory could be invoked to teach lessons for the present. Æthelwulf related the history of his monastery through a series of vignettes of its former abbots, teachers and holy men, each praised for his spiritual virtues, particularly for nightly prayer vigils and generosity, and especially in almsgiving to the poor.[58] The house's history was recalled in order to provide models of the holy life to inform the present. Alcuin's letters to the community of Wearmouth-

---

54. *Aldhelmi Opera*, ed. Ehwald, 493.
55. *Alcuin, The Bishops … of York*, 1394–1658; Alcuin's letters indicate group awareness on the part of pupils; for example, in *Epistolae*, no. 25 he informs his pupil Riculf of the dispersal of his other pupils (using their nicknames, another sign of camaraderie) and in no. 295 Alcuin holds up to a morally misled student the example of his co-pupil (probably Archbishop Eanbald II of York), who had become a bishop.
56. Æthelwulf, *De abbatibus*, c. 22, 54–63.
57. Alcuin, *Epistolae*, no. 19, 54.
58. Æthelwulf, *De abbatibus*: c. 7 – on the exemplary behaviour of the early brothers in prayer, in almsgiving and in fasting; c.8 describing Ultan as a model of teaching; c. 10 – Cwicwine praised for his almsgiving and exemplary devotion; c. 13 – Eorpwine admired for his generosity and fasting; c. 15 – portrays the generosity of Sigwine; c. 18 – Wulfsig who was notable for his vigils, psalm-singing and fasting; c. 19 – an account of Wynfrith's exemplary death.

Jarrow frequently urged the brothers to remember and imitate their forefathers, particularly Benedict Biscop and Ceolfrith, and to maintain the monastic life which they instituted.[59] The two histories of Wearmouth-Jarrow also demonstrate this point. The anonymous author portrays Ceolfrith as an ideal abbot, zealous for righteousness, stern in reproving sinners but gentle to the penitent, and praises Ceolfrith for his outstanding devotion to psalmody and the daily celebration of the Eucharist – a picture reiterated by Bede in his *Historia abbatum*.[60] Bede uses Abbot Eosterwine as a model of humility, emphasizing his indifference to his noble rank and rejection of the possible advantages which his blood relationship to Benedict Biscop could bring.[61] The venerated figures from a monastery's past both embodied the house's history and demonstrated to the present an exemplary way of life. Alcuin, for example, wrote to the community at Jarrow:

> Dearest brothers, remember your most noble leaders, the fathers and kindred who gave birth to you in Christ, and the most noble teachers whom you have possessed in the assembly of your brotherhood. Clinging to their teachings, living by their examples and following their rulings, you will most certainly be united in their blessedness in the future life. The place which has been worthy to have such teachers is blessed by God: and blessed are those who are occupied in preserving there their teaching.[62]

Their example was to be imitated and in this respect they were no different from the saints of the Church whose role within a monastic community was also to inspire imitation. Bede makes this point explicitly in his commentary, the *De Templo*, where he urges his readers to learn from the model of both dead and living saints:

> when through contemplating the life, sufferings and teachings of the saints, or reading of them in books, we are moved by their example ... we can also apply this to the saints who are still in

---

59. For example Alcuin, *Epistolae*, no. 67, which admonishes the brothers daily to be mindful of 'nobilissimi patris Benedicti, primi fundatoris vestri, et successoris eius Ceolfridi'. In no.19 these two are joined by Bede, who is described as not only a model teacher but also a model student. No. 282, 440: 'Exemplis sanctorum patrum Benedicti et Ceolfridi vivas, quatenus illorum merita sequens illorum mercede dignus efficiaris.' And see no. 284, and no. 288, 445: 'Recordamini, carissimi fratres, nobilissimos vestri patres et parentes, qui vos genuerunt in Christo, et nobilissimos magistros, quos habuistis in vestrae germanitatis congregatione. Horum doctrinis inhaerentes et horum exemplis viventes et horum statuta sequentes ...'.
60. Anon., *Vita Ceolfrithi*, cc. 19, 33, 394, 400; Bede, *HA*, c.16, 381.
61. Bede, *HA*, c. 8, 371-2.
62. Alcuin, *Epistolae*, no. 286, 445; Alcuin wrote in urging the young brothers at Wearmouth-Jarrow to apply themselves to their studies, 'Recogitate nobilissimum nostri temporis magistrum Baedam praesbiterum: quale in iuventute discendi studium, qualem nunc habet inter homines laudem, multo maiorem apud Deum remunerationis gloriam' (*Epistolae*, no. 19, 55).

this life. The purity of their love which makes them shine in the recesses of the heart before the Lord we cannot penetrate; nevertheless we find help for our salvation from those things which are externally visible whether in word or action or suffering.[63]

The two classes of widely venerated saints and local heroes could overlap – Cuthbert, for example, had been a prominent member of the Lindisfarne community and was refashioned by Bede as a model of monastic perfection whose miracles carried didactic lessons for disobedient and negligent monks. The gap between major and universally revered saints like Cuthbert and local figures, venerated by their own communities such as the scribe Ultan (at Æthelwulf's monastery) was slight in the age before official canonizations and in a monastic environment which concentrated upon imitatible virtues rather than wonder-working miracles.[64] Memories of such figures fused living recollection with textual models – the two prose lives of Cuthbert were shaped by hagiographical stereotypes which enabled the anonymous author and Bede to create a saint who conformed to contemporary norms of sanctity.

The revered figures of a community were therefore frequently remembered in an idealized and unindividualized form, described in the stock patterns of exemplary spiritual and ascetic practices, yet one moment in the lives is often recalled with some precision. The death of an individual, together with the illness leading up to it, formed a key moment in his or her memory. The hour of death occupied a very important place in Christian thinking since it could indicate the fate of a person's soul, heralded by angelic visitations or by demons gloating over their prizes, and was a crucial opportunity to prepare for the afterlife.[65] The dreadful demises in Bede's *Historia ecclesiastica* of the unrepentant craftsman monk or Cenred of Mercia's thegn who refused

---

63. *De Templo*, 164–5 (translation from S. Connolly, *Bede: On the Temple* (1995), 28). See too, Bede's teaching earlier in the *De Templo*, 154, 'Therefore, the stones which were laid as the foundation of the temple to bear the whole structure, are properly speaking the prophets and apostles who either visibly or invisibly received the word and the mysteries of truth from the very wisdom of God. Hence of us, too, who, in our modest way, strive to imitate the life or teaching of these men, the Apostle says we supported "on the foundation of the apostles and prophets"' (translated by Connolly, *Bede: On the Temple*, 14). This point is discussed further in my 'Universal and local saints in Anglo-Saxon England', in *Local Saints and Local Churches*, eds R. Sharpe and A. Thacker (forthcoming).

64. M. McLaughlin, *Consorting with Saints. Prayer for the Dead in Early Medieval France* (Ithaca and London, 1994), 64–7. And see again my 'Universal and local saints'.

65. On the Christian way of death and exemplary deaths in the early Middle Ages see P.-A. Février, 'La mort chrétienne', *Settimane*, 33 (1987), II, 881–952; M. Lauwers, 'La mort et le corps des saints. La scène de la mort dans les *Vitae* du haut Moyen Âge', *Le Moyen Âge*, 94 (1988), 21–50, H. Platelle, 'La mort précieuse. La mort des moines d'après quelques sources des Pays-Bas du Sud',

to confess his sins – both of whom perished miserably, aware of their inevitable damnations but unable to avail themselves of confession and forgiveness – were clearly intended to act as warnings.[66] These are the counterparts of the good deaths where the holy subjects are able to prepare for their ends through divinely revealed foreknowledge and often given long illnesses which purify them of their sins. The Whitby traditions concerning Hild and Caedmon recorded their deathbeds in some detail; Hild suffered a long illness before her death and was ready for her last day, fortified by the eucharist and able to give a deathbed oration to her nuns. Caedmon too was able to prepare himself by taking communion in an episode which indicated his foreknowledge of his death; he too made peace with his brothers and finished his life in tranquillity.[67] Æthelthryth of Ely's final illness, death and incorruption are included in the *Historia ecclesiastica* through her doctor's report.[68]

The topos of the deathbed scene acted as a frame for memories and was seen as an event to be recorded. Cuthbert's account of Bede's last days is moving in its personal detail, telling how both Bede and his brothers broke down in tears when singing the antiphon 'O King of glory, Lord of might'.[69] Wearmouth-Jarrow tradition carefully preserved memories of the deaths of its abbots and their preceding illnesses, not only those of Benedict Biscop and Abbot Sigfrith, but also of Eosterwine.[70] These accounts indicated something of the disruption to monastic routine which must have played its part in making the events memorable. These deaths were social, played out publicly among the community and important moments remembered for later instruction. Eosterwine, for example, aware of his imminent demise, continued to sleep in the monk's dormitory before finally removing to a more private place. When the end was close, he summoned all the brethren and gave them the kiss of peace. His death is recorded as taking place at night, while the office of matins was being sung, at a time therefore when the whole monastery was assembled together.[71] It is significant too that Alcuin's accounts of the demises of the bishops of York in his poem on York, *Versus de Patribus, Regibus et Sanctis Euboricensis Ecclesiae* are brief and generalized until

---

contd.
    Revue Mabillon, 60 (1982), 151–74, G. Scheibelreiter, 'The death of the bishop in the early Middle Ages', in *The End of Strife,* ed. D. Loades (1984), 32–43.
66. Bede, *HE,* V.13–14, 499–505.
67. Bede, *HE,* IV.23–4, 410–15, 418–21.
68. Bede, *HE,* IV.19, 394–7. Note too Wynfrith's exemplary death in Æthelwulf's *De abbatibus,* c.18.
69. Cuthbert, *Epistola de Obitu Bedae,* 582–3; on this see B. Ward, *Bede and the Psalter,* Jarrow Lecture 1991, 2–3.
70. Bede, *HA,* cc.11–13, 374–7. The timing and bare details of these deaths are recorded by the anonymous biographer but without elaboration (*Vita Ceolfrithi,* cc. 15, 17, 393–4).
71. Bede, *HA,* c. 8, 372–3. The social nature of early medieval death is noted by Lauwers, 'La mort et le corps des saints', 25 and by McLaughlin, *Consorting with Saints,* 46.

he reaches that of his old teacher, Ælberht, when he dwells upon his grief and the great funeral of the prelate.[72] The deaths of members of a community were significant moments when the fate of the individual could be assisted by the prayers of other members and were a lesson to all of mortality and transience.[73] Remembered as exemplary moments, these accounts still contain resonances of the emotional impact of the event and the disruption it caused in the normally unchanging routine of monastic life.

The power of the moment of death can be seen in the precision with which it was remembered. Many accounts report the exact time of death, often in terms of the liturgy which might recall Scripture particularly appropriate for the occasion or which provided spiritual solace. The psalm sung when Biscop breathed his last signified the entry of his soul into heaven. The place of death and the location of the dead person's remains were also important matters and this again can be readily seen in Bede's *Historia abbatum* which notes the place of burial and any subsequent reburials of its abbots and revered members.[74] These details are commonly recorded too in Bede's death notices of individuals in the *Historia ecclesiastica* not only because the tomb was the central miracle-working locus of a saint's cult but also because it provided a major focus for memory of an individual. Alcuin, in exhorting the brothers of Wearmouth-Jarrow to live in accordance with the spiritual standards of their forefathers reminded them that they prayed among their tombs.[75] The brothers of Bishop Cedd's monastery in the land of the East Saxons migrated to Lastingham where he died and was buried in order to 'live near the body of their father, or if the Lord so willed, to die and be buried there'.[76]

The significance attached to the last days of important members of a religious community and to the care of their remains and the weight carried by those memories stands behind the two accounts of the life of Abbot Ceolfrith. Both the anonymous biographer of Ceolfrith and Bede preserved and transmitted for the brothers at home a particularly detailed and vivid account of the abbot's death at Langres which could recreate it for those not present. The absence of Ceolfrith's body must have been a special anxiety for the brothers. Ceolfrith's successor,

---

72. Alcuin, *The Bishops ... of York*, 1569–96.
73. On the rituals of early medieval death see F.S. Paxton, *Christianizing Death: The Creation of a Ritual Process in Early Medieval Europe* (1990); McLaughlin, *Consorting with the Dead*; and D. Sicard, *La Liturgie de la mort dans l'église latine des origines à la reforme carolingienne*. Liturgiewissenschaftliche Quellen und Forschungen 63 (Münster, 1978).
74. Bede, *HA*, c. 14, 20, 378–9, 384–5; Anon., *Vita Ceolfrithi*, 18, 394.
75. Alcuin, *Epistolae*, no. 284, 443: 'Patribus oboedite vestris ... ut habeatis, qui super sepulchra vestra stare possint et intercedere pro animabus vestris. Considerate mentibus vestris, quales sint, qui modo in sepulchris iacent.' See also his letter to the York brethren in which Alcuin makes a similar comment about praying amid the community's tombs, *ibid.*, no. 43.
76. Bede, *HE*, III.23, 288–9.

Hwaetberht, on the assumption that the abbot would die in Rome, when writing to Pope Gregory II asked him to carry out the funeral arrangements for Ceolfrith's body and translate the remains of his predecessors Eosterwine and Sigfrith to a place nearer to those of Benedict Biscop.[77] Some of Ceolfrith's companions on his last journey 'in their undying love for him, remained to keep watch by his tomb in the midst of a people whose language they could not understand'. It is not surprising then that Ceolfrith's body was eventually brought back to his monasteries.[78] The production of not just one but two literary narratives of Ceolfrith's life and death must have been a response to a very deep sense of loss and disorder within the community, left bereft of the customary ways of remembering an essential figure in their monastic history and unable to fulfil the traditional duties in the care for the dead. The *Vita Ceolfrithi* and *Historia abbatum* formed Ceolfrith's literary remains, textual substitutes for his body.[79]

If death stands out as one of the central mnemonic moments in monastic life, physical objects must be seen as some of the chief vehicles for the transmission of monastic memory. The most powerful bearers of monastic memory were, of course, relics and reliquaries, and donations of land were another way in which both members of the community and others could seek to have their names commemorated in prayer. But gifts of church furnishings – altar vessels, crosses, pictures and books, for example – could also be used to ensure remembrance. Donors must have been at least partly prompted to make such gifts in the knowledge that their names would be forever associated with them, and some objects, like the Brussels cross, bear commemorative inscriptions to reinforce the message.[80] The accounts of Benedict Biscop by both the anonymous author and by Bede are much taken up with the enumeration of his many gifts to his

---

77. Bede, *HA*, cc. 19–20, 383–5; Anonymous, *Vita Ceolfrithi*, 30, 399–400.
78. Bede, *HA*, 21, 386 (translation from *The Age of Bede*, trans. J.F. Webb and ed. D.H. Farmer (revised edition, 1988), 207). Alcuin, *Bishops ... of York*, 1299–1300. It is interesting that Alcuin also exhibited a sense that he should be buried at York, among the community he had grown up in: 'O omnium dilectissimi patres et fratres, memores mei estote. Ego vester ero, sive in vita, sive in morte. Et forte miserebitur mei Deus, ut, cuius infantiam aluistis, eius senectute sepelietis. Et si alter corpori locus deputabitur, tamen animae – qualemcumque habitura erit – per vestras sanctas, Deo donante, intercessiones, requies vobiscum, credo, donabitur' (*Epistolae*, no. 42, 86).
79. For other (not necessarily conflicting) explorations of the reasons for the duplication of Ceolfrith's *vita* see W. Goffart, *Narrators of Barbarian History* AD *550–800. Jordanes, Gregory of Tours, Bede and Paul the Deacon* (Princeton, 1988), 275–80, 294–5; and Wood, *The Most Holy Abbot Ceolfrid*.
80. E. Okasha, *Handlist of Anglo-Saxon Non-Runic Inscriptions* (1971), no. 17 – a wooden cross from the tenth or eleventh century with an inscription which reads 'Æþlmær, and Aðel his brother, ordered this cross to be made to the glory of Christ, (and) for the soul of Ælfric their brother'. On the commemorative and other functions of free-standing crosses see I.N. Wood, 'Anglo-Saxon Otley: an archiepiscopal estate and its crosses in a Northumbrian context', *Northern*

foundations of books, church plate, altar vessels, pictures and relics. Ceolfrith too was a notable benefactor and indefatigable book collector, doubling the size of the library by his gifts.[81] At Æthelwulf's house, Abbot Sigfrith seems to have been largely remembered for his construction and adornment of a new church dedicated to St Mary which included a bejewelled golden chalice. Other members of the community are likewise remembered for their gifts of lavish church furnishings and Æthelwulf's poem conjures up the atmosphere of the darkened church, resounding with sacred singing, and gleaming with lamps and golden adornments associated with former abbots and donors.[82]

Æthelwulf's memories of his monastery's holy men and their gifts were inseparable from the setting of the church, as his closing vision of his masters Hyglac, Eadfrith and Wulfsig in a resplendent but imaginary church shows.[83] He recognizes, for example, his teacher Eadfrith at prayer at St Cuthbert's tomb. His recollection of his church is in turn dominated by the liturgy, the dominant ritual of monastic life and its chief method of commemoration. The power of prayer carried out through liturgical services was the single most important reason for the desire for earthly remembrance, and behind this stood the fear of death and divine punishment. Individuals desired to be remembered in prayer to ensure their ultimate salvation, and this anxiety dominates our sources. It found its fulfilment in the necrologies which contained the names of the dead to be prayed for and in their resulting liturgical commemoration in the mass when the names of the dead were read out at the most solemn moment in the canon.[84] The liturgy, therefore, with its combination of physical ritual, words and music, was an intensely powerful vehicle of memory. It carried too the commemoration of the saints, whose feasts were celebrated by special readings and prayers.

A monastery's identity was constructed out of many things: the nature of its foundation, whether royal or noble, its traditions of venerable fathers and founding figures, its buildings and their furnishings and its liturgy, including the saints culted. These combined

---

contd.

    History, 23 (1987) 26–30. See Remensnyder, 'Legendary treasure' for the shifting meanings and memories attached to objects.

81. Bede, *HA* c. 15, 379–80; Anon., *Vita Ceolfrithi* 20, 394–5.

82. Æthelwulf, *De abbatibus*, c. 20, 48–52.

83. *Ibid.*, 22, 54–63. On this vision see H.M. Taylor, 'The architectural interest of Æthelwulf's *De abbatibus*', *Anglo-Saxon England*, 3 (1974), 163–73.

84. McLaughlin, *Consorting with Saints*. The literature on necrologies and liturgical memoria is now vast; for insular *liber vitae* and necrologies, see J. Gerchow, *Die Gedenküberlieferung der Angelsachsen mit einem Katalog der 'libri vitae' und Necrologien* (Berlin, 1988) and S. Keynes (ed.), *The Liber Vitae of the New Minster and Hyde Abbey Winchester. British Library Stowe 944, together with leaves from British Library Cotton Vespasian A. VIII and British Library Cotton Titus D. XXVII*, Early English Manuscripts in Facsimile 26 (Copenhagen, 1996), 49–65.

to create distinctive identities for individual houses. Wearmouth-Jarrow's hallmark Roman – and other continental – identity could be seen in its stone and glass buildings, its hoard of exotic Mediterranean objects accumulated by Benedict Biscop and Ceolfrith, and its Roman liturgy learnt directly from the horse's mouth from John the Archchanter. Its well-furnished library and Italianate scriptorium also formed the house's reputation, as the letters of Boniface – anxious in their request for the works of Bede – and of Alcuin suggest.[85] The latter reminded the brethren of Wearmouth-Jarrow of their rich inheritance and their own obligation to live up to it: 'Remember that just as you have noble fathers so you should not be degenerate sons of such parents. Consider the treasure of books, ponder the adornment of the churches, the beauty of the buildings, the order of the regular life.'[86]

But the community's identity was dominated by its personal tradition of great men – the example given to its members by its abbots, chiefly Benedict Biscop and Ceolfrith. What of the houses' rule, the product of seventeen monasteries? Surely this was a key item in Wearmouth-Jarrow's identity. Curiously it is rarely mentioned outside the *Vita Ceolfrithi* and the *Historia abbatum*. The *Historia abbatum* cites the *Regula Benedicti* as laying down the practice for abbatial elections but does not mention a 'regula' drawn up specifically for Wearmouth-Jarrow.[87] Alcuin, as I cited above, exhorted the brothers to read the *Regula Benedicti* out at meal times for their moral instruction. Otherwise there is much discussion not of a written rule but of the 'regularis disciplina' and 'vita regularis' which in Alcuin's letters was established by the personal example of Benedict and Ceolfrith: 'Guard most zealously the observance of the regular life which the most holy fathers Benedict and Ceolfrith established for you'.[88] Alcuin seems to identify this with correct behaviour, devotion to prayer and pious behaviour, and the shunning of luxurious clothing and of indulgence in food and drink. The personal example and teaching of Benedict and

---

85. Boniface, *Epistolae*, nos. 75, 76, 116 and 125, 156–9, 250–2, 262–3; M.B. Parkes, *The Scriptorium of Wearmouth-Jarrow*, Jarrow Lecture 1982, esp. 15–17.
86. Ep. 19, 55. See too no. 286 which also reminds the brothers of the riches of their library.
87. Bede, *HA*, cc. 11, 16, 374–6, 380–1. P. Wormald, 'Bede and Benedict Biscop', *Famulus Christi*, ed. Bonner, 142–45, puts the question of a mixed versus Benedictine rule in perspective, commenting '... very little of what we can find out about Monkwearmouth-Jarrow is actually incompatible with the Benedictine Rule'. And see A.G.P. van der Walt, 'Reflections of the Benedictine Rule in Bede's Homiliary', *Journal of Ecclesiastical History* 37 (1986), 367–76 for its impact upon Bede's teaching.
88. For example Alcuin, *Epistolae*, no. 19, 54: 'Regularis vitae observationem quam statuerunt vobis sanctissimi patres Benedictus scilicet et Ceolfridus, diligentissime custodite ...'. No. 284, 443: '... in omnibus vitae disciplinis firmiter permaneatis, sicut patres vestri ... instituerunt'. And see too nos 282 and 286 where the regular discipline is mentioned but not associated with Benedict and Ceolfrith.

Ceolfrith handed down within the community's collective memory probably formed their 'rule', not a written text. The anonymous account of Benedict's establishment of his 'rule' suggests precisely this: '[Benedict] was accustomed to say that he learnt in seventeen ancient monasteries the rule which he taught, and whatever things he had seen most valuable anywhere, these he had brought to Britain as if hidden in the coffer of his breast and delivered them for us to follow'.[89] The Rule of Benedict clearly provided instructions for the liturgy and daily life as well as spiritual teaching for the community. But the necessary supplementation of this for the detailed requirements of everyday monastic life were contained in monastic customaries, probably then transmitted orally since our earliest written evidence for these dates from this period.[90] The supposed rule of Wearmouth-Jarrow was more likely to have been a customary – as Zelzer argued – which I suggest was transmitted through oral tradition concerning the example and teachings of Benedict and Ceolfrith.[91]

One final question remains. In this chapter I have drawn heavily upon written material from Wearmouth-Jarrow, a monastery whose atypical nature is signalled by precisely the wealth of texts surviving from it. Can this composite account of monastic memory be applied to less wealthy and rigorist establishments? Would it be true of double

---

89. Anon., *Vita Ceolfrithi*, c. 6, 390 (translation quoted from *English Historical Documents c. 500-1042*, ed. D. Whitelock (2nd edn, 1979), 760. Bede's version of this refers to the 'decreta' which he established for them which could mean written institutions, but does not necessarily (*HA*, c. 11, 374-5). (See K. Hallinger, 'Consuetudo. Begriff, Formen, Forschungsgeschichte, Inhalt', in *Untersuchungen zu Kloster und Stift*, Veröffentlichungen des Max Planck-Institut für Geschichte, 68, Studien zur Germania Sacra (Göttingen, 1980), 147, who remarks that the words *decreta* and *statuta* can mean a *consuetudo*.) Adalbert de Vogüé notes that the word *regula* can frequently mean not a written rule but rather 'l'autorité vivante d'un abbé'. 'Quand on lit ainsi, dans la vie d'un saint moine, qu'il se plaça "sous la règle" de tel ou tel "Père", il faut se garder d'imaginer une *regula* perdue dont cet abbé serait l'auteur', *Les Règles monastiques anciennes (400-700), Typologie des Sources du Moyen Age Occidental*, 46 (Turnhout, 1985), 12; and see his '*Sub regula uel abbate*. Étude sur la signification théologique des règles monastiques anciennes', *Collectanea Cisterciensia* 33 (1971), 209-41.

90. The earliest customaries are printed in *Initia Consuetudinis Benedictinae. Consuetudines Saeculi Octavi et Noni*, ed. K. Hallinger *et al.*, *Corpus Consuetudinum Monasticarum I* (Siegburg, 1963). Hallinger regards Benedict's *decreta* as lost (*ibid.*, xli). The earliest customaries date from the seventh century and the manuscripts of these from the eighth and ninth centuries; it seems reasonable therefore to suppose that much of this material (essential for the daily life of a monastery) was transmitted orally (*ibid.*, xxxix-xlix and 3-11; and see K. Hallinger, 'Consuetudo', 140-7 and L. Donnat, 'Les coutumes monastiques autour l'an mil', in *Religion et Culture autour l'An Mil: Royaume capétien et Lotharingie*, eds D. Iogna-Prat et J-C. Picard (Picard, 1990), 18). I am most grateful to Marilyn Dunn for her advice on these complex issues.

91. K. Zelzer, 'Zur Frage der Observanz des Benedict Biscop', *Studia Patristica, 20. Papers presented to the 10th International Conference on Patristic Studies Held in Oxford 1987*, ed. E.A. Livingstone (Leuven, 1989), 323-30.

houses or nunneries? The question cannot be fully answered because such houses left less copious evidence. Few communities would have possessed the riches of scriptural and exegetical books present at Bede's monastery and their spiritual and interpretative frameworks may have been less complex. The extent to which a house had contacts with the lay world must have varied and affected its memories. It is likely that monasteries founded by the nobility and charged with the responsibility of prayer for their dead kindred retained much stronger links with and memories of the secular world. On the other hand, communities of nuns may have been more insulated: a recent analysis of female hagiography suggests that these possessed a sense of time bounded by the monastery's walls, isolated from political developments and dominated by the ties of the family.[92] The traditions of clerical communities may also have been distinctively different because of their greater involvement with secular life and less exacting liturgical regime.[93] A house's memories would be shaped too by the movement of people from community to community – Bede's teacher, Trumberht, who had been at Lastingham brought with him recollections of Chad. Alcuin's letters suggest that the educational role of cathedral schools created strong personal links maintained even when students had moved on; indeed the memory of teachers may have been more powerful because of the dislocation of their pupils.

The question of the nature of Wearmouth-Jarrow's rule and the role of oral and written traditions in its observance of the monastic life encapsulates many of the themes of this study such as the interplay between oral, physical, gestural and written agents in the formation of community memory. Monastic memory was, as Coleman suggests, profoundly marked by written texts but these could be experienced in a number of ways – through the liturgy, for example, or through public reading in the refectory. Written teaching was inseparable from physical discipline in a monk's education; while texts could shape his understanding of, for instance, death or sanctity, they could not replace a monk's experience of the material world. Rather it was a fusion of the two which made the monastic life and its memories distinctive.

A community's traditions were dominated by its former abbots and founding fathers who were held to have established its way of life and who were interpreted according to textual norms as models of the monastic life. The dominant place of Benedict and Ceolfrith in the traditions regulating Wearmouth-Jarrow's life is in accordance with the centrality of former abbots in the narrative of monastic histories. Abbots dominated a community's memories just as they had dominated its daily life. However, a monastery's memories could be diverse,

92. J.M.H. Smith, 'The problem of female sanctity in Carolingian Europe c. 780-920', *Past and Present* 146 (1995), 20-8.
93. On clerical communities see my 'Pastoral care and conciliar canons', 208-9.

shared between different groups, and opposed. The works of Bede and the anonymous biographer of Ceolfrith represent deliberate refashionings of Wearmouth-Jarrow's memory, penned at a time of rupture after the deaths of its founders, Benedict and Ceolfrith.[94] A community's memories were held by the different groups within a monastery for different purposes and could be used to counter the abbot's authority – when the brothers of Fulda petitioned Charlemagne concerning their abbot, they invoked the ancient traditions of their monastery (and the *Regula Benedicti*) against the abbot's unpopular innovations.[95] Monastic communities were not monolithic institutions but bodies with a diverse membership and at times opposing aims, drawing upon varied memories.

Note

The material in this chapter was first presented as a paper at the 32nd International Congress on Medieval Studies, Kalamazoo, 1997. It was also presented at seminars and conferences at the University of Birmingham, the University of London and St Andrew's University in 1944 and 1995.

---

94. Goffart, *Narrators of Barbarian History*, 279–80 (a not wholly convincing political interpretation); for a richer account see Wood, *The Most Holy Abbot Ceolfrith*.
95. *Supplex libellus*, see, for example, cc. 10, 13, 18, 549–50.

Index

CPSIA information can be obtained
at www.ICGtesting.com
Printed in the USA
LVOW10*1622220218

567556LV00014B/414/P